Hawai'i

The Best of Paradise
An Insiders' Guide to Honolulu & Beyond

By Don W. Martin & Betty Woo Martin

DISCOVERGUIDES ● *Las Vegas, Nevada*

BOOKS BY DON AND BETTY MARTIN

Adventure Cruising • 1996
Arizona Discovery Guide • 1990, 1993, 1994, 1996, 1998
Arizona in Your Future • 1991, 1993, 1998, 2003
The Best of Denver & the Rockies • 2001
The Best of Phoenix & Tucson • 2001
The Best of San Francisco • 1986, 1990, 1994, 1997
The Best of the Gold Country • 1987, 1990, 1992
The Best of the Wine Country • 1991, 1994, 1995, 2001
California-Nevada Roads Less Traveled • 1999
Hawai'i: The Best of Paradise • 2003
Inside San Francisco • 1991
Las Vegas: The Best of Glitter City • 1998, 2001, 2003
Nevada Discovery Guide • 1992, 1997
Nevada In Your Future • 2000
New Mexico Discovery Guide • 1998
Northern California Discovery Guide • 1993
Oregon Discovery Guide • 1993, 1995, 1996, 1999
San Diego: The Best of Sunshine City • 1999
San Francisco's Ultimate Dining Guide • 1988
Seattle: The Best of Emerald City • 2000
The Toll-free Traveler • 1997
The Ultimate Wine Book • 1993, 2000
Utah Discovery Guide • 1995
Washington Discovery Guide • 1994, 1997, 2000

Copyright © 2003 by Don W. Martin and Betty Woo Martin

Printed in the United States of America. All rights reserved. No written material, maps or illustrations from this book may be reproduced in any form, including electronic media, other than brief passages in book reviews, without written permission from the publisher.

Library of Congress Cataloging-in-Publication Data
Martin, Don and Betty —
Hawai'i: The Best of Paradise
Includes index.
1. Honolulu—description and travel
2. State of Hawai'i—description and travel

ISBN: 0-942053-41-9

CHAPTER ILLUSTRATIONS • **Bob Shockley**, Mariposa, Calif.

MAPS & COVER DESIGN • **Vicky Biernacki**, Columbine Type and Design, Sonora, Calif.

JUST THE BEST; NOT ALL THE REST

This is a different kind of guidebook. Instead of saturating readers with details on everything there is to see and do in Honolulu and beyond, the authors have sifted through the Hawaiian Islands' hundreds of lures and selected only the ten best in various categories. This is more than a mere book of lists, however. Each listing is a detailed description, with specifics on location, hours and more.

Further, there is plenty from which to choose. *Hawai'i: The Best of Paradise* offers Ten Best lists in nearly fifty different categories. It is thus a great resource for visitors with limited time, visitors with lots of time and residents who would like to make new discoveries about their island paradise.

A guidebook that focuses only on the best must, by its very nature, be rather opinionated. Some would even suggest that it's impertinent. Further, many readers may not agree with the authors' choices, which is part of the fun of reading this book.

This is another in a series of "Ten Best" guides by Don and Betty Martin, winners of a gold medal in the prestigious Lowell Thomas Travel Writing Competition. Check your local book store for these other titles:

The Best of Denver & the Rockies
The Best of Phoenix & Tucson
The Best of San Francisco
Las Vegas: The Best of Glitter City
San Diego: The Best of Sunshine City
Seattle: The Best of Emerald City

These and other remarkably useful *DISCOVERGUIDES* also can be ordered on line at *www.amazon.com, bn.com* and *borders.com*. See the back of this book for the complete list.

CONTENTS

10 Odd ends: Assorted bits & pieces

11 The best of the rest of O'ahu

PART II: THE OUTER ISLANDS

12 Maui

13 The Big Island

14 Kaua'i

15 Moloka'i

16 Lana'i

MAPS

ALOHA, MARINE!

My first visit to Hawai'i—aboard a Japan-bound Marine Corps transport plane in the 1950s—left an indelible impression on my mind. I've not been able to erase it, nor would I want to.

We stopped to refuel at Hickam Field, a military airstrip adjacent to Honolulu's airport. It was near midnight and I could see little of these paradise islands. Yet, even out there on the tarmac, I could smell the perfume of tropical flowers. We had a few hours' layover, so several of us caught a bus to nearby Pearl City in search of a cup of civilian coffee. As we settled at a restaurant counter, several high school students—all formally attired—filed in, talking and laughing. It must have been grad night and they had come for a late snack after their prom. The guys were handsome in their tuxedos and the girls were gorgeous with their full-length gowns, leis and tropical flowers in their hair. They were a mixed lot of Asians, Caucasians, Polynesians and assorted blends thereof.

This was, at that time, an extraordinary sight. Even as the civil rights movement was exploding on the mainland, these kids seemed oblivious to the different colors of their skins. I decided that I wanted to live in these islands where ethnic blending was part of the culture.

Unfortunately, career paths drew me elsewhere and I never did return to live in Hawai'i. However, Betty and I were married there—grinning, nervous and lei-draped, standing on a beach at the Mauna Kea resort—and we have returned to the Islands many times.

To research this book, we spent several months there, exploring every idyllic corner of Hawai'i like curious, indulgent tourists. With minds free of the predilections of residents, we investigated, sampled and savored all that the state has to offer.

First, we prowled every street, back alley and beach in Honolulu and Waikiki, Hawai'i's most popular destination. We checked out the area's attractions and activities, and its most interesting restaurants and resorts. We then explored the rest of O'ahu, on a quest for the perfect shave ice, the best beaches and the finest vista points this idyllic isle has to offer.

From there, we hopped aboard a succession of jets and prop-jets and visited the other major islands. We checked out the busy resorts and hidden enclaves of Maui, the volcanic grandeur of the Big Island, the lush tropic gardens of Kaua'i, and the little visited retreats of Moloka'i and Lana'i.

After exploring every corner of America's paradise islands, we discovered the very best, just for you.

Don W. Martin
Checking out the view from Diamond Head

SURFING TO HAWAI'I
As opposed to surfing *in* Hawai'i

To learn all about these paradise islands, visit the Hawai'i Visitors Bureau's website at *www.gohawaii.com*. Webites for the individual island visitors bureaus are: HAWAI'I—www.bigisland.org; MAUI—*www.visitmaui.com*; KAUA'I—*www.kauaivisitors bureau.org*; LANA'I—*www.visitlanai.net*; MOLOKA'I—*www.molokai-hawaii.com*; and O'AHU—*www.visit-oahu.com*.

Some other useful websites are *www.planet-hawaii.com*, offering specifics on the various islands' attractions, shopping, dining, lodgings and such, with links to tourist-oriented firms; *www.maui.net*, featuring attractions, activities, hiking trails, golf courses, scuba, snorkeling and more; *www.islandcurrents.com*, focusing on Maui's arts and performing arts scene; *www.hotspots.hawaii.com*, which plays Hawaiian music and has shopping sites for CDs, cassettes and books on the islands; and *www.hawaiianlanguage.com*, with language lessons, a Hawaiian cultural events calendar and even hula lessons and lyrics to Polynesian songs. A site focusing on pop culture and entertainment is *www.e-hawaii.com,* featuring—among many other things—a pidgin English dictionary. And there's even a naughty website for you voyeurs, *www.hawaiisex.com.*

The state government's website is *www.state.hi.us*, with information on just about everything a visitor or newcomer might want to know.

Mahalo!

You will soon discover, upon arriving in Hawai'i, that "mahalo" means "thank you." And you will use that word often because Hawai'i's people are very friendly and hospitable. We use it here as well, to thank the many folks who assisted us, and therefore helped make this book possible. Unfortunately, we can't thank all of them in print, because the list would never fit.

However, we will find space to say "mahalo" to those who were especially helpful—the good people of the Hawai'i Visitors & Convention Bureau, and those of the visitor bureaus of the various islands.

We begin—because we couldn't have begun this book without her—with a big mahalo to **Cathy Pai** of McNeil Wilson Communications, the firm that represents the Hawai'i Visitors & Convention Bureau. Also extremely helpful were **Darlene T. Morikawa** of the HVCB, and **Maura L. Jordan** and **Arlene Abiang** of the O'ahu Visitors Bureau. Outer island folks who provided invaluable help included **Keli'i Brown** and his assistant **Roxanne Murayama** of the Maui Visitors Bureau (which includes Moloka'i and Lana'i), **Vivian Seeley** and **Laura Aquino** of the Big Island Visitors Bureau, and **Lori Michimoto** of the Kauai Visitors Bureau.

A BIT ABOUT THE AUTHORS

Don and Betty Martin have written two dozen travel books, mostly under their *DISCOVERGUIDES* banner and its predecessor, Pine Cone Press. When not tending to their publishing company in Las Vegas or retreating to in their second home in an historic California mining town, they explore America and the world beyond. Both are members of the Society of American Travel Writers. They are gold medal winners in the Best Guidebook category of the annual Lowell Thomas Travel Journalism Awards, North America's most prestigious travel writing competition.

Don, who provides most of the adjectives, has been a journalist since he was 16, when classmates elected him editor of his high school newspaper. (No one else wanted the job.) After graduating, he left his small family farm in Idaho, wandered about the country a bit, and then joined the Marine Corps. He was assigned as a military correspondent in the Orient and at bases in California. Back in civvies, he worked as a reporter, sports writer and editor for several West Coast newspapers, then he became associate editor of a San Francisco-based travel magazine. In 1988, he left to establish Pine Cone Press, Inc. He now devotes his time to writing, travel, sipping decent Zinfandel and—for some odd reason—collecting squirrel and chipmunk artifacts.

Betty, a Chinese-American whose varied credentials have included a doctorate in pharmacy and a real estate broker's license, does much of the research and editing for their books. She also has written travel articles for assorted newspapers and magazines and she has sold travel photos through a major New York stock agency. When she isn't helping Don run their publishing company, she wanders the globe—with or without him. Her travels have taken her from Cuba to Antarctica.

Closing introductory thoughts
Keeping up with the changes

Visions of Hawai'i seem almost eternal—swaying palms and swaying hips, tropical sunsets and exotic resorts. Yet Honolulu, Waikiki and the islands of Hawai'i are places of change. Each time we visit, we discover something new—a great little sushi parlor in a Honolulu alley or a hidden beach on the Big Island that we somehow overlooked before. If you discover something afresh during your visit, or if you find an error in this book, let us know, so we can fix it in the next edition.

Address your comments to:

DISCOVERGUIDES
P.O. Box 231954
Las Vegas, NV 89123-0033
e-mail: discoverhsd@earthlink.net

Hawai'i is what the rest of the world would like to be.
— **John F. Kennedy, during a visit to Honolulu in 1960**

Chapter One

AMERICA'S PARADISE

IT'S OKAY TO LOVE HONOLULU

It is fashionable among some travelers and travel writers to regard Honolulu and O'ahu as too congested and too touristy. They say that famous Waikiki Beach is tacky, crowded and commercialized. The real savvy travelers, they say, head for the outer islands.

Well, these two savvy travelers *love* Honolulu. It's the most attractive, cleanest and safest major city in America. The climate is year-around sunny and moderate and the sandy beaches are just steps from major commercial areas. If we could afford Honolulu's high cost of housing, we'd move there in a Las Vegas minute.

Waikiki, the world's best known beach, has undergone a multi-million-dollar facelift in recent years. Sidewalks of adjacent Kalakaua Avenue have been paved with flagstone and Waikiki's beach parks are dressed up with landscaping, fountains and occasional statues of legendary Hawaiians. Some of these bronze figures are draped daily with fresh flower leis—a really nice touch. Surfboard-shaped markers point out significant sites along a new Waikiki Historic Trail. Flower baskets hang from Victorian style lampposts and Kalakaua Avenue is lit at night by tiki torches at night. Further, it's no longer lined with tacky souvenir shops; it has become the smartest shopping street on O'ahu.

Is Waikiki crowded? Not like Coney Island or the beaches of coastal Los Angeles. And Waikiki is cleaner than both; it's kept spotless by a city that—like a vain woman—wants to stay pretty. Too commercialized? We have no problem with a few shave ice stands and beach boys offering outrigger rides and surfboard lessons, and we certainly like the grassy parks lining the beach. Waikiki is busy during the two high seasons—June through August and mid-December into April—and on weekends. However, I don't consider rows of bronzed sunbathing bikini-clad bodies as crowds; they're part of the scenery.

And remarkably, there are still open areas along the beach. Kapi'olani Park was set aside by King Kalakaua to honor his queen in 1877, long before developers could get to the land. And the U.S. Army grabbed a large chunk of Waikiki and built Battery Randolph as a coastal defense between 1908 and 1911. It's now the Army Museum of Hawai'i, and the surrounding lands—Fort DeRussy—were became a rest and recreation area for GI's during World War II. It's still army land although this large swatch of beach park is open to the public.

All of the above

So for all of the above reasons, this book is mostly about Honolulu. Further, the Honolulu section is mostly about Waikiki because this is home to ninety percent of O'ahu's hotel rooms. It is thus a safe assumption that ninety percent of O'ahu visitors spend a good part of their time there.

The book is designed to take readers by the hand and lead them to Honolulu/Waikiki's best attractions, activities, vista points, walking areas, restaurants, lodgings and more. After we have discovered all that this sun-kissed and surf-caressed city has to offer, we explore the rest of O'ahu. Then, since many visitors also fly to the outer islands, we follow with chapters on the best of Maui, the Big Island, Kaua'i, Moloka'i and Lana'i.

There are more comprehensive books about Honolulu and the rest of Hawai'i, but none that offers "quick lists" of things to see and do, places to eat and stay. These Ten Best lists feature more than fifty different categories, so this book is useful for those with limited time, and those with plenty of time.

Hawai'i rates high on lists of places people like to love. In a recent Harris Poll, it was ranked as America's third most desirable place to live, after Florida and California. When *Travel & Leisure* recently picked the world's top ten islands, three were in Hawai'i. Maui and Kaua'i were first and second and the Big Island was fifth.

The state lures more than seven million visitors a year; tourists outnumber residents nearly seven to one. Well over half the visitors—

about 4.25 million—spend their vacations on O'ahu, while Maui is the second most popular, with about two million. The Big island is third with 1.8 million, Kaua'i is fourth with just over a million, then comes Lana'i with 84,000 and Moloka'i, the least-visited with 70,000. And yes, those figures add up to more than 9.2 million. That's because many make multiple island visits, of course.

Aloha yourself!

Much of this love of Hawai'i is generated by an ethereal thing called the "aloha spirit." It's a wonderful concept—a term that encompasses friendship, warmth and caring. "Aloha" is a word of many meanings—hello, goodbye, welcome, "I love you," and maybe even "Have a nice day."

There's something almost sensual about lowering your head and grinning self-consciously while a pretty Hawaiian lass drapes a lei around your neck and whispers: "Aloha."

All of this aloha business leaves us with a warm and fuzzy feeling, although the word is overused. Aloha has become a brand name—from an airline to a moving company to a football bowl game to potato chips. Every employee in every resort on every island greets every guest every day with "Aloha." It seems requisite that most luaus and hula shows begin with the host/announcer insisting that attendees scream "Aloha!" as loud as they can. ("I can't heeeer you!" they bellow like angry Marine drill instructors. "Let's try it again!")

However, "aloha" wasn't originally used simply as a warm and fuzzy greeting. It was more of a statement of condition, of saying "I am here," and it could be loving, friendly or even guarded. Legend says the goddess A (pronounced "ahh") created the seas, then freed the force of Pele to create the lands. "Aloha" comes from *"alo"* ("presence") and *ha* (breath). It originally meant "divine breath" or to be in the presence of "A," the giver of life. It was thus a very spiritual word, not to be tossed about in hotel corridors.

Further, the original Hawaiians didn't always exhibit that aloha spirit. As Captain James Cook discovered the hard way in 1779, they were known to kick butt. Until King Kamehameha II abolished the *kapu* system in 1819, all but the highest ranking Hawaiians suffered under a rigid system of rules and punishments.

The word became romanticized only within the past few decades, mostly by tourist promoters who wanted to use "aloha spirit" to entice visitors to this friendly place. Indeed, the Hawai'i Visitors Bureau refers to the state as "The Islands of Aloha."

This notion of aloha spirit certainly does create a mood of welcoming friendship. Perhaps more importantly, it reflects a successful mixing of races and ethnic groups. These are small islands and its people have wisely learned to get along, to share their aloha spirit with one another. Hawai'i is the most comfortably integrated place on earth, and who's to quarrel with that concept?

THE STATE OF HAWAI'I: GETTING TO KNOW YOU

If you're a first-time visitor, you'll be struck by the fact that our fiftieth state is quite unlike the other forty-nine. And we aren't just referring to the obvious fact that it occupies several islands in the middle of the Pacific, or that it has sandy beaches and swaying palms. Florida, Louisiana and southern California have beaches and palm trees as well. However, Hawai'i is not Florida and it certainly is not southern California. It is a much more genteel place—that aloha spirit again—and life's pace is rather pokey here. Even traffic moves more slowly and speed limits seem extremely low for some of us mainlanders in a hurry.

Ethnically, Hawai'i is very different from the other states. Most of its residents have Asian roots and Caucasians are a minority. This is the result of early sugar barons importing thousands of Chinese, Japanese and Filipinos to work their fields. Many stayed, prospered and often intermarried. Thus the "Hawaiian" look is more of an Asian-Caucasian-Polynesian look. We've always felt that they're the most attractive of all Americans.

Hawai'i's culture is strongly influenced by its Polynesian roots although native Hawaiians comprise only about ten percent of the population. The hula, the lei and the luau are native to Hawai'i and other South Pacific islands. The food of Hawai'i is a delightful blend of Polynesian and Asian; its people were enjoying Pacific Rim cuisine long before the term was invented by some celebrity chef on the mainland.

The Hawaiian Islands

N

Kaua'i
Lihue
Kaua'i Channel
Kaulakahi Channel
Ni'ihau

O'ahu
Honolulu
Kaiwi Channel

Moloka'i
Pailolo Channel
Lana'i
Kaho'olawe

Maui
Lahaina
Haleakala National Park
Alenuihaha Channel

Hawai'i
Hilo Bay
Hilo
Hawaii Volcanoes National Park
Kawaihae Bay
Kona

The price of paradise

Hawai'i is not an inexpensive place to visit. Except for pineapples, papayas and poi, virtually everything must be brought in from somewhere else, so prices generally are higher than those on the mainland. Dining is rather expensive; figure on $30 to $40 per entrée at better restaurants. Attractions and activities tend to be costly as well; plan on spending upwards of $100 or more for snorkeling trips, para-sailing, catamaran cruises and such, and helicopter flights go beyond that.

You can do some bargain-hunting by checking through the many brochures and free tourist publications found in abundance in resort areas. Booking agencies and tourist booths also may have special discounts.

However, do your shopping carefully. Some of these "bargains" aren't what they seem, and many are come-ons. The $10-a-day snorkel rentals usually are for gear you wouldn't use in a kiddie pool, let alone in the ocean. Once you get to the dive shop, the better equipment will cost two to four times as much. Also, be wary of firms that make presentations at many hotels and resorts. They'll feed you a free breakfast buffet and offer special discounts and/or preferred seating for various activities and attractions. However, you often can get better prices by shopping around. And when you see *really* deeply discounted deals, the odds are you'll have to sit through a timeshare presentation to get those rates. (We'll admit guiltily that we've done this a time or two.)

As for hotel rooms—well, we're rather spoiled by prices in our hometown of Las Vegas. High end resorts on the islands start around $250 a night, compared with about $150 on the Las Vegas Strip. However, there are plenty of more moderately priced hotels and resorts.

And finally, as we demonstrate in Chapter Five, it is possible to enjoy an inexpensive vacation in Hawai'i. Many attractions are free or have very nominal admission prices. The islands abound with cheap restaurants and delis, and you can even find rooms near Waikiki Beach for less than $80 a night.

Kailua where?

Because the islands originally were ruled independently, duplicate place names are common. There is, for instance, a Kailua on the Big Island and Maui, and a Waimea on O'ahu, the Big Island and Kaua'i. The U.S. Postal Service doesn't permit duplicate town names, but the Kailuas and Waimeas were already in place when Hawai'i became a territory in 1898. Incidentally, the four major islands—O'ahu, Hawai'i, Maui and Kaua'i—are counties. Moloka'i and Lana'i are part of Maui County.

Hawaiian spoken here

When the first outsiders arrived in these islands, they found a people with a very lyrical spoken language but no alphabet. The early missionaries put their language to paper, and they found they needed only seven consonants—**h, k, l, m, n, p** and **w**—plus our five basic vowels.

Naturally, the first thing they translated into Hawaiian was the King James Bible.

Hawaiian consonant sounds are similar to ours, except that the **w** following an **e** or **i** has a *vee* sound. The vowels are pronounced as they are in Spanish—**a** is *ah*; **e** is *eh* or *ey*; **i** is *ee*; **o** is *oh* and **u** is *oo* as in *true*. The **u** is never pronounce *you*; that little stringed instrument Hawaiians like to plink is the *oo-ku-le-le*.

All words and syllables end in vowels, and the accent is usually on the next to the last syllable. And since the written language was adapted from a spoken language, there are no wasted silent letters.

Virtually every mainlander mispronounces most Hawaiian words—starting with the word "Hawai'i"—because they fail to separate some of the vowels. When the missionaries put the language to print, they used a single quote symbol (') with an ugly name—glottal stop—to indicate when paired vowels should be pronounced separately, or broken into two syllables. (In *Hawai'i: The Best of Paradise*, we use the ' in traditional place names but not in other reference containing Hawaiian words.)

Thus, this book is about *Ha-VA-ee*, not *Haw-wa-yuh*. And Honolulu is on the island of *Oh-AH-hoo*, not *O-WA-hoo*.

Not all vowels are pronounced separately. There are four compound sounds—**au** (*ow*), **ae** (*aye*), **ai** (*eye*) and **ei** (*ay*). Thus, there is no "hyena" in Lahaina; it's *La-HAI-nah*, not *La-ha-EE-na*. Note that **ae** and **ei** sound rather similar.

Obviously, you don't have to learn Hawaiian during your island visit, since English is the universal language. However, the above suggestions will be useful when you pronounce place names—Waimea, Lana'i, Kalakaua, Ka'anapali, Kapi'olani, Kahului, Wailuku and such. And you'll certainly want to sound like a local when you order an entrée of humuhumunukunuku'apua'a; it's a short fish with a long name.

If you want to learn a few Hawaiian words, or be able to say Pu'uhonua o Honaunau National Historic Park without tripping over your tongue, pick up a little yellow pocket-sized book called *Instant Hawaiian*. It's available at book stores, gift and souvenir shops throughout the islands.

Shakin' goin' on

If anything is more typical of Hawai'i than luaus and leis, it is the hula. It has been performed for centuries on several South Pacific islands, and likely was brought to the Hawaiian Islands by the Tahitians. They arrived here around the twelfth century A.D., several centuries after the first inhabitants had come from the Marquesas. The Tahitian hula is the most popular dance performed at most luaus and Hawaiian shows because it's faster and sexier than the more sedate and fluid Hawaiian hula.

Although the hula is sensual and erotic, its rooted in religious ceremonies. The original *hula kahiko* was performed only by men, with drums and chants, as a way of communicating with their gods and telling stories of the past. And never mind watching the hands; the chant was the most telling part of the early hula. The use of hand movements to relate a story evolved with the *hula auwana* of the late nineteenth century.

Early hula dancers usually were tattooed and they wore traditional *kapa* cloth garments, not grass skirts. They often performed in a sitting position. They danced to appease the hula goddesses Li'iaka and Laka, and then they solemnly offered the leis before their temples. Eventually, women were allowed to perform the dance and the hula became a mating ritual as well as a religious rite.

The first Westerners to visit the islands in the late 1700s must have enjoyed this spectacle of comely lasses with tattooed breasts, wriggling their hips, and clad in billowy *kapa* skirts. And did they wonder, as many wonder about my Scottish-kilted ancestors, if they wore anything underneath?

An abomination

However, when the first Protestant missionaries arrived on the Big Island in 1820, they were not amused. Calling the hula an abomination "performed by almost naked savages," they decreed that it be banned. Hawaiians who converted to Christianity stopped performing it, although the *hula kahiko* continued to be danced covertly in more remote areas. And randy whaling crewmen enjoyed rather raunchy versions of the hula in rowdy Honolulu and Lahaina bars in the 1800s.

The so-called grass skirt didn't arrive in Hawai'i until the 1870s, introduced by laborers from the Gilbert Islands. And they weren't made of grass, but of shredded coconut palm or *ti* leaves. King David Kalakaua, the champagne-loving "Merrie Monarch," is credited with bringing the hula back to popularity. He asked the islands' best dancers to perform at his coronation in 1883. In the years that followed, the more contemporary *hula auwana* evolved. As the islands became a popular tourist destination in the 1920s and 1930s, "hula maidens" greeted arriving ship passengers with leis and sensual dances, accompanied by ukuleles and guitars, musical imports from Portugal and Mexico.

The hula is coming full circle. At some of the better Polynesian shows and luaus, you'll see performers in more traditional dress—even topless, although properly covered with floral and maile garlands—dancing to traditional drum beats and chants. Most shows feature both men and women, performing dances from several South Seas societies. (See the index for various hula show listings.)

A quick geography lesson

The term "Polynesia" has come to mean the South Pacific in general, although there are actually three distinct island groups in the region—Micronesia, Melanesia and Polynesia. The latter is northernmost of these islands.

Hawai'i occupies Polynesia's northern tip and it's the most isolated island group in the world, 2,400 miles from the mainland and 4,900 miles from China. It's an archipelago of 132 islands, extending about 1,500 miles from southeast to northwest. However, its total land mass is small, about equal to Connecticut and Rhode Island combined. The eight major islands are gathered at the southeastern end, all within a few miles of one another.

Hawai'i is the southernmost American state; the larger islands are all within the Tropic of Cancer, which marks the northern edge of the tropical climate zone. A line drawn east from Kaua'i, the northernmost main island, would miss the mainland completely and pass through central Mexico. However, some of the outer islands such as Kure and Midway are in the temperate zone. Draw your line east from Midway and you'd nip through Texas and Florida.

The Hawaiian Islands literally rose from the sea, not drawn by some ancient Polynesian god but pushed upward by volcanic action. And they rose very slowly, building up over millions of years.

The oldest of the islands, Midway and Kure, probably broke the ocean's surface about twenty-five million years ago. More than twenty million years passed before the main islands emerged, starting with Kaua'i and Ni'ihau about five to six million years ago, and ending with Hawai'i, which is less than a million years old and still growing. Vents from Kilauea in Hawaii Volcanoes National Park have been erupting for more than two decades, adding more land as lava spills down to the shoreline. And Hawai'i isn't the *last* island. Even as we write this, a new volcano called **Loihi** is building toward the ocean's surface just south of the Big Island. Come check it out when it emerges in about 10,000 years.

GETTING THERE

Although Hawai'i is the globe's most isolated population center, getting there is easy if you're willing to take wing. Honolulu International Airport is served by about twenty-five domestic and foreign airlines. Some carriers have direct mainland flights to Maui, Kaua'i and Kona on the Big Island.

Hawai'i-bound U.S. carriers

Aloha Airlines, (800) 367-5250 or (808) 484-1111; *www.alohaairlines.com*—Flights from Oakland and Orange County, Calif., and Las Vegas; plus nonstops from Oakland to Maui and Kona, and Orange County to Maui.

American Airlines, (800) 433-7300; *americanair.com*—Service from Chicago, Dallas, San Francisco, San Jose and Los Angeles; plus direct flights to Maui.

Continental Airlines, (800) 231-0856; *www.continental.com*—Daily nonstops from New York/Newark, plus flights from other cities.

Delta Air Lines, (800) 221-1212; *www.delta.com*—Nonstops from several West Coast cities to Honolulu and Maui.

Hawaiian Airlines, (800) 367-5320 or (808) 835-3700; *www.hawaiianair.com*—Flights from several West Coast cities and Las Vegas to Honolulu, and nonstops from Los Angeles to Maui.

Northwest Airlines, (800) 225-2525; *www.nwa.com*—A daily nonstop from Detroit, plus flights from several other cities.

United Airlines, (800) 225-5825; *www.ual.com*—Hawai'i's major carrier, it has flights from many U.S. cities, including nonstops from the West Coast. In addition to Honolulu service, it has nonstops from Los Angeles and San Francisco to Kona, Maui and Kaua'i.

Inter-island travel is easy. **Aloha Airlines; Hawaiian Airlines** and **Island Air** (800-323-3345 or 808-484-2222) have frequent flights between and among the outer islands. Outbound planes leave Honolulu International—either from the main or the small Inter-Island Terminal—about every twenty minutes from early morning through late evening. The average inter-island fare is about $100. However, the carriers usually offer discounts, such as "six-pack" ticket books that cut each segment to about $65. Also, Aloha and Island Air has seven-day "all you can fly" travel passes for about $325. Seating is open on inter-island flights, so if you want a window, get in line early.

Honolulu International Airport is twelve miles or about twenty-five minutes from Honolulu, sharing space with Hickam air Force Base. Cab fare from the airport to Waikiki is about $25 and of course, the airport has outlets for all major rental car agencies. O'ahu's transit system, called **TheBus**, has service to the airport from early morning through late evening on routes 19 and 20. However, passengers are limited to carry-ons—only luggage that will fit on the lap or under the seat. (See "Getting about" below.)

Airport Waikiki Express buses, operated by Trans-Hawaiian Service, run between the airport and Waikiki hotels for $8 one way or $13 round trip. They leave every half hour or so and reservations aren't necessary, although you'll need to call for hotel pickup when it's time to fly out; (800) 533-8765 or (808) 566-7000; *www.transhawaiian.com*).

TRAVEL TIP: Check inter-island schedules as you plan your Hawai'i visit. If you're going from one outer island to the next, carriers often have direct flights, allowing you to bypass Honolulu. And if you're planning to visit O'ahu and one or more outer islands, you can fly into Honolulu and then return home from Maui, Kaua'i or Kona.

Rental cars

One of the few bargains in Hawai'i is rental car rates, which are among the lowest in the nation, except on Lana'i and Moloka'i. On the other islands, competition among national and local firms have kept prices down. Do some shopping, on-line or by phone, to get the best

O'ahu

Kahuku Point

Sunset Beach • Kahuku • Makahoa Point
Mormon Temple
Waimea • Laie • Polynesian Cultural Center
Kawailoa Beach • Waimea Falls Park
83
Waialua Bay
Kaena Point State Park • Mokuleia Beach • Haleiwa
Kaena Point • 930 • Mokuleia • Makalii Point
Kaena Point State Park • 803 • 99 • Kahana Bay
Kaaawa
Kaoio Point
Wahiawa
Kepuhi Point • 930 • Makaha • Kaneohe
Lahilahi Point • Mokapu Point
Pokai Bay • Waianae • H2 • 83 • 830 • Kaneohe M.C.A.S.
Maili
Malli Point • Nanakuli • 99 • Waipahu • Kailua
Pearl City • H3 • H3 • H3
H1 • Aiea • Maunawili • Waimanalo Bay
Pearl Harbor • U.S.S. Arizona • 63 • 72
78
Ewa • 61
Ewa Beach • H1 • Sea Life Park • Makapuu Point
Barbers Point • Honolulu • Hanauma Bay State Park
Mamala Bay • Waikiki
Diamond Head

Area of map → Honolulu

N

rates. Independent firms aren't always cheaper than the national chains. Also, most independents don't offer the convenience of airport service, so you may have to pay extra to get to the rental agency. This can be expensive. On Maui, for instance, it costs nearly $50 for a shuttle or cab from the airport to Lahaina.

Book rental cars well ahead; they can become very scarce during high season (summer and winter) and on weekends, particularly on the outer islands.

TRAVEL TIP: If you don't like the smell of tobacco smoke, make sure you request a non-smokers' vehicle. We've found that rental cars often are rank with tobacco odors, particularly on O'ahu. This is partly because many Japanese—who comprise about half of Hawai'i's visitors—are heavy smokers.

GETTING ABOUT

Since this book begins with Honolulu and O'ahu, this section focuses on driving and surviving in and around Hawai'i's capital city. Getting from the airport to Honolulu is simple; just follow signs to H-1 East. Then it starts getting complicated.

Hawai'i's only freeways are on O'ahu, and the main one is H-1, leading west from Honolulu toward the leeward (southwest) coast. In doing so, it passes within a few miles of nearly eighty percent of the state's total population. Thus, H-1 also is Hawai'i's most congested route. Avoid it during morning and evening rush hours, and on late weekend afternoons when locals swarm to and from the beaches. The

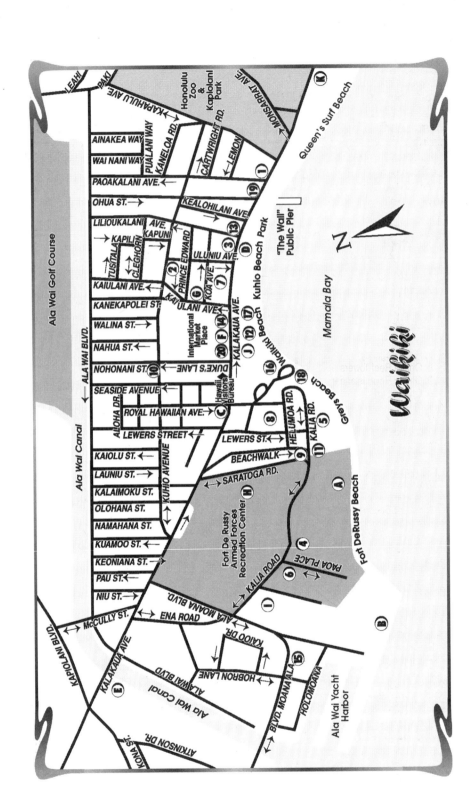

other freeways are H-2, which branches north from H-1 at Pearl City and goes halfway across the island toward Hale'iwa and O'ahu's North Coast; and H-3, which splits from H-1 above Honolulu, tunnels through the Ko'olau Range and winds up in Kane'ohe on the Windward (northeast) coast. A short freeway, Highway 79, bridges a bulge in H-1, offering a more direct route to downtown.

Although it's an appealing metropolis cradled between surf and mountains, Honolulu suffers traffic congestion just like ordinary cities. To improve traffic flow, engineers put one-way signs on many of the streets, and they seem to have done so with warped senses of humor. You may find yourself one-wayed into a corner, or having to take a wide loop and half a dozen turns to get from here to there. Further, because of the irregular topography, many of Honolulu's streets run at confusing angles.

Which way, Waikiki?

When you land at Honolulu International and fetch your rental car, we suggest that you take the slow way to Waikiki. Get onto eastbound H-1 and then exit onto the Nimitz Highway (Route 92). This travels along the waterfront and becomes Ala Moana Boulevard, which passes the edge of downtown, then blends into Kalakaua and *voile!* you're in Waikiki.

The Nimitz-Ala Moana route involves a lot of surface streets and stoplights, but you shouldn't get lost. When you become more familiar with street patterns, you can stay on H-1 and drop down into whatever part of Honolulu or Waikiki you wish to reach. The freeway was built through the area's already-populated foothills, so the on-ramps and off-ramps are rather jury-rigged. No clean-cut cloverleafs or classic diamond interchanges here!

Waikiki is two things—a famous beach and a specific area of Honolulu. It is *not* part of downtown Honolulu; that district is a couple or three miles northwest. Waikiki occupies an area between the beach and Ala Wai Canal.

Hotels

1. Aston Waikiki Beach Hotel
2. Aston Pacific Monarch
3. Aston Waikiki Beach Tower
4. Hale Koa Hotel (military only)
5. Halekulani
6. Hilton Hawaiian Village
7. Hyatt Regency
8. Ohana Reef Towers
9. Ohana Royal Islander
10. Ohana Surf
11. Outrigger Reef
12. Outrigger Waikiki
13. Pacific Beach Hotel
14. Princess Kaiulani Hotel
15. Renaissance Ilikai Waikiki
16. Royal Hawaiian
17. Sheraton Moana & Surfrider
18. Sheraton Waikiki
19. Waikiki Beach Marriott
20. Waikiki Beachcomber

Attractions, Shopping, Misc.

A. Army Museum of Hawaii
B. Atlantis submarines
C. DFS Galleria
D. Duke Kananamoku statue & Kuhio Beach stage
E. Hawaii Convention Center
F. International Market Place
G. King's Village
H. Post office
I. Rainbow Bazaar & Bishop Museum at Kalia
J. Royal Hawaiian Shopping Center
K. Waikiki Aquarium

The canal is about two miles long and only three streets cross it—Ala Moana, Kalakaua and McCully—so it tends to isolate Waikiki from the rest of Honolulu.

By studying maps and frequently getting lost, you'll soon realize that Waikiki's main thoroughfares are Kalakaua and Ala Wai Boulevard. Kalakaua is one-way southeast as it enters the Waikiki district and Al Wai is one-way northwest. Between them is Kuhio Avenue, which is thankfully two-way. Often, it will become your street-of-rescue when you're totally confused. Among and between these three main thoroughfares is a confusing grid of mostly one-way streets.

Go where?

Local folks have a quaint way of giving directions, telling visitors to "go makai" (east), "go Diamond Head" (south), go makua (west) and "go ewa" (north). However, we don't ask you to remember makai from makua. We keep it simple, using compass directions or just saying "go inland" or "go beachward."

To aid you further, each listing—except where the location is obvious—contains specific "GETTING THERE" directions. We assume you will have found your way to Waikiki before you begin exploring the area, so these directions will begin from Waikiki, or from H-1 just above it. If the listing is in Waikiki, we tell you the nearest cross street.

The Waikiki map will help you by showing the area's one-way street patterns. There are two relatively easy ways to reach H-1 from Waikiki. If you're going west, take one-way Ala Wai Boulevard west, then two-way McCully Street north and follow freeway signs; if you're going east, take two-way Kapahulu Avenue north from Kalakaua Avenue and follow signs to H-1.

Mapping things out

The best maps of Honolulu, O'ahu and the rest of the islands are produced by the American Automobile Association, although you have to be an AAA member to get one. If you are a member, pick up maps before you leave home, since AAA Hawaii has only one office. It's in Honolulu at 1270 Ala Moana Boulevard, between Pi'ikoi and Queen streets. It's open weekdays 9 to 5 (until 7 Thursdays) and Saturdays 9 to 2; closed Sundays; (800) 736-2886; *www.aaa.com.*

Most national rental car agencies provide drive guides with fairly useful maps, and many free tourist publications have maps as well. Among these are the magazine-sized *101 Things to Do* with editions for O'ahu, the Big Island, Maui and Kaua'i; and the slender, pocket-sized *Spotlight's Oahu Gold* and *This Week* magazines. *This Week* publishes editions for O'ahu, the Big Island, Maui and Kaua'i.

Public transit

TheBus, O'ahu's fine public transit system, recently was voted the best in the U.S. by the American Public Transit Association. It offers service throughout the island for $1.50 for adults and seventy-five cents for seniors with Medicare cards. There are no zones so you can travel throughout the island for a single fare. For schedule information call (808) 848-5555. Unlimited ride four-day visitor passes are available at ABC stores (see below, page 36).

Waikiki Trolley operates jolly old wooden trolleys in Waikiki, Honolulu and as far afield as Sea Life Park and the Polynesian Cultural Center. One-day passes are $18 and four-day passes are $30. The trolleys are best for sightseeing; they're not really useful if you're in a hurry. They follow convoluted, meandering routes, sometimes virtually doubling back on themselves. For route information call (800) 824-8804 or (808) 593-2822; *www.enoa.com.*

An UNAUTHORIZED HISTORY

The appearance of destitution, degradation, and barbarism, among the chattering, almost naked savages, whose heads and feet, and much of their sunburnt swarthy skins were bare, was appalling. Some of our number, with gushing tears, turned away from the spectacle... Can we throw ourselves upon these rude shores, and take up our abode, for life, among such a people, for the purpose of training them for heaven?

This entry from the journal of Hiram Bingham, who arrived with Hawai'i's first group of soul-savers in 1820, reflected more on the sanctimonious prejudice of the missionaries than the condition of the native people. It obviously did not occur to them that—then as now—the balmy climate did not require much attire. Barbaric? Not even by Western standards at this point in Hawai'i's history. The people were united under a single ruler, who just six months before had abolished the cruel *kapu* system. Had they still been barbaric, those pious Calvinists from Boston might have wound as missionary stew. Just forty-one years earlier, the Hawaiians had cooked Captain Cook.

However, the missionaries immediately set about to impose their rigid Protestant morality upon these "savages." Unlike the later-arriving Mormons who were willing to preserve the Hawaiians' cultural heritage, these dour Bostonians were determined to eradicate it. And they arrived at an opportune moment. The *kapu* system ruled by assorted gods had been abolished only a few months earlier.

As one historian put it: "This presented to the world the singular spectacle of a nation without a religion." The fourteen ministers had arrived with instructions for "raising up the whole people to an elevated state of Christian civilization; and bringing them to the mansions of eternal blessedness." They found a society confused, without gods and eager to be raised.

Of course, Hawai'i's human history did not start with the arrival of the missionaries, any more than it began when Captain Cook accidentally stumbled across the island chain in 1778. However, these two events did more to change Hawaiian society than anything else in their long history.

The first islanders

Hawai'i's true history began in the misty past, possibly as early as 200 A.D., when a group of Marquesans made an incredible 2,400-mile journey across an uncharted ocean in double-hulled canoes. How did they accomplish such a feat with no navigational equipment, and how did they know that the Hawaiian Islands even existed? The rest of the world didn't discover them until 1788, more than two centuries after most of the other Pacific islands had been identified.

Perhaps those early navigators didn't really know that islands lay ahead. Perhaps they had fled their homeland, driven out by war or famine and hoped to find landfall. Perhaps they were headed for South America—there is evidence that early Polynesians knew of that continent—and were blown off course.

The mystery of Hawai'i's discovery may never be solved, for the early Polynesians kept no journals, since they had no written language. Quotes Gavan Daws in *Shoal of Time* (© University of Hawaii Press):

By the time Westerners came to the Pacific the natives' long-distance canoe voyages had stopped. Legendary tales of migratory expeditions were still told, and the Polynesians could reel off genealogical chants that went back to the creation of the earth. But it was difficult to get the traditions of one group of islands to agree exactly with the traditions of another, and harder still to get the Polynesian idea of time to fit the Western historical calendar.

What *is* known is that the people of New Zealand, most of the South Pacific and even remote Easter Island were of the same root stock, spoke similar languages and lived similar lifestyles. The Hawaiian Islands were the last to be settled by the peripatetic Polynesians. Recent archeological finds and DNA studies indicate that the original Polynesians probably came from eastern Asia about 3,000 years ago, then gradually spread throughout the South Pacific. And since the region is comprised mostly of widely scattered islands, they obviously were among history's greatest navigators.

Accidental tourists

Hawai'i's written record began with the arrival of Captain Cook. The great explorer, on his third cruise to the Pacific, had been dispatched by England's Earl of Sandwich to find the fabled Northwest Passage. In late 1777, his two ships, *HMS Resolution* and *HMS Discovery*, struck northeasterly from the Society Islands, setting a course for the coast of western America. On the morning of January 18, 1778, the high profile of an island appeared on the horizon, then another. It was remarkable because charts showed no islands in this area.

As Cook's ships approached one of the islands—Kaua'i, as it turned out—several canoes approached. Since the English navigator had dealt with Polynesians on other Pacific Islands, he knew this was an opportunity to barter for food and fresh water. He tried to induce his visitors to come aboard; they refused, so he lowered trade items over the side. The canoers sent up fish and sweet potatoes in return.

Later, looking for a landing site, he dropped anchor for the night off the small village of Waimea. The next morning, a few of the locals worked up the nerve to come aboard. Cook wrote in his journal:

Their eyes were continually flying from object to object, the wildness of their looks and actions fully express'd their surprise and astonishment at the several new objects before them and evinced that they never had been on board a ship before.

Then their *hands* began flying from object to object. Cook soon realized that these folks, like many other Pacific islanders, had a penchant for theft. They tried to take practically everything that wasn't tied down. They particularly coveted anything made of iron—even simple nails—for they had no metal of their own.

As his crew tried to keep the natives from snatching whatever was loose on the ship, Captain Cook went ashore under marine guard. Hundreds awaited him and he was startled when they prostrated themselves as he stepped from his boat. Then they began showering him with gifts, so he offered goods in return.

His men, randy from weeks at sea, were pleased to find that the women were very willing sexual partners. Despite the celibate Cook's protests, they began romping with these bare-breasted maidens, even dressing them as men to smuggle them aboard. Thomas Edgar, master of the *Discovery*, wrote that when the men went ashore, the women "used all their arts to entice them into their houses & even went so far as to endeavor to draw them in by force." Unfortunately, this sexual freedom introduced to Hawai'i the first of many diseases that eventually would decimate the population.

Off to the passage

Captain Cook named the islands in honor of his patron, the Earl of Sandwich, then he sailed into the sunrise to continue his quest for the Northwest Passage. He failed to find it, of course; by early autumn, his way was blocked by a solid wall of pack ice in the Bering Sea. He decided—as millions would later decide—that the Sandwich Islands would be a nice place to spend the winter. He'd try for the Northwest Passage the following spring.

He got back in late November, this time putting ashore on Maui. The people were still friendly and willing to trade food and fresh water for metal. And they still tried to steal whatever they could lay their hands on. After several days cruising about Maui, Cook sighted a large island which the locals called Hawai'i, and decided to sail over for a look. On both islands, it was evident that these people knew of his earlier visit to Kaua'i. They came aboard the two ships without hesitation, often in such numbers that they threatened to capsize them. Some had venereal sores, yet they shared their women with the crew.

"The inhabitants thronged...to the ship with hogs and women," wrote Cook. "It was not possible to keep the latter out of the ship and no women I ever met with were more ready to bestow their favours."

He cruised around Hawai'i for six weeks, looking for safe harbor. He finally found it in a small bay called Kealakekua. Here, he again was greeted royally and the *ali'i* (chiefs) treated him to a lavish banquet. Cook noted that the *ali'i* and their priests kept using the word *lono*. He was taken to a second ceremonial feast in a *heiau* (temple) identified as "the house of Lono." Wherever he went in the company of the *ali'i*, commoners were ordered to prostrate themselves. Then it struck home: He was being worshiped as some deity named Lono!

On both visits, the arrival of his two ships had coincided with the annual festival of *Makahiki*, when folks put aside fighting and politics to honor the peaceful god Lono with processions, feasting and partying. The ships, with their tall masts and white sails, resembled the great canoes that had brought the first people to these islands. These canoes no longer existed, although the people knew of them from legends. And legends also said that Lono would return to them during the feast of *Makahiki*.

The imperfect storm

After two weeks of feasting, Cook felt he was overstaying his welcome; it seemed that his crewmen were eating everything in sight. So he set sail to explore more of the islands. Two days later, a howling gale broke one of the *Resolution's* masts and Cook decided to return to Kealakekua for repairs.

It was a fatal decision.

As crewmen worked on the mast, thefts continued, finally resulting in a violent confrontation. Sailors trying to retrieve some stolen tools were beaten and pelted with rocks; they obviously weren't being treated very royally. Then thieves took a cutter belonging to second-in-command Captain Clerke. An angered Cook went ashore and attempted to take the island chief Kalaniopu'u hostage, demanding that the boat be returned. An angry crowd gathered and shots were fired by Cook and his marines. As they attempted to reload, the mob descended on them. Cook was struck from behind, then stabbed in the neck and clubbed to death. Several men on both sides were killed in the brief but violent skirmish.

The crewmen retreated to their ships and Cook's body was dragged away by his attackers. The village was fired upon and later burned. Then a truce was established, at the request of several priests. Captain Clerke demanded the return of his leader's corpse and was given a bundle containing—much to his horror—a few body parts. The rest, he was told, had been burned and distributed among the priests and ali'i.

The saddened crew completed the mast repair and sailed away from Hawai'i on February 22, 1779, a week after Cook's death. Most historians believe that the deadly confrontation had occurred at the end of *Makahiki*, when the priests retreated to their *heiau* and the chiefs returned to the business of politics and combat.

Cook and other early visitors had noted that the Hawaiians, contrary to what the missionaries thought four decades later, were living a relatively good—if rather promiscuous—life. They tilled and irrigated fields and raised pigs, chickens and dogs—all for food—and they built ingenious shoreline fishponds with lava and coral walls.

However, they were a contradiction—friendly, gentle and welcoming, yet cunning, deceptive and sometimes vicious. Cook noted evidence that they practiced human sacrifice to appease their many gods, consecrate a new *heiau* and to mark the death of an *ali'i*. Later travelers and historians said some may have practiced cannibalism. Indeed, Cook was roasted, although there is no hard evidence that he became anyone's lunch.

The various islands were ruled as fifedoms by high chiefs and priests who fought among themselves for power. They imposed upon the common people a rigid system of *kapus*, which could bring death to anyone violating a complex set of laws. Women in particular were subject to these rules, and were forbidden—among many other things—to dine with men.

Kapus also required that commoners be obsessively servile around the *ali'i*. Posts of wood, bark and cloth—resembling padded jousting sticks—were placed wherever the *ali'i* went. According to an exhibit at Honolulu's Bishop Museum, these "were the signal for people to remove their clothes, squat, prostrate themselves or otherwise show deference."

To fail to do so often resulted in a quick and brutal death. Typical punishment for *kapu* violators included skull bashing or tying a person to a tree and drawing a strangulation cord around the neck, according to a Bishop Museum exhibit.

A not so merrie monarch

One of the warriors who had been present during Captain Cook's fatal visit to Kealakekua Bay was Kamehameha, the nephew of Chief Kalaniopu'u and a lessor *ali'i* from the Big Island's Waimea district. He supposedly took part in the fatal attack on Cook. Some historians say that he snatched a lock of the dead captain's hair as *mana*—a symbol of strength and prestige. He was a tall, powerful, brooding, ambitious and ugly man; one of Cook's officers said he had "as savage a looking face as I ever saw."

When Cook's crewmen sailed sadly from Hawai'i, they left behind not only body parts of their dead captain but several firearms that had been captured by the Hawaiians in the beach skirmish. These eventually would lead to a serious inter-island arms race.

News traveled slowly in those days, although word of the islands' discovery eventually reached Europe and America. Cook had opened up fur trading routes to North America and traders and whalers began calling on this valuable mid-Pacific landfall. The first ship arrived in 1786 and the numbers increased exponentially after that. Their crews bartered for food, firewood, fresh water and women. Then they realized that the *ali'i* mostly wanted weapons for waging war against one another. And when the Hawaiians couldn't barter for weapons, they tried to steal them. Several violent confrontations occurred; ships were attacked and plundered and villages were burned in reprisal. Still, greedy sea captains continued arming the natives, arriving with cargoes of muskets, knives and swords.

When old Kalaniopu'u died in 1782, his son Kiwalao was named as his heir. However, a power struggle followed, with several chiefs—including Kamehameha—fighting for control of the Big Island. A turning point in his violent career came in 1790 when he took possession of a small ship, the *Fair American*. Another *ali'i* had captured it after its sister ship, the *Eleanora,* had shelled a flotilla of canoes and a village, killing a hundred Hawaiians. In need of skilled crewmen, Kamehameha kidnapped two seamen—Isaac Davis, the lone survivor of the *Fair American* attack, and the *Eleanora's* boatswain John Young, who had come ashore just for a look around. They tried to escape but were recaptured and they eventually adopted Hawai'i as their new home.

Armed for battle

With a growing arsenal of weapons, and now a ship, a cannon and two able seamen, Kamehameha was ready to wage serious war. In 1782, even before he had secured all of his home island, he landed an invasion force on Maui. It was ruled by a powerful chief named Kaheliki, who had conquered O'ahu, Moloka'i and Lana'i. With Davis and Young firing the ship's cannon into the Maui warriors, Kamehameha routed the army and personally killed its leader. Kaheliki, who was on O'ahu at the time, was understandably stunned when he got the news.

However, more pressing matters called Kamehameha home; a chief named Keoua had invaded his lands. The two warring *ali'i* battled to a standstill, then Kamehameha committed one of his most dastardly acts. His followers had been building a *heiau* to his war god *Kukailimoku*. He invited Keoua there for peace talks, then stabbed him to death as he stepped onto the beach from his canoe. Kamehameha's men fell upon Keoua's small body of retainers and killed all but two of them with musket fire. Keoua's body was used to consecrate the new *heiau* in blood. Kamehameha was now ruler of the island of Hawai'i.

In 1791, Kaheliki invaded the Big Island, engaging Kamehameha in a clash of canoes in the pretty bay of Waipio. By now both had foreign gunners. The two adversaries fought to a draw in a conflict so bloody that it was called the Battle of the Red-Mouthed Gun. Kaheliki returned to O'ahu and died there three years later. Other chiefs began fighting over his lands and Kamehameha made his big move. He reconquered Maui, vanquish Moloka'i, seized Lana'i and headed with grim determination toward O'ahu.

The place of his greatest triumph is now a popular tourist stop. By rental car and tour bus, visitors head for Nu'uanu Pali, dramatic knife-edged cliffs above Honolulu. Kamehameha landed his forces at Waikiki in 1794 and—with muskets blazing and spears thrusting—he advanced against O'ahu's armies, which were led by a Maui chieftain. They sought the advantage of higher ground in the Nu'uanu Valley, but it proved their downfall. Savage and resolute, Kamehameha and his men cornered the enemy at the precipitous Nu'uanu Pali. Here, as exhibits tell today's tourists, he defeated the last of O'ahu's warriors, driving many of them over the sheer cliffs to their deaths.

The clever and ruthless campaigner now held dominion over all the major islands except Kaua'i, which he annexed in 1810 after years of negotiation. He had used the weapons and even the men of the Western world to defeat his enemies. However, history would demonstrate that—in the end—the Western world had used him.

In accepting the aid and weapons of the outsiders, Kamehameha was obliged to give them more influence over his domain. And in fact he wanted to adopt many of the ways of the West for his people. It seems odd in retrospect that he did not see this as the destruction of his society. Even as trade with the outside world increased and Kamehameha's people were obtaining Western luxuries and trappings, they were literally dying off.

White man's disease

Until Captain Cook arrived, the islanders had enjoyed something of a medical miracle, or at least a medical fluke. Isolated from the rest of the world, they had no communicable diseases and thus had built up no immunities. When the outsiders arrived, even simple maladies such as measles proved fatal; smallpox and typhus were devastating. The islands didn't even have mosquitoes until ships' crews dumped their stale, larvae-ridden water overboard to clean and refill their barrels. Malaria soon joined the list of white mans' diseases. Historians estimate that the native population shrank from an estimated 300,000 at the time of Cook's visit to about 60,000 in the 1860s.

Kamehameha died in 1919, leaving in place a British-style plan of royal succession. His son Liholiho became Kamehameha II, although he was hardly a worthy successor. A weak, boozing philanderer, he was exploited by Kamehameha's favorite wife, Ka'ahumanu. The powerful woman—who was not Liholiho's mother—used her strong will and her body to gain power within the new royal family. She slept with influential ali'i and manipulating the weaker ones. Ka'ahumanu despised the kapu system because it discriminated against women, so she convinced Liholiho to sit down and dine with the ladies. No lightning bolts struck, no volcanoes erupted, no tidal waves swept ashore.

The ruling ali'i realized that the gods they had feared for generations must have been false. Liholiho's timing couldn't have been better—or worse—depending on one's historical perspective. He paved the way for even more domination by outside forces. And this time, those forces were convinced they had been sent by God himself.

Hiram Bingham and his small band of Protestants stepped ashore from the brig *Thaddeus* at Waimea Bay on the Big Island on March 30, 1820. They had come to save the heathens from themselves. They were so blinded by their own vision of self-righteousness that they didn't even attempt to adapt themselves to Hawai'i's balmy climate. They continued wearing Boston black and gray in the tropical heat. They built New England style homes instead of the cooler, open-walled thatched dwellings of their converts.

Their missionary work was an ongoing sociological contradiction. They certainly were dedicated to the welfare of the Hawaiian people— at least as they interpreted it. They gave them an alphabet and thus a written language. They built schools and hospitals; they worked desperately to treat those suffering from white man's scourges, even as they accidentally inflicted them with these diseases. Most of the plagues, however, however, came from seaman in the liberty ports.

Not surprisingly, the missionaries and sailors were at constant odds. When the Calvinists tried to prohibit prostitution, their homes were fired upon by angry ships' crewmen. The Christians also clashed with a growing number of merchants and traders who came to Hawai'i to take, not to give. With the consent of greedy *ali'i*, traders virtually stripped the islands of sandalwood, shipping most of it off to China.

The royal Hawaiians

Throughout most of the 1800s, Hawai'i functioned as a constitutional monarchy, ruled by a succession of Kamehameha's descendants. Several foreign powers—particularly the United States, England and France—hungrily eyed these beautiful islands. Then in the mid-1800s, they agreed to respect Hawai'i's sovereignty, allowing the weak little kingdom survive for the moment. Its rulers continued looking to the West for advise, support and goods—particularly from the United States. Some *ali'i* even traveled overseas, visiting leaders in the Americas and Europe.

Some royal family members converted to Christianity, giving the missionaries considerable influence in shaping the island government. Eventually, the growing ranks of merchants, bankers and traders became more forceful in local politics, sometimes by marrying into Hawaiian royalty. And ironically, many of the most powerful merchants were sons of missionaries. In embracing the West, literally and figuratively, the Hawaiians had cast their fate to foreign winds. Hawaiian scholar David Malo wrote in 1837:

If a big waves comes in, large and unfamiliar fishes will come from the dark ocean, and when they see the small fishes in the shallows they will eat them up. White man's ships have arrived with clever men from big countries. They know our people are few in number and our country is small; they will devour us.

The tsunami and a sweet tooth

That foreign *tsunami* hit in 1848, ironically the same year that gold was discovered in California. This gold came in the form of land. The government, goaded by white businessmen, passed an act called the Great Mahele, which granted the *ali'i* the right to sell their land holdings. Until now, it had been understood that all land belonged to the chiefs, who shared its use with their subjects. The Mahele set up a Western system of deeded land ownership, and white merchants stepped in quickly to snap it up at bargain prices. The *ali'i* sold it willingly and greedily as they had given away their sandalwood; they wanted hard cash to buy more foreign luxuries.

Meanwhile, the missionaries were losing their grip on many of their flock as some members of royalty began encouraging them to return to their old ways. To worsen matters, the missions' home churches were strapped for cash and began withdrawing their support. Unlike the Spanish padres of early California, who created vast ranching enterprises, Hawai'i's missionaries had focused on tilling souls, not soils.

But there was soil to be tilled. The Great Mahele and intermarriage with the *ali'i* had given hundreds of thousands of acres to the whites.

Some new landowners realized they could cultivate a member of the bamboo family that grew wild in Hawai'i—sugarcane. Of course, agriculture is a labor-intensive business. The native people wouldn't do. Their ranks had been decimated by disease and alcoholism, and the survivors didn't take much to field work. In 1850, the government passed the Masters and Servants Act, allowing landowners to contract for foreign labor. Workers signed five-year contracts, giving them about $3 a month plus room, board and clothing.

First, the Chinese

The first to arrive were Chinese, imported from the war-torn and drought-ridden Canton province in 1852. The planters assumed that they would return to China after their contracts expired. However, most stayed and went into business, to become the first layer of Hawai'i's Asian dominated society.

The sugar industry grew, the Chinese left the fields to set up shops and the growers needed more workers. Deciding that Asians were too ambitious and really didn't know their proper place in a white world, they drew their next laborers from Portugal.

Europe was too far a reach for more immigrant labor, so the barons turned again to the Orient, importing Japanese workers starting in 1885, and Filipinos in 1910. Overall, they brought in nearly 400,000 laborers until importation dwindled in the 1930s. Nearly half of the laborers had come from Japan and the Japanese are today Hawai'i's largest ethnic group.

Each ethnic group was kept separate from the others in plantation work camps. The growers feared that interracial unity might lead to labor organizations. Within these camps, workers set up their own schools, churches or temples and even company stores. A typical work day would begin at 4 a.m. for the women, who rose to prepare breakfast and a field lunch for the men, who climbed from their beds at 5. Both men and women were in the fields by 6. They worked until 4:30 and returned to their huts, where it was lights out at 8:30.

The work was hard and the pay was bad. The growers' worst fears were realized in 1909 when Japanese workers staged the first of several strikes. Gradually, pay and working conditions improved and the labor camps continued well into the middle of the last century. Then foreign competition and sugar beets from the mainland eroded the Hawaiian sugarcane industry. Today, only two sugar mills still function—one on Maui and another on Kaua'i.

A collision course

Meanwhile, back in the previous century, it was evident that the royalists and planter-merchants were on a collision course. Kalakaua, Hawai'i's longest ruling monarch and its strongest leader since Kamehameha I, urged his people to resist further influence by the outsiders. And those "outsiders" wanted the monarchy gone so they could make their fortunes without interference. They plotted to have Hawai'i annexed to the United States, even though the U.S. had formally recognized its independence. In 1887, they forced a constitution onto Kalakaua that greatly favored the whites.

The popular monarch died in 1891 and his sister Lili'uokalani became queen. She was one of the most remarkable people in Hawai'i's history—proud to the point of arrogance, strong-willed and at the same time gentle and artistic. She was well-educated and she wrote poetry and music, including the sad farewell song *Aloha 'Oe*. Although she was a devout Christian, she was a champion of native Hawaiians' rights.

The good queen pushed her opposition too far and too fast. She proclaimed that she would nullify the constitution and restore a strong Hawaiian monarchy. This was all the excuse that the whites needed. They committed the brazen act of overthrowing a foreign power without the consent of their own government. A "Committee of Safety" of white citizens and a squad of Marines from the *U.S.S. Boston* surrounded the Queen's Iolani Palace in early 1893, held her captive and set up a provisional government.

Congress, shocked when it finally got news of this renegade action, refused to vote for annexation. The anarchists were faced with the embarrassing prospect of handing power back to the royalists. And the queen was so angry that she threatened to have them beheaded, although she later relented. The revolutionaries, led by Stanford Dole, the son of missionaries, refused to restore the monarchy.

In 1895, a group of royalists began stockpiling weapons to take the monarchy back by force, but their plot was discovered. They were arrested and Queen Lili'uokalani was charged with treason. She was sentenced to five years "hard labor," although she was confined to a room in the palace, and she was released after a few months. Two years later, in 1898, Congress annexed Hawai'i to the United States.

...and into the next century

Pineapples became an important cash crop at the start of the twentieth century, with the arrival of James Drummond Dole, a cousin of Stanford Dole, who was now territorial governor. He pioneered pineapple canning and eventually controlled eighty percent of the worlds' market. Dole bought the island of Lana'i in 1922 and turned it into one large pineapple field. It's still privately owned, although so few pineapples remain that residents supposedly have to borrow some from Maui for the annual Lana'i Pineapple Festival.

About the time of Dole's arrival, plantation owners, bankers and merchants—often the same people—created a monopoly called the Big Five. It controlled ninety-five percent of Hawai'i's agriculture and most of its business, banking and shipping. No surprise, each firm had at least one missionary descendent on its board of directors. They were—and in some cases still are—Castle & Cooke, Alexander & Baldwin, American Factors, Theo. Davies & Co., and C. Brewer & Co.

The twentieth century was a time of slow growth and gradual prosperity for the Territory of Hawai'i. The idyllic islands generally were overlooked by the rest of America, except for the wealthy few who could afford to take cruise ships there.

It was an odd time for Kamehameha's islands. Only five percent of the population was white at the turn of that century, yet they controlled ninety-five percent of the commerce. The Hawaiians themselves continued fading into the background, except as "local color" and novelty dancers for the growing tourist trade. Matson Lines, an offshoot of one of the Big Five, hauled tourists from San Francisco to Honolulu harbor, where they were met by hip-swaying hula maidens.

The grand hotels

The first major resort hotel, the Moana, opened at Waikiki on March 10, 1901, while there were still taro ponds and rice paddies on the beach. Gushed the *Honolulu Advertiser* about this pleasure palace:

The sounding splash of the surf on the sands of Waikiki, the strains of music and to the clinking glasses of bubbling wine, the beautiful Moana Hotel at Waikiki Beach was christened last night.

Waikiki's first resort hotel is still there, now part of the Sheraton chain. Meanwhile, assorted tent cabins, cottages and guest houses followed its opening. Then other large resorts were built, including the hideaway cottage complex, Halekulani (House of Heaven), opened in 1907 and since rebuilt as a highrise. The Moorish style Royal Hawaiian, dubbed "Pink Palace" because of its pink stucco façade, was completed in 1927. When it opened its doors, a local reporter wrote: "Gone are the days of a primitive people untouched by civilization."

Hawai'i had its first twentieth century celebrity when Waikiki beach boy "Duke" Paoa Kahanamoku won several Olympic Gold Medals for swimming from 1914 until 1920. He introduced surfing to the world and moved among real dukes and even presidents until his death in 1968 at the age of 78. Another twentieth century celebrity of sorts was Clarissa Haili, born October 28, 1901. Initially a school teacher, she changed her name to Hilo Hattie and became a comic hula character on the long running radio show, "Hawaii Calls." She died in 1979, although her name survives in a line of clothing and other Hawaiian style regalia.

Hawai'i's lighthearted innocence ended abruptly on Sunday morning, December 7, 1941. The expansionist-minded Empire of Japan had been spoiling for war with America since the mid-1930s and it came with a vengeance. More than 2,400 U.S. servicemen and civilians lost their lives when Japanese fighter planes from offshore aircraft screamed over O'ahu. They caught troops in their bunks, planes on the ground at Hickam Field and a good part of the American fleet at Pearl Harbor.

They came in so low that Army Colonel William Wheeler said: "I could see some of the Japanese pilots lean out of their planes and smile... I could even see the gold in their teeth."

My own recollection of the Pearl Harbor attack was as a kid listening wide-eyed to the radio on the front porch of our home in southern Oregon. I recall that mainlanders knew so little about Hawai'i that the announcer mispronounced O'ahu, calling it *O-hau.*

A pivotal role

Mainland America certainly was aware of Hawai'i from that point on. It became a major staging area for the Pacific theater. Officials were so fearful of a land attack that they placed the islands under martial law.

However, Hawai'i did not incarcerate its Japanese-American citizens, as did the western mainland states. It was impossible, for they represented nearly half the total population. And it was not necessary, either in Hawai'i or the American west. During the war, not one single act of sabotage was ever traced to a Japanese-American.

Quite the opposite. They were so eager to show their patriotism that they formed two all-Japanese combat units, the 442nd Regimental Combat Team and the 100th Infantry Battalion. They fought with such valor and ferocity in Italy and France that they became the most highly decorated fighting units of World War II. Eighteen Japanese-Americans from Hawai'i won the Medal of Honor, including young Lieutenant Daniel K. Inouye. He saved his pinned-down squad by wiping out two German machine gun nests, and he lost an arm in the process.

The Territory of Hawai'i emerged from World War II with a new attitude. Asians, still the majority, became more dominant in the business community. What began among the whites as a respect for

Japanese-Hawaiians blossomed into a broader acceptance of the islands' many ethnic groups. Aloha spirit was coming full flower. Hawai'i bloomed into America's fiftieth state in 1969, and the first Japanese-American was elected to the U.S. Senate—war hero Dan Inouye. "I got more votes among the haoles than my haole opponent," he once said.

Tourism began to flourish as flying became affordable. During the 1980s, investors from Japan—riding the crest of a booming economy—began buying up what their fathers had tried to take by force. Then Tokyo's stock market went into a tailspin and much of the business and resort ownerships were sold back to Americans.

A native Hawaiian movement gained momentum in the 1990s and continues today as they seek compensation for what was taken from them. There is talk of some kind of autonomy for Hawaiians and perhaps land redistribution, although it remains a complex and unresolved issue.

Tourism, Hawai'i's largest industry, continues to boom. It is ironic that it's glamorized with the lore of native Hawaiians—surfing, outrigger canoe rides, the lei, the hula and the luau. More than seven million people a year are drawn to these paradise islands. Tourism took a severe hit in the months following the September 11, 2001, terrorist attack, although it is coming back.

To ensure that those tourists keep coming, the state and the city of Honolulu spent several million dollars to return Waikiki Beach to that romantic image projected in the idyllic movies of the 1930s and 1950s.

And isn't this where we came in?

You know you're in Hawai'i...

1 When you see a bikini-clad surfer just off Waikiki Beach walking past the fashionable shops of Kalakaua Avenue, with her board tucked under her arm.

2 When you find flower petals instead of bird doo on your car if you park it under a tree.

3 When shave ice has its own section in the Yellow Pages. (The O'ahu phone book incorrectly calls it "shaved ice.")

4 When statues of famous citizens are draped with leis.

5 When sushi parlors serve Spam sushi rolls.

6 When you may see a pretty girl doing the hula on a busy city sidewalk, sometimes backed up by a ukelele and drums.

7 When McDonald's serves Spam, eggs and rice as one of its breakfast specials.

8 When you see as many Japanese tourists as American tourists, even though you're in America.

9 When you find lei-making shops instead of fortune cookie factories in Honolulu's Chinatown.

10 When you discover that ABC is a mini-mart, not a spelling primer. This Hawaiian chain sells groceries, liquor, snacks, aloha shirts, souvenirs, lots of macadamia nuts and other visitor essentials. There are thirty-eight outlets on Waikiki, plus stores on Maui, Kaua'i and the Big Island.

THE TEN BEST THINGS TO DO JUST BECAUSE YOU'RE IN HONOLULU

1 STROLL WAIKIKI BEACH AT SUNSET

Yes, it's busy and commercialized, yet Waikiki Beach is one of our favorite places, particularly at sunset. As the sun approaches the sea, Diamond Head is bathed in golden light and palm trees become silhouettes, moving in the breeze like slender hula dancers. Near the bronze statue of Duke Kahanamoku, dozens of people gather to witness this nightly spectacle. We all watch as the sun plays tag with the clouds. Many reach for their cameras as a sailboat passes in front of the golden disk; it happens often. And then the golden orb dips silently into the sea, issuing a tiny blue-green flash as it slips from sight. At nearby beachside resorts and along Kalakaua Avenue, tiki torches are lit.

2 HAVE A PINK DRINK AT THE PINK PALACE

Mai Tai Bar at the Royal Hawaiian, 2259 Kalakaua Ave., Waikiki; (808) 923-7311; www.royal-hawaiian.com. GETTING THERE: The hotel is behind the Royal Hawaiian Shopping Center, reached via Royal Hawaiian Avenue, off Kalakaua.

The Mai Tai Bar sits right on Waikiki Beach; it's a fine place for enjoying views of the surf, sunbathers and Diamond Head while sipping a Pink Palace. This Polynesian drink is a blend of Grand Marnier, light rum, cream of coconut and pineapple juice. It comes with a slice of pineapple and an orchid blossom, which your lady companion can thrust behind the appropriate ear. It's the left if she's married and the right if she's single and available. And if she's your wife and places it behind her right ear...?

3 VISIT CHINATOWN'S LEI STANDS

Along Maunakea Street between Beretania and King streets. GET-TING THERE: To reach Chinatown from Waikiki, head about 3.5 miles northwest on Ala Moana Boulevard. A quarter of a mile past Aloha Tower, turn right onto River Street, which borders a canal. Chinatown is to your right. Maunakea parallels River Street, two blocks east.

Most of the leis that are draped around tourists' necks as aloha greetings aren't made by native islanders. They're made by Chinese at several shops in Chinatown and many are along Maunakea Street. We counted six within three blocks. They're most active in the evening as workers prepare sweetly scented leis for the next day's use. They're open in the daytime, too, and they sell their leis at retail. You'll find a much better selection here—at much lower prices—than in tourist shops.

4 TOUR THE HISTORIC MOANA HOTEL

Sheraton Moana, 2365 Kalakaua Ave.; (808) 922-3111; www.shera-ton-hawaii.com. Tours are 11 and 5 on weekdays. GETTING THERE: The hotel is opposite the base of Ka'iulani Avenue.

The Sheraton Moana is the oldest luxury resort on the beach, opened in 1901 and restored to its original ionic columned splendor. Tours, which don't require reservations, begin in the History Room on the second floor just above the main lobby. Visitors watch a video about the hotel, then are taken on a walk past its historic sites.

If you don't take a tour, you can still learn about the Moana's storied past by viewing displays in the History Room and along corridors outside. You'll learn about "Boat Days" when well-heeled passengers arrived on Matson liners. Among exhibits are photos of early Waikiki and a radio script for "Hawaii Calls." It was broadcast from the hotel's Banyan Veranda for forty years until 1975, featuring Hawai'i's singing star Alfred Alpaca and comic hula girl Hilo Hattie.

5 CATCH THE DON HO SHOW

At the Waikiki Beachcomber, 2300 Kalakaua Ave.; (808) 923-3981; www.donho.com. Shows Sunday-Thursday; dinner seating at 7 and cock-tail seating at 8; see details in Chapter Six, page 113. GETTING THERE: The Waikiki Beachcomber is at the corner of Kalakaua and Duke's Lane.

After more than forty years onstage in Waikiki, "Mr. Hawaii's" voice is a bit rusty, and he chats and jokes with the audience more than he sings. However, that old "Tiny Bubbles" resonance is still there, and he still draws the faithful to his laid-back show.

6 DO THE ROYAL LUAU

Royal Hawaiian Hotel, 2259 Kalakaua Ave., Waikiki; (808) 931-7194; www.royal-hawaiian.com. Every Monday and Thursday with cocktails at 6 and the luau at 7; open bar with mai tais, piña coladas, beer and fruit punch; about $80.

Visitors debate as to which is the best luau on Oʻahu. Our favorite is the Royal Luau, the only one on Waikiki. The setting is fab—right beside the beach with a view of Diamond Head to the southeast and sunsets to the northwest. With flickering tiki torches, the moon and stars above, swaying palm trees and swaying hula girls, it provides one of the most romantic settings in the islands.

The luau doesn't include the ceremonial opening of the *imu* where the pig is roasted, although the onstage host explains the various foods served and their historic significance. Entertainment is a Polynesian mix of traditional dances and some contemporary Hawaiian songs. The show, like the historic Royal Hawaiian, has a pleasantly old fashioned flavor.

TRAVEL TIP: If the weather's troubling, call before you go, since the luau is outside and subject to cancellation during rain or strong winds. It is sometimes moved indoors in bad weather. In the off-season, it may be held on Mondays only. For other luaus, see the end of Chapter Two.

7 RIDE IN AN OUTRIGGER

On Waikiki Beach at C&K Beach Services, Aloha Beach Services, or Waikiki Prime Time Sports. FINDING THEM: All of these outrigger canoe operators are on the beach between Kuhio Beach Park off Kalakaua Avenue and Fort DeRussey park.

Two popular activities for Waikiki Beach visitors are riding outrigger canoes and surfing. We assume that most of our readers aren't surfers and may not be inclined to take lessons, so we'll suggest taking an outrigger ride instead. The only skill required here is paddling and your accompanying beach boy will show you the proper strokes. He'll help you try to catch a wave just like the surfers, and just like them, you'll likely get wet.

8 SLURP AN HISTORIC SHAVE ICE

Matsumoto's, 66-087 Kamehameha Hwy., Haleʻiwa; (808) 637-4827; www.matsumotosshaveice.com. Daily 8:30 to 6. GETTING THERE: Haleʻiwa is on Oʻahu's North Shore. From Waikiki, go northwest on H-1, then north on Highway 99 and follow signs to Haleʻiwa. Matsumoto's is on the eastern edge of the historic district.

Shave ice, which originated in China centuries ago and then traveled to Japan, was brought to Hawaiʻi by Japanese sugarcane workers.

The most popular outlet, although not the original, is Matsumoto's. It was established in 1951 by Mamoru and Helen Matsumoto as a grocery store. It still serves shave ice although it's is now a tourist and T-shirt shop, and no longer sells groceries. However the shave ice is fine, with a variety of flavors available, and they're all made on the premises. Among Matsumoto's customers have been Tom Hanks and former NFL stars Junior Seau and Ricky Watters.

The original shave ice, called *kakigouri* in Japanese, was made from packed snow, onto which sweetened soybean flour was poured. Then a machine was devised in Japan to shave powdery snow from a block of ice; thus the name "shave ice." Hawai'i's shave ice is much finer than mainland snowcones, which are usually made from finely crushed ice.

9 VISIT HILO HATTIE'S

700 N. Nimitz Hwy., (808) 535-6500; www.hilohattie.com. Daily 8 to 6; major credit cards. Free shuttle picks up shoppers from various Waikiki-area hotels daily from 8 to 5; call for the schedule. GETTING THERE: Follow Ala Moana Boulevard about three or four miles from Waikiki; it becomes the Nimitz Highway and Hilo Hattie's is on the right, at Pacific Street.

Hilo Hattie gained fame as a comic hula girl on the old "Hawaii Calls" radio show, then she lent her name to a line of colorful Polynesian sportswear. The firm has become the largest producer and retailer of such clothing in Hawai'i and maybe the world. The huge warehouse-sized flagship store on the Nimitz Highway is worth a visit.

As you enter the store, a pretty lady will drape a shell lei around your neck and invite you to have a free glass of punch or ice water. Hanging in the entry is a 160-inch-wide aloha shirt, logged in the *Guinness Book of Records* as the world's largest; it's labeled as a 400XL. Step inside and you're in a warehouse of gaudy Polynesian colors— aloha shirts, muumuus, sarongs and such. The store also has shelves brimming with wonderfully tacky Hawaiian souvenirs and specialty foods, including macadamia nuts and Kona coffee.

10 CATCH THE HONOLULU SYMPHONY AT THE WAIKIKI SHELL

Kapi'olani Park. For Waikiki Shell events, call (808) 527-2400 or (808) 591-2211, www.waikikishell.com; for Honolulu symphony information, call (808) 524-0815, www.honolulusymphony.com. GETTING THERE: From Kalakaua Avenue, turn north onto Monsarratt Avenue; the shell is on the right.

Every summer, the Honolulu Symphony presents free pops concerts at this outdoor band shell. Concert-goers can relax in the 2,400 seats or simply sprawl on the grass, enjoying the stars above and the silhouette of nearby Diamond Head. The crescent curve of the shell produces near perfect acoustics. It's also the site of many other concerts and assorted functions. The shell was opened in 1952 and for nearly half a century, it hosted the Kodak Hula Show, although it had been discontinued at press time.

SUPERLIST: THE VERY BEST OF HAWAI'I

After exploring Hawai'i on and off for years, and spending several months in intensive research for this book, we've developed our Superlist: the absolute best of paradise.

1 BEST ATTRACTION: Polynesian Cultural Center

At La'ie on O'ahu's North Shore, this living history center provides an excellent quick study of the cultures of Hawai'i and several other South Pacific islands. It's the state's most popular attraction. For someone on their first visit to Hawai'i, the Cultural Center offers a fine introduction to the people of paradise. **Chapter Two, page 43.**

2 BEST NATURAL ATTRACTION: Hawaii Volcanoes National Park

This is nature in motion. The Big Island's Hawaii Volcanoes National Park is one of the few places in the world where visitors may be able to see a volcano in action. The park also provides fine exhibits on volcanology, which is what the Hawaiian Islands are all about. **Chapter Thirteen, page 218.**

3 BEST SNORKEL AREA: Kealakekua Bay

This beautiful bay on the Big Island is an underwater preserve, so its reefs and fish are protected, providing Hawai'i's best snorkeling and diving. It's also one of the state's most historic spots, where Captain James Cook met his demise. **Chapter Thirteen, page 221.**

4 BEST ACTIVITY: Kaua'i helicopter flight

Many people say that Kaua'i is Hawai'i's prettiest island, with its imposing seacliffs and dramatic Waimea Canyon. And there's no better way to see it than by helicopter. **Chapter Fourteen, page 253.**

5 BEST BEACH: Polihale

And you thought we were going to say Waikiki! Polihale State Park on Kaua'i is one of the most beautiful and remote places in the islands.

Its broad sand dune beach is at the base of sheer cliffs, and the island of Ni'ihau is just offshore. And it's uncrowded, because you must drive over a sandy road to reach it. **Chapter Fourteen, page 251.**

6 BEST SCENIC DRIVE: West Maui

No, not the famous drive to Hana, but the lesser-known loop drive around the West Maui Mountains. You'll see more rugged seacliffs and a lot less traffic and rain. And it's all paved, although it's very narrow in spots. **Chapter Twelve, page 178.** If skinny roads intimidate you, a close runner-up is **Molokai's southeast coast,** from Kaunakakai to Halawa Bay. **Chapter Fifteen, page 274.**

7 BEST LUAU: Old Lahaina Luau

This Maui luau has it all—a gorgeous beachfront setting, fine Polynesian entertainment, one of the best luau food selections in the islands and Hawaiian cultural demonstrations. And did we mention the open bar? **Chapter Twelve, page 190.**

8 BEST RESTAURANT: La Mer

The Halukelani's award-winning Waikiki Beach restaurant is the most elegant in the islands, and the French cuisine is outstanding. Throw caution and wallet to the winds and go for the tasting menu with matching wines. **Chapter Three, page 66.**

9 BEST RESORT: Manele Bay Hotel

If it's good enough for Bill Gates, it's good enough for us. This Lanai resort, where he was married in 1994, is the most gorgeous and opulent retreat on all the islands. And because it's on the least-visited of the islands, it's far from madding crowds, not to mention tour buses. **Chapter Sixteen, page 288.**

10 BEST FAMILY RETREAT: Hilton Waikoloa Village

This large resort on the Big Island has everything for families—a large swimming complex, boat rides on a lagoon, even a monorail. It's all spread over 640 acres of beachfront and perhaps best of all, it's relatively affordable. **Chapter Thirteen, page 235.**

Chapter Two

HONOLULU & O'AHU LURES

BEING A TOURIST IN PARADISE

Oahu is a splendid place to vacation even if you plan only to luxuriate at a Waikiki resort and lie on sun-warmed sand. The island's many attractions are a pleasing extra, like getting free dessert with your entrée. In fact, O'ahu has more specific attractions than all of the other islands combined.

Although this section of the book is mostly about Honolulu and Waikiki, this chapter covers all of O'ahu. Many of the island's major attractions such as the Polynesian Cultural Center and Sealife Park and are outside the capital city and its famous beach.

We feature O'ahu's top lures in three lists—the Ten Best Attractions, the next Ten Best attractions and the Ten Best activities. Each list begins with our favorite, followed by the rest in alphabetical order. Thus, there are no losers in *Hawai'i: The Best of Paradise*; only winners and runners-up. We use this same procedure with other lists in this book, except when the items don't really relate to one another.

PRICING: Since prices frequently change, we use dollar sign codes to indicate the approximate cost of various attractions and activities: *$* = under $10; *$$* = $10 to $19; *$$$* = $20 to $29; *$$$$* = $30 to $39; *$$$$$* = $40 or more. And you already know that prices are almost always less for seniors and kids. **CREDIT CARDS**: Abbreviations are obvious, and "Major credit cards" indicates that an establishment accepts MasterCard and VISA plus at least two others.

☺ *KID STUFF:* This little grinning guy marks attractions and activities that are of particular interest to pre-teens.

NOTE: For a list of Oʻahu's Ten Best free lures, see Chapter Five. Also, for map locations of many of the listings in this chapter, see the Honolulu map in Chapter One, page 20.

THE TEN BEST OʻAHU ATTRACTIONS

Our list represents a mixed group, from museums to war memorials to natural attractions. We'd suggest visiting the first two shortly after you arrive for they will give you insight into everything else you will see and learn about Polynesian culture.

1 POLYNESIAN CULTURAL CENTER

55-370 Kamehameha Hwy., Laʻie; (877) 572-2347 or (808) 293-3333; www.polynesia.com. Monday-Saturday 11 to 9:30; may close earlier during slower seasons. Stores in the Treasures of Polynesia Shopping Plaza open at 11; access to villages starts at noon. Basic admission, including all village shows and activities $$$$; higher prices for tickets that include the Aliʻi luau, Horizons evening show and IMAX films. Round-trip shuttle from Waikiki $$. Major credit cards. GETTING THERE: The Polynesian Cultural Center is about thirty miles from Waikiki on the northeast Oʻahu coast. Easiest way is to catch the shuttle from Waikiki; check your hotel concierge for schedules. If you drive, head northeast from Honolulu on H-3, pick up Kamehameha Highway (Route 83) in Kaneʻohe and follow it north to Laʻie.

Operated by the Mormon church, the Polynesian Cultural Center is the best attraction in all of Hawaiʻi, and it's the most popular with visitors. It provides a sociological sampler not only of Hawaiʻi but the islands of Tonga, Fiji, Tahiti, Samoa, the Marquesas and Maori New Zealand. Each island is represented by an authentically reproduced village, where visitors watch traditional dances and arts and crafts demonstrations. The shows are quite authentic since the participants are native to the islands they represent; many are students at the adjacent Brigham Young University-Hawaiʻi.

Current focus of the village shows is more on lifestyles, costumes and cultures of the islands, instead of dancing. While very informative, they tilt more toward entertainment, often tinged with humor. Particu-

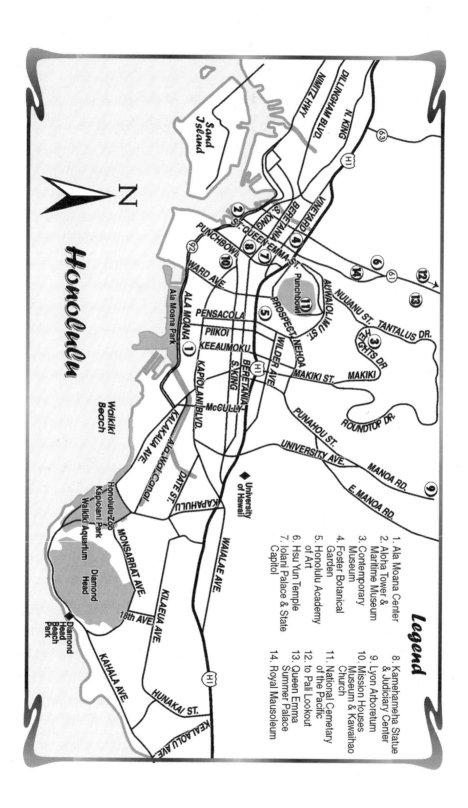

Honolulu

N

Sand Island

Waikiki Beach

Ala Moana Park

Legend

1. Ala Moana Center
2. Aloha Tower & Maritime Museum
3. Contemporary Museum
4. Foster Botanical Garden
5. Honolulu Academy of Art
6. Hsu Yün Temple
7. Iolani Palace & State Capitol
8. Kamehameha Statue & Judiciary Center
9. Lyon Arboretum
10. Mission Houses Museum & Kawaihao Church
11. National Cemetary of the Pacific
12. to Pali Lookout
13. Queen Emma Summer Palace
14. Royal Mausoleum

NIMITZ HWY.
N. KING
DILLINGHAM BLVD.
Punchbowl
BERETANIA
VINEYARD
S. KING ST.
QUEEN EMMA ST.
AUWAIOLIMU ST.
NUUANU ST.
TANTALUS DR.
PUNCHBOWL
WARD AVE.
ALA MOANA
ALA MOANA
PENSACOLA
PIIKOI
KEEAUMOKU
PROSPECT
NEHOA
WILDER AVE.
HEIGHTS DR.
MAKIKI ST.
MAKIKI
ROUNDTOP DR.
S. KING
BERETANIA
McGULLY
KALAKAUA AVE.
KAPIOLANI BLVD.
Ala Wai Canal
KAPAHULU
DATE ST.
University of Hawaii
PUNAHOU ST.
UNIVERSITY AVE.
MANOA RD.
E. MANOA RD.
WAIALAE AVE.
MONSARRAT AVE.
Honolulu Zoo
Kapiolani Park
Waikiki Aquarium
Diamond Head
18th AVE.
KILAUEA AVE.
Diamond Head Beach Park
KAHALA AVE.
HUNAKAI ST.
KEALAOLU AVE.

H1
H1
92
61
63

larly humorous is the Samoan village show, led by the Polynesian Cultural Center's top entertainer and poster boy, Chief Sielu Avea.

A daily highlight at the center is the midafternoon "Canoe Pageant" when islanders dance and sing on platforms rigged across double canoes that are poled along a moat.

The center's nightly Ali'i Luau is one of the most popular on the islands, and the food's not bad for this mass feeding of upwards of 400 people. The evening begins with a procession of brightly costumed "royalty," followed by a ceremonial uncovering of the *imu* pit where the pig is roasted. (It's not the one served to the assembled multitudes; the ceremony is mostly for show.) Entertainment during and following the feast is excellent, with the usual silly hula lessons for audience volunteers. There is no open bar; in fact no bar at all. These are good Mormon folk and only decaffeinated beverages are served.

TRAVEL TIPS: Get your seat on the lagoon bank for the Canoe Pageant at least half an hour early or you'll wind up standing. Also, get in line half an hour early for the luau for the best seating. (Some upgraded tickets include preferred seating.)

For a show that features much more South Seas dancing, catch the cultural center's "Horizons" program Monday-Saturday evening at 7:30; see Chapter Six, page 112.

2 BISHOP MUSEUM

1525 Bernice St., Honolulu; (808) 847-3511; www.bishopmuseum.org Open daily 9 to 5; $$. Major credit cards accepted in the gift shop. Planetarium shows at 11:30, 1:30 and 3; hula shows at 11 and 2 and crafts demonstrations from 9 to 2. One hour behind the scenes tours available. GETTING THERE: Go west on H-1, take the Houghtailing Street exit, go right to the first stoplight, turn left onto Bernice Street and follow it 2.5 blocks to the museum. To return from the museum, retrace your route but pass under the freeway, turn right onto King Street, right again onto Kalihi Street and follow H-1 signs east.

Simply put, this is the world's finest museum on Polynesian lore, with a splendid collection of artifacts and informative displays. The main building, a handsome cut-stone structure, houses the primary exhibits. It presents a quick study of the Polynesians' arrival in Hawai'i and the radical changes wrought by later intruders from the outside world. While historically accurate, the exhibits are a bit sanitized, with little reference to the subjugation of the Hawaiians and the decimation caused by "white mans' diseases."

Displays are on the main floor and three balconies. They cover the whaling period and the various ethnic groups drawn to Hawai'i by the sugar and pineapple industries. Other exhibits focus on the societies of Polynesia, Melanesia and Micronesia, and on Hawai'i's flora and fauna.

This is a labyrinthian place; about the time you think you've seen it all, you encounter a door or stairway leading to yet another display area.

Recent additions to the museum complex are the Castle Memorial Room, opened at the turn of this century and used for changing exhibits, and an outdoor hula garden, completed in 2003. The museum was founded in 1899 by Charles Reed Bishop in honor of his late wife, King Kamehameha descendant Princess Bernice Pauahi Bishop.

3 HAWAII MARITIME CENTER

Near the Aloha Tower at Pier 7 in Honolulu Harbor; (808) 536-6373; www.bishopmuseum.org. Daily 8:30 to 8, closes at 5 during off-seasons. GETTING THERE: Follow Ala Moana about 3.5 miles northwest from Waikiki; the Maritime Center is just short of Aloha Tower. ☺

Part of the Bishop Museum, this is one of Oʻahu's better archives, with a large warehouse full of maritime exhibits and the four-masted schooner *Falls of Clyde* berthed alongside. The *Clyde* is the star attraction, built in Scotland in 1878 and once used on the Matson Lines' Honolulu-San Francisco cruises. Visitors can poke into the captain's cabin and partially furnished staterooms, explore below deck and go forward to clutch the ship's wheel, pretending they're weighing anchor and catching a good breeze.

In the museum, several display cases are cleverly built into cutaway pontoons of a catamaran. The museum's varied exhibits concern voyages of early Polynesians, inter-island flying (started in 1929 by Hawaiian Airlines), whaling, and waterfront history. A large display focuses on Matson Lines' grand old days when its *S.S. Lurline* and other cruise ships brought pleasure-seekers to the islands. Particularly interesting to me as a former newspaperman was an exhibit about the *Honolulu Advertiser* and its coverage of the waterfront. First published in 1856, the *Advertiser* is the oldest American newspaper west of the Rockies.

4 HONOLULU ACADEMY OF ART

900 S. Beretania St., Honolulu; (808) 532-8700 or (808) 532-8701; www.honoluluacademy.org. Tuesday-Saturday 10 to 4:30 and Sunday 1 to 5; closed Monday; $; MC/VISA. GETTING THERE: From Waikiki, take McCully north to Beretania, turn left and follow it about 1.5 miles; the art museum is on the right, near Ward Avenue.

Known mostly for beaches and balmy climate, Honolulu is not regarded by visitors as a serious cultural center. Yet its recently renovated Academy of Arts is world class. Its thirty-three galleries—built around several courtyards—feature paintings, drawings, ceramics, sculptures and other fine art and folk art from all over the globe, with a special focus on Hawaiʻi and the South Pacific. It has a small, select collection of European and American masters. However, if your time is limited, hurry through these galleries and head for the outstanding exhibits from the Pacific and Asia.

Particularly intriguing is the East Meets West Gallery, showing cross-cultural influences on Asian and Western art. One of our favorite displays is a fanciful eighteenth century wallpaper panorama of Captain Cook's exploits in Hawai'i. It features idealistic drawings of bosomy maidens and tattooed men frolicking about and paying homage to their strange visitor. The panels are historically inaccurate but they're fun.

Brilliant Dale Chihuly glassworks decorate a courtyard beside the museum café and the entrance to the Doris Duke Gallery. Here, the focus is on past and present Hawaiian painters and artists who have visited Hawai'i. Polynesian galleries feature paintings of Hawaiian royalty, an impressive collection of calabash bowls, feathered body adornments and such. The Asian galleries offer snarling Indonesian masks, assorted Buddha figures, elaborate temple carvings from India and art from Japan, China and Korea. The James and Mari Michener Gallery displays their extensive collection of Japanese woodblock prints.

5 IOLANI PALACE STATE MONUMENT

King and Richards streets, Honolulu; (808) 522-0832. Open Tuesday-Saturday. Palace access by 45-minute guided tours only; 9 to 2:15; $$. Self-guiding tours of the Gallery Museum 9 to 4; $. Ticket office open 8:30 to 4:30; MC/VISA in the gift shop. Royal Hawaiian Band performs on the grounds every Friday at noon. GETTING THERE: From Waikiki, go north on McCully and then northwest on Beretania about three miles. Pass the state capitol and turn left onto Richards Street and left again onto King.

America's only former royal palace stands on a park-like fourteen-acre campus. It was completed in 1882 by Hawai'i's last, longest-serving and most colorful king, David Kalakaua. The opulent ten-room "American Florentine" mansion nearly bankrupted the monarchy. It has been meticulously restored, with many of the original furnishings on display. Its wooden floors are kept polished by visitors who are required to wear protective booties. Well-informed docents regale them with tales of Hawaiian royalty. The most elaborately furnished rooms are the opulent dining room set for a formal state dinner, and the combined throne and ball room with rose floral carpets, gold leaf framed mirrors and the original gold-leaf covered thrones.

The basement Gallery Museum contains the restored palace kitchen and several artifacts from Hawaiian royalty, including bird feather capes and original *ali'i* crowns, scepters and ceremonial swords.

Touring Iolani Palace, one gets the true sense of these remarkable people who evolved within a few decades from a stone age society to a European style monarchy with all the trappings of state.

NOTE: The adjacent royal residence, which for years has been used as the governor's mansion, is being restored as a museum, with the governor moving into a new mansion behind.

6 PACIFIC SUBMARINE MUSEUM & U.S.S. BOWFIN

111 Arizona Memorial Dr., Pearl Harbor; (808) 423-1341; www.bowfin.org. Daily 8 to 5. MC/VISA, AMEX; $; combined Bowfin/U.S.S. Missouri tickets $$. GETTING THERE: It's adjacent to the U.S.S. Arizona Memorial. Take exit 15-A from H-1 onto Kamehameha Highway, continue west for about a mile, then turn left at a sign onto Arizona Memorial Place. ☺

Although it shares the *U.S.S. Arizona* Memorial and *U.S.S. Missouri* complex, this attraction deserves its own listing. More than a sub on display, it's also a fine museum and park dedicated to the men and women of the "Silent Service." And the *U.S.S. Bowfin* was one helluva boat. During World War II, it sank forty-four enemy ships, more than any other American sub in history. It was one of only five U.S. Navy ships to win both a Presidential Unit Citation and Navy Unit Commendation during the war. Submarines represented about two percent of the Navy, although they suffered the highest percentage of losses; more than one in five subs never came back.

Self guided tours take visitors into the *Bowfin's* innards. It's a study in cramped efficiency where every cubic foot is taken up by snug quarters, battle stations, dials, gauges, levers and switches. The museum brims with submariner lore, including a detailed scale model of the *Bowfin*, insignia of various subs, artifacts, photos, graphics and stories of valor, including Medal of Honor winners. An interesting exhibit traces the history of submarines from primitive submersibles to modern nuclear subs.

7 SEA LIFE PARK

41-202 Kalaniana'ole Hwy., Waimanalo; (808) 259-7933; www.sealifeparkhawaii.com. Daily 9:30 to 5. MC/VISA, AMEX; $$$; various prices for interactive programs. GETTING THERE: The park is about fifteen miles northeast of Waikiki. Follow H-1 east, which blends onto Kalaniana'ole Highway (Route 72). The park is on the left, just beyond Makapu'u Point. ☺

Sealife Park is small when compared with aquatic parks in California and Florida such as Sea World, although it's an appealing place, tucked between brushy volcanic cliffs and the ocean. Visitors enter through the large Hawaiian Reef Tank. A walk spirals down through different levels that are busy with fish, rays, sharks, sea turtles and other creatures large and small. The park has three aquatic shows—

sea lions, dolphins and a combined sea life show that features dolphins with cameo appearances by a sea lion and a pair of "racing" Humboldt penguins. Of these, the combination show is best, since patrons can see the playful dolphins both above and below water through a large glass-walled tank.

TRAVEL TIP: If you have polarized sunglasses, you'll be able to see into the various aquarium tanks better, since they cut surface glare.

What makes this small park particularly fun is its interactive programs, available at additional cost. Guests can feed and touch dolphins at "Splash U" or the more extensive "Dolphin Adventure," swim with sting rays in the "Hawaiian Ray Encounter" and descend into the Hawaiian Reef Tank wearing "SNUBA" helmets for close encounters with sealife. They're given disposable waterproof cameras to try their skills at underwater photography.

8 U.S.S. ARIZONA MEMORIAL

On Ford Island at Pearl Harbor; (808) 422-0561 or (808) 422-2771; www.nps.gov/usar. Daily 7:30 to 5; last complete program/tour begins at 3; free. Waikiki shuttles from 6:50 a.m. to 1 p.m., $. Call (808) 839-0911 for pickup schedule. GETTING THERE: Take exit 15-A from H-1 onto Kamehameha Highway, continue west for about a mile, then turn left at a sign into Arizona Memorial Place.

Operated jointly by the U.S. Navy and the National Park Service, the Arizona Memorial is Hawai'i's most hallowed ground. Here, nearly 2,000 servicemen lost their lives in the Pearl Harbor attack on December 7, 1941. Most of the casualties were aboard the battleship *U.S.S. Arizona,* which sank nine minutes after a direct hit on its munitions store, before most of the crew could escape. It was among several ships moored at Ford Island; all were sunk or crippled during that "Day of Infamy." The battleship remains where it foundered, six feet below the surface, with a starkly simple white memorial structure built across its deck.

The haunting shadow of the ship is discernible beneath the sea, like a long and narrow rusting reef. The superstructure was removed, so only the remnant of a gun turret remains above water. A thousand or more years into the future, the ship will rust away and only memories will remain. All who visit here—and it is oddly popular with Japanese tourists—are moved by what they see and what they feel.

The memorial is just off Ford Island, reached by free shuttles operated by the Navy. Other facilities, all on the mainland side of Pearl Harbor, include a museum, visitor center, and a park with plaques describing the events of that terrible day. One learns an interesting fact in the museum: Of the sixty-seven Japanese ships in the carrier fleet that was involved in the Pearl Harbor attack, all but two were later sunk by American and British forces.

TRAVEL TIPS: Arrive early in the day, or you may spend hours waiting for the next available tour. Also, all passes for the day may be exhausted by the time you arrive.

Tours begin with a film about the attack. Sit near the theater exit so you can be among the first on the shuttle to the memorial. Sit on the right side of the shuttle for the best view of the city skyline and Ford Island. When you arrive at the Memorial, head straight for the Shrine Room at the rear, since others will linger at the memorial's main exhibits. By the time you've paid your respects in the Shrine Room, the exhibit area and windows to the sunken ship will be relatively free.

9 U.S.S. MISSOURI

Berthed at Ford Island's "Battleship Row" in Pearl Harbor, reached by shuttle from the U.S.S. Arizona/Bowfin parking area; (808) 973-2494; www.ussmissouri.com. Daily 9 to 5; ticket office 8 to 4. MC/VISA, AMEX; $$$; extra fees for guided tours and audio tours. Combined Bowfin/U.S.S. Missouri tickets available. ☺

Pearl Harbor's role in World War II came full circle when America's most famous battleship was opened as floating museum in January, 1999. The "Mighty Mo" missed most of that war, although it was Admiral William "Bull" Halsey's flagship, and it entered Tokyo Bay to become the site of Japan's surrender. (Its choice as the "surrender ship" was rather political; it was named for President Harry S Truman's home state and christened by his daughter.) The ship remained in service for decades more, seeing its final action during the Gulf War before being decommissioned in 1992.

Visitors can stroll about on their own or take one of several levels of guided tours. Onboard historical exhibits trace the "Mo's" history from its commissioning in January, 1944, to its role in Desert Storm, when it's big guns bombarded Kuwait. Tours end at the "surrender deck," where the document was signed at a simple mess table brought up from the galley. A bronze marker is embedded in the teakwood deck where the table sat. It reads: "Over this spot on 2 September 1945, the instrument of formal surrender of Japan to the Allied powers was signed, thus bringing to a close the Second World War." A couple of reproductions of the Instrument of Surrender are displayed in a glass case.

10 WAIMEA FALLS PARK

59-864 Kamehameha Hwy., Waimea; (808) 638-8511 or (808) 638-5300; www.atlantisadventures.net/hawaii. Daily 10 to 5:30. Major credit cards; $$$ plus additional fees for various activities and attractions. GETTING THERE: The park is about forty miles from Waikiki on O'ahu's North Shore. From Honolulu, go northwest on H-1 and then north on H-2 and Kamehameha Highway (Route 93). ☺

This long-popular attraction occupies a lush tropical valley, although it's misnamed. The "famous" falls are rather wimpy, dropping a mere forty-five feet drop over a rough lava ledge. In dry years, the falls dwindle to a trickle. Much more impressive here are the lush botanical gardens that decorate this valley. More than 6,000 plants from throughout the tropical world flourish in a series of thirty-five theme gardens, spread over 1,800 acres.

Waimea Falls Park is one of Hawai'i's finest tropical gardens although it's more expensive than most, since it's a commercial enterprise, owned by Atlantis Adventures (below). Most visitors come not to smell the flowers but to indulge in activities such as watching cliff divers and taking horseback rides, kayaking tours, conducted hikes and bike trips. The best deal—included in the gate admission—is a tram ride through the gardens, narrated by knowledgeable drivers. Ride down to the falls and then stroll leisurely back, pausing frequently to smell the flowers. And you might want to check out the Hawaiian Center, where you can learn about ancient Polynesian and watch an authentic *kahikio* style hula performance.

THE NEXT TEN BEST ATTRACTIONS

O'ahu has too many lures to fit into a single list. Our "B" list contains some that are overlooked by most visitors, including our favorite:

1 HAWAII'S PLANTATION VILLAGE

94-695 Waipahu St., Waipahu; (808) 677-0110; www.hawaiiplantationvillage.org. Hourly tours weekdays 9 to 3 and Saturdays 10 to 3; closed Sunday; $. GETTING THERE: Head west on H-1 past Pearl Harbor, then take exit 8-B into Waipahu; the route becomes Farrington Highway. After about a mile, turn right onto Waipahu Depot Street and follow brown directional signs to the complex. Leaving the village, take Waipahu Street east, following signs back to the freeway.

This large outdoor museum tells the story of those who made Hawai'i what it is today—a multi-ethnic brew of many cultures. When landowners began cultivating sugarcane, they imported nearly 400,000 foreign workers from the late 1800s through the 1930s. The village features a collection of original or replica homes of field workers from Portugal, Puerto Rico, Japan, the Philippines, Okinawa and Korea. They're furnished with the simple possessions of those hardworking people. The complex also includes a plantation store, infirmary and social hall. Visits are by guided tour, and some of the docents are former plantation workers who flavor their narrative with personal experiences.

A small museum has historic photos and graphics, with quotes from diaries and journals. It also exhibits artifacts from that era when hardworking men and women in a strange land arose at 5 a.m. to take up tools and head for the fields.

2 BISHOP MUSEUM AT KALIA

In the Hilton Hawaiian Village complex at 2005 Kalia Rd., Waikiki; (808) 947-2458; www.bishopmuseum.org. Daily 9 to 5; $$. GETTING THERE: Hilton Hawaiian Village is on the west side of Waikiki at Ala Moana Boulevard and Kalia Road. The museum is in the Kalia Tower, on the right just inside the village entrance.

This handsome facility is the Bishop Museum in a capsule, an appealing Waikiki annex to the famous Polynesian archive. Artifacts, graphics and old prints and photos trace the history, lifestyles, weapons and pleasures of early Polynesians. Particularly interesting is a model *hale* (house) with a *pili* grass thatched roof. One exhibit should bring a grin; it points out that flutes, rattles and percussion instruments were used to convey secret messages between lovers at night during the stern era of the missionaries. A major display—appropriate to the museum's location—focuses on the development of Waikiki Beach. Exhibits trace its history from its first days as a playground for the *ali'i*, through the "golden days of the thirties," to World War II when it was fenced off and open only to the military, and finally to the modern era of highrise hotels. A video focuses on Waikiki's history, with some interesting old black and white footage.

3 THE CONTEMPORARY MUSEUM

2411 Makiki Heights Dr., Honolulu; (808) 526-0232; www.tc-mhi.org. Tuesday-Saturday 10 to 4 and Sunday noon to 4; closed Monday; $. GETTING THERE: From Waikiki, go north on McCully, then northwest on Beretania about half a mile to Punahou Street and turn right. Cross H-1 and, after less than half a mile, go left on Nehoa Street for two blocks. Turn right (uphill) on Makiki Street and fork left onto Makiki Heights Drive; the museum is on the right.

Normally, art museums—modern or otherwise—appeal mostly to the artistically inclined. However, the Contemporary Museum is interesting even if you don't know Dale Chihuly from Dale Carnegie. It occupies an elaborately landscaped Asian garden terraced into steep hills above Honolulu. The garden was part of an estate built in the 1920s. Some really strange sculptures occupy the grounds, which cascade downhill into a shallow ravine. Paths lead to hidden stone-lined creches and reflection pools; they're nice places to sit and contemplate the beauty and silence of the garden—but take your mosquito repellent. The museum's permanent exhibit, in a building below the main gallery, is a whimsical three-dimensional "construction" patterned after a set for a children's opera, *L'enfant et les Sortileges*. (It's easier seen than explained.) Several other galleries feature changing exhibits, with an obvious focus on the modern art of Hawai'i and beyond. Other facilities include an appealing little café and a gift shop.

4 DOLE PLANTATION

64-1550 Kamehameha Hwy., Wahiawa; (808) 621-8408; www.doleplantation.com. Daily 9:30 to 5:30. Free admission; modest fees for the Pineapple Express and World's Largest Maze. GETTING THERE: The plantation is about forty-five miles from Waikiki. Drive northwest on H-1, then north on H-2 until it becomes Highway 80 and then 99. Just beyond Wahiawa, watch for the plantation complex among pineapple fields on your right. ☺

The "plantation" is essentially a large specialty foods and gift store surrounded by Dole pineapple fields. It grew from a roadside fruit stand that opened in 1950. Featured attractions are the cute "Pineapple Express" that takes riders through fields where plants are in various stages of growth, and the "World's Largest Maze" made of hedges and other plants. Registered in the *Guinness Book of World Records*, the maze covers 100,000 square feet, with 1.7 miles of pathways.

Other facilities include a garden with pineapple varieties from around the world, a series of plaques detailing the history of Hawai'i's pineapple industry (which started with the arrival of James Drummund Dole in 1899), and an activity center with lei-making and other crafts demonstrations. The Plantation Store sells all sorts of things pineapple, including specialty foods, souvenirs, tasty smoothies and waffle ice cream cones.

5 FOSTER BOTANICAL GARDEN

50 N. Vineyard Blvd., Honolulu; (808) 522-7060 or (808) 522-7066; www.co.honolulu.hi.us/park/. Daily 9 to 4; $. Guided tours weekdays at 1. GETTING THERE: The garden is at the corner of Vineyard and Nu'uanu Street. Follow H-1 about two miles northwest from Waikiki, take the Vineyard exit and continue briefly west to Nu'uanu.

This collection of local and international flora occupies a fourteen-acre botanical island surrounded by busy Honolulu. It's not a quiet retreat since it's bordered by the freeway, yet it is a pleasant place to stroll about. A specialty here—if that's a proper word for a botanical garden—is a collection of huge tropical trees, including a Chinese banyan, a kapok tree of Africa, an earpod tree from tropical America with big bunions, and a particularly towering smooth-trunk quipo tree from Panama. Some of these giants date from the 1850s, when they were planted by German botanist William Hillebrand.

At a gift shop, visitors can buy things botanical, including plants and seeds approved for mainland export and books on such heady subjects such as *Natural Insect Repellents*.

TRAVEL TIP: While you're in the neighborhood, check out the adjacent **Kuan Yin Temple** at 170 N. Vineyard, open daily 8:30 to 2. It's quite impressive with its red and gold embellishments and distinctive floral patterned coffered ceiling.

6 HONOLULU ZOO

151 Kapuhulu Ave., Waikiki; (808) 971-7171; www.honoluluzoo.org. Daily 9 to 4:30; $. GETTING THERE: It's in Kapi'olani Park at the corner of Kalakaua and Kapuhulu avenues. Metered parking is available in a lot off Kapuhulu. ☺

While not a world class zoo, Honolulu's critter park is quite appealing. And the term "zoological garden" is appropriate, since it's richly endowed with tropical foliage. Larger than it appears from the outside, the 43-acre zoo has a cast of several hundred animals, mostly from Asia and Africa, with a special focus on Hawai'i's fauna. Here, one can be guaranteed a nene sighting; that's the much endangered state bird. Most of the enclosures are rather small and the zoo still has many old fashioned cages. However, this is the little zoo that could; several projects are underway to expand and improve its facilities, including a large tropical rainforest. And this modest zoo offers a lot of bellows for the buck; admission fees are very modest.

Visitors are first greeted by a flamingo habitat near a huge banyan tree and an inviting lawn area. From here, paths meander throughout this lushly landscaped complex. The zoo's best lure is the African Savanna, where one can smile at a Nile crocodile. And don't fail to miss the Volunteer Compost Garden.

7 LYON ARBORETUM

3860 Manoa Rd., Honolulu; (808) 988-0456; www.hawaii.edu/lyonarboretum. Monday-Saturday 9 to 3; visitors can remain until gates close at 4; $. Guided tours Tuesday at 10 and Saturday at 1; reservations advised. GETTING THERE: The arboretum is tucked into steep hills above Honolulu. From Waikiki, go north on McCully, then northwest on Beretania less than half a mile to Punahou Street and turn right. Punahou crosses H-1 and blends onto Manoa Road. Follow it about three miles to its end, just beyond Paradise Park. (About two-thirds of a mile from the freeway, make sure you fork to the left to avoid East Manoa Road, which will lead you astray.)

This very attractive botanical preserve is operated by the University of Hawaii. Not just another garden with labeled plants, it's part of a dense rainforest that crawls high up into the Manoa Valley. It's often soggy and damp in this lush 194-acre habitat; visitors should the accept the gift shop manager's offer of mosquito repellent. The arboretum is a gorgeous place thick with more than 5,000 varieties of tropical native and introduced plants. Birds chirp and caw and rustle the leaves of its trees. Its trails are very steep, so an arboretum visit is a good workout.

They're also very complex. A sign says: "You're back to nature now, and therein lies the adventure." Part of that adventure may include getting lost on the trail system, but it's a pretty place in which to be misplaced.

8 MISSION HOUSES MUSEUM

553 S. King St., Honolulu; (808) 531-0481; www.missionhouses.org. Tuesday-Saturday 9 to 4; $. Guided tours at 10, 11:15, 1 and 2:45. Gift shop, visitor center and tea room open Mondays 9 to 4 although the houses are closed that day. GETTING THERE: From Waikiki, go northwest on Beretania, left on Punchbowl for one long block, then left again on King; the complex is immediately on the right.

"Children of the missionaries remained influential and controversial in the islands for generations." That graphic in the visitor center targets the mission of the Mission Houses Museum—to preserve elements of that controversial era. What it preserves are three furnished buildings that survive from the Honolulu Mission Station, established here in 1820. At its peak it had several coral and wood frame homes, a printing office, book bindery, storehouse and of course a church. The surviving structures are the 1820 *Hale La'au*, a typical woodframe house shipped in pieces from New England; the 1831 coral block Chamberlain House; and the Printing House, where the first Hawaiian translation of the Bible was printed.

While not a part of the Mission Houses Complex, the adjacent 1842 Kawaihao Church at King and Punchbowl streets is worth a look; see Chapter Five, page 100. Its cornerstone was laid by Hiram Bingham, who brought the first group of missionaries to these islands. They first landed on the Big Island, then they established their headquarters at this Mission Houses site.

9 QUEEN EMMA SUMMER PALACE

2913 Pali Hwy., Honolulu; (808) 595-3167; www.daughtersofhawaii.org. Daily 9 to 4; $. GETTING THERE: Follow the Pali Highway about two miles northeast from H-1 above Honolulu.

Once the summer retreat of Queen Emma and her husband Kamehameha IV, this 1848 Greek Revival structure rivals Iolani Palace for its elegant interior and nineteenth century furnishings. The palace was the personal property of Queen Emma, left to her by her uncle John Young II, and many of the furnishings and artifacts are original. Particularly impressive is a three-tiered cabinet standing more than nine feet tall, stocked with Blue Willow china. Among the good queen's personal possessions are her sleigh bed, an 1801 piano, and items of jewelry and clothing. Tours through the palace are conducted whenever four or more people arrive, or visitors can browse about on their own.

10 WAIKIKI AQUARIUM & KAPI'OLANI PARK

2777 Kalakaua Ave., Waikiki; (808) 923-9741; www.waquarium.org. Daily 9 to 5; $. GETTING THERE: Waikiki Aquarium is in Kapi'olani Park on the eastern end of Waikiki Beach. ☺

Waikiki Aquarium eventually may be replaced by a $250 million facility in Kaka'ako Waterfront Park in Honolulu. Until then, this small facility operated by the University of Hawaii will remain open. It's a fine aquarium with several glassed-in galleries, plus videos and interactive exhibits. The newest exhibit is "Corals are Alive," a fine study of coral reefs and the gorgeously colored fishies that inhabit them. Other interesting displays include a tankful of fluorescent blue moon jellyfish, moray eels in plastic see-through tubes for a better look, plus cuttlefish and octopi. Out back are the Edge of the Reef exhibit, an open pond with see-through windows; and a habitat for rare monk seals.

The surrounding **Kapi'olani Park** is one of the largest urban parks in Hawai'i. It has more than half a mile of beachfront, spacious and tree-shaded lawns and picnic facilities. And it provides nice views of Diamond Head and Waikiki highrise resorts. Two small bathing beaches form sandy bookends to a seawall that fronts most of the park. Inland from the beach is the **Waikiki Shell**, an outdoor bandstand that hosts Honolulu Symphony concerts and other special events; see Chapter Six, page 112.

THE TEN BEST THINGS TO DO ON O'AHU

After you've seen O'ahu's sights and attractions, you may want to take in some of its activities. There is much here than in King Kalakaua's day, when Waikiki was "a hamlet of cottages...its excitement caused by the activity of insect tribes and the occasional fall of a coconut." We begin with our favorite activity—not watching coconuts fall—and then we list the remaining nine choices in no particular order, not even alphabetical.

1 CRUISE AMONG THE FISHES

Atlantis Submarines; at Hilton Hawaiian Village pier, Ala Moana Boulevard and Kalia Road, Waikiki; (800) 548-6262 or (808) 973-9811; www.atlantisadventures.net/hawaii. One-hour cruises daily from 8 to 3. Major credit cards; $$$$$. ☺

The Atlantis submersibles take passengers down more than 100 feet to explore the waters off Waikiki. This is a fun fish-spotting outing for people who don't dive or snorkel and even for those—like us—who do. The venture begins with a boat ride out to the sub—which is about a mile offshore—with nice views back to Waikiki and Diamond Head. Once aboard the sub, passengers cruise past a series of artificial reefs that were placed on the ocean's bottom several years ago. They include a deliberately scuttled former Navy maintenance ship and the fuselage and wings of a couple of aircraft. These *faux* reefs attract hundreds of fish, so passengers can expect good sightings. On a sunny day, visibility is remarkably clear, even down to 100 feet.

Everybody gets a window seat and we saw hundreds of fish on our cruise, including a squadron of three rays flying in formation, and a giant sea turtle lounging on the deck of the sunken "reef ship." Some of the fish came right up to the windows, apparently watching us watch them.

2 LEARN TO SURF

Various beach boy huts along Waikiki. GETTING THERE: These beachside surf schools are between Kuhio Beach Park and Fort DeRussy Beach Park.

Ever had the desire to hang ten? Or at least learn what "hanging ten" means? Several beach boy huts along Waikiki Beach and elsewhere in the islands offer surfing lessons. Waikiki is a good learning place, since the waves are large enough to get the novice surfer up on the board, but not so large as to pose any real risk. The best of these is the **Hans Hedemann Surf School** with locations on the beach in front of the Outrigger Reef and Sheraton Waikiki hotels, plus a showroom at 2586 Kalakaua Avenue in the Park Shore Hotel. They're open daily 8 to 5; (808) 924-7778; *www.hhsurf.com.*

Among other Waikiki beach huts offering lessons—reading northwest from Kuhio Beach Park—are **Pacific Beach Services, Palekaiko Beach Club** and **C&K Beach Services,** all close together. Next is **Aloha Beach Services** in front of the Outrigger Waikiki, next to Duke's Barefoot Bar & Restaurant; **Wetcetera Sun Care Center** in front of the Shore Bird Beach Bar at the Outrigger Reef Hotel; **Da Company** just beyond; then **Waikiki Prime Time Sports** with two locations on Fort DeRussy Beach. Most of these places close at 5; opening hours vary but they'll all be in business by 9.

3 RIDE AN OUTRIGGER CANOE

Along Waikiki Beach; see listing above. ☺

Don't feel up to getting up on a surfboard? Take an outrigger canoe ride; you simply sit and paddle as you splash through the breakers. Expect to get a little wet and have a lot of fun. Several Waikiki beach huts offer these rides. They don't have specific schedules; they simply push off as soon as four to six people show up.

These are some of the same places that give surfing lessons (above), and again we list them walking northwest from Kuhio Beach. You'll first encounter **C&K Beach Services** opposite Kuhio Park, then **Aloha Beach Services** at the Outrigger Waikiki. **Hans Hedemann** has an outrigger in front of the Sheraton Waikiki; and finally, you can catch a Polynesian canoe at **Waikiki Prime Time Sports** on Fort DeRussy Beach.

4 RIDE THE WAIKIKI TROLLEY

Stops throughout Waikiki Beach and Honolulu; (808) 593-2822; www.waikikitrolley.com. Trolleys operate daily from 8:30 a.m. to 11 p.m. Single rides $, one-day passes $$, and four-day $$$$.

Jolly old fashioned open-air trolleys serve most Waikiki/Honolulu attractions and shopping areas. Passengers with passes can hop on and off at will; trolleys come by about every half hour. The system is quite complex, with four different lines covering much of the city and extending to major attractions such as Diamond Head, the Polynesian Cultural Center and Sea Life Park. Operators point out places of interest and chat about Hawaiian history and folklore.

The trolleys are best for sightseeing and getting to major attractions and shopping areas; they're not particularly useful for anyone in a hurry. They follow very convoluted, meandering routes, sometimes almost doubling back on themselves.

5 DRIVE THE FOREST RESERVE

Round Top and Tantalus drives in the Honolulu Watershed Forest Reserve. GETTING THERE: To begin this scenic drive, go north on McCully Street from Waikiki, then northwest on Beretania about half a mile to Punahou Street and turn right. Cross H-1 and, after less than half a mile, go left on Nehoa Street for two blocks. Turn right (uphill) on Makiki Street and fork right for Round Top Drive.

The Round Top-Tantalus drive takes you within minutes from urban Honolulu into a rainforest in the foothills of Ko'olau Range. Along the route, the lush vegetation parts occasionally to offer fine views back down to Honolulu and Waikiki. The drive passes beneath thick canopies of banyan and other tropical trees, some with creepers that nearly brush the cars as they pass. The road also passes several trailheads, should you want to hike into this Polynesian jungle; see "The Ten Best walks and hikes" in Chapter Nine.

To begin, follow Round Top uphill through a neighborhood of luxury homes. Climbing higher into the reserve, you'll pass a few more forest-shrouded homes, then you'll encounter the turnoff to **Pu'u Ualaka'a State Park** (daily 7 to 6:30; no fee). Its vista point provides grand views of Honolulu, from Diamond Head and Waikiki to the Punchbowl and beyond. To reach it, drive past the first parking area (unless you need to use the restrooms there) and continue to a second parking lot, where a short walk takes you to the lookout.

Back on Round Top, if you're in a hiking mood, watch for the **Molika** and **Manoa Cliff** trailheads on opposite sides of the road, just beyond a five-mile marker. Then just over summit, where the road name changes from Round Top to Tantalus, watch for the **Pu'u Ohia** trailhead, marked by green posts. Parking is on the left and the trail is on the right. A bit farther down, after you pass the four-mile marker, watch for a parking area for the other end of the **Manoa Cliff Trail**, which leads down into a lush creeper-draped canyon.

As you emerge from the woodland on Tantalus and return to residential areas, turn left onto Makiki Heights Drive, which will take you past the **Contemporary Museum** (see above) and complete your loop. Or stay with Tantalus and follow signs to the **Punchbowl** and **National Cemetery of the Pacific**, see Chapter Five, page 101.

6 TAKE THE WAIKIKI HISTORY WALK

Waikiki Historic Trail; (808) 841-6442; www.waikikihistorictrail. com. Monday through Saturday, starting at 9 a.m.; free.

The Waikiki Historic Trail consists of twenty-one surfboard-shaped markers placed along Waikiki Beach, Kalakaua Avenue and the Ala Wai Canal. Completed in late 2000, it covers about two miles. Docents of the Native Hawaiian Hospitality Association conduct free two-hour walks over two different portions of the trail. One begins at the Visitor Information Station at the corner of Kalakaua and Kapahulu avenues. The other starts at the Bishop Museum at Kalia, in Hilton Hawaiian Village, on the corner of Kalia Road and the Hilton complex entrance.

Docents discuss the history of Waikiki and the lifestyles of early Hawaiians, and they help visitors get oriented to the trail. Brochures available at visitor centers outline the trail but they lack detail, so it's difficult to find all of the markers. The two guided walks don't cover the trail's full length. We cover some of this walk in "The Ten Best walks and hikes" in Chapter Nine, page 137.

7 GO DIAMOND HEAD!

Diamond Head State Monument, C/o Department of Land & Natural Resources, Honolulu; (808) 587-0285 or (808) 587-0300. Park open 6 a.m. to 6 p.m.; token entry fee. GETTING THERE: From Waikiki, go southeast on Kalakaua to Kapi'olani Park, then fork left onto Monsarrat Avenue, which becomes Diamond Head Road. Follow it about a mile, and the turnoff into to the Diamond Head parking area is just beyond Kapi'olani Community College. ☺

Locals have a quaint way of telling directions. The expression "go Diamond Head" means to go in the direction of that noted promontory. We urge you to go Diamond Head because it's more than just a world-famous landmark; it's an interesting place to explore. It's a tilted volcanic crater whose real name is *Le'ahi*. Its upper edge forms the famous profile which—from most vantage points—looks like a ridge instead of a crater.

Within Le'ahi's shallow crater is a park—part grassy and mostly brushy—and a trail leading to the crater's stiff upper lip. Displays at a small visitor center near the parking lot tell you about Diamond Head. It was created by a single eruption either 150,000 or 300,000 years ago. (Two different signs contradict one another.) A trail was built to the crater's upper rim in 1908 so mules and men could haul materials for a fortification. Completed in 1910, this bunker with five underground levels was called Fire Control Station Diamond Head.

Scores of folks hike that steep trail every day to enjoy a predictably pretty panorama of Waikiki, Honolulu and much of O'ahu's south shore. We describe the hike in detail in Chapter Nine, page 140.

TRAVEL TIP: Take water because the hike is very steep, with an altitude gain of 560 feet in less than a mile. And take a flashlight, since the route passes through two dark tunnels and an even darker spiral staircase within the fortification. Start early in the day; it'll be less crowded and cooler. Also, avoid Diamond Head on weekends, when it's swarmed by locals and visitors. You'll have trouble finding a place to park, and there'll standing room only at the small observation point at the top.

8 LEAN AGAINST THE SCENERY AT PALI LOOKOUT

Nu'uanu Pali State Wayside, above Honolulu. Park open daily 4 a.m. to 8 p.m.; free. GETTING THERE: The Wayside is about five miles up the Pali Highway (Route 61) from H-1.

For a particularly scenic drive highlighted by a splendid view from one of the world's windiest overlooks, head up the Pali Highway toward the knife-edge ridges of the Ko'olau Range. The route takes you past attractive hillside homes and then quite suddenly into an area of lush vegetation. The vista is mostly to the wet side of O'ahu and Kane'ohe Bay, with those dramatically fluted cliffs in the foreground. Mark Twain once called this the most beautiful view in the world.

Graphics explain what you're seeing at this windy place, pointing out that half of the Ko'olau Volcano slid into the sea about two million years ago, leaving the sharp ridge of the Ko'olau Range, with its 2,000-foot cliffs. Another display discusses Kamehameha's final battle here that united most of the Hawaiian Islands in 1794. His troops cornered an army lead by a Maui chief and in the bloody fracas, many were forced off the steep cliffs.

As you head back toward Honolulu, you can drive through an even thicker rainforest by taking a left hand turn across Pali Highway onto Nu'uanu Pali Drive. It takes you through botanical tunnels where creeper-laden trees have clasped branches above the road like leafy joined hands. After about a mile, the road rejoins the Pali highway.

9 SNORKEL AT HANAUMA BAY

Hanauma Bay State Underwater Park, in Koko Head Regional Park off Highway 72; (808) 396-4229. Daily except Tuesday, 6 a.m. to 6 p.m. GETTING THERE: It's about seven miles east of Waikiki on the Kalaniana'ole Highway.

This astonishingly pretty crescent bay was formed when the outer edge of a small crater eroded, allowing the sea to enter. It's one of Hawai'i's best snorkeling spots, with calm water and schools of tropical fish meandering among coral formations. Since it's a short drive from Honolulu, this also is Hawai'i's most crowded beach park. About the only way to avoid cheek-to-cheek sunbathers and schools of snorkelers is to go early in the morning on a weekday. Don't *even* think about coming out here on a weekend. For starters, you'll be lucky if you can find a place to park. Hanauma Bay gets more than a million visitors every year.

The bay is a nature preserve and the rules are simple—look but don't touch anything under water. Visitors are required to view a brief video about preserving the reef and its fish before they're allowed down to the beach, which is reached by a steeply tilted road from the visitor center. The elderly and those heavily laden with beach toys can catch a tram. Once there, one can rent snorkel gear and other beach equipment. The beach is quite appealing, with fine-grain sand, palm trees and shaded picnic areas.

10 DO A LUAU

Well of course you have to do a luau when you vacation in Hawai'i. Although now thoroughly touristified, the luau descends from a rich tradition of feasting and togetherness. Early luaus were both religious and social rituals, to celebrate such events as the birth of a child, the christening of a new canoe or a successful battle. The feast was called the *'aha'aina,* literally translated as "to gather together" (*'aha*) and "eat a meal" (*'aina*). If the early Hawaiians were having just a few folks over to uncover the roast pig, yams and other good things from the *imu,* the gathering was called *pa'ina.* This would be more akin to our Sunday dinner.

Tourist promoters had trouble pronouncing *'aha'aina* or *pa'ina,* so the word "luau" became popularized. Originally, *lu'au* referred to young taro leaves, traditionally cooked as greens and always served at the *aha'aina* and *pa'ina.*

Assorted versions of this uniquely Hawaiian feasting ritual are held throughout the state. Here are the major ones on O'ahu. All feature traditional Polynesian drinks, most with open bars, except the Polynesian Cultural Center luau, which serves no alcohol. All except Waikiki's Royal Hawaiian luau offer transportation to their sites.

GERMAINE'S LUAU — *Held on a private beach on Barber's Point east of Honolulu; (800) 367-5655 or (808) 949-6626; www.germaines-luau.com.* ☐ Popular for generations, this "family style" luau features the unearthing of the pitted pig from the *imu*, followed by pigging out and Polynesian singing and dancing.

PARADISE COVE LUAU — *On a 12-acre beach near Barbers Point; (800) 775-2683 or (808) 842-5911; www.paradisecove.com.* ☐ In addition to the typical Polynesian entertainment, this luau features traditional Hawaiian games, coconut plucking, a *hukilau* (fish net pulling) and lessons in lei-making.

POLYNESIAN CULTURAL CENTER ALI'I LUAU — *In La'ie on the North Shore; shuttles available from Waikiki; nightly at 6; (877) 572-2347 or (808) 293-3333; www.polynesia.com.* ☐ This luau features a re-creation of a traditional *ali'i* feast with costumed "royalty," followed by pig unearthing, dining and typical Polynesian music and dancing; see above on page 45.

ROYAL LUAU — *Royal Hawaiian Hotel; (808) 931-7194; www.royal-hawaiian.com.* ☐ It's our favorite O'ahu luau and the only one on Waikiki Beach. The show includes an introduction and explanation of typical luau foods, a mix of traditional and contemporary Polynesian songs and Polynesian dances; see Chapter One, page 37.

The only reason I eat poi at my age is to keep my body stuck together.
— **Don Ho, age sixty-something**

Chapter Three

DINING HONOLULU
PACIFIC RIM FARE AHEAD OF ITS TIME

Hawai'i's dining scene reflects the state's rich ethnic diversity—a savory blend of Asian and Polynesian with American and even some Portuguese accents. As we noted in the first chapter of this book, the islanders were enjoying Pacific Rim fare long before it became fashionable on the mainland. Here, it's called Hawaiian regional cuisine.

Hawai'i has its share of celebrity chefs, notably Roy Yamaguchi, whose Roy's restaurants have spread to many mainland cities. Among chefs who have gained local fame are Alan Wong, George Mavrothalassitis of Chef Mavro's, Russell Siu of 3660 on the Rise, Hiroshi Fukui of L'Uraku, D.K. Kodama of Sansei Seafood and Sam Choy.

Incidentally, if you're a night owl or you like late lunch, you may go hungry in Hawai'i unless you plan ahead. Most restaurants close earlier than in mainland cities; many kitchens turn off their stoves around 9 p.m. Some do stay up late, and we use the phrase "late dinner" in our listings to identify these. Also, many Hawai'i restaurants that serve

The Spam® what am?

Obviously, Hawaii's eating habits have been influenced by the many people who came from elsewhere, bringing their ethnic dishes and customs. Perhaps the strangest food fad from the outside world is good old fashioned Spam. And it was brought not by immigrants but by American servicemen stationed here before and during World War II. This salty canned pork product produced by Hormel Foods was a staple in most B-ration and C-ration packages. Troops in the field ate Spam at least once a day. (As a former Marine, I'm well qualified to comment on this subject.)

Since locals already liked pork, Spam caught on quickly and it remains today one of Hawaii's most popular food products. In fact Hawaii consumes more Spam per capita than any other state, around four million cans a year. That's three and a half times as much as the national average, about six cans per person! Some sushi parlors and *okazuya* delis serve Spam sushi rolls and McDonald's outlets in Hawaii feature a Spam, eggs and rice breakfast on the menu. And if you want to cook with Hormel the Hawaiian way, get a copy of one of Ann Kondo Corum's two cookbooks: *Hawaii's 2nd Spam Cookbook* (© 2001) or her earlier *Hawaii's Spam Cookbook* (© 1987). They're available at local book stores or from The Bess Press, 3565 Harding Ave., Honolulu, HI 96816; (808) 734-7159; *www.besspress.com*.

lunch and dinner close in midafteroon. (We recall arriving in Kameula on the Big Island at 2 p.m. and every restaurant of note was already taking its afternoon siesta. We had to resort to a Foodland deli.)

Restaurants tend to be a bit more expensive in Hawai'i than on the mainland and it's not really their fault. They must rely heavily on imports and small-scale farming for their ingredients. That doesn't mean you can't afford to dine out here. Quite the contrary; Hawai'i has scores of affordable places, mostly ethnic and mostly Asian. You'll find our ten favorite "Cheap Eats" listed in Chapter Five.

Pupu and grinds

You'll often encounter two dining expressions in Hawai'i—*pupu* (or *pu'u pu'u*) and "grinds." *Pupu* refers to appetizers offered by many restaurants and cocktail lounges. Specifically, *pupus* are a mixed platter, similar to Spanish *tapas*. However, many places use the term to identify any appetizers, from Buffalo wings to spring rolls. "Grinds" simply means food, usually referring to inexpensive local fare.

And speaking of grinds, we particularly like the many *okazuya*, which are small delis dishing up hearty servings of inexpensive food. Most are open just for lunch, although a few keep their doors open until early evening. Some have seating; others are take-out only. For more on *okazuya*, see Chapter Five, page 102.

Honolulu's dining scene

Until the last decade or so, Hawai'i's dining scene was focused primarily in Honolulu and particularly the Waikiki Beach area. However, many of the islands' best restaurants are now in Maui, lured by the its growing visitor popularity. A few others thrive in the better resort areas of the Big Island, Kaua'i and Lana'i. In the latest Zagat Survey, eight of Hawai'i's top-rated restaurants were on Maui, compared with only six on O'ahu.

Still, by sheer numbers of restaurants and diners, Honolulu is where most of the culinary action is. Many of its restaurants are in Waikiki, since that's where ninety percent of the island's visitors stay. There are notable exceptions. Among our off-Waikiki selections below are Alan Wong's, Chef Mavro's, 3660 on the Rise, L'Uraku and Sansei. They draw much of their support from locals, although visitors find their way to these places—with the help of guidebooks such as ours.

The *Honolulu Advertiser* publishes an insert, *Hawaii's Best 150 Restaurants* each December. Included with home-delivered editions of the newspaper and available at many restaurants, it's a relatively useful guide for visitors. It offers a good cross section of Hawai'i restaurants—mostly on O'ahu—with locator maps. And no, we don't know why McDonald's earned praise in the last edition.

If you like your restaurants in groups, Honolulu's Waterfront Plaza on Ala Moana between Punchbowl and South streets has more than half a dozen dining spots on its **Restaurant Row**. Among them are Sunset Grill, American fare, (808) 521-4409; Payao Thai Cuisine, (808) 536-4204; Jose's Cantina, Mexican, (808) 528-3859; Ruth's Chris Steak House, (808) 599-3860; Sansei Seafood, Pacific Rim fare, (808) 536-6286 (see below, page 74); and Phillip Paolo's, Italian, (808) 538-6643. In the midst of all these is a mostly outdoor bar simply called The Row.

The way things work

Our restaurant selections come from our own dining experiences and reliable recommendations from other sources. These *do not* include throw-away tourist publications. Our choices are based more on overviews of food, service and décor, not on the proper doneness of a specific 'opakapaka fillet. We don't attempt to judge a restaurant by a single meal, for your dining experience may be quite different from ours. The chef might be having a bad night, or your waitress might be recovering from one.

PRICING: Dollar sign codes indicate the price of a typical dinner with entrée, soup or salad, not including drinks, appetizers or dessert: *$* = less than $10 per entrée; *$$* = $10 to $19; *$$$* = $20 to $29; *$$$$* = $30 to $40; *$$$$$* = "Did you say you were buying?" **CREDIT CARDS:** Abbreviations are obvious, and "Major credit cards" indicates that an establishment accepts MasterCard and VISA plus at least two others.

THE TEN VERY BEST RESTAURANTS

Our choices feature mostly regional fare, since we assume you aren't going to Hawai'i to search out Italian or Mexican restaurants. Asian, yes, and they're on our next list.

1 LA MER

The Halekulani, 2199 Kalia Rd., Waikiki; (808) 923-2311; www.halekulani.com. French-continental with Polynesian accents; full bar service. Dinner nightly. Major credit cards; $$$$ to $$$$$. Reservations recommended; jackets or long-sleeved collared shirts for gentlemen. GETTING THERE: The Halekulani is on Waikiki at the corner of Kalia Road and Beachwalk.

La Mer provides Hawai'i's best dining experience; it's the only restaurant on O'ahu with a rare AAA Five Diamond rating. The look is elegant Hawaiian plantation, with bamboo trimmed wall panels with decorative insets suggestive of sepia batik prints. Located in the legendary House Without a Key, the restaurant offers views of Waikiki through French shutters that are almost always pulled back. Sink into cushioned bamboo chairs before tables set with bud vases and tiny oil lamps, and prepare to be spoiled. Presentations and dinnerware are works of art, with a different style of china for each course.

You can place your fate and credit card in the hands of the chef and the attentive staff by partaking of a multi-course tasting menu with appropriate wines. When we dined, the *prix fixe* menu consisted of sautéed duck liver garnished with truffles, sautéed John Dory fillet, mussel soup with saffron, roasted squab and a fine selection of French cheeses and desserts. Off-the-menu entrées include duck breast with lavender honey, roasted veal chop, rack of lamb with Dijon mustard crust, Scottish salmon with salmon tartar, and three-fish sampler in a rosemary sauce crust.

2 ALAN WONG'S

1857 King St., Honolulu; (808) 949-2526; www.alanwongs.com. Hawaiian regional; full bar service. Dinner nightly. Major credit cards; $$$ to $$$$. Reservations recommended. GETTING THERE: It's just west of McCully, on the third floor of a small building. From Waikiki, go inland on McCully, cross King (which is one-way the wrong way), then take lefts on Young, Pawa'a and King; the restaurant is on the right. Wong's is rather hard to spot at night since there's no neon.

Local celeb chef Alan Wong's restaurant is a lively, upbeat place with an open kitchen. It's stylishly done with slender drop lamps, muted colors and black and white prints on the walls. Balcony seating is available although the view is of King Street; no Waikiki sunsets here. If someone else is buying, try the five-course Menu Sampling, with or without matching wines. Regular menu choices may include ginger-crusted *onaga*, grilled beef tenderloin, macadamia coconut-crusted lamb chops, or grilled chicken and shrimp with chicken hash in jaded ginger sauce. Portions are generous and the entrées are artfully presented. Preceding the above, try one of Wong's interesting starters such as a potsticker salad or Chinese quesadilla. And to end all of this, the banana-raspberry-oatmeal crumbcake is fantastic.

Should you want to try this at home, the chef-owner has a cookbook called *Alan Wong's New Wave Luau* available at the restaurant. Incidentally, Wong's features a good selection of tropical drinks such as Polynesian Paralysis (four layers of rum with tropical fruit juices), plus an extensive wine list.

3 BALI BY THE SEA

Hilton Hawaiian Village, 2005 Kalia Rd., Waikiki; (808) 949-4321; www.hiltonhawaii.com. American-Pacific Rim; mostly seafood; full bar service. Dinner nightly except Sunday. Major credit cards; $$$ to $$$$. Reservations recommended. GETTING THERE: The Hilton is at the corner of Ala Moana Boulevard and Kalia Road; turn right onto Kalia, then right again into the Hilton complex.

This pleasing restaurant has a cool modern look with soft green and beige fabrics, pastel Polynesian prints and potted palms. It is indeed by the sea, right on the beach and open to the breezes. Come before sunset to enjoy the splendid views of Waikiki. This is quite a romantic spot, with candle-lit tables set with tiny flower vases. The menu is mostly seafood, with some chicken, pork, beef and lamb dishes. Some examples are tiger prawns with scallops and spears of crisp asparagus, macadamia nut-crusted 'opakapaka (pink snapper) set on a bed of mashed purple yams with kaffir lime sauce; and *ahi* tuna with scallions and tempura crust.

The wine list is fashionably overpriced and very extensive, with French, German, Italian and a goodly selection of California labels. We declined dessert despite the tempting choices, then we were surprised with the presentation of a chocolate Diamond Head, "steaming" with dry ice and with two chocolate truffles in the crater. "We present this to all of our patrons to thank them for dining with us," said our waiter.

4 CHEF MAVRO

1969 King St., Honolulu; (808) 944-4714; www.chefmavro.com. French-Polynesian; full bar service. Dinner nightly except Monday. Major credit cards; $$$$ to $$$$$. Reservations recommended. GETTING THERE: The restaurant is on the corner of McCully and King. Simply take McCully inland from Waikiki.

This is an expensive favorite for locals and visitors, with an elegantly simple and restful interior of beiges, off-white, peach and apricot. Candle-lit tables are graced with tropical flowers in bud vases. The fare is stylishly presented and excellent—an intriguing mix of French and Pacific Rim, although portions are small for the hefty prices. Try one of the tasting menus, available with or without matching wines. Chef-owner George Mavrothalassitis gathers frequently with staff members and friends, tasting more than dozen wines to choose the proper ones. (I applied for a job, but all positions were taken.)

The menu changes every few days. Recent examples include potato-crusted 'opakapaka; breast of duck with vegetable stirfry and hearts of palm, and lamb loin with marjoram purée. The service is casually friendly and perfectly timed. The waitstaff senses precisely when to deliver the next course, proceeded by the wine service. Desserts are incredibly rich, and some sit in the best raspberry purée I've ever tasted. The chocolate-pecan tart matched Betty's wildest chocoholic dreams.

5 HOKU'S

Kahala Mandarin Oriental, 5000 Kahala Ave., Waikiki; (808) 739-8888; www.mandarin-oriental.com/kahala. American/Pacific Rim; mostly seafood; full bar service. Lunch and dinner daily. Major credit cards; $$$$. Reservations recommended. GETTING THERE: Go southeastward along Waikiki, shifting from Kalakaua Avenue to Diamond Head Road to Kahala Avenue. Remain on Kahala for just over a mile, continuing into the Wai'alae Country Club; the Mandarin is at the end of the road.

The simple elegance of the Mandarin Oriental is reflected in this restaurant over Kahala Beach, with dark cane-back chairs, steeply-pitched dark wood cathedral ceilings and modernistic wall sconces. Zagat readers rate it among the top twenty restaurants in all the islands for food, although some complain that the large open kitchen makes it a bit too noisy. Ask to be seated some distance away if that's an issue; this is a rather large restaurant.

Menu offerings include wok-fried locally raised Maine lobster and clams, crisp whole island fish with sweet and sour and black bean sauce, Chinese braised duck with Asian vegetables, Hawai'i-spiced chicken with green beans, pepper-crusted New York steak with a purée of sweet potatoes and caramelized Maui onions, and wok-seared jumbo prawns.

6 KINCAID'S FISH, CHOP & STEAK HOUSE

Ward Warehouse at 1050 Ala Moana Blvd., Honolulu; (808) 591-2005. American; full bar service. Lunch and dinner daily. Major credit cards; $$ to $$$. Reservations accepted. GETTING THERE: It's in the far end of the Ward Warehouse complex. Go north from Waikiki on Ala Moana Boulevard, turn right onto Ward, right onto Auahi Street, then right yet again into the first parking area. The restaurant is on the second floor.

Local foodies may roll their eyes at our selection of Kincaid's as one of Honolulu's Ten Best restaurants. However, the food is fine, the portions are generous and it's very affordable. It's favored by locals, and it ranks high in Honolulu restaurant polls. Kincaid's is a popular business lunch place and the bar is a singles gathering spot. This is Honolulu's closest thing to a classic American steak and chop house. The décor would fit comfortably in Chicago or San Francisco—plank wood floors, exposed ventilation ducts and upholstered booths. And it offers something of a view, across Ala Moana Boulevard to the Honolulu waterfront.

Despite its classic American look, Kincaid's menu is mostly Hawaiian regional, featuring fresh local seafood, babyback ribs with Hawaiian barbecue sauce, coconut tiger prawns with Cajun marinade, plus lots of steaks. A specialty is "shellstock linguine" with Thai crabcakes, sea scallops, Manila clams and roasted tiger prawns.

7 ROY'S HONOLULU

6600 Highway 71, Honolulu; (808) 396-7697; www.roysrestaurant.com. Pacific Rim; full bar service. Dinner nightly. Major credit cards; $$$ to $$$$. Reservations advised. GETTING THERE: Follow Highway 71 four miles north from the end of H-1 freeway, turn left onto Keahole Street then immediately right into the Hawaii Kai Center. The restaurant is on the corner of Highway 71 and Keahole.

Since starting in Honolulu in 1988, Roy Yamaguchi has opened restaurants far and even wide—throughout the islands and to several mainland cities. There were more than thirty at last count. His success is based on a blending of Asian and Polynesian cuisine, which he calls "Hawaiian fusion." He's not the first to do so, although he seems to be the most marketable.

Roy's Honolulu isn't his original restaurant although it's now his flagship. It has a sleekly modern look; this isn't Don, the Beachcomber's. The spacious dining room looks across Highway 71 to Maunalua Bay. The frequently-changing menu recently offered macadamia nut mahi mahi in lobster butter sauce, sea scallops with black bean sauce and garlic and teriyaki grilled chicken with portobello oyster sauce.

8 SHIP'S TAVERN

Sheraton Moana, 2365 Kalakaua Ave., Waikiki; (808) 922-3111; www.moana-surfrider.com. American-continental; full bar service. Dinner Tuesday-Saturday; closed Sunday-Monday. Major credit cards; $$$

to $$$$. Reservations advised. GETTING THERE: The Sheraton Moana is in the heart of Waikiki, opposite the International Market Place.

Appropriate to its second-floor location in the classic Moana hotel, Ship's Tavern is a classically elegant, old fashioned restaurant. With its warm paneled woods and beveled glass suggestive of a fine old ship's drawing room, it is one of Waikiki's most refined spaces. Indeed, the look suggests a grand restaurant in San Francisco, except that the view through its window walls is of Waikiki Beach and Diamond Head.

The fare is hearty and traditional, yet with some interesting Asian seasonings. Some recent examples were garlic rosemary-crusted rack of lamb, sautéed jumbo shrimps with soy-cilantro vinaigrette, a seafood potpourri and several serious steaks.

9 THE SURF ROOM

Sheraton Royal Hawaiian, 2259 Kalakaua Ave., Waikiki; (808) 931-7194; www.royal-Hawaiian.com. American with Asian accents; full bar service. Breakfast buffet, plus lunch and dinner daily. Major credit cards; $$$ to $$$$. Reservations advised. GETTING THERE: The hotel is behind the Royal Hawaiian Shopping Center, reached via Royal Hawaiian Avenue.

This attractive restaurant is done in the fun pinks that are the Pink Palace's trademark. However, most of the Surf Room's décor is the beach and Diamond Head; it offers the best views of any Waikiki restaurant. A covered veranda has a few sheltered tables, although most of the dining is outdoors, under pink and white awnings.

The menu is American-Hawaiian without being too cutesy; no air-dried tomatoes or sun-dried beef here. (Or is it air-dried beef and sun-dried tomatoes?) Try the Art of Food and Wine tasting menu, with courses such as pan-roasted squab, kettle-braised red wine cabbage, and braised tenderloin tips, each with a matching wine, followed with pumpkin crème brûlée for dessert. Other menu items include teriyaki braised filet, sautéed mahi mahi, apple-smoked bacon tenderloin, and roast Chilean sea bass. And if you really want to fill your platter with fish fare, go for the Friday night seafood buffet.

10 3660 ON THE RISE

3660 Wai'alae Ave., Honolulu; (808) 737-1177. Asian fusion; full bar service. Dinner nightly except Monday. Major credit cards; $$$ to $$$$. GETTING THERE: From lower Waikiki, take Kapahulu Avenue inland about 1.5 miles to Wai'alae Avenue (crossing under H-1), then go right about a mile to a street called Wilhelmina Rise.

Russell Siu's award-winning restaurant isn't on a rise, nor is it rising. It's on the ground floor of an office building at the corner of Wai'alae Avenue and that street with the odd name. Although the building is modern, the surrounding neighborhood is rather scruffy. The restaurant is quite sleek, with light natural wood furniture, frosted glass partitions to break up the dining room and stylish little drop lamps over comfy booths.

Siu says he serves a fusion of "European, Pacific Rim and island-style cuisine." What's Euro-Pacific-Hawaiian? How about medallions of beef tenderloin with asparagus and lobster meat, macadamia nut rack of lamb with cabernet mint sauce, or seafood and mushroom linguine with shiitake mushroom and lobster cream sauce? Prices are modest for such complex and interesting dishes. Even the three-course tasting menu is less than $40, with just $10 more for three wine pairings. (Some of the tonier Waikiki restaurants charge that much for a single entrée.) When we last checked, this "Taste of 3660" consisted of marinaded scallops, calamari spinach salad, beef tenderloin medallions and dessert.

THE BEST ASIAN/PACIFIC RIM RESTAURANTS

O'ahu's large Asian population has produced an interesting mix of restaurants. Several, which local foodies call Hawaiian regional, make the Ten Very Best list above. The choices below are more Asian than Hawaiian; some are ethnically specific while others reflect Hawai'i's mix of Asian cultures.

1 THE GOLDEN DRAGON

Hilton Hawaiian Village, 2005 Kalia Rd., Waikiki; (808) 949-4321; www.hiltonhawaii.com. Chinese; mostly seafood; full bar service. Dinner nightly except Monday. Major credit cards; $$$ to $$$$. Reservations recommended. GETTING THERE: See Mer listing above.

The Golden Dragon was a pleasant surprise for my Chinese wife, who questioned whether a resort restaurant could get serious about traditional Chinese food. The Golden Dragon does. Its Szechuan and Cantonese fare is excellent, reasonably priced for a resort restaurant and the portions are large. The extensive menu contained some tempting creations. However, we chose more familiar fare as a true test of the kitchen's Chinese cookery—*mushu* pork, lemon chicken and stir-fried bok choy. The *mushu* arrived pre-assembled in the pancakes, with a tasty plum sauce on the side; lemon chicken was perfectly lemony and the stir-fried veggies were fresh and lightly done.

The décor is Chinese opulent but not overdone, with a few Asian artifacts and paintings. The restaurant entrance is guarded—not by golden dragons—but by a pair of snarling lions. "They're friends of the dragons," the hostess explained. The dining room and its adjacent patio overlook the Hilton Lagoon. If the timing is right, it's a nice place for watching the sunset.

2 KEO'S IN WAIKIKI

2028 Kuhio Ave., Waikiki; (808) 951-9355; www.keosthaicuisine.com. Thai/Hawaiian; full bar service. Breakfast, lunch and late dinner daily. Major credit cards; $$ to $$$. Reservations accepted. GETTING THERE: The restaurant is in the Ambassador Hotel building, where Kuhio forks left off Ala Moana.

This attractive restaurant has been feeding locals and visitors for nearly a quarter of a century—and winning awards. *Bon Appetit* and *Gourmet* magazines called it America's best Thai restaurant and *Travel Holiday* picked it as Honolulu's best dining value. It's a pleasing space with Southeast Asian décor, cushioned wicker chairs and tables set with small oil lamps and bud vases with orchid blooms. With such intimate settings, we also picked it as one of Honolulu's ten most romantic restaurants in Chapter Seven, page 128.

The fare is artfully prepared and, as *Travel Holiday* said, very reasonable, with many entrées in the low teens. Some items have Thai roots with American-Hawaiian accents, such as Thai style pork chops with lemon grass and parsley sauce, barbecue ribs with Western barbecue sauce, and garlic beef or shrimp with mushrooms. The menu also features more traditional cashew nut chicken, sautéed chicken with lemongrass, and Bangkok duckling. It also offers some lively curries, and patrons can choose their temperature rating.

3 LEGEND SEAFOOD

Chinese Cultural Plaza in Chinatown, 100 N. Beretania; (808) 532-1868. Chinese; full bar service. Lunch weekdays, breakfast through lunch weekends and dinner nightly. Major credit cards; $$ to $$$. To reach Chinatown from Waikiki, head 3.5 miles northwest on Ala Moana Boulevard. A quarter of a mile past Aloha Tower, turn right onto River Street and follow it to Beretania. The Cultural Plaza is between River and Maunakea streets.

The look of the Legend is Chinese *moderne* excess; it's one of those cavernous Asian restaurants that manages to look both stark and gaudy at the same time. A huge beaded chandelier dominates the barn-sized dining room and a massive medallion hangs from one wall; otherwise the décor is rather sparse.

However, people come for the food, not the trimmings. While not inexpensive for a Chinatown restaurant, it's reasonably priced and portions are ample. The monster menu lists 145 items, plus a few interesting and unlisted desserts. Our stir-fried chicken in black bean sauce was excellent and the bok choy was fresh, crisp and lightly done. Other good choices include steamed fresh fish (one of the few really expensive dishes), steamed chicken with ginger and green onions, and stir-fried Chinese broccoli with dried flounder.

4 L'URAKU

1341 Kapiʻolani Blvd., Honolulu; (808) 955-0552; www.luraku.com. Japanese/Pacific Rim; full bar service. Lunch and dinner daily; Major credit cards; $$ to $$$. Reservations recommended. GETTING THERE: From Waikiki, go northwest on Ala Wai Boulevard, turn right onto Mc-Cully Street and then left onto Kapiʻolani Boulevard. Follow it about a mile to Piʻikoi and the restaurant is just beyond, on your left.

This Asian fusion restaurant is favorite of locals and the few visitors who discover its odd location on the ground floor of a condominium building. Dinner entrées range into the high $20s and beyond, although you can sample chef Hiroshi Fukui's "Euro-Japanese" fare for less by catching one of the "Weekender Luncheons." When we last dined, they were only $16 for appetizer, salad, entrée, dessert and a non-alcoholic drink. Our starters were tofu with bay shrimp and ginger and a mixed green salad. Among main course choices were pan-seared fresh salmon filet, soft-shelled crab sandwich, an eggplant and chicken hash sandwich, almond-crusted catch of the day, pork chop or lamb chop. The fare was excellent, servings were both artfully presented and large, and service was attentive almost to the point of being doting. With your tea or coffee, liquid sugar is provided to keep you from going stir crazy.

The evening menu offers some of the same items, plus miso-yaki butterfish with pea sprouts and ginger, salmon with Maui onion and teri cream sauce, and several pastas. L'Uraku's wine list has earned a *Wine Spectator* award. The restaurant's décor is whimsically modern. Walls are splashed with almost childlike multicolor designs and the ceiling is hung with hand-painted upside-down umbrellas.

5 MEKONG THAI

1295 S. Beretania St. (between Keʻeaumoku and Piʻikoi), (808) 591-8842; and 1726 S. King St. (between McCully and Pauwʻa); (808) 941-6184. Thai; wine and beer. Lunch weekdays and dinner nightly. Major credit cards; $$ to $$$.

Honolulu's two Mekongs Thai are pleasing little places with café curtains, floral prints on the walls and table vases with orchids. The large menu offers a good choice of soups, salads and appetizers and a variety of spicy entrées. Vegans will appreciate a good selection of vegetarian dishes.

A favorite of ours is Panang curry with beef, chicken or seafood in coconut milk. Other good choices are the Evil Jungle Prince with beef, chicken or pork sautéed with basil spices and coconut milk; and ginger beef, chicken or pork with spices, green beans and coconut milk. For variety, order three or four appetizers instead of a main dish; servings are generous and modestly priced. We tried the fish cakes, deep fried calamari with a spicy dipping sauce, and do-it-yourself spring rolls that you wrap in crisp lettuce.

6 SAM CHOY'S

Asian/Pacific Rim; mostly seafood; full bar service. Major credit cards; $$ to $$$; www.samchoy.com.

Chubby, smiling Sam Choy has promoted himself to celebrity chef status without really making any major culinary breakthroughs. His two restaurants do offer interesting and affordable fare, and he has authored some cookbooks. How could he resist naming one *The Choy of Cooking*?. The first of his two Honolulu restaurants is more tourist-oriented; the second is more favored by locals.

SAM CHOY'S BREAKFAST, LUNCH & CRAB, *580 N. Nimitz Hwy., Honolulu; (808) 545-7979. Breakfast, lunch and dinner. GETTING THERE: From Waikiki, go northwest 3.5 miles, passing Honolulu Harbor and Aloha Tower. The restaurant is near Pacific Street, where Nimitz has split into two sections.*

This house of Choy occupies an industrial-strength building, with a large open kitchen and high ceilings. It would be excessively noisy except the place is so cavernous that much of the babble is lost in the rafters. This also is a brewery, producing suds with names like Ehu Ale and Kiawe Honey Porter. The menu offers several crab and lobster dishes plus a good selection of seafood. Our steamed *ahi* with apricot sauce and garlic mashed potatoes was quite tasty and portions were huge. However, you might want to ask that the fish be lightly done if that's important to you. On one visit, we had to send ours back twice.

Sam Choy's Diamond Head, *449 Kapahulu Ave., Honolulu; (808) 732-8645. Dinner nightly plus Sunday brunch. GETTING THERE: Going inland from Waikiki and look for the restaurant on a long block between Ala Wai and Date, in a street-front mall.*

You can't see Diamond Head from Choy's Diamond Head restaurant, although it's closer to that famous promontory than the Nimitz Highway place. This house of Choy is a bit more stylish and less gimmicky, with a pleasant Chinese bamboo décor. The menu is similar although it features more regional dishes, such as Hawaiian-style seafood bouillabaisse, seafood *lau lau* and a seafood sampler.

7 SANSEI SEAFOOD RESTAURANT

500 Ala Moana Blvd., in Waterfront Plaza's Restaurant Row, Honolulu; (808) 536-6286; www.sanseihawaii.com. Japanese/Pacific Rim; full bar service. Lunch weekdays and late dinner nightly. Major credit cards; $$$ to $$$$. Reservations recommended. GETTING THERE: From Waikiki, follow Ala Moana northwest 2.5 miles. Waterfront Plaza is on the right, at the corner of Punchbowl.

Chef D.K. Kodama's two Maui restaurants met with such success that he opened a third in Honolulu. While the Maui places are Japanese rustic, the local version is more modern. The décor consists mostly of Sansei's press notices. The Honolulu restaurant, like its Maui cousins, can get noisy. Come for camaraderie, not for Japanese serenity. Sansei is a four-in-one place—a main dining room, a sushi bar, a cozy cocktail lounge and a large bar that resonates with karaoki most nights.

Kodama's menu changes frequently, although you might encounter savories such as roasted Japanese jerk chicken with garlic mashed potatoes, scaloppini of pork tenderloin with Asian sweet and sour glazed fig chutney, or grilled mahi mahi with greens and Japanese plum vinaigrette. For the budget-minded, Sansei offers a 25 percent early bird dinner discount from 5 to 5:30 and a 50 percent late bird pupu and sushi discount from 10 p.m. to 2 a.m.

8 SEAFOOD VILLAGE

Hyatt Regency Waikiki, 2424 Kalakaua Ave.; (808) 971-1818; www.hawaiisbusiness.com/seafoodvillage/. Chinese; full bar service. Lunch and dinner daily. Major credit cards; $$ to $$$$. Reservations accepted. GETTING THERE: It's in the Hyatt shopping complex near the corner of Kalakaua and Kanekapolei.

Other guidebooks ignore this somewhat overly decorated place, but not local diners. They voted it Honolulu's best Chinese restaurant in the annual *Honolulu Advertiser's* I'lima Awards. The interior is pleasingly too busy with lots of laminated wood, red and gold lacquer and Chinese screens. Tables are set with sexy pink nappery.

During lunch, Seafood Village serves some of the best Kong style *dim sum* in Honolulu. Evening menu items include crispy deep fried oysters, kung pao shrimp, prawns with honey glaze walnuts, scallops sautéed with broccoli, spicy calamari with peppery salt, and chili garlic prawns. Among its seafood specialties are live—and expensive—lobster, salmon, sea bass and sunfish, plus fresh abalone.

9 ROYAL GARDEN

Ala Moana Hotel at 410 Atkinson Dr., Honolulu; (808) 942-7788; www.alamoanahotel.com. Chinese; primarily Cantonese; full bar service. Lunch and dinner daily. Major credit cards; $$ to $$$. GETTING THERE: From Waikiki, drive northeast to Ala Moana Shopping Center, go right on Atkinson Street briefly then turn left into the hotel.

This is one of those upscale Chinese restaurants whose décor stops just short of being overdone. It's a busy study in crystal chandeliers, dark woods, plush carpeting and soft autumn colors. Fortunately, there are no snarling dragons, gold shields or red tassel lanterns. The menu is formidable, listing 160 items, and that's not counting desserts.

Among the Royal Garden's featured entrées are minced pork wrapped in lettuce (its version of *mushu* pork), sautéed shrimp and boneless chicken in a potato basket, stuffed eggplant in a bell pepper with tofu and black bean sauce, and shredded mixed meat with mushrooms and mustard cabbage.

10 YANAGI SUSHI

762 Kapi'olani Blvd., Honolulu; (808) 597-1525. Japanese; full bar service. Lunch and late dinner daily. Major credit cards; $$ to $$$$. GETTING THERE: From Waikiki, go inland briefly on McCully Street, turn left onto Kapi'olani and follow it 1.5 miles. Shortly after crossing Ward Avenue, watch on your right for the restaurant at the base of Dreier Street. It's in a low rise building, in an area that's fastly becoming highrise.

Yanagi has the look of a comfy Japanese country inn—rice paper wall panels and bamboo accents, with cozy little booths and tables. Immodestly calling itself "the finest Japanese restaurant in Honolulu," it serves a full range of entrées in addition to more than two dozen types of sushi. And is it really immodest? The Zagat Hawaii survey raves about its "authentic sushi" and "outstanding *udon* and *shabu shabu*." It has been in business more than two decades and has lured the likes of Gene Hackman and Michael Jackson; theirs and other celebs' photos are part of the décor.

Should you need to know, *udon* is a Japanese noodle soup and *shabu shabu* is a stir of thin sliced beef with vegetables and noodles. Yanagi also serves the requisite *sukiyaki* and tempura, several combo dinners and, for those with no Asian persuasion, New York steak.

THE TEN BEST SPECIALTY RESTAURANTS

These selections are listed in no particular order, since each category is different.

1 THE BEST VIEW RESTAURANT:
Hanohano Room

Atop the Sheraton Waikiki, 2255 Kalakaua Ave.; (808) 922-4422, ext. 73620. Continental and Hawaiian regional; full bar service. Breakfast Monday-Saturday, Sunday champagne brunch and dinner nightly. Major credit cards; $$$$ to $$$$$. Reservations advised. GETTING THERE: The Sheraton is adjacent to the Royal Hawaiian, reached via Royal Hawaiian Avenue off Kalakaua. An outside elevator to the restaurant is just to the left of the main entrance.

No other Honolulu skyroom can match the splendid view from the thirtieth floor of the Sheraton Waikiki—the lofty perch of the stylish Hanohano Room. Its window walls offer a panoramic sweep from Diamond Head down to Waikiki Beach and northwest toward Honolulu. And since it towers over its neighbors, nothing obstructs the vista, particularly toward Diamond Head. With such a panorama, come for a breakfast buffet and then dinner to catch sunup and sundown. Saturday breakfast buffet is by reservation only, when a live radio show broadcasts from this sky high perch.

The fare is an interesting mix of classic continental with Hawaiian regional accents. Some examples are shiitake-crusted mahi mahi, 'opakapaka with lobster sauce, and sautéed tiger prawns. The Hanohano Room is simply decorated, since the view of Waikiki and Diamond Head rivals anything an interior designer could match. We've also rated it as Honolulu's most romantic restaurant; see Chapter Seven, page 126.

HONORABLE MENTIONS: If you like aerial views with your dinner, check out these other restaurants on high.

AARON'S: *Ala Moana Hotel, 410 Atkinson Dr.; (808) 955-4466; www.alamoanahotel.com. American-continental; full bar service. Dinner nightly; late night supper Friday and Saturday. Major credit cards; $$ to $$$$. GETTING THERE: From Waikiki, drive northeast to Ala Moana Shopping Center, go right on Atkinson Street briefly, then turn left into the hotel.* □ The views of downtown Honolulu, the ocean and the mountains are fine, although growing highrises have hidden Diamond Head from this attractive restaurant. Come early, since Honolulu from on high is much more attractive in daylight than darkness. You want dazzling lights, go to Las Vegas. Among Aaron's menu offering are grilled rack of lamb, seared *ahi* in Cajun sauce and crabcakes.

SARENTO'S TOP OF THE "I": *Renaissance Ilikai Waikiki Hotel, 1777 Ala Moana Blvd.; (808) 949-3811; www.ilikaihotel.com. Italian; full bar service. Major credit cards; $$$ to $$$$. GETTING THERE: The Ilikai is at Ala Moana and Hobron Lane on the northwest end of Waikiki. A direct elevator to Sarento's is forward and to the left as you enter the Ilikai's main lobby.* □ Winner of several local awards including best all around restaurant, this hotel-topper offers an fine panorama. It rivals the view from the Hanohano Room although neighboring high rises interfere somewhat with the vistas. The fare includes some interesting pastas, plus stuffed pork chops with prosciutto and fontana cheese, chicken stuffed with prosciutto, and pan-seared Atlantic salmon with roasted tomatoes and pesto risotto. The budget-minded can catch discounted early bird dinners.

TOP OF WAIKIKI, Waikiki Business Plaza at 2270 Kalakaua Ave.; (808) 923-3877; www.ambassadorwaikiki.com/dining. Asian/Pacific Rim; full bar service. Dinner only. Major credit cards; *$$ to $$$. GETTING THERE: It's at the corner of Kalakaua and Seaside avenues.* □ This is the least expensive of the city's skyrooms and the only one that revolves. Since it's off the beach, its twenty-third floor perch doesn't offer Hanohano's or Sarento's views. However, you do see a full panorama, for what comes around goes around. And everyone gets a good view, since tables are terraced in three tiers.

Some menu items are mahi mahi with shiitake mushrooms and ginger cilantro, roast duck breast with *hoisin* honey glaze, ribeye steak, roast beef and veal piccata. The restaurant's look spartan Tokyesque; it sits atop a box-like highrise like a giant Kodak slide carousel.

2 THE BEST BEACH RESTAURANT: Duke's Waikiki

Outrigger Waikiki, 2335 Kalakaua Ave.; (808) 923-0711; www.dukeswaikiki.com. Hawaiian regional; full bar service. Breakfast, lunch and dinner. Major credit cards; $$ to $$$. GETTING THERE: The Outrigger Waikiki is on the beach, between the Sheraton Moana and Royal Hawaiian, opposite the International Market Place.

This large and popular café, busy with palm thatch and other retro-Hawaiiana décor, was named for Hawai'i's most beloved athlete, Duke Kahanamoku. He won several Olympic medals for swimming and he was the father of international surfing. Its walls are busy with old Waikiki memorabilia, surfing regalia and photos of the Duke smiling with local and international celebs. And of course, the restaurant is right over da beach, man. It occupies the site of the former Outrigger Canoe Club; the local surfing legend rode the waves just offshore. The adjacent Barefoot Bar is a popular place for locals to suck 'em up. Both the bar and restaurant offer fine Waikiki views.

The menu features regional fare such as Big Island pork ribs, stir-fried chicken cashew, garlic-baked fish and teriyaki style fish. A specialty is seafood Thai style—shrimp, fish and scallops sautéed in Asian spices and coconut curry over white rice. Entrées are modestly priced for a beachside resort restaurant. They include a salad bar, baked muffins and sourdough bread.

3 BEST BREAKFAST PLACE: Eggs 'n Things

1911-B Kalakaua Ave., Waikiki; (808) 949-0820. American; no alcohol or credit cards; $ to $$. Open late evening the following midafternoon Thursday-Sunday, then early morning to midafternoon Monday-Wednesday. GETTING THERE: *It's at the foot of McCully Street between Ena Road and Ala Moana Boulevard.*

This is your place if you feel the need for an omelet at midnight or beyond—at least from Thursday through Sunday, when it's open from 11 at night until 2 the next afternoon. Eggs 'n Things is a bright and cheerful little diner on the ground floor of the Kalakauan building. It serves the usual assortment of omelets, waffles, pancakes and such; crepes suzette are a specialty. If you want a Hawaiian breakfast, go for the banana crepes suzette, or coconut or macadamia nut waffles or pancakes. They're particularly tasty, since the syrups are made in house. The menu features fried breakfast Spam, but please don't pour syrup on it.

4 BEST BUFFET: Pikake Terrace

Sheraton Princess Ka'iulani, 120 Ka'iulani Ave., Waikiki; (808) 931-4667; www.sheraton-hawaii.com. American; full bar service. Breakfast and dinner buffets plus Sunday brunch and light lunches. Major credit cards; $$ to $$$$. GETTING THERE: The Princess is just off Kalakaua Avenue in the heart of the Waikiki district.

This is our favorite buffet both for the extensive food selection and the setting, in a palm-lined courtyard near the Sheraton's swimming pool. Live Polynesian entertainment is presented nightly and tables are candle lit to create a rather romantic scene. Each evening buffet has a theme—seafood on Sunday, Tuesday and Thursday; steak and seafood Monday; seafood and ribs Wednesday; seafood, lobster and steak Friday; and seafood, crab and prime rib Saturday. Steak, ribs and lobster come right off the barbecue, and prime rib is served every night. Finish off the evening at the dessert section and ice cream sundae bar.

5 THE BEST SUNDAY BRUNCH: Banyan Veranda

Sheraton Moana, 2365 Kalakaua Ave., Waikiki; (808) 922-3111; www.moana-surfrider.com. American; full bar service. Breakfast and dinner daily. Major credit cards; $$$$. Reservations advised. GETTING THERE: The Sheraton Moana is in the heart of Waikiki, opposite the International Market Place.

The Banyan Veranda claims to serve "Hawai'i's best Sunday brunch" and we agree. This is a splendid space, just off the beach and shaded by a giant banyan tree planted in 1904. The terrace and adjacent Beach Bar offer views of Waikiki and Diamond Head. The Sunday brunch selection is the most extensive of any on the island. We counted—and attempted to sample—eleven hot entrées, seven cold selections and seven salads. There's also a tempting seafood display, several soups, pastries, and omelette and waffle stations. A macadamia nut waffle drowned in coconut syrup is the way to start your Waikiki day.

6 BEST SEAFOOD RESTAURANT WITH A SEAFOOD VIEW: Neptune's Garden

Pacific Beach Hotel, 2490 Kalakaua Ave., Waikiki; (808) 921-6112; www.neptunesgardenrestaurant.com. Asian/Pacific Rim; full bar service. Dinner nightly; live entertainment Tuesday-Saturday. Major credit cards;

$$$ to $$$$. Reservations accepted. GETTING THERE: The hotel is across Kalakaua from the beach, between Kealohilani and Lili'uokalani avenues.

Several tables in this mostly seafood restaurant are adjacent to Hawai'i's largest indoor aquarium, a fish-busy 280,000-gallon Plexiglas tank. The restaurant has an appealing Asian modern look with curving room dividers, potted plants and sleek drop lamps over booths and tables that are dressed in pink nappery. The best fish-view tables are along a railing. Kitchen offerings include steamed island snapper, pan-fried *moi*, sautéed garlic shrimp, seared *ahi*, seafood bouillabaisse and for non-fish eaters, beef tenderloin and macadamia nut-crusted rack of lamb.

7 BEST LOCAL HANGOUT: Matteo's

364 Seaside Ave., Waikiki; (808) 922-5551; www.hawaiibusiness.com/matteos/. Italian; full bar service. Late dinner nightly. Major credit cards; $$$ to $$$$. Reservations advised. GETTING THERE: It's at the corner of Seaside and Kuhio adjacent to the Marine Surf Hotel, a few blocks off Waikiki Beach.

Some local foodies call this long-established place "faded," although it's hardly that for many locals, who come for hearty Italian food and idle chat with tuxedoed waiters. It's a favorite hangout of Don Ho and his daughter Hoku, who may stroll over with a few friends and band members after his show at the nearby Waikiki Beachcomber. Other local celebs and news anchors get their pasta fixes here as well. The place has the look of a fine old American-Italian restaurant with dark paneled walls, plush curved booths and dim lighting.

Matteo's isn't inexpensive although you can catch an early bird special between 5:30 and 6:30 for about $10. Menu items include steak and peppers "Frank Sinatra", Moloka'i herbal rack of lamb, several seafood dishes, cioppino and the usual pastas. A specialty is seafood tuttanesca—shrimp, scallops, clams, fresh fish, mussels and anchovies in a tomato sauce, served on a bed of linguine.

8 BEST GRINDS: Ono Hawaiian Food

726 Kapahulu Ave., Honolulu; (808) 737-2275. Traditional Hawaiian; no alcohol or credit cards; $. Lunch through early dinner Monday-Saturday; closed Sunday. GETTING THERE: Follow Kapahulu inland from Waikiki for about a mile. It's on the left between Kamuela and Date, just beyond Ala Wai Golf Course.

You needn't go to a luau to get *lau lau*. Typical luau fare is served at this charmingly funky little joint at a considerably less cost. In fact, we also nominate it as one of the Ten Best cheap places to eat in Chapter Five, page 106. You can pig out on *kalua* pig and other native Hawaiian fare by ordering a luau plate, or select from several àla carte choices such as *lomi lomi* salmon, chicken long rice, or chicken *lau lau*, plus beef stew and beef curry. Portions are huge; our favorite is chicken *lau lau*—chicken steamed off the bone in a thick bundle of taro leaves.

Ono has been serving hearty Hawaiian fare for forty years. Founder Sueko Oh Young, well into her eighties, is retired although she still stops by to help in the kitchen. Ono's walls are busy with scores of photos of celebs and snapshots of regular customers, and that's about it for décor. There's often a line at lunch; the place is so small that patrons are asked to wait out on the sidewalk until a table clears.

9 BEST 'BURGER JOINT: Cheeseburger in Paradise

2500 Kalakaua Ave., Waikiki; (808) 923-3731; www.cheeseburger-waikiki.com. American; full bar service. Breakfast through late dinner daily. Major credit cards; $ to $$$. GETTING THERE: It's across from Waikiki Beach on the corner of Kealohilani.

This beach shack-funky restaurant with rattan walls and ceiling fans serves the best 'burgers on O'ahu. And they're served by a waitstaff—both guys and gals—wearing skimpy grass skirts, fortunately with khaki shorts underneath. The signature cheeseburger—not inexpensive but worth the price—has Colby, jack or Swiss cheese, prime Angus beef, tomatoes, lettuce and onions, served on a sesame seed or whole wheat bun. And the buns are done in house. This burger paradise also has several other sandwiches, salads and assorted tropical drinks. It features live entertainment most nights.

The word is that Jimmy Buffet of *Cheeseburger in Paradise* musical fame wasn't happy about the name selection when this place opened a few years ago, but apparently the issue has been settled.

10 BEST TOURIST RESTAURANT: Don Ho's Island Grill

Aloha Tower Marketplace, 101 Aloha Tower Dr., Honolulu; (808) 528-0807; www.donho.com/grill. Hawaiian regional; full bar service. Lunch and dinner daily. Major credit cards; $$ to $$$. GETTING THERE: The Marketplace is at the base of Aloha Tower, about three miles northeast of Waikiki, off Ala Moana Boulevard.

Honolulu teems with tourists, mostly from the mainland and Japan, so we decided to end this chapter with the Best Tourist Restaurant. And what's more appropriate than one named for Don Ho? He has been entertaining tourists for nearly half a century—not here but in Waikiki. Zagat's Hawai'i survey readers agreed with our selection, although in a mean-spirited way, calling it a "tacky tourist trap."

No, Don Ho doesn't do the cooking, and perhaps he should, since the fare is rather ordinary. However, prices are reasonable for this harbor-view location and portions are generous. Entrées include wok-seared garlic chicken, Asian chicken *mushu*, grilled island style guava chicken and seafood curry, plus assorted pizzas. The restaurant is dressed in unsubtle Polynesian décor, with distressed bamboo chairs and thatched roofs. The Tiny Bubbles Bar hangs right over the waterfront, so come for a drink and a view if the menu doesn't impress you.

Chapter Four

THE BEST RESORTS
PLAYGROUNDS IN PARADISE

Waikiki Beach is *the* paradise with pillows. O'ahu has more beachside and beach-view hotels than any other place in America except Florida, and ninety percent of these are in Waikiki. And why not? It offers one of the country's best beaches, and the cosmopolitan lures of Honolulu are but a short drive away.

It could be said that Waikiki's role as a resort started shortly after Kamehameha I conquered O'ahu in 1794 to unite most of the Hawaiian Islands. He established his capital at Honolulu and the royal family soon began relaxing on this marshy, spring-fed beach area. (*Waikiki* means "spouting water.") However, its history goes back even further. Archeological evidence suggests that a village occupied Waikiki about 600 A.D. Try to picture—at the base of Diamond Head—a thatched-hut village with taro patches and fish ponds!

Throughout their nearly one century of rule, Hawaiian *ali'i* relaxed at summer retreats here. White settlers saw its resort value as well. The United State annexed Hawai'i in 1898 and the first luxury hotel—the Moana—opened on Waikiki three years later.

The Moana is still there, since joined by dozens of other resorts. Only a few stand right on the sand; the rest are just inland, creating a highrise area greater than downtown Honolulu. They're crowded together like kids along a parade route, all straining for a view.

That view doesn't come cheap. Room rates in the better Waikiki Beach hotels start around $250 a night and ocean view rooms are considerably higher—often more than double. Surprisingly, Waikiki also has some relatively inexpensive hotel rooms, although not on the beach. We begin our choices of playplaces with the Ten Best luxury resorts, then follow with ten more affordable hotels. And in the next chapter, we even managed to find ten Waikiki-area hotels and hostels with rooms for less than $90 per couple during high season.

All but one of the selections below are on or near Waikiki. If you like quiet, remote beaches, you're in the wrong city and maybe even on the wrong island. We like the tempo and the excitement here.

PRICING: Dollar sign codes indicate room price ranges for two people, based on high season (summer and winter) rates: *$* = a standard two-person room for $99 or less; *$$* = $100 to $149; *$$$* = $150 to $199; *$$$$* = $200 to $249; *$$$$$* $250 or more. **CREDIT CARDS:** All of the below listed cards accept most major credit cards.

NET-SURFING: The rates listed below were provided by the hotels, although you may get lower prices by booking via the internet. Check the hotels' websites for specials, particularly during the off-season. Also, check travel sites such as *www.hotels.com*; *www.travelocity.com* and *www.expedia.com*.

TRAVEL TIP: Kalakaua Avenue, Waikiki's main street, is usually busy with traffic and it can become particularly noisy with revelers on Friday and Saturday nights. Bear this in mind when booking hotels along the avenue. Rooms over the street can be rather noisy, even though they may offer fine beach views.

THE TEN BEST RESORT HOTELS

In keeping with our Ten Best theme, we have selected only O'ahu's finest hotels. Not everyone, including the authors of this book, can afford such luxury. However, these elaborate resorts are attractions unto themselves, even for non-guests. We enjoy prowling about these grand hideaways, sampling the restaurants, window shopping the shops and enjoying cocktails with views of beach and sea. Our selections are based on overall resort appeal, not the opulence of individual rooms.

1 HILTON HAWAIIAN VILLAGE

2005 Kalia Rd., Honolulu, HI 96815; (800) HILTONS or (808) 949-4321; www.hiltonhawaii.com. Largest resort complex on Waikiki Beach with 3,432 rooms and suites; $$$$ to $$$$$. GETTING THERE: The *village is on the corner of Ala Moana Boulevard and Kalia Road. Turn right onto Kalia and then right again into the village.*

The Hilton is the largest resort in the state and the largest beachfront resort in the world. Its 31-story Rainbow Tower is one of Waikiki's best known landmarks; mosaic rainbows on either end are listed in the *Guinness Book of World Records* as the world's largest murals. The Hilton Hawaiian Village is an extensive complex, a virtual vacation campus alongside the shore.

The décor in the public areas and rooms is Polynesian floral with Asian accents. Some of Waikiki's best views are from its hotel towers. This is indeed a village—an extensive complex of highrises, shops, gardens, two mini-golf courses, two spas, five swimming pools and other "water features" spread over twenty-two acres. It's also home to the Bishop Museum at Kalia, an annex to the world-renowned museum in nearby Honolulu.

The Hilton has nearly twenty restaurants and cafés, including Bali by the Sea and the Golden Dragon; see Chapter Three, pages 67 and 71. Thirsty? There are eight bars and lounges, many with beach views. The village is a virtual shopping center as well, with more than ninety shops and stores, including a streetful lining the main drive into the complex. Room amenities include data ports with internet access, voicemail, refrigerators and lanais or balconies.

2 THE HALEKULANI

2199 Kalia Rd., Honolulu, HI, 96815-1988; (800) 367-2343 or (808) 923-2311; www.halekulani.com. An opulent Waikiki beachside resort with 456 rooms and suites; $$$$$. GETTING THERE: Take Lewers Street off Kalakaua Avenue, follow it to the end and go briefly left.

The Halekulani is a superb study in elegance and client care; it's the most luxurious hotel on Waikiki Beach. No other resort in Hawai'i—yea, perhaps in the world—treats its guests with such indulgence. They're escorted to their rooms by a receptionist, not a bellman, and a basket of goodies arrives soon after. Staff members—from the concierge to waiters to maids—call patrons by their names and no, we don't know how they remember them all. Hotel guests also are guests of the Iolani Palace, Bishop Museum, Honolulu Academy of Art and the Contemporary Museum; room keycards provide free admission.

The Halekulani's centerpiece is a large oval pool with a stunning orchid blossom of blue ceramic tiles on the bottom. Fine works of art and stylish shops line the hotel's wide corridors. Its rooms are gorgeous, with tropical décor, soft colors, marble baths and Berber carpets. The Halekulani was built in 1907 as a series of garden bungalows. When new owners demolished them to build hotel towers in 1981, they saved and carefully restored the legendary House Without a Key, a classic South Seas plantation style structure.

Longtime locals and visitors—we among them—like to relax in wicker chairs in its Lewers Lounge and reminisce about the old days, when the Halekulani was the last low-rise resort on Waikiki. The "House" also contains the hotel's three restaurants—the namesake House Without a Key, and the La Mer (Chapter Three, page 66) and Orchid (Chapter Seven, page 129).

3 HYATT REGENCY WAIKIKI

2424 Kalakaua Ave., Honolulu, HI 96815; (800) 233-1234 or (808) 923-1234; www.hyattwaikiki.com. A 1,230-room twin-towered highrise hotel across from Waikiki Beach; $$$$ to $$$$$. GETTING THERE: The Hyatt is between Ka'iulani and Uluniu avenues. The motor entrance is on Uluniu, which is one-way outbound. To reach it, turn left onto Ka'iulani, right on Koa Avenue and then right again onto Uluniu.

With its octagonal forty-story towers, the Hyatt offers some of Waikiki's finest views, since it sits opposite Kuhio Beach Park. This sleekly modern complex is a fine place to explore, covering almost a full city block. Its ground floor breezeway is a large shopping arcade accented with a pair of waterfalls that cascade down two floors into a pool. The hotel lobby is classic Hyatt Regency—a landscaped atrium rising ten stories. A balcony hanging over Kalakaua offers nice views of palm-lined Kuhio Beach Park.

Rooms are spacious, with the usual resort amenities, and nearly all have views of something interesting—beach, Diamond Head, the heart of Waikiki or inland mountains. Rooms and suites on the Regency Club floors include continental breakfast, evening snacks and cocktails and access to a private rooftop sun deck. Hotel amenities include a large spa, swimming pool, a "Camp Hyatt" for kids and several restaurants. We like the casual Terrace Grille with views of Waikiki.

4 KAHALA MANDARIN ORIENTAL

5000 Kahala Ave., Honolulu, HI 96816-5498; (800) 526-6566 or (808) 739-8888; www.mandarin-oriental.com/kahala. Elegant beachside resort with 364 rooms and suites; $$$$$. GETTING THERE: Press southeastward along Waikiki, shifting from Kalakaua Avenue to Diamond Head Road to Kahala Avenue. Remain on Kahala for just over a mile, continuing into the Wai'alae Country Club; the Mandarin is at the end of the road.

If you want to get away from the ruckus of Waikiki, but not too far away, head briefly east for one of Hawai'i's most opulent hotels. Tucked between the Wai'alae Country Club and Kahala Bay, the Mandarin is a place of quiet retreat. The hotel tower looks a bit odd, framed in vertical and horizontal beams as if it hasn't been uncrated. However, the interior definitely as been. Massive modernistic chandeliers mark the large lobby and adjacent Veranda Lounge. Elegant shops line wide corridors that play silent host to select works of art. Rooms are done in dark mahogany, with four poster beds, teak parquet floors and oversized marble bathrooms. Guests are escorted to their rooms, then continually spoiled until they reluctantly depart.

Water courses flow through the extensive, beautifully landscaped grounds, with tropical reef fish, sea turtles and—oh my!—dolphins. They're part of the Dolphin Quest "swim with dolphins" program. They cruise contentedly about the lagoon between "Quests," to the delight of guests. The lagoon complex also has adult and kids swimming pools. Kahala Beach is adjacent, sandy and inviting; a breakwater keeps the surf gentle. The Mandarin's dining venues—all properly stylish—are the Plumeria Beach Café, Tokyo Tokyo; the informal Veranda and Hoku's (Chapter Three, page 68).

5 OUTRIGGER WAIKIKI

2335 Kalakaua Ave., Honolulu, HI 96815-2941; (800) OUTRIGGER or (808) 923-0711; www.outrigger.com. Luxury beachside highrise with 530 rooms and suites; $$$$ to $$$$$. GETTING THERE: The hotel is on the beach between the Sheraton Moana and the Royal Hawaiian.

Outriggers are among the more affordable of the Waikiki's nicer resorts; not inexpensive but less pricey than most of the other better hotels. (The company also has an inexpensive division called Ohana Hotels; see below.) The flagship of this chain has a prime location, in the heart of Waikiki and right on the sand. The lobby—on the second floor—is comfy and appealing with floral carpeting, overstuffed couches and a beautiful lacquered outrigger canoe, a signature item in Outrigger resorts. The hotel is home to the small International Surfing Museum, with boards, trophies, photos and other items from some of the world's top surfers, plus ongoing surfer videos. The Outrigger also is home to "The Society of Seven," a musical and comedy show (Chapter Six, page 115).

The three restaurants—all with Waikiki views—are Duke's Canoe Club (Chapter Three, page 78), Sunset Terrace, and Chuck's Steakhouse. Rooms are nicely done with cheerful Polynesian décor; most have balconies. Resort facilities include a guest laundry, pool and spa, fitness center, beach activities hut and a kids activity center.

6 RENAISSANCE ILIKAI

1777 Ala Moana Blvd., Honolulu, HI 96815; (800) 468-3571 or (808) 949-3811; www.ilikaihotel.com. High rise resort hotel above Ala Wai Harbor; 783 rooms and condos; $$ to $$$$. GETTING THERE: The Ilikai is on Waikiki's west end, at the corner of Hobron Lane.

Like the Outrigger, this is one of the more affordable of Waikiki's resorts. It's not quite on the beach although the sand is a short walk away, down an access ramp. The rooms are attractive and spacious, the result of a recent $27 million renovation. Because of the Ilikai's height and location, eighty percent of them have ocean views; all have balconies. Many of its units have full kitchens. Facilities include a kids' activity center, a large lagoon/swimming complex, tennis courts, fitness center and guest laundry.

A gurgling fountain with a pair of happy bronze whales designed by noted Hawai'i artist Wyland greets guests at the entrance. The appealing open lobby has several shops and a water feature with a stream cascading over lava rocks. Dining options include Sarento's Top of the "I" (Chapter Three, page 77), Canoes with indoor/outdoor tables and views of the marina and ocean, Tanaka of Tokyo and the poolside Paddles bar. There are several other restaurants in the adjacent marina complex.

7 ROYAL HAWAIIAN/SHERATON WAIKIKI

Royal Hawaiian: 2259 Kalakaua Ave., Honolulu, HI 96815-2578, (800) 325-3589 or (808) 923-7311, www.royal-Hawaiian.com; Sheraton Waikiki: 2255 Kalakaua Ave., Honolulu, HI 96815-2579; (808) 782-9488 or (808) 922-4422; www.sheraton-hawaii.com. The Royal Hawaiian has 527 rooms and suites; the highrise Sheraton has 1,710; $$$$$. GETTING THERE: Both hotels are on Waikiki Beach, reached from Kalakaua via Royal Hawaiian Avenue.

These side-by-side hotels are operated by Sheraton, although they're hardly twins. The Sheraton is curvy modern with a light, contemporary Polynesian look; the Royal Hawaiian is the legendary Spanish-Moorish style "Pink Palace." It was opened in 1927 by Matson Navigation Company with "400 lavishly decorated rooms" to house the cruise line's passengers. It was touted as "the finest resort hostelry in America." Despite being rimmed by high rise hotels and its own Royal Hawaiian Shopping Center, the Pink Palace remains something of an island, isolated by spacious, nicely landscaped lawns fore and aft.

Inside, ornate beams hold up lofty lobby ceilings hung with teardrop crystal chandeliers. Free historic tours are conducted Monday, Wednesday and Friday at 2; reservations aren't necessary. The Royal Hawaiian hosts one of the island's best luaus Monday and Thursday (Chapter One, page 37) and conducts a Hawaiian theme high tea every afternoon from 1 to 4. Its main dining venue, the Surf Room, is one of Waikiki's top restaurants. It and the adjacent Mai Tai Bar offer fine Waikiki and Diamond Head views.

The bold sweeping curves of the adjacent Sheraton Waikiki tower high above the beach. Its spacious, flagstone-paved lobby is dramatically modern, done in yellow and hot pink with a tropical motif. The main restaurant is the Hanohano Room, atop the hotel's thirtieth floor; see Chapter Three, page 76. Just off the lobby is Esprit, Waikiki's only beachside nightclub, offering live entertainment and dancing; see

Chapter Six, page 116. Down by the sea is the Sandbar, an informal café and poolside bar.

Both hotels have long swatches of beach; low chains draw a line in the sand to separate hotel beach from public strand.

8 SHERATON MOANA & SURFRIDER

2365 Kalakaua Ave., Honolulu, HI 96815-2943; (800) 782-9488 or (808) 922-3111; www.sheraton-hawaii.com. Historic Waikiki hotel with low-rise wings and a highrise tower; 793 rooms and suites; $$$$$. GETTING THERE: It's at the foot of Ka'iulani Avenue.

Waikiki's first major resort, the Moana still stands proudly between Kalakaua Avenue and the beach. It's a splendid retreat with a blend of Hawai'i plantation and Beaux Arts styles. Ionic columns support the elegant lobby's lofty ceiling. The Banyan Veranda, surrounding a creeper-draped giant of a tree, is a popular gathering place. The Beach Bar is adjacent, just off the sand and thus enjoying fine Waikiki and Diamond Head views. The History Room on the second floor of the main building tells of the early days of Waikiki and this grand old hotel (Chapter One, page 37). Property tours are conducted Monday, Wednesday and Friday, starting from here at 11 and 5.

A modern hotel tower, the Surfrider, reaches skyward just to the west of the original Moana, which is now called the Banyan Wing. The resort's dining facilities include the historic Ship's Tavern (Chapter Three, page 69); the Banyan Veranda (Chapter Three, page 79) and the Beachside Café. Amenities at the Moana and Surfrider include a beachside swimming pool, fitness center, Keiki Aloha Club for children, a salon and spa.

9 TURTLE BAY RESORT

57-091 Kamehameha Hwy., Kahuku, HI 967831; (800) 203-3650 or (808) 293-8811; www.turtlebayhotel.com. A 485-unit low-rise resort complex on O'ahu's northern shore; $$$ to $$$$$. GETTING THERE: The resort is about forty miles from Honolulu. Take H-1 west, then H-2 north. Blend onto Kamehameha Highway at the end of the freeway and follow it north along the coast for about twelve miles.

Occupying an 880-acre peninsula on O'ahu's famed North Shore, Turtle Bay Resort is like one of the expansive outer island retreats. With plenty of room to roam, it offers a 36-hole golf course, tennis courts, riding trails, a large spa and five miles of shoreline. It's the ideal retreat for those who want to escape the madding—if happy—crowds of Waikiki. Further, its rooms are cheaper than at most of the high end Waikiki hotels. Recently renovated, the resort is surrounded by handsomely landscaped grounds and all of that beachfront—some of it sandy and some craggy lava.

Window walls of the large open lobby offer dramatic ocean panoramas. Several shops line the lobby and adjacent corridors and a pair of macaws oversee the area. Dining venues are the Palm Terrace, cascading down from the lobby to a swimming pool, the Surf Room; the beachside Terrace Café and a gourmet room called 21° North. Our favorite spot here is the outdoor Hang Ten pool bar, overlooking a beach where those mighty North Shore breakers roll in. Folks gather on the sloping grass above the beach every winter to watch international surfing competitions.

10 WAIKIKI BEACH MARRIOTT RESORT

2552 Kalakaua Ave., Honolulu, HI 96815-3699; (800) 367-5370 or (808) 922-6611; www.marriottwaikiki.com. A 1,310-room high rise in the heart of Waikiki; $$$$$. GETTING THERE: It's at the corner of Ohua, across Kalakaua from Kuhio Beach Park.

Fresh from a $60 million renovation, the Marriott is one of Waikiki's largest resorts. Its two towers—one rising thirty-three floors—offer vistas of the beach, Diamond Head and distant downtown Honolulu. The hotel's interior courtyard shelters visitors from the busy-ness of surrounding Waikiki. Palms soar high in the sky and hotel towers with scalloped balconies soar much higher. Historic photos line a corridor leading to the main lobby, an appealing space with a flagstone floor. Its centerpiece is Hawai'i's oldest existing outrigger canoe, built in 1890.

Among the Marriott's restaurants are Kuhio Beach Grill, the Mauna Terrace on the third level pool deck with views of Waikiki, and Restaurant Run (sushi and other Japanese fare). The rooms are Polynesian *moderne* with floral prints, wood furniture and marble-floored bathrooms with granite counter tops. The Marriott's many amenities include two swimming pools, fifteen shops, a fitness center and *Keiki Kids* program.

Special mention: Aston Waikiki Tower

2470 Kalakaua Ave., Honolulu, HI 96815; (800) 922-7866 or (808) 926-6400; www.astonhotels.com. A highrise luxury condo complex with ninety-six suites; $$$$$. GETTING THERE: The tower sits just back from Kalakaua, off Lili'uokalani Avenue. Turn left from Kalakaua onto Lili'uokalani, then left again into the parking entrance.

If you'd like a luxury apartment in the heart of Waikiki, this is your place. All units in this 39-story tower are fully furnished condos with kitchens, living rooms, wet bars, one or two bedrooms and large outside balconies with patio chairs and tables. There's even a pass-through from the kitchen to the balcony. And the views! There are only four units per floor and many offer vistas in both directions—to Waikiki from the living room, kitchen and balcony; and to the mountains from the bedrooms.

These are luxury units with all the amenities of an upscale resort, which of course it is. The hotel has a fourth deck swimming pool and a workout room, and it offers free guest parking, a rarity in Waikiki.

THE TEN BEST MEDIUM-PRICE HOTELS

Can't afford the $250 or more a night charged by most of Waikiki's leading resorts? You can still stay near the beach by choosing one of several modestly priced hotels. Most have rooms ranging between $100 and $200; some of our choices are closer to the $100 mark. All of our chosen hostelries are within a short walk of Waikiki.

Two firms, Aston Hotels & Resorts and Ohana Hotels & Resorts, specialize in budget-priced properties and some have made our list, including our very favorite.

1 ASTON WAIKIKI BEACH HOTEL

2570 Kalakaua Ave., Honolulu, HI 96815; (800) 922-7866 or (808) 922-2511; www.astonhotels.com. A 25-story 716-room hotel across from the beach; $$$ to $$$$$. GETTING THERE: It's on the eastern side of Waikiki at the corner of Kalakaua and Paoakalani Street. Turn left off Kalakaua then quickly right for parking.

Our favorite affordable Waikiki retreat is a newly renovated hotel with a modern and almost whimsical South Seas theme. Guest rooms have beaded "hula girl" curtains on the closets and bright lava red or sunshine yellow bedspreads. All units have small refrigerators and balconies. The location is excellent, just across Kalakaua from the beach and adjacent to Kapi'olani Park. Since the resort stands alone at the far end of Waikiki's "hotel row," most rooms have at least a partial beach view. The hotel's "social center" is an elevated pool deck and the adjacent Tiki's Grill & Bar; both overlook the beach. Tiki's offers live entertainment most nights. A Wolfgang Puck Express and an ice cream parlor called Coldstone Creamery are on the ground floor.

A special hotel feature is "Breakfast on the Beach." Guests find a plastic picnic bag in their rooms, which they can fill with pre-wrapped goodies from an extensive morning buffet. They can dine on the pool deck, at Tiki's outside tables or—as the name says—carry their booty across Kalakaua Avenue for a picnic on the beach.

2 ASTON PACIFIC MONARCH

2427 Kuhio Ave., Honolulu, HI 96815; (800) 923-9805 or (808) 923-9805; www.astonhotels.com or www.pacific-monarch.com. A 34-story hotel with 140 studios or one-bedroom units; $$$ to $$$$. GETTING THERE: The hotel is two blocks off the beach at Kuhio and Uluniu. Fork left onto Kuhio from Kalakaua Avenue and follow it fourteen blocks to Uluniu; hotel is on the northwest corner.

This attractive, recently renovated hotel is in the eastern part of Waikiki, close to the beach and Kapi'olani Park. Units are fairly roomy and all have kitchenettes or full kitchens; many have lanais. Facilities include a small pool, sauna and hot tub, guest laundry, cocktail lounge and gift shop. Units on higher floors—and the rooftop pool—offer Waikiki vistas.

3 'ILIMA HOTEL

445 Nohonani St., Honolulu, HI 86815; (800) 367-5172 or (808) 923-1877; www.ilima.com. A condo hotel with ninety-nine units; $$ to $$$$. GETTING THERE: The hotel is near the corner of Ala Wai about three blocks from the beach. From Kuhio Avenue, take three lefts—onto Nahua Street, Ala Wai Boulevard and Nohonani. The hotel is on your left.

This older, well-kept nine-story hotel just off the Ala Wai Canal offers some of the best rates in the Waikiki area. Studio units start around $100; one and two bedroom suites go up from there, although not much beyond $200. All units are quite roomy and each has a full kitchen with microwave and lanai; some have spa tubs. If you can afford normal Waikiki rates, you can get a 1,500-square-foot three-bedroom penthouse for less than $400. It has two kitchens, two bathrooms and a washer/dryer. Hotel facilities include a pool, sauna, exercise room and sun deck. The small lobby is cozy and inviting, with koa wood trim and paintings of Hawaiian mythology on the walls.

4 MARINE SURF WAIKIKI HOTEL

364 Seaside Ave., Honolulu, HI 96815; (888) 456-SURF or (808) 931-2424; www.marinesurf.com. Small 23-story all-studio hotel; $ to $$$. GETTING THERE: It's at the corner of Kuhio and Seaside. Turn left off Kalakaua Avenue and go inland two blocks to Kuhio.

Rooms in this hotel just off the beach are a little weathered although they're neat and clean and fair-sized. All have kitchenettes, handy for longer stays. Oddly, non-smoking rooms are more expensive, unless that strange policy has changed. Units have small balconies and some of the uppers have nice views. There's a small pool and sun deck on the fourth floor and a washer and dryer on each floor.

5 OHANA ROYAL ISLANDER

2164 Kalia Rd., Honolulu, HI 96815-1937; (800) 462-6262 or (808) 922-1961; www.ohanahotels.com. A midsize highrise hotel with 101 rooms; $$ to $$$. GETTING THERE: The hotel is at the corner of Kalia and Saratoga. Either turn left from Ala Moana Boulevard and follow Kalia around Fort DeRussy Park, or turn left from Kalakaua Avenue onto Saratoga.

This small hotel has very clean and nicely decorated if quite snug rooms. All have small balconies and refrigerators; some have full kitchens with microwaves. A few rooms have views of Waikiki; oddly, the hotel's best view is from the eleventh floor laundry room. Guests have access to the Outrigger Reef swimming pool and other facilities, just across Kalia Road.

6 OHANA SURF

2200 Kuhio Ave., Honolulu, HI 96815-2699; (800) 462-6262 or (808) 922-5777; www.ohanahotels.com. A midsize sixteen-story hotel with 251 rooms; $$ to $$$. GETTING THERE: The hotel is at the corner of Nohonani Street. Parking is on Nohohani, which is one-way beachward; to reach it, drive west on Ala Wai and turn left.

This older, well-kept hotel is about a block from the beach, opposite the inshore side of the International Market Place. A small pool is elevated above the street. All rooms have balconies, refrigerators and microwaves; some have views. They range from reasonably roomy to quite snug and they're cheerfully decorated, with floral print spreads and matching drapes, Hawaiian prints on the walls and blonde wood furniture.

7 PACIFIC BEACH HOTEL

2490 Kalakaua Ave., Honolulu, HI 96815; (800) 367-6060 or (808) 923-4511; www.pacificbeachhotel.com. A high-rise resort across from the beach, with 837 rooms; $$$ to $$$$. GETTING THERE: The hotel is opposite Kuhio Beach Park between Lili'uokalani and Kealohilani avenues. Turn left from Kalakaua onto Lili'uokalani, and then turn right for the hotel.

This is one of the larger and more elaborate hotels that qualifies for our modest price list. Rates begin just above $200 although they're often lower with specials. A wide corridor lined with shops leads to the hotel's spacious lobby, whose centerpiece is Hawai'i's largest indoor aquarium. Tropical fish—some huge—are visible from the lobby and from two of the hotel's restaurants—Five Fathoms and Neptune's Garden (Chapter Three, page 79). The hotel's other restaurant is Shogun's, with Japanese and Pacific Rim fare. Comfortable rooms feature Polynesian décor and many have Waikiki views. The Pacific Beach Hotel's amenities include a tennis court, swimming pool, salon and spa, and a business center.

8 SHERATON PRINCESS KA'IULANI

120 Ka'iulani Ave., Honolulu, HI 96815; (800) 782-9488 or (808) 922-5811; www.sheraton-hawaii.com. Very attractive 1,150-room highrise hotel; $$$ to $$$$$. GETTING THERE: It's just off Kalakaua Ave-

nue, with a pedestrian entrance near the Princess Food Court. The auto entrance is off Ka'iulani, which is one-way inland.

Most Sheratons in Waikiki are too pricey for this list, although this appealing resort is one of the area's better bargains. Some room prices start well under $200, although most are higher. It was named in honor of Princess Ka'iulani, whose home once stood on this spot. She was heir apparent to the throne until the monarchy was overthrown, then sadly, she died shortly after at the age of twenty-two. Old black and white photos of her and other *ali'i* are displayed in the hotel's public areas, particularly on the eleventh floor Stevenson Room. The Scottish author became quite enamored with her during his stay in Hawai'i.

The hotel was built in 1955, although virtually none of the original remains. However, in keeping with earlier times, Hawaiian crafts people and artists set up daily displays on long tables between the swimming pool terrace and the lobby entrance. Dining venues are the Pikake Terrace (Chapter Three, page 79), Homoyama (Japanese), and the inexpensive Princess Food Court on Kalakaua Avenue (Chapter Five, page 103). Amenities include a swimming pool, fitness center and children's program. The hotel is home to a nightly show called "Creations: A Polynesian Journey" (Chapter Six, page 115). Historical tours of the property are given weekdays at 4.

9 WAIKIKI BEACHCOMBER

2300 Kalakaua Ave., Honolulu, HI 96815-2938; (800) 622-4646 or (808) 922-4646; www.waikikibeachcomber.com. A 550-room highrise across Kalakaua from the beach; $$$ to $$$$$. GETTING THERE: It's at the corner of Duke's Lane; turn left off Kalakaua.

Like the Princess Ka'iulani, this attractive highrise resort is in the higher end of our "modest" price range. Rack rate start above $200, although cheaper package deals are common. The hotel lobby, a small pool and restaurant are elevated above Kalakaua Avenue, sitting atop Macy's Waikiki. Rooms are fair sized and nicely furnished; all have refrigerators and balconies; many offer views. Its main dining venue is the Hibiscus Café, serving Hawaiian regional fare. Hotel amenities include a pool and spa.

The Beachcomber is Waikiki's major entertainment center, with three theaters hosting long running shows—the Don Ho Show, "Magic of Polynesia" and "Blue Hawaii: The Show"; see Chapter Six for reviews. Often, several cast members of the Polynesia show stage a free and rather lively preview in the hotel's driveway, beside Duke's Lane.

10 WAIKIKI ROYAL SUITES

255 Beachwalk, Honolulu, HI 96815; (800) 535-0085 or (808) 926-5641; www.marcresorts.com. A small condo hotel with all kitchen units;

$$$*. GETTING THERE: The hotel is just off Kalakaua Avenue; turn left onto Beachwalk and it's on the left.*

Part of the Marc Resorts Hawai'i chain, this small hotel is two blocks from Waikiki Beach. It features clean, well-kept and nicely furnished studios and one and two bedroom units. All units have full kitchens and balconies and some offer Waikiki vistas. Hotel facilities include a guest laundry, sundry shop and free parking. A restaurant is adjacent.

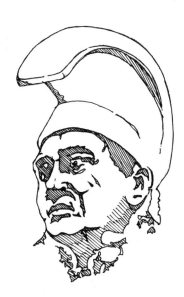

Being poor is no disgrace, but it's no great honor either. — **Will Rogers**

Chapter Five

PROUD PAUPERS
AN AFFORDABLE GUIDE TO HONOLULU

What? You can't afford that $3,000 a night beachfront suite at the Kahala Mandarin Oriental? Or the $100 multi-course tasting menu at Halekulani's La Mer restaurant?

As we commented earlier, although Honolulu/Waikiki is not an inexpensive vacation destination, bargains do abound here. The area offers many free attractions, and with a little searching, one can find very inexpensive restaurants and cheap places to stay—even in the Waikiki area.

THE TEN BEST FREE ATTRACTIONS
Including some often overlooked gems

Honolulu's best free attraction is its most famous—Waikiki Beach. All of Hawai'i's beaches are public and its beach parks and even inland state parks are free. Our favorite freebie is right off Waikiki Beach. In fact, the structure in which it is housed was established to defend it.

☺ *KID STUFF:* This little grinning guy marks attractions and activities that are of particular interest to pre-teens.

NOTE: For map locations of many of the listings in this chapter, see the Honolulu map in Chapter Two, page 44.

1 ARMY MUSEUM OF HAWAII

In Fort DeRussy on the corner of Kalia and Saratoga roads, Waikiki; (808) 438-2821. Daily except Monday, 10 to 4:15. GETTING THERE: Turn left onto Kalia from Ala Moana Boulevard or left onto Saratoga from Kalakaua Avenue.

This very professionally done museum housed in an old artillery battery traces the history of the U.S. Army in Hawai'i and the Pacific. It features a military timeline and exhibits concerning Hawai'i's role in assorted wars. The museum is housed in various rooms and bunkers of Battery Randolph, built between 1908 and 1911 for coastal defense. A major exhibit focuses on the Pearl Harbor attack and—interestingly— it examines it from a Japanese perspective, detailing its planning and execution. Other displays concern homefront defense during World War II, the role of Hawai'i's Japanese-Americans in that war, and Hawai'i's participation in the Korean and Vietnam conflicts.

A short film, "The Military Heritage of Hawaii," traces the state's military history from Kamehameha's battles to the Vietnam War. It's narrated by the deep baritone voice of World War II Medal of Honor winner, Senator Daniel K. Inouye. Another theater, the Bora Bora Bijou, shows military documentaries and Hollywood films, mostly concerning the Pacific War. The Gallery of Heroes honors Hawai'i's military men who have won medals for valor, including eighteen Medal of Honor winners. Most of these were Japanese-Americans who fought in Italy and France World War II.

2 ALI'IOLANI HALE & JUDICIARY HISTORY CENTER

417 S. King St., Honolulu; (808) 539-4999. Weekdays 9 to 4; closed weekends. GETTING THERE: It's at the corner of King and Mililani streets, across from Iolani Palace. From Waikiki, go north on McCully and then northwest on Beretania about three miles. Pass the state capitol and turn left onto Richards Street, then left again onto King to Mililani; it's on your right.

A golden-robed statue of Kamehameha I stands guard over Aili'iolani Hale, home to Hawai'i's supreme court and the Judiciary History Center museum. The ornate Italianate structure was built in 1874 and housed the legislature during the final years of Hawai'i's monarchy. Some may recognize it as a site for TV's *Magnum PI* series. The Judiciary History Center occupies a large room and a rear hallway, with displays about Hawaiian jurisprudence, from the kapu system to contemporary courts. Exhibits focus on the often difficult transition from ancient Hawaiian to modern law. An interesting display concerns the problem with divorce, not today but more than a century ago, when polygamy was abolished and Hawaiian men had to learn to live with just one woman.

Adjacent to the museum is a restored courtroom where displays keyed to school children explain how the legal system works. An exhibit in a back hallway focuses on wartime Hawai'i with yet another legal angle—the temporary declaration of martial law.

3 DAMIEN MUSEUM & ST. AUGUSTINE'S CATHOLIC CHURCH

130 Ohua Ave., Waikiki; (808) 923-7024 or (808) 923-2690; www.smcenter.org/staugustine. Museum open weekdays 9 to 3; church open daily 8 to 5 and during services. GETTING THERE: The church is just off Kalakaua Avenue near the eastern end of Waikiki. Enter the parking lot from Ohua Avenue. The Damien museum occupies a small building across the lot from the church.

Historic photos and a few artifacts in this modest museum trace the life of Father Damien and his work with Moloka'i's leper colony. It includes some of his personal belongings and a sad last photograph taken a month before he died in 1889, showing a face puffy and misshapen with leprosy. A film traces the history of the Kalaupapa leper colony and Father Damien's work there. It's informative although it contains many unpleasant photos of leprosy victims.

Adjacent St. Augustine's is particularly dramatic, a fine example of modern church architecture. Its soaring green copper A-frame rooflines are wedged with brilliant stained glass triangles of biblical scenes. The façade facing Waikiki is even more striking, with a towering stained glass window. People passing on Kalakaua Avenue often miss this imposing church because, unfortunately, it's fronted by a Burger King and an ABC store.

4 FORT DeRUSSY

Along Waikiki Beach, framed by Ala Moana Boulevard, Kalakaua Avenue and Kalia and Saratoga roads. ☺

It's called a fort, but DeRussy is a recreation area, established as a rest and rehabilitation center during World War II. Now open to the public, this U.S. Army facility offers expansive tree-shaded lawns, picnic tables, barbecues, children's play areas, fresh water showers, tennis and volleyball courts and one of the best stretches of beach on Waikiki. Because it isn't fronted by a hotel that spills its human contents onto the sand, this is one of the least crowded sections of Waikiki, and it has a relatively unobstructed view of Diamond Head. A beach equipment rental hut is open daily 9 to 5, and a small refreshment stand is adjacent. A shaded arbor is nearby, with tables and benches.

5 FREE WAIKIKI AQUARIUMS

The Waikiki Aquarium isn't very expensive (Chapter Two, page 56), but if you're really on a budget, you can see two big fish tanks absolutely free. ☺

THE TUBE: *At Beyond the Reef Shop in DFS Galleria, corner of Kalakaua and Royal Hawaiian avenues in Waikiki; (808) 931-2655; www.dfsgalleria.com. Daily 9 a.m. to 11 p.m.* ❑ You'll first notice this Plexiglas aquarium as you're walking along the Kalakaua sidewalk. Enter DFS Galleria, step inside the Beyond the Reef shop and you can walk through a fish tube that delivers you to the shop's second floor. En route, you'll see lots of fish close up and—really intriguing—distorted images of downtown Waikiki through the aquarium tank. Look up as you walk through the tube and you may see a huge ray that seems to be hovering in space over your head; it's actually sitting on the tube. Despite its name, Beyond the Reef Marine Store isn't a dive shop; it's a souvenir and T-shirt store.

PACIFIC BEACH HOTEL OCEANARIUM: *2490 Kalakaua Ave., between Kealohilani and Liliʻokalani avenues in Waikiki; (808) 923-4511; www.pacificbeachhotel.com.* ❑ A 280,000-gallon aquarium dominates the lobby and mezzanine of this highrise hotel. You can even watch fish while dining on fish, at the Five Fathoms or Neptune's restaurants. The Oceanarium is an impressive thing for a hotel lobby— three stories high, fifty-two feet long and thirty-two feet wide. Some of its residents are impressive, too, such as a ninety-pound stingray. Divers appear at noon, 1, 6:30 and 8:15 Monday-Saturday and at 10:45, 12:45, 1:45, 6:30 and 8:15 Sunday to feed the fish and give them a few strokes.

6 HAWAIʻI STATE CAPITOL

415 S. Beretania St., Honolulu; (808) 586-0178; www.state.hi. us/about/capitol.hsm. Weekdays 7:45 to 4:30. For information on public tours, call (808) 586-7256. GETTING THERE: It's between Punchbowl and Richards streets. From Waikiki, go north on McCully and then northwest on Beretania about three miles; the capitol is on your left.

Everything about Hawaiʻi's capitol building has architectural significance, which may or may not escape the eye of the beholder. Completed in 1969, it's a large quadrangle supported by columns and surrounded by a moat (in need of cleaning when we last looked) with an inner courtyard open to the sky. A large mosaic in the center symbolizes changing colors and patterns of Hawaiʻi's surrounding ocean. The columns supposedly resemble palm trees and the house and senate chambers are conical to suggest volcanoes that formed the islands.

Most of the building's intrigue is in its unusual design; the public areas are otherwise rather spartan. A statue of Father Damien stands near the southwest entrance, square shaped as if he's wearing a milk carton. The sculpture was not greeted with universal enthusiasm when it was unveiled. A more realistic statue of Queen Lili'okalani graces the other entrance.

7 HSU YUN TEMPLE

42 Kawananakoa Place, Honolulu; (808) 536-8458. Daily 7 to 5; donations appreciated. GETTING THERE: Follow H-1 about three miles from Waikiki and take the westbound Vineyard Boulevard (Highway 98) exit. Continue west about half a mile and turn right onto Nu'uanu Avenue. Cross under the freeway, then within a few blocks, turn left onto Kawananakoa and go right into the temple parking lot. The eastside temple door generally is the only one open.

This gorgeous Buddhist temple operated by the Chinese Buddha Association of Hawai'i is O'ahu's most elaborate religious shrine. It's a splendid study in ornate red and gold columns and glossy green tile roofs with turned-up eves, where temple lions perch to scare away bad spirits. Inside, the stunning altar is done in red and gold lacquer, with three seated gold-plated Buddha images. Four other altars in the main temple hold smaller Buddha figures. We like to stand quietly in this imposing edifice to contemplate its elaborate beauty and smell the incense. If you want to learn the story of Buddha's life, old fashioned prints with English legends line the walls.

8 KAWAIHAO CHURCH

957 Punchbowl St., Honolulu; (808) 522-1333. Weekdays 9 to 3 and Sunday morning during services. Donations appreciated. GETTING THERE: It's at the corner King and Punchbowl streets, across from the Mission Houses Museum. From Waikiki, go north on McCully and then northwest on Beretania about three miles to Punchbowl, turn left and go a block to King.

Dedicated in 1842 by Hawai'i's first missionary leader Hiram Bingham, this imposing coral block structure is the state's oldest permanent Christian church. Five years in the building, it's constructed of huge coral slabs hewn from offshore reefs by Hawaiians who had to dive down ten to twenty feet with hammers and chisels. Why would anyone want to do that? Because they were ordered to by Kamehameha III, who had converted to Christianity.

The interior is spartan, with dark wood pews, a wooden truss ceiling and rather austere walls and altar. What are impressive are plush burgundy, velvet and stained wood royal pews at the back of the church; they originally were on either side of the altar. In the church cemetery, some grave markers date back to the 1850s.

9 NATIONAL CEMETERY OF THE PACIFIC

In Punchbowl crater, just north of downtown Honolulu. Gates open daily 8 to 5:30. GETTING THERE: From Waikiki, go north on McCully and then northwest on Beretania about three miles. Turn right onto Queen Emma Street, cross over H-1 and follow signs.

"These men were part of the price that free men have been forced to pay to defend human liberty," says a plaque at the entrance to Hawai'i's national cemetery. The most hallowed place in Hawai'i after the U.S.S. Arizona Memorial, it occupies a bowl-shaped crater that inspired its nickname.

More than sacred ground for fallen heroes, it's a major monument to the war in the Pacific. Walls of the large Honolulu Memorial building are lined with distinctive crushed-glass murals tracing the history of the that war from the Pearl Harbor attack to the conquest of Okinawa and Japan's surrender. Another series of murals focus on the Korean War. To the left of the memorial as you face it, an inclined path leads up to a large terrace that provides panoramic views of Honolulu. The walkway is lined with several smaller monuments to various American military units.

10 ROYAL MAUSOLEUM

2261 Nu'uanu Ave., Honolulu. Weekdays 8 to 4:30; closed weekends and holidays. GETTING THERE: Follow directions toward Hsu Yun Temple (above), then just before you reach it, turn right through a black wrought iron gate.

This park-like facility is where most of the heavy hitters of Hawaiian royalty are entombed, including Kamehamehas II through V. Now a state monument, it was completed in 1865 as a final resting place of the kings and high chiefs, primarily the Kamehameha and Kalakaua families. A somber gray stone chapel stands in the middle of extensive tree-shaded grounds. It originally served as the mausoleum, but remains later were removed to crypts elsewhere on the site. The chapel generally isn't open, although you can peer through windows to the dark wood varnished pews.

Most members of the royal family rest beneath a tall black granite pillar near the chapel; steps lead down to the crypts. The last entombment at the Royal Mausoleum was 1953, when David Kalakaua Kawananakoa was interred.

Free wiggles

Several free Polynesian shows are presented each week around Waikiki. Unfortunately, the legendary Kodak Hula Show at Aloha Bowl has closed, although there are still a number of other Hawaiian entertainments in the area.

DFS Galleria presents its Hawaiian Music and Dance Revue Wednesdays and Fridays at 7 p.m. at Kalakaua Avenue and Royal Hawaiian.

International Market Place features Hawaiian and contemporary entertainment nightly except Sunday and Tuesday, usually starting at 7. It's at 2330 Kalakaua Avenue between Duke's lane and Ka'iulani Avenue.

Kuhio Beach Park is the setting for a torch lighting ceremony and hula show Thursday through Sunday from 6 to 7 p.m. It's held at the Hula Mound at the foot of Ulunui Avenue, beside the Duke Kahanamoku statue and a giant banyan tree. A conch shell is sounded, tiki torches along Kalakaua Avenue are lighted, then the show begins.

Sunset on the Beach is presented at Queen's Surf Beach at Kalakaua and Kapahulu avenues Saturday and Sunday between 4 and 9 p.m. This festive event includes live entertainment—usually Polynesian—followed by a free outdoor movie projected on a large screen. Folks sit in the sand or on an adjacent pier. Local restaurants set up food booths. Artists and artisans conduct a "Hawai'i Made" handicraft fair, starting about 9 in the morning.

THE TEN BEST CHEAP EATS

We define a cheap meal as a dinner entrée with a side dish and non-alcoholic drink for under $10. Of course, you can eat for less at any of the fast food chains in the Waikiki area. McDonald's Happy Meals and Jack In the Box combos are under $10. But did you really come all the way to Hawai'i to eat overcooked hamburgers? If must have a 'burger, try Cheeseburgers in Paradise at Kalakaua and Kealohilani; see our listing in Chapter Three, page 81.

Among the very cheapest places to eat in Hawai'i are *okazuya*, Asian delis with strong Polynesian accents. They're great for hearty, inexpensive meals. Most are open during midday only, although a few are open from midmorning to early evening. Some have tables; others are take-outs only. You'll find several along King Street in Honolulu, and along Kamehameha Highway in Kane'ohe. We list our favorite *okazuya*, Masa & Joyce, below.

The name is Japanese; *okazu* is a side dish and *ya* is a place or a shop. However, the food is an Asian-Hawaiian mix. Typical dishes are Japanese *saimen* (soup) and sushi, Chinese *chow fun* (wide noodles stir-fried with vegetables), Okinawan *anagi* (fried doughnuts), Korean *kim chee* (spicy pickled cabbage), Filipino *lechon kawali* (crispy pork) and Hawaiian dishes such as *lomi lomi* (salmon ceviche), *lau lau* (meat or chicken roasted in *ti* leaves), *kalua* pig (roasted and shredded) and mashed native sweet potato.

Pick up a copy of *The Okazu Guide* by Donovan M. Dela Cruz and Jodi Endo Chai (© 2002), a directory to dozens of *okazuya* on O'ahu.

They've also written *The Puka Guide* to O'ahu's hole-in-the-wall diners (© 2001). Most O'ahu book stores carry them, or contact: Watermark Publishing, 1000 Bishop St., Honolulu, HI 96813; (866) 900-BOOK or locally (808) 587-7766; *www.watermarkpublishing.net.*

Another inexpensive eating tradition drawn from Hawai'i's ethnic mix is the plate lunch, fast food served in small family diners or from lunch wagons. It usually begins with dollops of rice and/or macaroni salad, followed by assorted meats such as beef teriyaki, shoyu chicken, beef curry or mahi mahi, drenched with a ladle of gravy. A Japanese version of the quick lunch is the *bento*, a small partitioned box with rice, pickled vegetables and a variety of other foods.

And now, let's eat—cheaply.

1 PRINCESS FOOD COURT

Corner of Kalakaua and Kai'ulani avenues in Waikiki; part of the Sheraton Princess Kai'ulani hotel complex; (808) 922-5811; www.sheraton-hawaii.com. American/Hawaiian fare; beer. Breakfast through late dinner. Major credit cards.

This simple cafeteria is our favorite budget food place for a few good reasons—it's in a great location just across from Waikiki Beach, it's neat and clean, and the food isn't bad. Several full dinners are under $10. Some examples are half roasted chicken with mashed potatoes or fries and corn on the cob; hot pork sandwich with mashed potatoes and gravy; rotisserie pork with rice or potatoes and corn on the cob; fish filet with French fries and a small salad; and curry *katsu* chicken with white rice. There's also a Baskin-Robbins and Dunkin' Donuts in the court.

2 BA-LE FRENCH SANDWICH & BAKERY

Various locations in Honolulu, including the Fort Street Mall near Beretanina downtown; in Chinatown at 150 N. King St. (between River and Kekaulike streets); and near Sears in the Ala Moana Shopping Center at Ala Moana Boulevard and Atkinson Drive. Vietnamese; no alcohol or credit cards. Most are open daily 9 a.m. to 7 p.m.; some outlets are closed Sunday.

Despite the name, these are Vietnamese cafés and they don't just serve sandwiches, although that's the specialty and they're huge and hearty. Other fare includes tofu noodles, egg rolls, imperial rolls, shrimp rolls and soups, which can be combined to make a meal for much less than $10. Or go for the spaghetti with meat sauce or meat balls. Ba-Le also serves several plate lunches, such as garlic shrimp, pork chops, combined pork chop and lemongrass chicken, and curry chicken. They're about $5 and all come with rice.

3 CURRY HOUSE COCO

2310 Kuhio Ave., Waikiki; (808) 922-9441. Curries and more; no alcohol or credit cards. Lunch through late dinner daily. GETTING THERE: It's at the corner of Nahua Street in the central Waikiki area.

Although it's Japanese, this tiny place specializes in curries and virtually everything here is within our price range. And you don't have to settle for a mere bowl of curry—although it's very tasty. Several inexpensive combination plates include spinach curry with chicken cutlets, squid curry with stewed shrimp and cheese curry with fried chicken.

4 EASTERN CHINESE FOOD CENTER

118 N. King St., Chinatown; (808) 536-4121. Mostly Cantonese; no alcohol or credit cards. Breakfast through dinner daily. GETTING THERE: To reach Chinatown from Waikiki, go 3.5 miles northwest on Ala Moana Boulevard. A quarter of a mile past Aloha Tower, turn right onto River Street. The restaurant is between River and Keikauliki streets.

The name sounds more impressive than it is. This is a basic hole-in-the-wall diner with a takeout counter and a few tables. Yet it has won raves from the local press. It's noted for mild Cantonese fare and particularly for its roast duck and steamed fish. Among offerings from its rather large menu are crispy chicken on rice, ginger chicken on rice, and shrimp with vegetables. Most of these items are around $5 to $7, so two of you can share three different dishes for about $20.

5 EZOGIKU

Three outlets in or near Waikiki: 2420 Koa Avenue, behind the Hyatt Regency, (808) 922-2473; 2546 Lemon Road, near Paoakalani Street, behind the Hawaiian Regent Hotel, (808) 923-2013; and 2146 Kalakaua Avenue, near Beachwalk, (808) 926-8616. Japanese; no alcohol or credit cards. Lunch through late dinner daily.

These tiny cafés feature hearty bowls of *ramen* (Japanese noodle soup). You can get a big bowl plus six pieces of *gyoza* (small potstickers) and a cup of tea for under our $10 limit. Among other budget items are beef curry rice and fried noodles. These are simple places, usually with a few counter stools set before open kitchens, and some tables outside.

6 GLOWING DRAGON SEAFOOD RESTAURANT

1023 Maunakea St., Chinatown; (808) 521-4492. Chinese; wine and beer. Lunch through late dinner daily. Major credit cards. GETTING THERE: See directions to Eastern Chinese Food Center above. Maunakea

Street is two blocks to the right of River Street and the restaurant is between Hotel and King streets.

Glowing Dragon—we love that name!—is a remarkably attractive place for a budget diner. It's decorated with large Oriental prints and a few Chinese artifacts, and the food is excellent. The best bargain is a three-course dinner plate of roast duck, lemon chicken, beef broccoli, wonton and rice for about $7. Also, a dining couple can share two regular entrées and a soup and stay within our budget per capita.

And the menu is *huge*, featuring 184 different items. Although it's mostly Chinese, the restaurant features *shabu shabu*, a Japanese-style stir fry of thick noodles, meat and vegetables. The Glowing Dragon is one of few restaurants in Honolulu/Waikiki that stays open *really* late—until 2 a.m. when we last checked.

7 HONG CAFÉ

1145 Maunakea St., Chinatown; 538-0775. Vietnamese, wine and beer. Lunch through dinner daily; MC/VISA. GETTING THERE: It's a block from Glowing Dragon; see above.

Hong sounds Chinese although this small place is Southeast Asian. Like the Glowing Dragon, it's remarkably cute for a budget café, with lacquered medallions on the walls and carved-back wooden chairs. A planter wall divides the small dining room, making it even cozier. Among Hong's specialties are rice plates and most are a mere $6. Some examples are pork chops, barbecued chicken, lemongrass chicken, chicken curry, fried prawns, and pork with fried prawns. Two tasty hot pot dishes of sautéed fish and sautéed shrimp also are under our budget ceiling.

8 MASA & JOYCE

45-582 Kamehameha Hwy., Kane'ohe; (808) 235-6129. Weekdays except Tuesday 9 to 6, Saturday 9 to 4 and Sunday 9 to 2. MC/VISA. GETTING THERE: From H-1, take the Likelike Highway (Route 63) northeast to Kane'ohe, then go right briefly on Kamehameha. The restaurant is near an Aloha service station, at the corner of Luluku Road.

You'll have to drive about ten miles to reach or favorite *okazuya*. It's one of the few that has places to sit and is open beyond lunchtime. Masa & Joyce is so popular with locals that you may find it a chore to get into the parking lot around noon. Among its specials are Hawaiian plates of chicken or pork *lau lau*, *kalua* pork, chicken long rice, *lomi lomi* salmon, and *shoyu* pork, all served with poi or rice.

We like to choose a variety of individual items, such as fish cake, chicken long rice, Spam sushi roll and sesame chicken. Combined, they're well under our budget of $10 per person and more than enough for two.

9 ONO HAWAIIAN FOOD

726 Kapahulu Ave., Honolulu; (808) 737-2275. Hawaiian; no alcohol or credit cards. Lunch through early dinner daily except Sunday. GETTING THERE: Follow Kapahulu inland from Waikiki for about a mile. Ono is on the left between Kamuela and Date, just beyond Ala Wai Golf Course.

We nominated this hole-in-the-wall in Chapter Three as the best place for "grinds"—traditional Hawaiian food. It's also worthy of our Ten Best Cheap Eats list, since virtually everything is under $10, and the portions are formidable. You can pig out on *kalua* pig, *lomi lomi* salmon or other Hawaiian fare without flattening wallet or purse. See details on page 80.

10 PHÒ OLD SAIGON

2270 Kuhio Ave., Waikiki; (808) 922-2668. Vietnamese and some American dishes; wine and beer. Lunch through late dinner daily. Major credit cards. GETTING THERE: It's in the central Waikiki area between Seaside Avenue and Nohonani Place.

This small café just two blocks off the beach offers big bowls of *phò* (noodle soup) for about $7. Combined with a one dollar bowl of rice, they make a hearty dinner. Many other dishes are within our $10 limit as well. Some examples are crispy fried noodles with seafood, rice noodle soup with seafood, and beef steak with salad and rice. Phò is a slightly cute place, with white cane-back chairs and bamboo forest wallpaper covering an accent wall.

Cheap eats in plural

A couple of food courts, one at the Ala Moana Shopping Center and another in Chinatown, will stretch your dining budget. At both, you can fill up for under $10, while going on an international dining spree.

MAKAI MARKET FOOD COURT: *Ala Moana Shopping Center, Ala Moana Boulevard and Atkinson Drive; (808) 955-9517. Daily 9:30 to 9:30. GETTING THERE: From Waikiki, follow Ala Moana northwest for less than a mile. The food court is at ground level on the Ala Moana Boulevard side.* □ About two dozen food stalls occupy this large shopping center's food court. Some are pretzel, ice cream and cookie joints, although most are ethnic takeouts. What's your international pleasure? Choices include Ala Moana Poi Bowl and Lahaina Chicken (Hawaiian), Donburiya Dondon, Naniwa-ya Ramen, Tsuruya Noodle Shop and Oishii Teppanyaki (all Japanese), Panda Express and Patti's Kitchen (Chinese), Sbarro and Mama's Spaghetti House (Italian), Senor Pepe (Mexican), Little Café (Thai), Orleans Express (Cajun) and Yummy Korean BBQ. If you arrive with an adult thirst, you can get a serious drink from the Cove Bar, which occupies an island surrounded by all these food outlets.

MAUNAKEA MARKETPLACE: *In Chinatown, extending between Hotel and Pauahi streets, flanked by Maunakea and River streets; (808) 524-3409. Most food stalls open morning through early evening. GETTING THERE: See directions to Chinatown in the Eastern Chinese Food center listing above.* ☐ This lively, colorful marketplace has an all-Asian food court with stalls selling a variety of inexpensive dishes. Among them are Triple One (Chinese and Singaporean-Malaysian), Jackie's Corner (Asian mix), Korean Kitchen, 888 Vietnamese Fast Food and Malee (Thai-Vietnamese), Masa's Sushi (Japanese *bento* box lunches), and four different Filipino places. For your sitdown dining pleasure, several small tile-topped tables run down the middle of this long and narrow food court. Expect them to be crowded during the lunch hour and any time on weekends.

TEN CHEAP SLEEPS

We don't use the term "Ten Best" here because some of these places are really rather weathered, so there's nothing "best" about them. However, the ones we selected are clean. We define a cheap sleep as a comfortable and clean hotel or motel room for under $90 for two people during high season, and this was a real challenge in Waikiki. Our choices range from some a couple of surprisingly attractive mini-resorts to some very spartan hostels.

TRAVEL TIPS: Many of these budget places appeal to students and other young travelers, so expect them to get a bit partyish in the evenings. If you seek peace and quiet, these may not be your style. Also, most of the hostels require proof that you have an airline ticket off the island, so dorms and rooms won't be used as crash pads by local flunkies. Further, not all of the below-listed places have air conditioning or parking, although most do. Before committing to a reservation, call to check these features and to confirm the current price.

Some of the better budget priced hotels such as the Hawaiiana and Royal Grove book up *months* in advance, so act accordingly.

We list these places not alphabetically, but in the order of their appeal, with the most spartan cheapies at the end. Our favorite cheap hotel nudges our upper price range and it may exceed it by the time you arrive. Hopefully, you'll agree that it's worth the higher tariff.

1 HAWIIANA HOTEL

260 Beachwalk, Honolulu, HI 96815; (800) 367-5122 or (808) 923-3811; www.Hawaiianahotelatwaikiki.com. A small low-rise hotel two blocks from the beach. Rooms from $85 to $190; major credit cards.

GETTING THERE: Turn left onto Beachwalk from Kalakaua Avenue and it's just on your left.

This well-kept hotel is built around a pair of swimming pools in a landscaped courtyard. It's one of the few low rises left on Waikiki, and it's remarkably quiet. Further, it's one of the few hotels in this price range with a pool. The look is early Hawaiian, with louvered windows and doors. Rooms are decorated in cheerful Polynesian colors. The Coffee Chalet has designer coffees and light snacks, open morning through early evening.

2 ROYAL GROVE HOTEL

151 Ulunui Ave., Honolulu, HI 96815; (808) 923-7691; www.royal-grovehotel.com. A small low-rise hotel about two blocks from the beach. Rooms from $60 to $75; major credit cards. GETTING THERE: It's in the eastern Waikiki area. Turn beachward from Kuhio Avenue onto one-way Ulunui, and it comes up shortly on your left.

The Royal Grove rivals the Hawaiiana as one of Waikiki's best budget-priced hotels, and weekly rates make it even more affordable. It has fair-sized and clean if basic rooms in a simple cinder block structure. Amenities include a comfortable lobby, a lounge and a pool courtyard. It's pink, so think of it as a poor man's Pink Palace. All units have kitchenettes, TV and lanais; some rooms are at poolside and some are air conditioned.

3 THE BREAKERS

250 Beachwalk, Honolulu, HI 96815; (800) 426-0494 or (808) 923-3181; www.breakers-hawaii.com. Low-rise courtyard style hotel. Rates start at just under $100; major credit cards. GETTING THERE: It's between Saratoga Road and Beachwalk; take either street beachward from Kalakaua Avenue.

Just two blocks from the beach, the Breakers is quite attractive for a budget hotel, and it's one of the few with a full-service restaurant. The two-story hotel is built around a swimming pool and courtyard. Fair-sized Hawaiian-Oriental style rooms have small kitchens, desks, patios or decks, and they're quite neat and clean. Breakers Bar and Grill is open for breakfast, lunch and dinner.

4 INTERCLUB WAIKIKI HOSTEL

2413 Kuhio Ave., Honolulu, HI 96815; (808) 924-2636; www.hostels.com/interclubwaikiki/. A 20-unit hostel with shared rooms for less than $20 and private rooms for about $50; MC/VISA. GETTING THERE: It's in central Waikiki on the beachward side of Kuhio, near the corner of Ka'iulani Avenue.

This is one of Waikiki's best hostel buys—very clean with air conditioned rooms, and close to the beach. All units have refrigerators, TVs and private baths. Private rooms have patios, microwaves and hotplates. This well-run hostel even provides beach gear.

5 WAIKIKI BEACHSIDE HOSTEL

2556 Lemon Rd., Honolulu, HI 96815; (808) 923-9566; www.hokondo.com. MC/VISA. Dorm units start at $20, semi-private rooms at $50 and private units are $85; MC/VISA. GETTING THERE: Follow Kapahulu Avenue one block inland from Kalakaua Avenue and take the first left onto Lemon Road; the hostel is immediately on your right.

No, Waikiki Beachside Hostel isn't at beachside, although it's just a block from Waikiki and it's very neat and clean. It has basic dorms, semi-private rooms with shared kitchens and private units with TV and full kitchens. The hostel has daily maid service, a guest laundry, parking and high speed internet access at the Beachside Café.

6 WAIKIKI PRINCE HOTEL

2431 Prince Edward St., Honolulu, HI 96815; (808) 922-1544. A small hotel two blocks from the beach; all kitchen units. Rooms start at $50; MC/VISA. GETTING THERE: It's on the eastern end of the Waikiki district. From Kuhio Avenue, turn beachward on Ulunui Avenue, then go right onto Prince Edward and it's immediately on your left.

It isn't nearly as princely as its name, although the rooms are reasonably clean and equipped with stoves, refrigerators and microwaves. All have balconies and cable TV. A negative here is that rooms have louvered windows, which aren't good sound barriers so they can get a bit noisy, although the hotel is on a lightly traveled street.

7 SEASIDE HAWAIIAN HOSTEL

419 E. Seaside Ave., Honolulu, HI 96815; (866) 924-3303 or (808) 924-3303; www.seasideHawaiianhostel.com. A small complex in central Waikiki, about four blocks from the beach. Dorm rates start at $15; semi-private rooms start at $40; discounts for weekly rates; MC/VISA. GETTING THERE: Turn inland off Kuhio Avenue onto one-way Seaside; it's about a two blocks away, on your right, between Kuhio and Ala Wai Boulevard.

This low-rise hostel is built around an attractive courtyard shaded by a large banyan tree. It offers free breakfast, internet access and airport shuttle. Rooms have microwaves, fridges and TV. Facilities include a communal kitchen and family activity room. The hostel is set back in an alley so it's very quiet. It's also easy to miss; look for a yellow surfboard sign.

8 ISLAND HOSTEL/HOTEL

1946 Ala Moana Blvd., Honolulu, HI 96815; (808) 942-8748. Small facility with dorms around $20 and private rooms starting at $50; weekly and monthly rates; MC/VISA. GETTING THERE: The hostel is across from Fort DeRussy, near the Kalakaua-Ala Moana junction.

Rooms at this hostel/hotel on Waikiki's west side are very basic although they're slightly neater than the cluttered hostel office. Private rooms have a range, refrigerator, TV and air conditioning. That cluttered office complex has a communal TV, washer/dryer, microwave and other kitchen facilities.

9 CENTRAL YMCA

410 Atkinson Dr., Honolulu, HI 96814; (808) 941-3344; www.centralymcahonolulu.org. Basic "Y" units; shared rooms (men only) are $30 for one and private rooms (men and women) are $53 for two; major credit cards. Reservations required, at least two weeks in advance; no walk-ins. GETTING THERE: The "Y" is across from the Ala Moana Shopping Center. Take Ala Moana Boulevard northwest from Waikiki, turn right onto Atkinson and it comes up shortly on the right.

Rooms are spartan but clean in this well-run YMCA, which is less than a block from Ala Moana Park and beach. Private rooms have bathrooms, beds and dressers. Common facilities include an Asian restaurant, swimming pool, TV lounge, internet access and the usual abundance of YMCA activities and classes.

10 HALE ALOHA HOSTEL

2417 Prince Edward St., Honolulu, HI 96815; (808) 926-8313; www.hiayh.org. A 63-bed hostel two blocks from the beach, with a few private rooms. Dorms are about $20, rooms $50; MC/VISA, AMEX. GETTING THERE: It's on the eastern side of Waikiki. From Kuhio Avenue, turn beachward on Ulunui Avenue, then turn right onto Prince Edward and it's on your left, just beyond the Waikiki Prince Hotel (above).

This member of Hostelling International has <u>very</u>—and we underline that word—spartan units. The few private rooms have beds, bedstands, small bathrooms and not much more. The location is good, however, within a couple blocks of the beach. It offers a communal kitchen, TV room and laundry facilities.

TRAVEL TIP: If you're retired or still-active military, you can get very good rates at **Hale Koa Hotel** in Fort DeRussy, a short stroll from Waikiki Beach. It has an attractive lobby, several shops, and a swimming pool with a poolside bar—all the facilities of a resort hotel, which it is. For information: Hale Koa Hotel, 2055 Kalia Rd., Honolulu, HI 96815-1998; (800) 367-6027 or (808) 955-0555; *www.halekoa.com*.

Waikiki is a hamlet of plain cottages...its excitements caused by the activity of insect tribes and the occasional fall of a coconut
— **Description of Waikiki in the 1890s**

Chapter Six

NIGHTSIDE
WHAT TO DO AFTER A HAWAIIAN SUNSET

Waikiki is considerably more exciting today than it was in the late eighteenth century, when it was a quiet place of relaxation for King Kalakaua and other *ali'i*. It's very active at night, busy with clubs and pubs and several live shows at various resorts. Further, this tropical paradise is no cultural desert. Honolulu has three major performing arts venues—the Blaisdell Concert Hall, the Hawaii Theatre and the Waikiki Shell (see below). O'ahu is home to the highly regarded Honolulu Symphony, Hawaii Opera Theater, and several drama groups including the Diamond Head Theatre, plus four ballet companies.

The Friday *Honolulu Advertiser* contains an insert appropriately called *tgif*. It covers the arts and entertainment scene on all the islands, including theater, ballet, dance, concerts, clubs and pubs, fairs and festivals, the local and international pop music scene, dining and restaurant reviews, and movies.

GETTING TICKETED: The largest O'ahu ticket agency is **TicketsPlus**, selling ducats for the Blaisdell Concert Hall, Waikiki Shell, Aloha Stadium and other venues. Tickets-by-phone numbers are (888)

355-4411 or (808) 526-4400. **Blaisdell Concert Hall** ticket number is (808) 591-2211; the **Honolulu Symphony** number is (808) 792-2000; and the **Hawai'i Theatre** box office is (808) 528-0506.

Performing arts venues

Much of what happens in Honolulu's performing arts scene happens at one of three places:

Blaisdell Concert Hall is part of the Neal S. Blaisdell Center, which also includes an arena and exhibition hall. It's parallel to Ward Avenue, stretching from Kapi'olani Boulevard to King Street, with the concert hall at Ward and King. The box office is open Monday-Saturday 9 to 5; (808) 591-2211; *www.blaisdellcenter.com.*

The Hawai'i Theatre is a 1922 beaux-arts structure at 1130 Bethel Street, reopened in 1996 after a $22 million renovation. Most of that money was spent inside; the plain façade is rather austere. It hosts everything from major traveling groups and performers to the annual Hawaiian International Jazz Festival. To reach it, head northwest from Waikiki on Ala Moana Boulevard for about three miles, turn right onto Bethel and drive three blocks; the theater is on the left, at the corner of Pauahi. The box office is open Tuesday-Saturday 9 to 5; (808) 528-0506; *www.hawaiitheatre.com.*

Waikiki Shell is an outdoor amphitheater in Kapi'olani Park. It hosts free Honolulu Symphony pops concerts every summer and it's used for assorted other entertainments. Built in 1952, it has 2,400 seats and another 6,000 people can sprawl on the surrounding grass; (808) 924-8934; *www.waikikishell.com.*

PRICING: We use dollar sign codes to indicate the approximate cost of adult admission to various activities: *$* = under $10; *$$* = $10 to $19; *$$$* = $20 to $29; *$$$$* = $30 to $39; *$$$$$* = $40 or more.

THE TEN BEST SHOWS & CONCERTS

This is a mixed list of Honolulu's best live entertainment, from Waikiki production shows to theater and dance. We begin with our favorite Hawaiian dance show, then list the rest in no particular order, except that we group performing arts at the bottom.

TRAVEL TIP: When Waikiki shows have an option of dinner (usually a buffet) or cocktail seating, the best seats go to the diners since they stay put, and the cocktail crowd gets the leftovers.

1 HORIZONS SHOW

Polynesian Cultural Center, 55-370 Kamehameha Hwy., La'ie; (800) 367-7060 or (808) 293-3333; www.polynesia.com. Nightly except Sunday at 7:30. Major credit cards; $$$$. Combination tickets available for cultural center admission, the luau and/or IMAX theater and Horizons *cultural center admission, the luau and/or IMAX theater and Horizons show. Round-trip shuttle from Waikiki available. GETTING THERE: The Polynesian Cultural Center is about thirty miles from Waikiki on the northeast O'ahu coast. The easiest approach is to catch a shuttle from Waikiki; call the cultural center for schedules. If you drive, head northeast from Honolulu on H-3, pick up Kamehameha Highway (Route 83) in Kane'ohe and follow it north to La'ie.*

Horizons is the world's largest Polynesian dance revue, with more than 100 performers from Hawai'i and several other South Pacific cultures. It's a complex production with an elaborate set that includes a waterfall, fake smoke, fire and occasional brimstone. This is easily the best show of its type in the islands. The choreography is excellent and the dancers and singers are skilled and colorfully costumed. They range from glaring Maoris and war-chanting Tongans to graceful Hawaiian hula dancers and sexily gyrating Tahitians who demonstrate a considerable amount of wiggle room.

The show ends with a Samoan troupe that mixes traditional song and dance with comedy. Four guys demonstrate that one should never try firewalking while wearing a grass skirt. (We hope they were also wearing asbestos shorts.) Samoa's Chief Sielu Avea, the Polynesian Cultural Center's lead performer, closes the show. He cracks a few jokes and twirls his fire knives; it's quite impressive in the darkened theater.

2 THE DON HO SHOW

Waikiki Beachcomber, 2300 Kalakaua Ave., Waikiki; (877) 693-6646 or (808) 923-3981; www.donho.com. Sunday-Thursday at 8:15, with dinner seating at 7. MC/VISA; show only, $$$; dinner and show, $$$$. GETTING THERE: The Waikiki Beachcomber is at the corner of Duke's Lane; turn left off Kalakaua.

"Mr. Hawaii" has been performing on Waikiki for more than four decades. He's now in his sixties, and his show, which was always laid back, is even slower paced than before. He spends more time interacting with his audience and telling slightly naughty jokes than singing. ("This guy overdosed on Viagra and died making love; they couldn't get the coffin lid closed"). We'd have preferred more singing and less patter, since most of his pleasantly resonate voice is still there. Of course, he begins the show with his trademark *Tiny Bubbles,* and he ends with it as well.

"I do it twice because I forget that I've already sung it." A pause, then: "I've been singing it for forty years. I hate that song."

Between Ho's songs and patter, members of his band do solos, everything from country ballads to a Louis Armstrong impersonation to high-tenor Hawaiian songs. It's a pleasant evening but don't hurry your mai tai. As we said, the show's pace is *very* slow.

3 BLUE HAWAII: THE SHOW

Waikiki Beachcomber Hotel, 2300 Kalakaua Ave.; (808) 923-1245. Nightly except Tuesday, with dinner seating at 5 and the show at 6:15. MC/VISA; show only, $$$; dinner and show, $$$$. GETTING THERE: See above.

There are hundreds of *faux* Elvises in our hometown of Las Vegas, and we now we've found one on Waikiki. Much taller than most of the Vegas versions, Jonathan Von Brana has the appropriate shock of dark hair and dimpled cheeks. His voice is strong and pleasant enough to be a non-Elvis singer.

And what's The Pelvis got to do with Waikiki? The original Elvis made a couple of movies here, including *Blue Hawaii,* and a TV special, *Elvis: Aloha from Hawaii.*. Von Brana belts out several songs from these shows and he does a powerful rendition of *Viva Las Vegas* that made us briefly want to be back home. *Blue Hawaii: The Show* also features four fetching ladies who open with a sexy Tahitian hula number. Then they return in assorted and usually skimpy costumes appropriate to whatever Von Brana is singing. This *faux* Elvis is hardworking, sweats easily, and has a gracious way with the audience. One couldn't expect more from any of the Elvises in Las Vegas where, incidentally, he once worked.

4 MAGIC OF POLYNESIA

Waikiki Beachcomber Hotel, 2300 Kalakaua Ave.; (877) 971-4321 or (808) 971-4321; www.robertshawaii.com. Two shows nightly, one with dinner at 5 followed by the show at 6, then a cocktail only show at 8. Major credit cards; show only, $$$$; dinner and show, $$$$$. GETTING THERE: See above.

The show is aptly named, since it's magic with an upbeat Polynesian theme. It's relatively short; island-born magician John Hirokawa performs only a few tricks, although they're elaborately staged. The production begins with the rumbling of a volcano, flashing lights, *faux* smoke and a seat-rattling soundtrack. An attractive brace of Polynesian dancers squiggle onstage to wiggle their fannies to a Tahitian hula. They're the sexiest dancers we've seen in Waikiki, amply endowed behind coconut cup bras. Lucky coconuts. The star arrives in a blast of fire and brimstone, beheads a grinning tattooed Mauri and reassembles him, then he performs assorted other tricks. In the show's best bit, he's squished together in a box, then he emerges and hops around on the stage like a stepped-on toad. He later levitates a pretty lady and explodes her into streamers.

Hirokawa performs no breakthrough magic, although the staging is elaborate and the show is fast-paced and entertaining. Since the show is nightly, he takes a break on Sunday and Monday, when magician Michael Villoria takes over.

5 SOCIETY OF SEVEN

Outrigger Waikiki, 2335 Kalakaua Ave., (808) 922-6408 or (808) 923-SHOW; www.outriggerentertainment.com. Nightly except Monday; dinner seating at 7 and show at 8:30. Major credit cards; show only, $$$$; dinner and show, $$$$$. GETTING THERE: The hotel is between the Sheraton Moana and the Royal Hawaiian, across Kalakaua from the International Market Place.

Now, let's try to get this straight. A group of energized, funny and innovative entertainers called the Society of Seven have performed at the Outrigger for more than thirty years. Now, they've gone to Las Vegas for an indefinite run at the Aladdin Hotel. They've been replaced in Waikiki by a new group called the Society of Seven Las Vegas, which doesn't perform in Las Vegas. Got that?

This is best show in Waikiki. While Don Ho may gently lull you, this wired group will keep you alert and usually laughing. Their show is a witty mix of quick-take impressions, upbeat music, some rather good singing and just plain silliness.

Some of their numbers include an impersonation of an out of sync In Sync; a wonderfully irreverent Woopie Goldberg "Sister Act" and twin Polynesian Elvises doing "Jailhouse Rock." We don't normally care for audience participation, but the group's "One Minute School of Elvis Impersonators" with three volunteers is really funny. And are you ready for Willie Nelson, Ray Charles, the Osmond Brothers and Kathryn Hepburn singing "Over the Rainbow"?

If there's a fault here, it's the theater: the floor is too flat and the stage is too low, so short folks may have a problem seeing the conclusion of some of the pratfalls.

6 CREATION: A POLYNESIAN JOURNEY

Sheraton Princess Ka'iulani, 120 Ka'iulani Ave., Waikiki; (808) 931-4660; www.sheraton-hawaii.com. Tuesday, Thursday, Friday, Saturday and Sunday, with dinner seating at 5:15 and cocktail seating at 6. Major credit cards; show only, $$$$; dinner and show, $$$$$. GETTING THERE: It's at the corner of Ka'iulani and Kalakaua avenues. There's a pedestrian entrance off Kalakaua and the auto entrance is off Ka'iulani, which is one-way inland.

Yes, but what is it creating? This show displays the requisite female navels and male muscles as it portrays Polynesian legends in song and dance. It's well produced, nicely staged and executed with lots of verve. However, it has a problem with focus. It presents creation legends of several Polynesian societies, but it gets sidetracked with laser talking heads and some really pointless magic tricks. A properly grizzled old story teller, who looks and sounds like a Polynesian Orson Wells, leads the audience through several of these "creation" scenarios. They begin with a Polynesian Adam and Eve rising out of a taro patch, which is nicely done. Then you've got your assorted pretty hula girl navel engagements, your whirling poi balls, and your fierce stage-stomping Mauri warriors, most of whom seem to be having bad hair days.

And suddenly you're on Waikiki Beach and our mysterious voyager is wearing an aloha shirt. This provides the proper excuse for assorted Hawaiian hulas and even an Elvis number, *Hula Baby Rock*. Fortunately, it does not employ an Elvis impersonator.

7 ESPRIT

Sheraton Waikiki, 2255 Kalakaua Ave.; (808) 922-4422; www. sheraton-hawaii.com. Esprit is on the ground level, open nightly from early evening past midnight. The Randy Smith show is Friday and Saturday at 7:45. Major credit cards; $$$; cover for live entertainment other nights $. GETTING THERE: Follow Royal Hawaiian avenue beachward from Kalakaua.

This darkly modern lounge is the only nightclub on Waikiki Beach, with nice views thereof—although it's open mostly after sundown. It's a serious entertainment venue with a bandstand and excellent sound system. Entertainer Randy Smith was doing Frank Sinatra impersonations on Fridays and Saturdays when we last checked. His show included Broadway singer Kathy Foy, pop guitarist Johnny Valentine and hula performer Joni Albao. On other nights, local bands play music for listening and dancing.

Performing arts

8 HONOLULU SYMPHONY

Performs primarily at the Blaisdell Concert Hall, corner of Ward Avenue and King Street. Symphony box office is in the Dole Cannery, Suite 202, at 650 Iwilei Rd., open 9 to 9. GETTING THERE: To reach the Blaisdell Concert Hall, take Ala Moana Boulevard to Ward Avenue, turn inland, drive just over half a mile to King Street, turn right and then go right again into the parking area.

Established in 1900, the Honolulu Symphony is Hawai'i's oldest and most honored performing arts group. It's also the oldest American orchestra west of the Rockies. It presents concerts in the large, attractive Blaisdell Concert Hall, and a summer series in Waikiki Shell.

Hong Kong-born conductor and musical director Samuel Wong presents an ambitious season of classic and pops concerts, with featured artists such a Lou Rawls, Dave Koz and Michael McDonald. He has gained an international reputation, having wiggled his baton before some of the globe's finest symphony orchestras.

Opened in 1964, Blaisdell Concert Hall is an ideal venue for the symphony's orchestrations. Acoustics are excellent and steeply tiered seating provides everyone with a good view. This is where Hawaiians come for a night of fine music, although they don't come dressed to the nines, or even the sevens. Folks here are casual about their culture.

9 DIAMOND HEAD THEATRE

520 Makapuʻu Ave., Honolulu; (808) 733-0274. Shows usually run Thursday through Saturday at 8, with matinees some weekends. MC/VISA; $$ to $$$$. GETTING THERE: From Waikiki, go inland on Monsarrat just under 1.5 miles and turn left onto Makapuʻu at the lower edge of Kapiʻolani Community College.

This community theater group presents five Broadway musicals and a drama each season. It performs in a refurbished movie theater across from the community college. The box office is open weekdays 10 to 6, plus Saturdays 10 to 2 when a show is running.

10 BALLET

Ballet Hawaiʻi, (808) 988-7578 or (808) 521-8600, www.ballethawaii.com; and Hawaiʻi State Ballet, (808) 947-2755, www.hawaiistateballet.com.

Hawaiians don't just do the hula; Oʻahu has several dance troupes including four ballet companies. Best known of these are Ballet Hawaiʻi, established in 1975; and Hawaiʻi State Ballet, founded in 1983. Both stage several productions each year. Ballet Hawaiʻi generally performs at the Blaisdell Concert Hall, and it joins with the Honolulu Symphony each holiday season for the *Nutcracker*. Hawaiʻi State Ballet performs at Ala Moana Centerstage at Ala Moana Shopping Center and the Mamiya Theatre at 3124 Waiʻalae Avenue.

THE TEN BEST PLACES TO SUCK 'EM UP

Honolulu is not a bar town to the measure of San Francisco, New York or Chicago. There are too many things to do here, other than perching on a bar stool and nursing a martini or even a mai tai. Folks would rather hit da beach during the cocktail hour, man!

The best of Honolulu's bars are on Waikiki Beach, mostly in resorts. And it's here that folks perch on a barstool or at a beachside table, admiring the views and nursing a mai tai, or even a martini.

1 SHORE BIRD BEACH BAR

Outrigger Reef Hotel, 2169 Kalia Rd., Waikiki; (808) 922-2887; www.outrigger.com. Lunch through late evening. GETTING THERE: It's on the beach, adjacent to the Halekulani. From Kalakaua Avenue, take Beachwalk to Kalia and turn right.

While we really enjoy sunsets and romance at the Royal Hawaiian's Mai Tai Bar, the Shore Bird is our favorite Waikiki hangout. Come join us and admire the profile of Diamond Head and the profiles of bronzed bodies lying within a cocktail napkin's toss of your table. The Shore Bird is more upbeat than most resort beach bars, with lively and usually live music that attracts a youngish crowd. Quaint belt-driven ceiling fans give the Bird an old fashioned look. Lunch and dinner menus offer essential American fare with Polynesian accents, and the restaurant features a "You're the Chef" barbecue, permitting you to burn your own meat or fish.

2 THE BEACH BAR

Sheraton Moana, 2365 Kalakaua Ave.; (808) 922-3111; www.sheraton-hawaii.com. Lunch through late evening. GETTING THERE: The Sheraton Moana is at the foot of Ka'iulani Avenue.

The Beach Bar is on the outer edge of the historic Moana's Banyan Veranda. It's one of the best view bars on Waikiki, since its tables practically nudge the sand. The bar is an attractive open air lounge shaded by trees and beach umbrellas. It serves light fare, such as grilled vegetable platter and Paniolo babyback ribs. The adjacent Banyan Veranda serves Sunday brunch and nightly dinner; see Chapter Three, page 79, and Chapter Seven, page 127.

3 DUKE'S BAREFOOT BAR

Outrigger Waikiki, 2335 Kalakaua Ave.; (808) 923-0711; www.outrigger.com. Lunch through late evening. GETTING THERE: The hotel is on the beach between the Sheraton Moana and the Royal Hawaiian.

This is the consummate beach pub, with palm-thatched umbrella tables and a thatched drop roof over the serving bar. It's an upbeat place attracting a young crowd, with live entertainment almost nightly. And it's a virtual Duke Kahanamoku museum, with old photos and memorabilia of the "father of surfing," Hawai'i's famous athlete.

4 GORDON BIERSCH

Aloha Tower Marketplace, Honolulu; (808) 599-4877; www.gordon-biersch.com. Mid-morning through late evening. GETTING THERE: From Waikiki, follow Ala Moana Boulevard 3.5 miles northwest; Aloha Tower is on your left.

Gordon Biersch was one of America's first brewpubs, started in Palo Alto, near San Francisco, in 1988. Outlets have spread to five Western states and the Aloha Tower version is Hawai'i's first brewpub. It's an attractive place with warm woods, large brewing kettles behind glass walls and lots of open air tables overlooking Honolulu Harbor. The pub brews and serves hearty German style lagers, with sturdy fare to match, such as Cajun pasta, marzen barbecued ribs and beer battered fish and chips. Appropriate to its Honolulu location, this Gordon Biersch also serves Polynesian *pupu* appetizers.

5 HANOHANO LOUNGE

Sheraton Waikiki, 2255 Kalakaua Ave.; (808) 922-4422, ext. 73620; www.sheraton-hawaii.com. Cocktails from 4 p.m.; late night entertainment Friday and Saturday. GETTING THERE: Follow Royal Hawaiian avenue beachward from Kalakaua.

The cocktail lounge of the thirtieth floor Hanohano Room offers absolutely splendid views of Waikiki. The bar counter faces Diamond head, and patrons look beyond the barkeep through floor-to-ceiling picture windows. Just to the left of the bar are several small tables including—if you feel romantic—a pair of tables for two. For more on the Hanohano Room, see Chapter Three, page 76, and Chapter Seven, page 126.

6 HOOTERS OF HONOLULU

Aloha Tower Marketplace, (808) 524-4668; www.hootershawaii.com. GETTING THERE: See Gordon Biersch listing above.

The first Hooters was born in Clearwater, Florida, in 1983, and the name supposedly comes from its owl logo, but we know better. The various Hooters—including the one in Honolulu—are decorated with pretty young lasses wearing orange hotpants and scoop-necked tops. They serve smiles, strong drinks and hearty bar fare such as chicken strips, steamed clams and assorted sandwiches. Hooters are popular sports bars with a dozen or more TV monitors tuned to the current games. Like many Honolulu pubs and restaurants, this Hooters is mostly open to the outdoors, with views of Honolulu Harbor.

7 MAI TAI BAR

Royal Hawaiian Hotel, 2259 Kalakaua Ave.; (808) 923-7311, www.royal-Hawaiian.com. Lunch through late evening. GETTING THERE: Follow Royal Hawaiian Avenue beachward from Kalakaua.

This was Waikiki's first beachside bar and it has the best views of the strand and Diamond Head. It's a popular place for sunset-watchers. In keeping with the Royal Hawaiian's primary colors, outdoor tables are shaded by pink and white umbrellas. The bar serves assorted Polynesian drinks including its signature "Pink Palace," and even a pink beer. Menu offerings include hamburgers, small pizzas, salads, quesadillas, Buffalo wings, a seafood sampler, and *pupu* platters.

8 THE SAND BAR

Sheraton Waikiki, 2255 Kalakaua Ave.; (808) 922-4422; www.sheraton-hawaii.com. Lunch through late evening. GETTING THERE: Follow Royal Hawaiian avenue beachward from Kalakaua.

Yet another of Waikiki's popular beachside cocktail lounges, the Sand Bar sits beside two bodies of water—the beach and the hotel swimming pool. And of course it has those grand vistas. Its extensive bar menu features hot wings, barbecued chicken sandwiches, ahi steak sandwiches, babyback ribs and other light fare.

9 TIKI'S GRILL & BAR

Aston Waikiki Beach Hotel, 2570 Kalakaua Ave., (808) 922-2511; www.astonhotels.com. Lunch through late evening. GETTING THERE: It's on the eastern side of Waikiki at the corner of Kalakaua and Paoakalani Street. Turn left off Kalakaua then quickly right for parking.

This lively bar on the hotel's elevated open deck looks across Kalakaua Avenue to Kuhio Beach Park. Pick a railing table for the best Waikiki view, or you can sit near the hotel pool, which shares this large deck. The bar-restaurant is decorated with bamboo and tribal masks for that proper tiki look, and tiki torches blaze from its perimeter at night. The restaurant serves American-Hawaiian fare and the bar has lighter *pupu* appetizers.

10 YE OLDE FOX & HOUNDS PUB & GRUB WAIKIKI

1778 Ala Moana Blvd.; (808) 947-3776. Breakfast through late evening daily. GETTING THERE: It's across Ala Moana from the Renaissance Ilikai hotel in Discovery Bay Center, near Hobron Lane.

If you're looking for an old fashioned bar—complete with smoky atmosphere, check out this cellar place. The décor suggests a Hawaiian version of an English pub, with white lattice accents, ceiling fans, beer logos and sports banners. A couple of pool tables and electronic dart boards are off the main bar. Those seeking quiet can adjourn to a cozy side room with high back rattan queen's chairs. A few tables occupy a sunken brick patio out front. The fare is mostly Brit, including Cornish pasties, fish and chips, bangers and mash and shepherd's pie—with thirty-five beers on tap to wash it all down.

Her islands here, in southern sun,
Shall mourn their Ka'iulani gone,
And I, in her dear banyan shade,
Look vainly for my little maid.

From a poem by Robert Louis Stevenson,
dedicated to Princess Ka'iulani in 1889

Chapter Seven

ROMANCE
..AND OTHER PRIMAL URGES

Hawai'i is one of the world's most romantic places, identified with the sensual hip movements of the hula, a lei presented with a warming smile, the verbal caress of the word "aloha." Sunsets on the sea, palm fronds rustled by the warm tradewinds, a candle-lit dinner at a beachside restaurant—these things spell romance.

A wedding in paradise?

Thousands come to these islands each year to get married, as did Betty and I many years ago. Or they come to spend their honeymoon after being married at home, or to renew their vows or have a second honeymoon, or maybe just to mess around. They come because this is a place to kindle new passions or rekindle old ones. We've always liked the sight of newlyweds in white bridal gown and dark tux, posing on a beach for wedding photos, in stark contrast to the tanned sunbathers lying about.

Hawai'i has more weddings per capita than any other state except Nevada. (Somehow, we sense that Hawai'i-bound couples are driven by romance while those headed for our home state are driven more by lust.) The most recent statistics show that Hawai'i has about 25,000 marriages per year, and more than 16,000 of these are non-residents.

Feeling the itch to get hitched? It's as easy in Hawai'i as it is in Las Vegas. There is no residency or citizenship requirements, no blood test and no waiting period. About the only prerequisite are to be at least eighteen years old, have a valid ID such as a driver's license or birth certificate, and have $60 in your pocket for the marriage license. You can even marry a second cousin, but not a first. And no, that's not where the term "calabash cousin" came from. It refers to someone who is informally adopted into a family. It's an old Hawaiian expression, comparing the spreading of a calabash vine to the outreach of an *'ohana* or family.

To learn more—about Hawaiian marriages, not calabashes—call the Hawaii Department of Health at (808) 586-4545 or log onto *www.go-hawaii.com* and click on "weddings & honeymoons."

Whether you're coming to Hawai'i to get married or just for a little hanky panky, we present twenty best places for romance among the palms.

THE TEN BEST PLACES TO SNUGGLE WITH YOUR SWEETIE

O'ahu receives more than four million visitors a year, many of them looking for love in all the right places. Obviously, those places have become very crowded, and it's often difficult to be alone together. However, we've found ten spots where you *can* be alone, or at least where romance is expected, and you can ignore those around you.

1 WAIKIKI BEACH

Kuhio Beach Park, off Kalakaua Avenue at the base of Ohua Avenue.

What? We've selected Hawai'i's most popular beach as the best place to snuggle with your sweetie? Yes, if you're willing to wait until after sunset. Crowds line the beach every evening to watch the day end, something the two of you might do to get into a romantic mood. However, within a few hours, Waikiki is practically deserted. After all, you can't get a suntan at night, right?

For a romantic snuggle in the sand, we particularly like an area reached by a sloping concrete walk just behind a bronze statue of Prince Kuhio in Kuhio Beach Park. It's across Kalakaua Avenue from the Waikiki Marriott. The beach slopes sharply downward here, forming a low berm. Sitting with your back against this sand ridge, you're out of sight of strolling pedestrians on the nearby street. You may be tempted to slip into the calm water here, which is sheltered by a concrete seawall. Don't say we didn't warn you that nude swimming is illegal on Waikiki Beach.

2 KUHIO BEACH PIER

Off Kalakaua Avenue at the base of Kapahulu Avenue, opposite the Aston Waikiki Beach Hotel.

One of our favorite nighttime sweetie snuggle places is a pedestrian pier called "The Wall," part of a protective seawall that creates a sheltered swimming area on Waikiki. Tiki torches light the pier and the roof lines of a small shelter at the end are trimmed in beaded lights, so the place isn't too dark and scary. There are no benches on this pier, although the two of you can sit on a low encircling railing. You can watch the surf roll in, admire the lights of Waikiki's highrise hotels and, on a moonlit night, even perceive the subtle outline of Diamond Head.

3 LYON ARBORETUM

3860 Manoa Rd., Honolulu; (808) 988-0456; www.hawaii. edu/lyonarboretum. Monday-Saturday 9 to 3; visitors can remain until gates close at 4; modest admission fee. GETTING THERE: The arboretum is tucked into steep hills above Honolulu. From Waikiki, go north on Mc-Cully, then northwest on Beretania less than half a mile to Punahou Street and turn right. Punahou crosses H-1 and blends onto Manoa Road. Follow it about three miles to its end, just beyond Paradise Park. (About two-thirds of a mile from the freeway, make sure you fork to the left to avoid East Manoa Road, which will lead you astray.)

This attractive hillside botanical garden operated by the University of Hawaii is a fine sweetie snuggle place. However, be sure to accept the gift shop manager's offer of mosquito repellent. This is essentially a rainforest crawling up a steep hillside, entwined with a network of trails. It's thick with native and introduced plants. Benches along the trails—and the fact that the arboretum gets few visitors—make this a fine sweetie snuggle place. Particularly appealing is a pagoda-roofed gazebo beside a koi pond, with a spillover fountain. It's just below the gift shop/visitor center.

4 THE MOVIE MUSEUM

3566 Harding St., Honolulu; (808) 735-8771. Open noon to 8 p.m. Thursday-Sunday; modest fees for films. GETTING THERE: It's in the Wai'alae area, between Eleventh and Twelfth avenues. From Waikiki, go inland on Kapahulu Avenue about 1.2 miles, cross under H-1, go right on Wai'alae Avenue for just under a mile and turn right onto Eleventh.

This "museum" is actually a cozy theater with nineteen recliner chairs before a ten-foot screen. Owner Dwight Damon shows movies

Thursday through Sunday, drawing from his collection of 3,000 videotapes. Most are Hollywood and foreign classics. What's so romantic about this, other than cozying up in overstuffed recliners? When the theater isn't open to the public, you can rent it for about $200 and have it all to yourselves. Can you watch naughty movies? You'll have to discuss that with Dwight.

5 MOUNT TANTALUS

Part of the Honolulu Watershed Forest Reserve above the city. Pu'u Ualaka'a State Park is open daily 7 to 6:30. GETTING THERE: From Waikiki, go north on McCully Street, then northwest on Beretania about half a mile to Punahou Street and turn right. Cross H-1 and, after less than half a mile, go left on Nehoa Street for two blocks. Turn right (uphill) on Makiki Street and fork right for Round Top Drive.

A rainforest cloaks the southern slopes of Ko'olau Range, and its dark green thickets offer lonely refuge for you and your sweetie. Honolulu Watershed Forest Reserve doesn't sound very romantic, but the Round Top/Tantalus scenic drive that loops through it certainly is. Trails lead from the road at several points, and your disappearance into thick undergrowth can be quick. Although these are popular trails, we rarely encounter hikers on weekdays. We're almost always alone, surrounded by jungle, listening to the calls of unseen birds and the soft rustling of the wind. There are a few benches for sitting and snuggling, or any fallen log will do.

If you prefer a panoramic vista instead of solitude, stop at Pu'u Ualaka'a State Park, on your left as you drive up Tantalus. Turn into the park and continue past a pottie and picnic area to the end of the road, where you'll encounter the lookout. The view takes in much of southern O'ahu from Diamond Head and Waikiki to downtown Honolulu and Punchbowl Crater.

6 DIAMOND HEAD LOOKOUT

Diamond Head State Monument, open from 6 a.m. to 6 p.m.; token entry fee. GETTING THERE: From Waikiki, go southeast on Kalakaua to Kapi'olani Park, then fork left onto Monsarrat Avenue, which becomes Diamond Head Road. Follow it a mile and the turnoff into to the Diamond Head parking area is just beyond Kapi'olani Community College.

Think of this as a conditional snuggle place. Further, it's one that must be reached by hiking nearly a mile up a switchback trail and then climbing 280 steps. The lookout on Diamond Head crater's highest crest is usually busy with other visitors, and it's often quite windy up there. However, it's a great place to watch the sunrise and you'll likely be alone together at that hour of the morning. The sun appears around the corner of the island behind Waikiki, then it begins its dramatic light and shadow act on the resort towers of the famed beach below you. If the lookout becomes too crowded, you can always retreat to a quiet bunker or a darkened spiral staircase just below.

TRAVEL TIP: The hike passes through two dark tunnels, and that spiral staircase is *really* dark, so take a flashlight. Also carry water since this is a tough climb, or even better, a bottle of champagne.

7 WAIKIKI HAU TREE

On Waikiki Beach between the Halekulani and Sheraton Waikiki. GETTING THERE: Take Lewers Street off Kalakaua Avenue, follow it to the end and find a place to park. There's beach access between the Halekulani and Sheraton.

Hau's that? A massive hau tree that sprawls over the sands of Waikiki can serve as a retreat for lovers, even though the area is quite public. As we established above, the beach is not crowded at night, and the two of you can practically disappear among the branches after sunset. No, you don't have to climb. The noble old tree has been topped and its thick branches grow across on the sand like a great gnarled hand. Many of these horizontal limbs are at the proper level for sitting, or you can settle into the sand and use a branch as a back rest. From your protective shelter, you can look west toward the sunset and east toward Diamond Head.

8 MAI TAI BAR

Royal Hawaiian Hotel, 2259 Kalakaua Ave.; (808) 923-7311, www.royal-Hawaiian.com. GETTING THERE: Follow Royal Hawaiian Avenue beachward from Kalakaua.

We keep coming back to this outdoor lounge because it's one of our favorite places on Oʻahu. The Royal Hawaiian was the third major hotel built on Waikiki, so it occupies a prime piece of beach. Patrons of the Mai Tai Bar and adjacent Surf Room restaurant have fine views of Diamond Head to the east and Waikiki to the west. It is thus a grand place to watch the sunset. And the bar—as if designed with lovers in mind—has several tables-for-two along an outer railing, right above the sand. Tiki torches are lighted and candles are placed on the tables just before sundown. What could be more romantic?

TRAVEL TIP: Get there at least an hour before sundown to ensure getting a beachside table.

9 WAIMEA FALLS PARK

59-864 Kamehameha Hwy., Waimea; (808) 638-8511 or (808) 638-5300; www.atlantisadventures.net/hawaii. Daily 10 to 5:30; entrance fee. GETTING THERE: The park is about forty miles from Waikiki on Oʻahu's North Shore. From Honolulu, go northwest on H-1 and then north on H-2, which blends onto Kamehameha Highway.

Waimea Falls Park (Chapter Two, page 51) is a popular commercial operation and not uncrowded. However, you can shed those crowds by tucking yourselves into the several botanical gardens that line the main road. Most visitors ride a tram from the entrance, gawk at the falls—which aren't very impressive—then take part in one of the many activities offered. That leaves just the two of you to explore the gardens, which are quite impressive and interlaced with paths.

If you happen to be on O'ahu on the Friday closest to a full moon, you can take part in the "Moonwalk at Waimea Park," when it's uncrowded and dimly romantic. Watch the moon glitter off the falls, and into your lover's eyes.

10 KAWELA BEACH

Off Kamehameha Highway on O'ahu's North Shore. GETTING THERE: Follow directions to Waimea Falls Park above, and continue another six miles. The beach is just beyond the hamlet of Kawela. No sign marks it, so if you reach Turtle Bay Resort, you've missed it by 1.5 miles. If you're coming from the other direction, it'll be the first beach you see after passing the resort.

Kawela is one of the most romantic beaches on all the islands, particularly for watching the sunset. It's a pretty little crescent of sand, accented by lava outcroppings and shaded by fine-needled casuarina trees. A tiny isle sprouting a few trees is just offshore. You'll find several cozy snuggle spots here, against a sandy slope, down out of sight of the highway. The surf is rather rough, so use this beach for snuggling, not swimming.

THE TEN MOST ROMANTIC RESTAURANTS

Is there anything more romantic than a sunset dinner beside the beach? We don't think so. However, our number one choice isn't on the beach; it's high above it.

PRICING: Dollar sign codes indicate the price of a typical dinner with entrée, soup or salad, not including drinks, appetizers or dessert: **$** = less than $10 per entrée; **$$** = $10 to $19; **$$$** = $20 to $29; **$$$$** = $30 to $40; **$$$$$** = $41 and beyond.

1 THE HANOHANO ROOM

*Atop the Sheraton Waikiki Hotel & Resort, 2255 Kalakaua Ave.; (808) 922-4422, ext. 73620. Continental and Hawaiian regional; full bar service. Breakfast Monday-Saturday, Sunday champagne brunch and dinner nightly. Cocktails from 4 p.m.; late night entertainment Friday and Saturday. Major credit cards; **$$$$** to **$$$$$**. Reservations advised. GETTING THERE: The Sheraton is adjacent to the Royal Hawai-*

ian, reached via Royal Hawaiian Avenue off Kalakaua. An outside elevator to the restaurant is just to the left of the main entrance.

Our favorite romantic restaurant is as high as your lover's expectations. The thirtieth-floor Hanohano Room is a very intimate place for a sunset dinner, particularly at one of its tables-for-two. Gaze at the view—and into one another's eyes—and listen to the soft tinkling of a piano, issuing from somewhere. Even the ride up in the outside elevator can be romantic, for it offers a view of downtown Waikiki. If you're here on a Friday or Saturday night, linger over dinner; live music for dancing starts around 9. We also chose the Hanohano Room as Honolulu's best view restaurant; see Chapter Three, page 76.

2 BANYAN VERANDA

Sheraton Moana, 2365 Kalakaua Ave.; (808) 922-3111; www. moana-surfrider.com. American; full bar service. Breakfast and dinner daily; afternoon tea Monday-Saturday. Major credit cards; $$$$. Reservations advised. GETTING THERE: The hotel is in the heart of Waikiki, opposite the International Market Place.

The Banyan Veranda is a very romantic dining spot. Settle into a comfortable cane and wicker chair at a lamp-lit table within view of the beach, listen to soft Hawaiian music and watch a hula girl writhe sensuously. This place was even more romantic from 1935 until 1975, when the radio program "Hawaii Calls" originated from here. Appropriately, the evening meal is called the "Romantic Sunset Dinner." It's *prix fixe*, and choices when we last checked were seafood linguine, New York steak, *nori*-wrapped island snapper, pan roasted chicken breast or Maine lobster.

3 INDIGO

1121 Nu'uanu Ave., Chinatown; (808) 521-2900; www.indigo-hawaii.com. Chinese/Pacific Rim; full bar service. Lunch Tuesday-Friday and dinner Tuesday-Saturday; closed Sunday-Monday. Major credit cards; $$$ to $$$$. Reservations accepted. GETTING THERE: To reach Chinatown from Waikiki, head 3.5 miles northwest on Ala Moana Boulevard. Just past Aloha Tower, turn right onto Smith Street, go inland four blocks, then go right on Pauahi and right again on Nu'uanu.

Dine under the stars in the quiet courtyard of this Chinese modern restaurant, which is surrounded by the unmodern brick and masonry of old Chinatown. Tiki torches and candles cast soft glows onto tables-for-two beside a koi pond. If you dine inside, you'll relax in a cool atmosphere of blues and bamboos, potted plants and tasseled umbrellas. Chef/owner Glenn Chu calls his cuisine "Eurasian," and it features such diverse entrées as Sumatra peppered beef with coconut curry, lamb shanks with curry, and roasted duck glazed with raspberry *hoisin* sauce. For appetizers, order one of Chef Chu's special *dim sum* dumplings for your little dumpling.

4 KEO'S IN WAIKIKI

2028 Kuhio Ave.; (808) 951-9355; www.keosthaicuisine.com. Thai/Hawaiian; full bar service. Breakfast, lunch and late dinner daily. Major credit cards; $$ to $$$. Reservations accepted. GETTING THERE: The restaurant is in the Ambassador Hotel building, where Kuhio forks left off Ala Moana.

With its appealing Southeast Asian décor, Keo's is a good place for romance on a stormy night. The folding window walls onto Kuhio Avenue may be pulled shut, thus stifling the traffic noise. Otherwise, the more romantic tables are against inside walls away from the street. Several tables-for-two sit beneath framed works of art. Cushioned wicker chairs, bud vases with orchid blooms, small oil lamps and green and white nappery provide the proper setting for intimate dining. Keo's also is one of the Ten Best Asian/Pacific Rim restaurants in Chapter Three; see page 72 for menu details.

5 MATTEO'S

364 Seaside Ave., Waikiki; (808) 922-5551; www.hawaiibusiness.com/matteos/. Italian; full bar service. Late dinner nightly. Major credit cards; $$$ to $$$$. Reservations advised. GETTING THERE: It's at the corner of Seaside and Kuhio adjacent to the Marine Surf Hotel, a few blocks off Waikiki Beach.

This local favorite also is a favorite for lovers, with its plush curved brocaded booths, dark paneled walls, dim lighting, soft music and tuxedo-clad waiters. Curiously interesting and somehow sensuously appealing is a large wine rack in the back dining room, outlined in beaded lighting. The appropriate wine should be in there to loosen your lover's inhibitions. We also selected Matteo's as the best local restaurant in Chapter Three. For suggestions on what dishes to order for your favorite dish; see page 80.

6 NEPTUNE'S GARDEN

Pacific Beach Hotel, 2490 Kalakaua Ave. (808) 921-6112; www.neptunesgardenrestaurant.com. Asian/Pacific Rim; full bar service. Dinner nightly; live entertainment Tuesday-Saturday. Major credit cards; $$$ to $$$$. Reservations accepted. GETTING THERE: The hotel is across Kalakaua from the beach, between Kealohilani and Lili'uokalani.

You and your lover can dine on fish while watching fish in Neptune's Garden. Several tables in this restaurant are adjacent to Hawai'i's largest indoor aquarium, a fish-busy 280,000-gallon tank. While there's nothing really sexy about an aquarium, watching those fish swim about can be quite soothing. And the Tokyoesque look of the restaurant *is* rather sensuous, with drop lamps over booths, sexy pink nappery, candle-lit tables, potted plants and curving room dividers. From the kitchen emerges fish of course—steamed island snapper, pan-fried *moi*, sautéed garlic shrimp, seared ahi tuna and seafood bouillabaisse.

7 NICK'S FISHMARKET

Waikiki Gateway Hotel, 2070 Kalakaua Ave.; (808) 955-6333; www.waikiki-gateway-hotel.com. Seafood with Italian accents; full bar service. Dinner nightly. Major credit cards; $$$ to $$$$. Reservations accepted. GETTING THERE: It's at the corner of 'Olohana in the northwestern area of Waikiki.

Although the Waikiki Gateway isn't exactly a high end hotel, its restaurant is regarded by local foodies as one of the area's best. Several awards are posted at the entry, although most are a few years old. Like the hotel, Nick's could use a tuck here and there, although it's still an attractive and rather romantic dining venue. It's dimly lit, with cozy curved booths, and several tables-for-two with high curved-back chairs that almost embrace the sitters.

After your leisurely meal, you can embrace on the dance floor; there's live music several nights a week. The menu is rather traditional; no sun-dried beef, air-dried tomatoes or raspberry purée. Among Nick's entrées are shellfish bouillabaisse, crab leg basket, abalone with walnuts, salmon with honey and saké marinade, and sesame seed-encrusted swordfish.

8 ORCHIDS

The Halekulani, 2199 Kalia Rd.; (808) 923-2311; www.halekulani.com. American/Pacific Rim; full bar service. Breakfast, lunch and dinner, and Sunday brunch. Major credit cards; $$$$ to $$$$$. Reservations recommended for dinner. GETTING THERE: The Halekulani is on Waikiki at the corner of Kalia Road and Beachwalk.

Settle into the comforts of old plantation Hawai'i in this handsome restaurant in the House Without a Key. This is the only building surviving from original garden style resort, which opened in 1907. Dim lighting, white nappery, bud vases and tiny lamps add the proper level of intimacy. Outdoor tables under a covered veranda are particularly appealing, with views of Diamond Head, Waikiki Beach and tropical sunsets. Service is attentive and never hovering. The two of you will be left alone, although the slightest nod will summon someone.

The menu is as mature as your romance, without a lot of silly sauces and relishes. Some recent entrées were Madras seafood curry, mixed grill in tarragon butter, roasted lamb chops with Port wine glaze, and filet mignon with lobster tail.

9 SUNSET TERRACE

Outrigger Waikiki, 2335 Kalakaua Ave., (808) 971-3595; www.out-rigger.com. American; full bar service. Breakfast, lunch and dinner. Major credit cards; $$ to $$$. Reservations accepted. GETTING THERE: The Outrigger is on the beach between the Sheraton Moana and the Royal Hawaiian.

Are you saving for the ring, or did you already spend too much on it? Sunset Terrace is remarkably inexpensive for a major Waikiki restaurant, with dinner entrées starting in the low teens. And it's certainly romantic. When the sun sets, the lights are dimmed and candles flicker on cozy tables. Relax and enjoy the view over the hotel's swimming pool to the palm-lined beach. Soft music adds to the romantic charm of this scene. Seating is indoors and out, with tables-for-two on an outside railing. Among menu items are grilled guava chicken, grilled salmon, several steaks and fresh fish of the day. But don't order Grandma Jesse's meatloaf; that's not very romantic.

10 THE SURF ROOM

Sheraton Royal Hawaiian, 2259 Kalakaua Ave.; (808) 931-7194; www.royal-Hawaiian.com. American with Asian accents; full bar service. Breakfast buffet, lunch and dinner daily. Major credit cards; $$$ to $$$$. Reservations advised. GETTING THERE: The hotel is behind the Royal Hawaiian Shopping Center.

Pink is the color of romance—or at least of babies generated by romance—and you'll certainly think pink as you dine at the Surf Room. The color is in the scalloped awnings, the nappery, the menu cover and the texture of the grand old Spanish-Moorish architecture rising about you. Tiny oil lamps on the tables add touches of intimacy. Come for a romantic sunset dinner when old sol sizzles into the sea and the majestic profile of Diamond Head fades to a dark silhouette. This is one of the few beachside restaurants with a clear view of that famous profile. We've also selected the Surf Room as one of O'ahu's Ten Very Best Restaurants in Chapter Three; see page 70.

An extravagance is anything you buy that is of no earthly use to your wife.   **— Franklin P. Jones**

Chapter Eight

CREDIT CARD ABUSE

SHOPPING UNTIL YOU'RE DROPPING

Visitors come to Hawai'i not just for sun, surf, sand and luaus; they come to shop. They buy everything from pineapples to chocolate covered macadamia nuts to Hawaiian handicrafts, plus uncounted numbers of dashboard hula girls and refrigerator magnets.

Among the more popular items are Hawaiian fashions—aloha shirts and mumus and other brightly colored resort wear popularized by outlets such as Hilo Hattie. Inspired by a former comic hula dancer, the firm has several stores on O'ahu and most of the outer islands; see Chapter One, page 39.

Vacationers also shop for art in Hawai'i. The islands' two best known artists, Christian Lassen (*www.lassen-hawaii.com*) and the single-named Wyland (*www.wyland.com*) have galleries on Waikiki and elsewhere. Several O'ahu galleries feature the works of other local artists; notable among these is Diamond Head Gallery, with three outlets on Waikiki; (808) 971-2800.

THE TEN BEST MALLS & SHOPPING AREAS

Our choices range from large and small malls to major shopping districts. Although there are several large malls on O'ahu, our focus is the Honolulu-Waikiki area. We begin—as usual—with our favorite, followed by the rest in alphabetical order.

1 ALA MOANA SHOPPING CENTER

1450 Ala Moana, Honolulu; (808) 955-9517; www.alamoana.com. Most stores open Monday-Saturday 9 to 9 and Sunday 10 to 7; restaurant hours vary. GETTING THERE: Follow Ala Moana northwest from Waikiki and the shopping center starts at the corner of Atkinson Drive.

This is Hawai'i's largest mall, two blocks long and occupying three levels. It is so large, in fact, that newcomers can expect to get lost there. This sprawling center targets both the budget-minded and the high end shopper. Its major department stores are Macy's, Sears, Neiman Marcus, Japan's Shirokiya and JCPenny (although it may close). It's an attractive facility, with tropical landscaping set in stone planters and ponds occupied by huge koi. The center is open to the sky, with overhangs to provide quick shelter from Honolulu's sudden and usually brief rainstorms.

Ala Moana Centerstage on the lower level near Waldenbooks is often the site of live entertainment and other special events. Adjacent are several tables set with chess sets to invite relaxing. The Makai Market Food Court reflects Honolulu's international flavor with Thai, Chinese, Japanese, Korean, Filipino, traditional Hawaiian and even Mexican fare; see Chapter Five, page 106.

TRAVEL TIP: Alamoana Shopping Center's parking is very complex, occupying several levels. Make sure you note where you've parked or you may never find your car again.

2 ALOHA TOWER MARKETPLACE

1 Aloha Tower Dr., Honolulu; (808) 566-2337; www.aloha-tower.com. Most shops open Monday-Saturday 9 to 9 and Sunday 9 to 7; restaurant hours vary. GETTING THERE: Follow Ala Moana Boulevard three miles northwest and Aloha Tower is on your left.

More than seventy shops occupy a two-story open air complex at the historic Aloha Tower on the Honolulu waterfront. Many are tourist-oriented, featuring Hawaiian wear, art and artifacts, curios and souvenirs. Worth a look is Hawaii Pacific Arts & Crafts, with a nice selection of Polynesian items. The center has several restaurants, including three featured elsewhere in this book; check the index for Gordon Biersch, Don Ho's Island Grill and Hooters.

The star attraction here is the 184-foot **Aloha Tower**, opened in 1926 to greet arriving cruise ship passengers. Until steamships were replaced by aircraft, many a visitor's first impression of Hawai'i was to step ashore at Aloha Tower and receive a lei greeting from a pretty Hawaiian lass. The tower was the tallest structure in the islands until the 1960s. Its observation deck is open to the public daily from 9 to 5. Ride an old fashioned elevator that saunters leisurely to the tenth floor observation deck for a fine view of the waterfront, city, ocean and mountains. Signs tell you what you're seeing. Near Aloha Tower Marketplace is the **Hawaii Maritime Center** operated by the Bishop Museum; see Chapter Two, page 46.

3 HILTON HAWAIIAN VILLAGE

2005 Kalia Rd., Waikiki; (808) 949-4321; www.hiltonhawaii.com. Shop hours vary. GETTING THERE: The complex is on the corner of Ala Moana Boulevard and Kalia. Turn right onto Kalia Road and then right again into the village.

More than ninety shops are part of the 22-acre Hilton Hawaiian Village complex, the largest resort on Waikiki. They sell everything from Hawaiian fashions to Panama hats to ukeleles to fine jewelry to souvenirs. Most are in the Rainbow Bazaar, where two dozen shops and boutiques line the village's main drive. Tapa Concourse in the heart of the village has another dozen shops, and others occupy the base of the new Kalia Tower, Diamond Head Tower, Rainbow Tower, and Ali'i Plaza at the base of the Ali'i Tower.

4 HYATT REGENCY WAIKIKI

2424 Kalakaua Ave., Waikiki; (808) 923-1234; www.hyatt-waikiki.com. Shop and restaurant hours vary. GETTING THERE: The Hyatt is between Ka'iulani and Uluniu avenues.

The Hyatt Shops occupy three levels—a ground floor open breezeway and two balconies above. It's an appealing complex, with a pair of waterfalls that cascade from the upper floors into a ground floor lagoon. Stores a mix of designer and specialty shops and galleries. Five restaurants—Seafood Village, Chao Mein, Musashi, the Colony and Terrace Grille—are within the shopping complex.

5 INTERNATIONAL MARKET PLACE

2330 Kalakaua Ave., Waikiki; (808) 971-2080; www.international-marketplacewaikiki.com. Most stores and restaurants open 10 to 10:30. GETTING THERE: It's in the heart of Waikiki, between Duke's Lane and Ka'iulani Avenue.

The ultimate tourist trinket shopping center, this busy open air market was started in 1955 by entrepreneur Donn Beach. He built it around his Don, the Beachcomber restaurant, on land once owned by Queen Emma, widow of Kamehameha IV. This complex of 130 shops, carts and kiosks is attractively landscaped by palms, huge banyan trees and fountains. It is *the* source for sunglasses, T-shirts, plastic leis, Kamehameha decorative candles, Hawaiian girlie calendars, puka shell necklaces, and wiggly-waisted hula girl and hula boy clocks. A food court has a dozen takeouts, and free Hawaiian shows are presented each evening except Tuesday and Sunday on an outdoor stage.

6 KAHALA MALL

4211 Wai'alae Ave., Honolulu; (808) 732-7736; www.kahalamall-center.com. Most stores open Monday-Saturday 10 to 9 and Sunday 10 to 5. GETTING THERE: Head east on H-1, take the Wai'alae exit, turn right onto Kilauea Avenue and right again into the mall.

Not far from Waikiki and easily reachable via H-1, this midsize mall is anchored by Macy's and a large Barnes & Noble book store. It has about ninety other shops, plus a Star supermarket and a multi-screen theater complex. Shops are in the medium to upper medium price range and they're all under cover, with a few potted palms, and benches for shoppers to rest weary feet.

7 KALAKAUA AVENUE

Between Kalaimoku Street and Ulunui Avenue.

This stretch of Kalakaua is O'ahu's trendiest shopping area. Stores along the avenue, intermixed with resort hotels, range from fancy boutiques and a large Macy's to souvenir booths. Among it's high end stores are Cartier, Fendi, Louis Vuitton, Burberry, Chanel, Tiffany & Co., Gucci and Yves Saint Laurent. The eastern part of this area has been dressed up with flagstone sidewalks and tiki torches.

Kalakaua also is home to three shopping complexes listed elsewhere on these pages—Hyatt Regency Shops, Royal Hawaiian Shopping Center and the lovable old International Market Place. Another large complex is **DFS Galleria Waikiki** at the corner of Kalakaua and Royal Hawaiian avenues, with about fifty specialty shops and restaurants and a duty free shop. Particularly interesting here is an 65,000-gallon aquarium called The Tube; see Chapter Five, page 99. Shops are open daily 9 to 11; (808) 931-2655; *www.dfsgalleria.com.*

8 KING'S VILLAGE

131 Ka'iulani Ave., Waikiki; (808) 677-7111. Most shops and restaurants open at 10; closing hours vary. GETTING THERE: It's between Koa Avenue and Prince Edward Street, behind the Hyatt Regency Hotel.

This cute little has complex has an ornate kingdom of Hawai'i look with Polynesian-accented European style architecture. Forty clothing, jewelry and specialty shops and restaurants are tucked into three levels, linked by rambling alleys and landscaped patios. Chairs and tables offer respite from the busyness of nearby Waikiki which—within the village—seems far away.

In keeping with its Hawaiian Royalty theme, a changing of the guard is performed at 6:15 nightly by "sentries" dressed in replica uniforms of the King Kalakaua's 1875 Royal Palace Guards. The village occupies land that once was the home of Princess Ka'iulani and no, we don't know why it isn't called Princess Village.

9 ROYAL HAWAIIAN SHOPPING CENTER

2201 Kalakaua, Waikiki; (808) 922-0588; www.shopwaikiki.com. Most shops open 10 to 10. GETTING THERE: It's at the base of Duke's Lane, stretching for three blocks along Kalakaua.

Not actually part of the Royal Hawaiian, this complex in fact shields the historic hotel from Kalakaua Avenue. A nice focal point of this large center is an impressionistic sculpture of a Hawaiian spearfishing, on Kalakaua at the base of Seaside Street. This is one of Hawai'i's largest shopping complexes, with nearly 140 stores and eighteen restaurants and cafés on three levels. Scores of shops line the Kalakaua sidewalk and scores more stand along a parallel corridor inside. A couple of walkways, almost hidden by the ranks of shops, lead to the Royal Hawaiian Hotel. There are no anchor stores here, only a wide range of shops offering everything from high style clothing and surfboards to jewelry and fine art.

10 VICTORIA WARD CENTERS

1210 Auahi, Honolulu; (808) 591-8411; www.victoriaward.com. Various hours for shops and restaurants; Ward Farmers Market open Monday-Saturday 7 to 5 and Sunday 7 to 1. GETTING THERE: From Waikiki, go northwest 1.5 miles on Ala Moana Boulevard, turn right on Kamake'e Street and left on Auahu and you're in the heart of the Ward complex.

Talk about shopping 'til you're dropping! This huge facility contains several individual complexes, with 1.3 million square feet of building space spread over sixty-five acres. This was part of a 100-acre piece of Honolulu owned by early entrepreneurs Curtis and Victoria Ward. The Ward Center includes the **Ward Warehouse** with mostly specialty and tourist shops and a few restaurants and takeouts; **Wards Village Shops** with more specialty stores; **Ward Centre**, a covered shopping complex; and **Ward Entertainment Center** with a multi-screen theater. Our favorite here is **Wards Farmers Market,** an old fashioned food market with meat, fish and produce sections, plus Hawaiian and other ethnic fare in a large cafe and food court complex.

Chapter Nine

GETTING PHYSICAL
SHEDDING THOSE LAU LAU LUNCHES

Too much poi, boy? One of the pleasant risks of an enjoyable Hawai'i vacation is putting on a bit of weight. Those luaus tend to go to waist. However, you can work off extra poundage by taking one or more of our Ten Best walks and hikes. These are mostly relatively level walks, not really challenging hill climbs. If you want to do some serious hiking, check local book stores for these two guidebooks—*Oahu Trails* by Kathy Morey; Wilderness Press; and *Hawaii's Best Hiking Trails* by Robert Smith, Hawaiian Outdoors Adventures.

Note: **Bold face** listings marked with ❖ are described in more detail elsewhere in this book; check the index for page numbers.

OAHU'S TEN BEST WALKS & HIKES

Our first seven selections are in or about Waikiki and Honolulu and the hills above. The final three workouts are on the North Shore and the Leeward Coast.

1 WAIKIKI BEACH WALK

About two miles one way; all level. GETTING THERE: The walk's starting point is the Memorial Natatorium in Kapi'olani Park, just beyond the Waikiki Aquarium. Follow Kalakaua Avenue east into the park.

You might consider taking this walk soon after you arrive, since it provides a good overview of Waikiki and most of its parks, resorts and attractions. Wear sandals and maybe even a swimsuit, since you'll be plodding through sand part of the way and you may be tempted to splash into the surf.

A brochure available at the **Aloha Kiosk** visitors informatiion stand at Kalakaua and Kapahulu avenues describes the ❖ **Waikiki Historic Trail**. It's a walking route with twenty-three sites designated by surfboard-shaped markers. We follow it in some areas, although the route is rather erratic and the brochure lacks sufficient detail to keep you on track.

Docents of the Native Hawaiian Hospitality Association conduct free walks over two portions of the historic trail Monday through Saturday, starting at 9. One begins at the Visitors Information Stand, and the other starts at the Bishop Museum at Kalia at Hilton Hawaiian Village, corner of Kalia Road and the Hilton complex entrance; (808) 841-6441. (www.waikikihistorictrail.com)

TRAVEL TIPS: See the Waikiki map on page 20 for details on the area. Start your walk early in the morning for a few good reasons. You usually find free parking on the seaward shoulder of Kalakaua; you'll be walking with the sunrise at your back; and it'll be cool.

This is a fairly simple walk. It follows Waikiki Beach through Kapi'olani Park, then alongside Kalakaua Avenue and then onto the beach in front of its famous resorts. Our walk begins near the abandoned but soon-to-be-refurbished **Memorial Natatorium.** From here, follow a walking path just above the beach in Kapi'olani Park, past the ❖ **Waikiki Aquarium**. The path merges with Kalakaua Avenue at the base of Kapahulu, and you may want to skitter across the street to stock up on brochures at the **Aloha Kiosk**. Or skitter to the opposite curb to stock up on caffeine at a Starbucks.

On the beach side of Kalakaua, note the charming bronze monument of a surfer paddling along and chatting with a sea lion. For the next several blocks, your path will be the Kalakaua sidewalk, with ❖ **Kuhio Beach Park** on your left and high rise hotels and assorted shops on the right. At the corner of Ohua Street, note the statue of **Prince Jonah Kuhio Kalanianaole.** He went from royal family member to revolutionary to leading statesman for the new U.S. territorial government after the overthrow of the Hawaiian monarchy. Check out ❖ **St. Augustine's Catholic Church** just inland from Kalakaua at 130 Ohua Avenue, with its imposing green copper A-frame roof lines. The small ❖ **Damien Museum** honoring the Moloka'i leper colony martyr is to the left of the church.

At the western edge of Kuhio Beach, across from the ❖ **Hyatt Regency Waikiki**, note the large bronze statue of ❖ **Duke Kahanamoku**. Just beyond the statue, at the Honolulu Police Waikiki Substation, leave Kalakaua and head for the beach to begin trudging through sand. You'll shortly encounter a narrow concrete walk; follow it to the backside of the grand Beaux Arts style ❖ **Sheraton Moana**. An inviting patio area just off the beach is shaded by a giant banyan tree. Next door is the modern ❖ **Sheraton Surfrider**, and then the ❖ **Outrigger Waikiki**.

From here, take a narrow beach access alley inland between the Outrigger and Sheraton, and cross Kalakaua to the wonderfully tacky ❖ **International Market Place**. Note the hand-carved statues of a very bosomy hula girl and a pot-bellied beach boy on the sidewalk just to the right of the entrance. From the market, cross Kalakaua and explore the ❖ **Royal Hawaiian Shopping Center** and the ❖ **Royal Hawaiian** itself, then return to the sand.

As you continue along the beach, the route shifts up to an elevated concrete walk that passes in front of the ❖ **Sheraton Waikiki**. The concrete ends and you'll shuffle through sand in a narrow section where you may get your feet wet at high tide. It's back to concrete in front the ❖ **Halekulani**, then you're in sand again as you slog past the ❖ **Outrigger Reef** with its beachside ❖ **Shorebird Bar**.

Just beyond the Outrigger, follow a concrete sidewalk between the beach and parklands of ❖ **Fort DeRussy**. The ❖ **Army Museum of Hawaii** in a former coastal bunker just up from the beach is worth a pause. From here, return to the beach and continue to the ❖ **Hilton Hawaiian Village** and its Hilton Lagoon. This marks the end of Waikiki Beach. You may want to finish with a drink or snack at one of the village's outdoor bars or cafés, and explore its extensive grounds.

If you're too weary to walk back, you can summon a cab at the Hilton or follow Kalia Road to Kalakaua Avenue and pick up a city bus. Most that run along here will return you to your starting point. They usually shift from Kalakaua to Kuhio Avenue and follow it back to Kapi'olani Park.

2 ALA WAI CANAL STROLL

Just over two miles one way; completely level. GETTING THERE: Start at the Visitors Information Stand at Kalakaua and Kapahulu.

If you're looking for a level place to jog or stride, a recreational path follows the banks of the Ala Wai Canal. This is best as an early morning walk, since the sun will be behind you. Pick up a designer coffee at Starbucks across from the visitor kiosk, then start your stroll on the east side of Kapahulu, since it has a walking/biking path. Follow it inland alongside ❖ **Kapiʻolani Park** and the ❖ **Honolulu Zoo**. You'll catch occasional glimpses of ❖ **Diamond Head** to your right and the fluted ridges of the Koʻolau Range ahead, with uptilted wedges of homes crawling into some of the shallow valleys.

At the first traffic light, where Ala Wai Boulevard and Paki Avenue converge on Kapahulu, the bike route peels off to the right. You are to peel to the left, crossing Kapahulu onto Ala Wai. You'll follow a park strip briefly and then reach the start of the **Ala Wai Canal** and its walking path. An historical marker points out that this was once the estate of Queen Liliʻuokalani. This walking/jogging path continues alongside the canal for about a mile and a half. It's not an unbusy route, since traffic rumbles immediately to your left. But ignore all that and enjoy your stroll along this landscaped, palm-lined path. You may see folks in small outriggers or kayaks paddling along the canal's calm waters. You'll also see splish-splashes as fish zap careless bugs.

You'll eventually reach McCully, one of the few streets that crosses the Ala Wai Canal. Cross with it, then continue your walk on the inland side of the canal. This takes you through a nicely landscaped park strip. You'll soon reach Kalakaua Avenue where—unfortunately—there's no crosswalk, so either retreat to the nearest intersection or cross with caution. The canal-side path then passes under a canopy of trees beside the **Hawaii Convention Center**; this is the most pleasant part of the walk.

The walkway ends at Ala Moana Boulevard and the **Ala Wai Yacht Harbor**. You can follow Ala Moana and Kalakaua back to your starting point or grab a cab or city bus. As we noted above, most buses along here go to Kapiʻolani Park. You'll have to walk the equivalent of about three city blocks to reach nearest bus stop, which is at Hobron Lane, near the ❖ **Renaissance Ilikai Hotel**.

3 CHINATOWN RAMBLE

About a mile, all level. GETTING THERE: Drive 3.5 miles northwest on Ala Moana Boulevard. A quarter of a mile past Aloha Tower, cross River Street and a canal, then make an immediate right along the canal bank and go left into the Aʻala parking lot. Chinatown is just across the canal and our walk begins here.

Chinatown is best seen afoot since parking is rather scarce within this congested community. This is a typical Asian-American enclave, a slightly scruffy and busy commercial brew of produce, poultry and fish markets, small cafés, herbal shops, accupucturists and more. Most of its sidewalks still have overhangs built many decades ago. The developers of modern Honolulu next door have foolishly not used these shady shelters from the tropic sun.

Incidentally, Chinatown isn't just Chinese. The community is an Asian ethnic mix with several Vietnamese, Thai, Korean, Japanese and Filipino shops, markets and cafés.

Once you've parked, walk up to King Street, turn right, cross back over the canal and into the busy heart of Chinatown. Worth a browse are the **Downtown Market** and **Oahu Market**, both with several shops under one roof and both on your right. After a block, turn left onto Kekauliki Street, which becomes a pedestrian mall lined with more markets and shops. Another multi-tenant complex, **Kekauliki Market**, is on your right.

Cross Hotel Street and you'll enter ❖ **Maunakea Marketplace**, built around a courtyard. Your walk through the market will take you into its busy food court, a good place for an inexpensive lunch. Continue through the market and exit onto Pauahi Street. Turn left and walk half a block to River Street, then go right to follow a canal-side walk lined with brilliant bougainvillea. Cross Beretania Street and continue along the canal on a pedestrian mall that borders the **Chinatown Cultural Plaza**, fronted by a bronze statue of Dr. Sun-Yat Sen. Take a right turn into the mall to check out more shops and restaurants, including ❖ **Legends Seafood Restaurant**, which we reviewed in the dining chapter. The cultural plaza is rather austere. It could use a bit of sprucing up and a brighter paint job. Think of it as Asian sterile.

Exit the cultural plaza on Beretania, cross to Maunakea street and walk back into the heart of Chinatown. Maunakea is the ❖ "**street of leis**"; more than half a dozen lei stands provide the floral garlands used at many Waikiki resorts and island luaus. Pause to watch the ladies threading delicate orchids and other flower blossoms into strands, and buy a lei for your lady; they're much cheaper here than elsewhere.

Check on your right for **Hawaiian Hula Bread Bakery** at 974 Maunakea, between Puhuahi and Hotel streets. It sells sweetish white "Hula Bread" and other bread specialties; buy some for a walking lunch. If you've worked up more of an appetite, you might try the second-floor **Wo Fat Seafood Restaurant** on your right at 115 N. Hotel St.; (808) 521-5055. It's Hawai'i's oldest restaurant, opened in 1882—and we suspect that's the last time the stairway carpet was changed. However, it's neat and clean inside and the food is okay.

For a walking dessert, a block beyond is our favorite Chinatown goodie takeout, **Shung Chong Yuein Chinese Cake Shop**. It's at 1027 Maunakea, between Hotel and King streets, on the left. This bakery issues traditional moon cakes, melon cakes and other Chinese pastries, plus candied ginger, pineapple rings, taro root and even candied carrots and squash. Next door is ❖ **Glowing Dragon Café**. When you reach King Street, hang a right, cross the canal and you're back at your starting place.

4 DIAMOND HEAD HIKE

About 1.5 miles round trip. Steep hike on a well-marked hard surface trail, with some switchbacks and lots of steps; all of it is railed. Diamond

Head State Monument is open from 6 a.m. to 6 p.m., with a modest admission fee; (808) 587-0285. GETTING THERE: Follow Kalakaua Avenue southeast through Waikiki then, in Kapi'olani Park, fork left onto Monsarrat Avenue, which becomes Diamond Head Road. Follow it about a mile and the turnoff into Diamond Head State Monument is just beyond Kapi'olani Community College.

This is a popular, tough and mercifully short hike up the "Gibraltar of the Pacific," one of world's most famous promontories. A lookout atop an old artillery bunker at the upper crest of Diamond Head crater offers Waikiki's most sweeping view.

The trail is hacked out of lava rock, rising steeply through a brushy, thin *kiawe* forest. On the upper end, you must climb a calf muscle-straining 280 steps and then pass through a dark tunnel and an even darker iron spiral staircase. You'll emerge into one of the bunkers, duck out under a low ceiling and finally climb to a surprisingly small viewing area. On a weekend, it can get quite crowded up here.

Graphics tell you what you're seeing, and you learn that this is a tuff cone whose real name is *Le'ahi*. It was created by a single eruption about 300,000 years ago. (However, another sign says 150,000 years ago.) This fortification, called Fire Control Station Diamond Head, was completed in 1910. Think of the commute those coast watchers had, getting to work every day!

TRAVEL TIP: Take plenty of drinking water, since the hike is very steep, with an altitude gain of 560 feet in less than a mile. And take a flashlight for the dark tunnels and spiral staircase. Start your hike early in the day, both because it's cooler and to avoid periodic afternoon showers. Also, don't try this hike on weekends when Diamond Head is swarmed with locals as well as visitors.

5 DIAMOND HEAD ROAD STROLL

A one mile round trip, mostly level, plus a short downhill walk to Kuilei Cliffs Beach and back. GETTING THERE: Follow Kalakaua Avenue east through Kapi'olani Park. After a mile or so, you'll hit a stop sign where the route changes its name to Diamond Head Road. Continue another half mile past beachside homes until you reach an open area where houses no longer block the view, then find a place to park.

This stroll alongside Diamond Head Road follows an asphalt path on a coastal bluff. Walk east from the parking area, enjoying vistas down through brambly *kiawe* and gnarled banyan trees to sandy beaches rimmed with lava. **Diamond Head** is just across the road, although from this angle, it looks more like a rough, brushy cliff face than a volcanic cone. You'll shortly pass **Diamond Head Light**, built in 1917 and still lighting the way for approaching ships. It's now automated and not open to the public. A bit beyond, you'll enter **Diamond Head Lookout Recreational Park**. The scenery doesn't change; only the designation. After passing a parking turnout, you'll see an asphalt path tilting down to **Kuilei Cliffs Beach**. A favorite of surfers, it's missed by most tourists, so it's relatively uncrowded. Once down there, you can walk for some distance along the shore, going to the right over lava tidepools or to the left over smooth sand. If the surf's not too rough and you decide to take a dip, there's a shower here for rinsing off the salt.

Back up on top, you'll pass a landscaped park strip with shady trees and inviting patches of grass. Just beyond is another parking turnout with a monument marking Amelia Earhart's flight between North America and Hawai'i on January 11, 1935. (It doesn't mention that she crash-landed.) And just beyond that is another parking area, where you can start back, since more cliffside homes block the view beyond this point.

6 MANOA CLIFFS HIKE

A 3.5-mile round trip; moderate with some steep upgrades. The trailhead is off Round Top Drive above Honolulu. GETTING THERE: Go north on McCully Street from Waikiki, then northwest on Beretania about half a mile to Punahou Street and turn right. Cross H-1 and, after less than half a mile, go left on Nehoa Street for two blocks. Turn right (uphill) on Makiki Street and fork right for Round Top Drive. Shortly after passing the Pu'u Ualaka'a State Park entrance, watch for a Manoa Cliffs Trail sign; it's just beyond a five-mile marker. Parking is on the left and the trail begins across the road.

Although Honolulu is noted for its dry climate, the flanks of the Ko'olau Range just above the city are cloaked in thick forest. A large swatch of this greenery has been set aside as the Honolulu Watershed Forest Reserve and it's criss-crossed by hiking trails. Two roads, ❖ Round Top and Tantalus, loop through this area, providing one of Honolulu's most popular scenic drives. (It's actually one road with a name change.) Our favorite hike in this area, the Manoa Cliffs Trail, rambles through the rainforest and loops around the two portions of the road.

Starting from the roadside parking area, you'll immediately begin a rather steep climb up gravel-filled steps, diked with boards to prevent erosion. After a series of switchbacks, the trail levels out and winds along a cliff face, offering splendid views of the forested valleys below and the Ko'olau Range above. Just after you cross a small gully, you'll see a bench; it's a nice place to pause and enjoy some of the yellow strawberry guavas growing wild along the trail. The route continues winding along the crest, offering more fine views—including a glimpse over a ridge to the windward side of the island.

You're essentially winding over—and high above—the point where Round Top and Tantalus roads merge. Your path also merges—joining the Pu'u Ohia Trail and then separating from it. Keep to the left to stay with the Manoa Cliffs Trail. It starts winding downhill from here—with views of west Honolulu and the harbor and airport. You'll encounter a few unauthorized "goat trails" as you descend; keep alert to stay with the main route. You'll know you're on course when you encounter a couple of benches, where you can pause and enjoy the view. The trail emerges onto Tantalus Drive at a huge banyan tree, near a Hawaiian Telephone facility. From here, you can retrace your route or take the shorter road back to your car.

7 MANOA FALLS HIKE

About two miles round trip; moderate to moderately steep. The trailhead is in the hills above Honolulu. GETTING THERE: From Waikiki, go north on McCully, then northwest on Beretania less than half a mile to Punahou Street and turn right. Punahou crosses H-1 and blends onto Manoa Road. Follow it about three miles, just beyond Paradise Park. You'll see the trailhead parking area just before the road goes left up to Lyon Arboretum.

Although it's in a rainforest, this isn't a wilderness trail. It's one of the most popular hikes on O'ahu, so don't expect to be alone in the jungle, George. The trail is gentle at first and then it tilts upward, leading to a sixty-foot waterfall that spills into an inviting pool. Manoa Falls Trail is well maintained and relatively easy to hike, but wear serious hiking shoes since it's usually muddy. This is a pleasant hike, shaded most of the way by a canopy of vines and creeper-clad trees as it follows the babbling, rocky course of Manoa Creek.

TRAVEL TIP: The trailhead parking lot is a high theft area and vehicle break-ins are common. Don't leave anything of value in your car.

Walks & hikes outside Honolulu/Waikiki

8 KAILUA BEACH & BAY

A two-mile round trip; all level except for a brief scramble up a slope. GETTING THERE: Follow Likelike Highway (Route 61) from Honolulu to the community of Kailua on O'ahu's northeastern shore. Drive through the business district and turn right onto Kalaheo Road. The beach park is about two-thirds of a mile away.

This is one of the few beaches in Hawai'i with hardpacked sand, so it's ideal for strolling. Kailua Beach Park on Kailua Bay comes in two sections separated by a lagoon and linked by a paved path. From the main parking area, follow the path to your left. It bridges the lagoon and takes you to the beach park's smaller section, called Kalala. This is a popular area for windsurfers and kiteboarders. Kiteboarding is a new sport in which participants stand on chubby surfboards and are pulled along by large kites that resemble half-parachutes.

After watching them at play, follow the shoreline along Kailua Bay. Walk back to the main beach and continue for about half a mile along this hard-packed sand. Toward the upper end, the beach becomes a mix of sand and lava ridges. You'll soon hit a lava outcropping where homes in a neighborhood called Lanakai stand on a bluff above. A stone wall supporting them discourages further beach walking. To make this a round trip, scramble over some low lava ridges and then up a grassy slope up to Mokulua Drive

You can turn this walk into a four-mile round trip by continuing along Mokulua to its end, passing those beachside homes. However, you won't see much because they hog the view. Otherwise, head back toward the Kailua Beach Park on Mokulua Drive, which provides slightly elevated views of the coastline.

9 WAIMEA-PUPUKEA BEACH LINK

Mostly level; about two miles round trip. GETTING THERE: The two beach parks are in the town of Waimea on O'ahu's North Shore, near Waimea Falls Park. From Honolulu, go northwest on H-1 and then north on H-2 and Kamehameha Highway (Route 93).

If you intend to visit ❖ Waimea Falls, you'll find this stroll to be a pleasant diversion. Waimea Beach Park, across the road from the Waimea Falls Park entrance, is bordered on the highway side by a concrete walking path. Walk east and you'll link up with small ❖ Pupukea Beach Park in the village of Waimea. This park is interesting for a low lava ridge just offshore; huge waves slam into it, sending great sprays of foamy water high into the sky.

To do this short walk, plant your car at Waimea Beach, then follow the path eastward out of the parking lot. After leaving the park, the path becomes a pedestrian bridge, crossing a small gully created by Waimea lagoon and creek. Your route then follows the shoulder of the highway, toward the town of Waimea. As you reach Pupukea Beach Park, you'll pick up another paved path leading into that facility. If you feel the need for fuel, a Foodland market and a Starbucks are just across the highway. From here, retrace your route back to Waimea Beach Park.

10 KA'ENA POINT HIKE

About six miles round trip, starting from Ka'ena Point State Park. GETTING THERE: Follow H-1 west from Honolulu until it blends onto Route 93 expressway (Farrington Highway) just beyond Barbers Point. Then simply stay with the highway to its end. The park is about forty miles from Honolulu.

No paved roads reach Ka'ena Point, O'ahu's westernmost tip. However, you can reach it by hiking along one of two rough jeep trails. One leads from the Windward Coast west of Hale'iwa; the other from the Leeward Coast north of Wai'anae. We prefer the latter because it's more scenic, the hike is a bit shorter and it's easier to reach from Waikiki.

The hike begins at the end of the pavement in Ka'ena Point State Park. The vistas are splendid here—gray-green terraced bluffs above, and a wildly rugged lava coast just below. This unruly shoreline is busy with lava ridges, tidepool terraces, cobblestone beaches, coarsely scalloped coves and offshore seastacks. The trail stays above the shore for the most part, although you can carefully scramble down to the beach to explore tidepools. Do so with great caution and watch for incoming breakers.

Just short of Ka'ena Point, the road forks to the right and a sandy path leads left toward **Ka'ena Point Lighthouse**. Follow this neat, pebble-lined trail through sand dunes toward an overlook. This is a wild and beautiful area, where swells converge at O'ahu's jagged western tip. Huge albatrosses and other seabirds swirl overhead; many nest in the sand dunes among vines and shrubs with purple, white and pale blue blooms. This is a nature preserve, so nothing should be disturbed.

I got the notion that Hawaii was one, long sweet song.
— James Drummund Dole, on arriving on O'ahu in 1899

Chapter Ten

ODD ENDS
ASSORTED BITS & PIECES

Hawai'i offers a bounty of attractions, activities, experiences, flavors, sights and sounds. This chapter gathers up loose ends and places them in lists that don't fit into other lists.

THE BEST PLACES TO SIT & DO NOTHING

What we really mean is the Ten Best places to watch the rest of the world go by. We have turned the relaxing pastime of people-watching into a fine art, and Hawai'i is one of the best places in the world to practice it. It offers so many tempting places to loaf—beaches, beachside bars, plush resort hotel lobbies, palm-shaded parks, open-air shopping centers. And where but in Hawai'i can you see a bikini-clad girl with a surfboard, walking past an Yves Saint Laurent store?

Other than hanging out on our favorite Waikiki avenue, these are listed in no particular order.

1 ALONG KALAKAUA AVENUE

From Lewers Street to Kapahulu Avenue.

This busy thoroughfare opposite Waikiki Beach is the best people-watching place in all of the islands. You can lounge at a bench or table in Kuhio Beach Park opposite the surf, or adjourn to the other side of Kalakaua, where happy tourists stroll in and out of highrise hotels.

Kalakaua Avenue is particularly great for people watching at night. Tiki torches blaze along the street and the adjacent beach is lighted, casting warm glows on the white foam of incoming breakers. The sounds of music issue from hotel lobbies and bars, mixing with the laughter of nighttime revelers on the sidewalk. In front of the International Market Place, "living statues" in metallic grease paint stand stock still on their pedestals or they move in wind-up toy fashion, mutely soliciting tips. You might encounter an impromptu hula dancer writhing to the measure of a guitar and bongo drums, a Chinese lady playing a harmonica and singing Chinese songs badly, or a native Hawaiian playing bagpipes. Kalakaua Avenue at night—particularly a Friday or Saturday night—can be quite a carnival.

2 IN THE SAND, MAN!

Anywhere along Waikiki Beach.

If you like your beaches uncrowded and remote, head for Oʻahu's North Shore or one of the outer islands. However, for a great people-watching beach, Waikiki is the place to be. Although we enjoy playing in the surf as well as the next, what prefer doing most on Waikiki is nothing—except watching other people doing something.

The sights never end; never stop changing—children squealing in pretend fright at gentle incoming breakers, surfers catching waves farther out, tourists riding outriggers and catamarans, overdressed Japanese visitors rolling up their trouser legs and giggling as they splash in the surf. You're likely to see a wedding couple in stark formal contrast to the sunbathers, posing for photos. Most activity stops at sunset as nearly everyone squints toward the west, hoping to catch that brief blue-green flash when ole Sol heads for the other side of the earth.

3 TAPA BAR

Hilton Hawaiian Village, 2005 Kalia Rd., Waikiki. GETTING THERE: The Hilton is on the corner of Ala Moana Boulevard and Kalia. Turn right onto Kalia Road and then right again into the village.

This large outdoor bar is in the heart of the extensive Hilton complex, near the base of the Aliʻl Tower. It's a crossroad in this 22-acre complex, beside a swimming pool and between the Aliʻi Tower and main hotel lobby. Settle down with a mai tai and watch the tourist tide ebb and flow. Listen to happy splashes from the pool, piped-in Hawaiian music and the distant murmur of the surf.

4 HYATT REGENCY SHOPS

2424 Kalakaua Avenue. In Waikiki, between Ka'iulani and Uluniu avenues.

Waterfalls cascade from two balconies into a landscaped lagoon at the Hyatt Regency shops. Several chairs and tables here invite lingering. It's a pleasant place to watch people pass, while listening to the pleasant sounds of falling water. A small bar is nearby, should you to prefer people-watching with drink in hand.

5 MOANA HOTEL FRONT PORCH

Sheraton Moana, 2365 Kalakaua Avenue. In Waikiki, across from Ka'iulani Avenue.

The inviting "front porch" of the historic Moana Hotel is a fine place to sit and do nothing. Settle into one of the old fashioned white rocking chairs and watch the pedestrians—and traffic—of Kalakaua Avenue. Pick up a cup of designer caffeine from the hotel's coffee bar and the morning newspaper. Then lean back and relax, enjoying this decidedly upscale version of loafing on the front porch.

6 ALA MOANA SHOPPING CENTER

1450 Ala Moana Boulevard. GETTING THERE: Follow Ala Moana northwest from Waikiki; the shopping center starts at the corner of Atkinson Drive.

There are plenty of people-watching places in Hawai'i's largest shopping center and of course, there are always plenty of people. Our favorite place to pause from shopping is on the third level between Emporio Armani and Tommy Bahama's, opposite Neiman Marcus. There's a specialty coffee takeout here, and several tables and chairs along a railing. You'll be right above Ala Moana Centerstage, where you might see live entertainment simply by leaning over and looking down. To reach this spot, enter the shopping center through its food court from the Ala Moana Boulevard side, then continue into the main mall, going up two escalators until you reach the third level.

7 INTERNATIONAL MARKET PLACE

2330 Kalakaua Avenue. Between Duke's Lane and Ka'iulani Avenue.

Just inside the Kalakaua entrance to the market place, you'll find a single stone bench at the base of a banyan tree. It's beside a decorative waterfall and koi pond. Sit and watch tourists such as yourself browse through the trinket shops. (They never seem to buy anything. Will you?) There's only one bench here, so you'll have to take turns. If it's occupied, you can perch on one of the decorative lava boulders rimming the koi pond.

8 HALEKULANI HOTEL LOBBY

2199 Kalia Road in Waikiki. GETTING THERE: Take Lewers Street off Kalakaua, follow it to the end and go briefly left.

The gorgeous Halekulani lobby, with its bold squared pillars, glossy marble floors and crystal chandeliers, is a fine place to watch the beautiful people pass. Settle into a deeply cushioned wicker chair by a gurgling fountain just inside the main entrance, and pretend you can afford to stay here.

9 MAI TAI BAR

Royal Hawaiian Hotel, 2259 Kalakaua Avenue. GETTING THERE: Head toward the beach on Royal Hawaiian Avenue from Kalakaua.

Any area along Waikiki Beach is a great people-watching place, particularly for you guys who like to watch young female people in bikinis. If you prefer bikini-watching while sitting upright, step from the sand onto the terrace of the Mai Tai Bar, which opens at 10 a.m. It offers the best Waikiki vistas of any bar on the beach. You can enjoy grand views of the great curving sweep of surf, sea and Diamond Head from here—when you can take your eyes off the curves on the beach. The bar of course offers assorted tropical drinks and some tasty light fare. If you aren't thirsty or hungry, or you're just too cheap to buy something, you can sit in the sand, leaning back against a low pink wall that separates the bar from the beach.

10 THE WAIKIKI TROLLEY

Stops throughout Waikiki Beach and Honolulu; (808) 593-2822; www.waikikitrolley.com. Trolleys operate daily from 8:30 a.m. to 11 p.m.

How about sitting and people-watch while going somewhere? The Waikiki trolleys—old streetcars mounted on truck chassis—travel throughout Waikiki, Honolulu and beyond, taking visitors to various attractions and shopping areas. It's not a practical transit system like TheBus, since the trolleys follow rather convoluted routes. They take their time getting from here to there and back to here again. However, if you don't mind a rather bumpy ride—since these are trucks in disguise—they pass the most interesting sites of Waikiki and the rest of Honolulu. And, like San Francisco's cable cars, they're open to the breeze, so they're fine people-watching platforms.

THE TEN BEST VISTA POINTS & PHOTO ANGLES

The beaches, mountains and volcanic crests around Waikiki and Honolulu provide impressive vista points and photo spots. We offer separate lists of five each, starting with our favorites.

The five best vista points

1 BEST OVERALL VIEW: Diamond Head

Diamond Head State Monument. Park open 6 a.m. to 6 p.m.; token entry fee. GETTING THERE: From Waikiki, go southeast on Kalakaua to Kapi'olani Park, then fork left onto Monsarrat Avenue, which becomes Diamond Head Road. Follow it about a mile and a half, and the turnoff into to the Diamond Head parking area is just beyond Kapi'olani Community College.

From the view platform on the highest point of Diamond Head crater, you'll get the full sweep of O'ahu's northwestern shore. The vista extends from Waikiki to downtown Honolulu at the base of the Ko'olau Range, to Pearl Harbor and the low ridge of Barbers Point in the distance. Of course, you must climb a steep trail to get there. See details in Chapter Nine, page 140.

2 THE BEST VIEW OF DIAMOND HEAD: Kapi'olani Park

Various places on the inland area of the park. GETTING THERE: Kapi'olani Park is on the east end of Waikiki, starting at the corner of Kalakaua and Kapahulu avenues.

If you walk inland from Kalakaua Avenue, away from the beach and into the heart of Kapi'olani Park, you'll see fine views of Diamond Head with nothing in the foreground to interfere—no buildings, cars or utility poles. This vantage point also makes a nice photo; it's best as a late afternoon horizontal. You can dress it up by framing it in foreground foliage.

3 THE BEST PLACE TO WATCH SURFERS PLAY: Turtle Bay Resort

57-091 Kamehameha Hwy., Kahuku. GETTING THERE: The resort is on O'ahu's North Shore, about forty miles from Honolulu. Take H-1 west, then H-2 north. Blend onto Kamehameha Highway at the end of the freeway and follow it north along the coast for about twelve miles.

This large resort occupies a peninsula reaching northward into the wild breakers of the North Coast. Settle in the grass or onto a chair at a lawn area between the resort's swimming pool and the beach, and watch the surfers ride the really big ones. If you're here in November or December, you may see a surfing competition, with some of the world's top boarders riding those legendary North Shore pipelines.

4 BEST VIEW OF WINDWARD O'AHU: Pali lookout

Nu'uanu Pali State Wayside, above Honolulu. Park open daily 4 a.m. to 8 p.m.; free. GETTING THERE: The Wayside is about five miles up the Pali Highway (Route 61) from H-1.

From this windy viewpoint—hold onto your hat and any small children—the vista is a dramatic panorama of the wet side of O'ahu and Kane'ohe Bay. Fluted green-clad cliffs of the Ko'olau Range in the foreground add more drama to this splendid vista. Mark Twain once called this the most beautiful view in the world.

5 BEST PLACE TO WATCH THE SUNSET: Kawela Beach

It's just west of Turtle Bay Resort, off Kamehameha Highway on the North Shore. GETTING THERE: Follow directions toward Turtle Bay Resort (above), but don't go all the way. The beach is just beyond the hamlet of Kawela. No sign marks it, so if you reach Turtle Bay, you've missed it by 1.5 miles. If you're coming from the other direction, it'll be the first beach you see after passing the resort.

This pretty little beach shaded by lacy casuarina trees is a fine place to watch day's end. It's a cozy crescent of sand, accented by lava outcroppings, with a tiny island just offshore. At certain times of the year, the sun dips behind that minuscule isle; at other times it sets on sea. Don't forget to watch for the blue-green flash. For more on Kawela Beach, see Chapter Seven, page 126.

Shooting Hawai'i

Since photographs are two-dimensional, good photographers apply several techniques to give them depth. You can suggest dimension in a scenic view by framing it with an overhanging palm frond or other object in the foreground, and perhaps something in the middleground. On the other hand, if you're focusing on a single subject, don't clutter your photo with framing; let the viewer see nothing but that object.

Most outdoor photos are predominately blue, green and brown, the colors of the sky and the earth. With Hawai'i's abundance of water and vegetation, you'll get plenty of blue and green in your photos. To brighten them, add colors from the warm side of the spectrum—reds, yellows and oranges. Dress Auntie Maude in a bright yellow dress or place a brilliant flower in the foreground of your photo, off to the side where it won't interfere with the main subject.

When you photograph people, don't force them to squint into the sun. Position them with the sun behind you but to the right or left so it strikes them at an angle, accenting their features. Also, have your subjects interact with the setting instead of just staring morosely at the camera or—worse—wearing a silly grin.

Light and shadow are key elements in photography, giving two-dimensional photos more a feeling of shape and contour. Early morning and late afternoon are the best times to shoot, when shadows are stronger. This is particularly true for structural photos and skylines. At midday when the sun is shining straight down, objects appear flat, washed out and uninteresting. Further, in the late afternoon, the atmosphere attains a golden quality, giving warm tones to your pictures.

If clouds are drifting about the horizon—and they almost always are in these islands—watch for the likelihood of a spectacular Hawaiian sunset. And to make it even more spectacular, place something in the foreground, such as a palm tree or tiki torch. You'll like the effect.

The five best photo stops

You can get good results at these picture spots with an adjustable camera (we're partial to Canons), a simple point and shoot or even a disposable camera. If you have an adjustable camera, a 28mm to 80mm zoom lens will greatly improve your photo opportunities.

If you use a digital camera, you already know that you can cheat, manipulating the results with your computer. You can even eliminate Auntie Maude's red-eye or remove an offending garbage can from your favorite beach shot.

6 BEST SHOT OF DIAMOND HEAD: from Duke's at the Outrigger Waikiki

2335 Kalakaua Avenue. GETTING THERE: The hotel is on the beach between the Sheraton Moana and the Royal Hawaiian.

This is a great angle for photographing Diamond Head, with a curving slice of Waikiki Beach and several resort hotels in the foreground and middleground. It's best as a horizontal and you may want to use a medium range telephoto for a tighter shot. With a bit of maneuvering, you can get a palm tree or perhaps a colored outrigger canoe and maybe a beach bunny in the foreground. Take your photo in the late afternoon to capture those long shadows.

For a really cool early evening shot, step onto the Outrigger's flagstone beach patio and try to position burning tiki torches in the foreground. They're usually lit just before sundown.

7 BEST OVERALL SHOT OF WAIKIKI & HONOLULU: from Diamond Head

See "Best overall view" above.

This is a pretty obvious photo and nearly everyone takes it. Honolulu's best viewpoint also is its best photo stop. Often, high-angle shots tend to flatten the scenery, but not in this case, since it's only 760 feet above the surf line, providing a relatively low trajectory. There are three levels to the observation deck, so you can easily get Auntie Maude in the foreground. Put her off to one side, with the whole sweep of western O'ahu below and behind her. It's best as an early morning shot, since you're shooting northwest; you'll want to avoid the washed-out look of high noon or the incoming glare of the afternoon sun.

8 BEST SHOT OF HONOLULU'S WATERFRONT & SKYLINE: piers 16 or 17

From Waikiki, follow Ala Moana Boulevard about four miles northwest until it blends into the Nimitz Highway. The piers are immediately beyond River Street, opposite Flora-Dec Craft Floral & Party Supplies.

A couple of wharfs reaching into the harbor provide nice vantage points for a layered shot of the Honolulu waterfront. You can get the highrises of downtown in the background, Aloha Tower in the middleground and perhaps a boat or two in the foreground. If a cruise ship is in port, you can photograph the tower peeking over its superstructure. This is a horizontal photo, using a medium to moderately wide angle lens. It's best taken in late afternoon when the sun's over your shoulders.

A sign on the piers warns: "No persons or private vehicles allowed on state piers unless authorized by the harbormaster," although no one bothered us. The worst some anxious piermaster would do, we suppose, is ask you to leave. This isn't a military base, f'gawdsake!

9 BEST SHOT OF THE PINK PALACE: from Kuhio Beach

Waikiki's Kuhio Beach Park breakwater, across Kalakaua from the base of Ulunui Avenue.

Waikiki's Royal Hawaiian Hotel, the legendary "Pink Palace," stands in the shadow of surrounding highrises, so it's difficult to isolate it for a photo. The best angle is from the north breakwater at Waikiki Beach, with a medium range telephoto. You'll get the Palace crouching below lofty hotel towers, with a broad sweep of the beach in the foreground, perhaps with some brightly-painted outriggers.

10 BEST COASTAL PHOTO: just east of Hanauma Bay

Off Highway 71. GETTING THERE: From the end of H-1, follow Highway 71 east about six miles, then park at a roadside turnout just beyond the entrance to Hanauma Bay Underwater Park Preserve. For the best view down the coast, walk along the shoulder of the road for several hundred feet, back toward Hanauma Bay.

This is the O'ahu shoreline's best picture stop—a gorgeous view eastward along the beach. It takes in a series of crescent bays on a black lava coastline, with the surf slamming into low cliffs, sending spray high into the sky. The twisting curves of Highway 71 add a nice element to the photo. On windy days, rooster tails skitter up from the crests of waves; salt particles suspended in the air may give the coast a misty, ethereal look. This can be either a vertical or horizontal. Experiment with different angles with your zoom lens. It's best as an early morning shot, when sun's slanting rays accentuate the incoming surf and the lava shapes.

THE TEN BEST SPECIALTY GUIDES

Now that you've purchased this guidebook—assuming you're not still standing in the book store taking a free read—we can recommend several specialty guides to Hawai'i. These are generally available only at bookstores in the islands. We've listed addresses of the publishers, so you can order copies in advance of your trip. However, check on shipping costs and possible price changes first. They also may be available on the web at *www.amazon.com, www.bn.com* or *www.borders.com*. Since we have no favorite guides other than our own, these are listed alphabetically.

1 ADVENTURERS HAWAII

By Peter Caldwell, Taote Publishing, P.O. Box 22660, Honolulu, HI 96823; $15.95.

Busy with color photos, this book offers details on where to hike, bike, dive, snorkel, swim and otherwise explore the physical side of Hawai'i. The author calls it "an invitation to see the Hawaiian Islands beyond the world of the tourist brochure."

2 BEST PLACES TO STAY: HAWAII

By Kim Grant, Houghton-Mifflin Co., 215 Park Ave., New York, NY 10003; 420 pages; $19.

This is a comprehensive guide to lodgings on the major islands, and it has specialty lists of romantic hideaways, intimate and affordable inns, best bargains, best snorkeling and diving, best restaurants worth a detour and more.

3 BEST PLACES TO KISS IN HAWAII

By Linnea Lundgren, Beginning Press, 13075 Gateway Dr., Suite 300, Tukwila, WA 98168; 212 pages; $14.95.

It's "A Romantic Travel Guide" to the most intimate inns, hotels, restaurants, parks and scenic drives, covering the major islands.

4 A HAWAIIAN READER

Volumes I and II, edited by A. Grove Day and Carl Stroven, Mutual Publishing, 1215 Center St., Suite 210, Honolulu, HI 96816; www.mutualpublishing.com; 340 and 360 pages; $6.95 each.

These are anthologies of writings by famous authors about Hawai'i's history, culture and beauty. Among authors included are Mark Twain, Robert Louis Stevenson, Jack London and James A. Michener.

5 HAWAI'I'S BEST BEACHES

By John R.K. Clark, University of Hawaii Press, Honolulu, HI 96822-1888; www.hawaii.edu/uhpress/; 148 pages; $19.95.

Scenic color photos decorate this guide to more than fifty beaches on Hawai'i's main islands. Listings include driving instructions, descriptions and specifics on beach facilities.

6 HAWAII'S BEST HIKING TRAILS

By Robert Smith, Hawaiian Outdoor Adventures Publications, 102-16 Kaui Place, Kula, HI 96790; www.maui.net; 310 pages; $15.95.

This detailed guide to thirty-eight hiking trails on the main islands has trail descriptions, maps, and black and white photos, plus listings of camping areas and cabins.

7 HAWAII OFF THE BEATEN PATH

By Sean Pager, Globe Pequot Press, Guilford, CT 06437; www.globe-pequot.com; 310 pages; $13.95.

While not really taking readers off the beaten path, this guidebook features detailed driving routes throughout the main islands. It features interesting attractions, historic bits, trivia and places to dine.

8 THE "REVEALED" SERIES

Andrew Doughty and Harriet Friedman, Wizard Publications, Inc., P.O. Box 991, Lihu'e, HI 96766-0991; www.wizardpub.com.; various page lengths; $14.95.

These books about Maui, the Big Island and Kaua'i are the most comprehensive island guidebooks available, covering sights, activities, lodgings, shopping and history. They're busy with color photos and maps.

9 ROADSIDE GEOLOGY OF HAWAI'I

By Richard W. Hazlett and Donald W. Hyndman, Mountain Press Publishing Co., P.O. Box 2399, Missoula, MT 59806; 304 pages; $20.

The forces that shaped Hawai'i's islands are the focus of this scholarly guide. It points out interesting features along roads and highways of the main islands, while providing an overall view of the state's volcanic geology.

10 SHOAL OF TIME

By Gavan Daws, University of Hawaii Press, Honolulu, HI 96822-1888; www.hawaii.edu/uhpress/; 494 pages; $13.95.

Author Daws presents a scholarly yet highly readable history of Hawai'i, from the arrival of Captain James Cook to the present. He deals briefly with the islands' formation and their discovery by the early Polynesians, although the main focus of his book is Hawai'i's recorded human history.

THE TEN BEST RADIO STATIONS

What turns you on when you turn the radio on? Mellow sounds, rock, jazz, news and talk or Hawaiian music as soft as an offshore breeze? Our favorite O'ahu station, in fact, is called "The Breeze."

1 KHUI—FM 99.5

"The Breeze" plays a soft mix of Hawaiian and mainland music; it's a good easy listening station.

2 KSSK—FM 92.3

"Adult contemporary" best describes this station's mix of popular and light rock.

3 KQMQ—FM 93.1 & AM 690

The "Q" plays past and present rock and pops.

4 KZUH—FM 90.3

This station plays jazz and alternative sounds.

5 KXME—FM 104.3

Its format is contemporary pops and light rock.

6 KHPR—FM 88.1

Hawai'i's public radio station offers classic music, a little jazz and the usual PBS news and features

7 KCCN—FM 100 & AM 1420

Hawai'i calling? This station plays traditional and contemporary Hawaiian music.

8 KHCM—AM 940

Of course Hawai'i has cowboys, called *paniolos,* and this station plays country music.

9 KHVH— AM 990

It's O'ahu's most popular news and talk station, with traffic, sports and weather.

10 KKEA—AM 1420

For sports of all sorts, this is O'ahu's ESPN station.

The island of Oahu...looms up in the distance, displaying gray and red rocky hills, unrelieved by a single shade of green, forbidding enough in aspect.
— **Laura Fish Judd, Leaves from a Missionary's Diary, 1828**

Chapter Eleven

O'AHU
THE BEST OF THE REST OF THE ISLAND

O'ahu is considerably more appealing today than it was in 1828 when missionary doctor Laura Fish Judd first sighted it from the deck of a ship. As the most populous and most visited of all the islands, it certainly is no longer "forbidding in aspect." She had seen the southeast coast, which was rather dry and barren, although it's now part of Honolulu's growing eastern suburbs. She continued in her diary:

Now we pass the old crater, Diamond Head, and we can see a line of coconut trees stretching gracefully along the sea beach for a mile or more. There! I see the town of Honolulu, a mass of brown huts, looking precisely like so many haystacks in the country.

Ms. Judd ought to see Honolulu and O'ahu now!

This island is called "The Gathering Place," and we have gathered in this chapter a quick overview of paradise beyond Honolulu and Waikiki, with a pair of driving trips. We then present a list of the island's best beaches.

TO LEARN MORE: Contact the O'ahu Visitors Bureau, 735 Bishop St., Suite 35, Honolulu, HI 96813; (877) 525-OAHU or (808) 524-0772; *www.visit-oahu.com.*

DRIVING O'AHU

You can discover much of what's interesting about O'ahu beyond Honolulu and Waikiki by taking two easy-to-follow driving trips around the island's windward and leeward coasts. Both routes end at different sections of Ka'ena Point State Park. At each terminus, jeep trails lead to Ka'ena Point itself, which is O'hu's westernmost tip.

NOTE: Listing in **Bold face** marked with ❖ are described in more detail elsewhere in this book; check the index for page numbers.

THE WINDWARD COAST

Begin your coastal trek by taking Kalakaua Avenue east from Waikiki. You'll pass through ❖ **Kapi'olani Park**, with the ❖ **Honolulu Zoo** on your left and ❖ **Waikiki Aquarium** on your right. The route, which changes its name to Diamond Head Road, then skirts the lower flanks of ❖ **Diamond Head**, passing through an area of opulent beachfront homes, with occasional glimpses of the ocean. This region is ❖ **Diamond Head Lookout Recreational Park** on the edge of Maunalua Bay. Several turnouts offer a chance to pause and enjoy views of O'ahu's scenic coastline.

About five miles from Waikiki, you'll hit a stop sign with a sign indicating Highway 72 to the left; it's the main road around the island. First, however, continue straight ahead through a "Dead End" sign. You'll pass the **Wai'alae Country Club**, some luxury condos and at the road's end, you'll reach the opulent ❖ **Mandarin Oriental.**

Exit this place of envy and drive about a mile inland to route 72, the Kalaniana'ole Highway. Watch on your right for a postage stamp size bit of green called **Wailupe Beach Park**, with nice views of Maunalua Bay, a few picnic tables and a rocky beach.

As you skirt Maunalua Bay, notice the elegant homes perched on steep slopes above. To reach this attractive neighborhood and enjoy views back down to the coast, go left onto Hawai'i'kai Drive. It's about three miles beyond Wailupe Park, opposite **Paiko Lagoon Wildlife Sanctuary** and **Kuliu'u Beach Park**. Follow it inland through an area of rather modest homes built around **Kapua Pond**, once royal a fish pond. Loop around for more than a mile, then go left at a stoplight to stay with Hawai'i'kai. Just beyond, at a double right turn arrow, continue straight ahead (through a "No outlet" sign), then within a block turn left at a small "Mariner's Ridge" sign at Kaluanui Road. After winding about a mile up through a steeply tilted residential area, you'll reach a dead end, where a trail leads up a brushy hill.

From this area, you'll have fine views back down to that fish pond community and two craters, **Koko Head** and **Koko Crater**. The vistas get better if you hike up the trail; it eventually leads to a viewpoint with a nice panorama of the surrounding countryside. Although not well maintained, it's a relatively easy trail, with a few eroded areas.

Back in your car, retreat down Mariner's Ridge, go right on Hawai'i'kai, then turn left onto Wailua Street shortly after passing a post office. Follow Wailua across a narrow section of the pond, then go right onto Lunalilo Home Street. It takes you back to Kalaniana'ole Highway. Turn left to continue your coastal cruise.

Shortly beyond is the entrance to ❖ **Hanauma Bay Nature Preserve**, an almost circular bay formed from a crater whose seaward side eroded away. One of O'ahu's most popular beaches and snorkeling areas, it's open daily except Tuesday from 6 to 6. Beyond Hanauma Bay, the highway hugs the shoreline, and views of this lava-strewn coast are particularly impressive. Just over a mile from the Hanauma Bay entrance, watch for a turnout on your left for the **Halona Blowhole**, where incoming surf blasts skyward through an old lava tube.

The highway continues above this rugged wind and water sculpted coast, then it drops down to a broad plain, passing long and slender ❖ **Sandy Beach Park**. It swings inland and uphill, bypassing Makapu'u Point, O'ahu's easternmost tip, then it returns to the coast at Waimanalo Bay. You've rounded the corner, leaving O'ahu's southeast shore and entering the Windward Coast. On your left is one of the island's major attractions, ❖ **Sea Life Park**, open daily 9:30 to 5; (808) 259-7933; *www.sealifeparkhawaii.com*. On your right, down by the sea, is **Makapu'u Beach Park**.

A change of scene

From here, terrain and vegetation change dramatically, from the gentle, semi-arid slopes of the southeast coast to the dramatically fluted and green-clad cliffs of the Ko'olau Range. You'll pass several beach parks, and then enter the pleasantly scruffy little beach town of **Waimanalo**, along the edge of the bay by the same name. Opposite the town's school, pause for a look at **St. George Catholic Church**, a modern structure with a cut lava stone façade and window walls.

Highway 72 skims the western edge of **Kailua** and **Kane'ohe**, two towns set at the base of those incredibly steep, accordion-creased cliffs. Although the towns are ordinary, they enjoy one of the most imposing settings in the state. If you'd like to visit a very attractive beach park, detour into Kailua by turning seaward from Highway 72 onto Highway 61 (Kailua Drive). Go just under two miles to Kalaheo Avenue, turn right and follow it to ❖ **Kailua Beach Park**, with rolling lawn areas, shady trees and a beach of tawny sand.

Retrace your route, but remain on Kalaheo Avenue, following it through Kailua, along the edge of Kailua Bay. After about two miles, it becomes Kane'ohe Bay Road and crosses the narrow neck of the Mokapu Peninsula just below **Kane'ohe Marine Corps Air Station**. Then it crosses H-3 freeway and enters the town of Kane'ohe, situated on broad, calm Kane'ohe Bay. The road hugs the bayfront for about 3.5 miles. Then it goes briefly inland to a major junction, where it becomes Likelike Highway, which leads across the island to Honolulu. The cross street here is Kamehameha Highway, which will be your main route for most of the rest of this drive.

Go left on Kamehameha Highway briefly, then turn right onto Luluku Road and follow it toward the Ko'olau cliffs to **Ho'omaluhia Botanic Garden,** an lush swatch of green on a sloping hill above Kapani Wai Reservoir. It's open daily 9 to 4; free; (808) 233-7323. A road and several paths meander through these extensive gardens.

An ornate temple

Now return to that major junction and go left on Likelike Highway, following it briefly inland to Kahekili Highway, where you'll turn right. Follow this about 2.5 miles and turn left into the **Valley of the Temples,** a memorial park set against those 2,000-foot Ko'olau cliffs. Its centerpiece is the ornate **Byodo-In Temple** set amidst elaborately landscaped grounds with koi ponds adrift with black swans. It's open daily 8 to 4:30, with a modest admission fee; (808) 239-8811. Other structures in this large memorial park are an A-frame chapel and mausoleum, a Catholic garden and three individual shrines. The most impressive of these is a lava stone and laminated beam memorial dedicated to a wealthy Hong Kong banker and shipping magnate.

From here, retrace your route on Kahekili Highway for 1.5 miles, then turn left onto Ha'iku Road and go left again to rejoin Kamehameha Highway. You'll skirt the edge of Kane'ohe Bay, passing **He'eia State Park** and then **Laenami Beach Park,** both occupying small peninsulas. He'eia is on a bluff with nice views across Kane'ohe Bay while Laenami is down at beach level. Immediately beyond Laenami, Kamehameha and Kahekili highways merge as Route 83. Continue along the edge of the bay, passing through alternate areas of thick tropic vegetation and surprisingly modest and sometimes scruffy shoreside homes with million dollar views.

About five miles beyond Laenami Park is ❖ **Kualoa Regional Park**. It occupies a generous slice Kane'ohe bayfront, with picnicking and camping facilities and about a mile of sandy beach. The very recognizable seastack called **Chinaman's Hat** is just offshore. Pressing onward, you'll see the ruins of an 1864 brick sugar mill on your left, vine-clad and suggestive of a Mayan ruin.

You'll pass through a scattering of tiny towns and public beaches, and then encounter **Kahana Valley State Park** opposite Kahana Bay. It's a curious combination of a lushly vegetated valley and shabby old homes, although it's historically significant. Lands owned by the *ali'i* often were long, tapered wedges called *ahupua'a* which ran from the highest ridges to the beach, providing a variety of landforms and a fresh water source from the mountains. Kahana is a former *ahupua'a* and about thirty families still live here. Park officials sometimes involve them in living history programs, particularly for school groups. The drive into this long and slender state park is interesting mostly for its novelty value, and you'll encounter speed bumps every few yards. More impressive is a palm grove at the park's entrance and—across the highway—a shaded, sandy beach with lacy-needled casuarina trees, picnic areas and some campsites.

Just beyond is **Sacred Falls State Park,** which has been closed indefinitely because of a fatal landslide several years ago. It's worth a pause if it's open, with a two-mile trail leading up a lush green valley to the 87-foot-high waterfalls. Beyond here, the shoreline highway passes rows of homes and stretches of beach; some are regular beach parks while others are just little bits of unnamed strand.

Hawai'i's top attraction

About three miles past Sacred Falls, you'll reach Hawai'i's most-visited attraction, the ❖ **Polynesian Cultural Center.** It's in La'ie, with the campus of **Brigham Young University-Hawaii** next door. The cultural center is open daily except Sunday from noon to 6; (808) 293-3333; *www.polynesia.com.*

Just beyond, turn right onto Naupaka Street opposite La'ie Shopping Center and follow it to rugged, wave-splashed **La'ie Point.** From this rocky promontory, you'll enjoy fine views up and down O'ahu's northeast coast and inland to those gorgeous cliffs. Incoming breakers slam into the peninsula's craggy flanks and crash over tiny islands offshore. Most travelers miss this dramatic landspit; you're only companions likely will be a few fishermen.

Back on Kamehameha Highway, look inland for the stately, gleaming white **Mormon Temple,** at the end of a tree-lined drive. The landscaped grounds and a visitor center are open to the public daily from 1 to 6:30. Guided tours leave every few minutes from the Polynesian Cultural Center; (808) 293-9297.

Malaehana State Recreation Area is just beyond, with soft sandy beaches at the base of wooded hills. **Goat Island,** a bird sanctuary, is offshore. The next item of interest along Kamehameha Highway is the large, rustic and rusting corrugated **Kahuku Sugar Mill,** which active from 1893 until 1971. It was open to visitors until 2001, when it was closed for safety reasons. As a result, several stores and shops around the complex are slowly dying; they're either shuttered or used for secondary non-tourist related business. There's a post office here in case you need to send postcards. Light fare is available at the funky **Kahuku Sugar Mill Restaurant,** open for lunch and dinner.

More interesting is the **"Famous Kahuku Shrimp Truck"** alongside the highway. It's a takeout installed in an old delivery van that has made its last delivery, except for fried shrimp and calamari through its service window. Picnic tables are adjacent, under a canvas awning, and the side of the truck is covered with invited graffiti from patrons. This "famous" takeout is open daily 9:30 to 6. It accepts cash only, but a little cash goes a long way. You can get a huge lunch plate of shrimp or calamari with rice and macaroni salad, sufficient for two people for $10.

If you're still hungry, you'll see several roadside stands in this area selling coconuts, pineapples, bananas and assorted local produce. You'll also encounter several farmers' markets on weekends.

A couple of miles past the sugar mill and shrimp truck is the entrance to ❖ **Turtle Bay Resort**, an extensive complex occupying a small peninsula. Just over a mile beyond, watch for ❖ **Kawela Beach**, our choice as the prettiest little beach on the North Shore. No sign marks it, although it's the first beach park you'll see after the highway passes Turtle Bay.

You're now on the O'ahu legendary North Shore, home of those massive, curling breakers that are the dramatic exclamation points of surfer movies. Regarded by many as the world's top surfing area, ❖ **Sunset Beach** stretches for two miles along here, starting near a traffic signal in the hamlet of **Kahikilani**. It's a rather narrow beach, lined with palms and casuarina trees. A few surfer shops, cafes and businesses are along the inland side of the highway. You'll be pressed to find a parking space near this beach on weekends, or any winter day when the incoming surf is at its wildest. It's particularly crowded in December, when surfing competitions are held. Sunset Beach the home of the ❖ **Banzai Pipeline**, which is both a place and a condition. It describes a curling wave so high that expert surfers drop down into its base and "ride the pipeline." Banzai's biggest waves break just southwest of **Ehukai Beach Park**, at the lower end of Sunset Beach.

A pair of pretty parks

Four miles beyond, in the pretty hamlet of **Waimea** are two attractive coastal parks linked by a walking path, ❖ **Pupukea Beach Park** and **Waimea Bay Beach Park**. Pupukea, on a low bluff, is a fine wave-watching spot, since breakers often crash over a lava ridge just offshore. Waimea Bay Beach Park is in a pretty, sheltered cove just beyond. Inland is another of O'ahu's major attractions, ❖ **Waimea Falls Park,** open daily 10 to 5:30; (808) 638-5300; www.atlantisadventures.net/hawaii.

Moving right along, you'll pass large **Hale'iwa Beach Park**; fork to the right onto Route 830 for the funkily historic town of **Hale'iwa**. (Kamehameha Highway goes inland here, headed across O'ahu to Honolulu.) This former sugar town has become a major surfing and minor art center, with a score or more shops, boutiques and galleries. Many occupy old false front woodframe buildings. Find a place to park and explore its small business district.

Check out the **North Shore Surfing Museum** in the North Shore Marketplace, with displays about the beginning surfing in Hawai'i and its eventual spread around the world. It's open daily 9 to 7; (808) 637-8888. Nearby is **Lili'uokalani Church**, built in 1832 and later named in honor of Hawai'i's favorite queen, who sometimes attended services there. Nearby is ❖ **M. Matsumoto Grocery Store**, famous for shave ice. It's no longer a grocery store but a tourist shop, and it can be jammed with shave ice patrons on warm weekends. Hale'iwa must be the shave ice capital of the world; there are half a dozen such places along here.

Continuing beyond town, you'll reach a roundabout; spin off to the right for **Waialua**. You will pass some old fashioned south seas style homes built on stilts to entice ocean breezes, with cars and assorted odds and ends parked underneath. Within about a mile, turn left in front of a school onto Goodwin Avenue, following a Ka'ena Point sign. After a block, go left onto Kealohanui Street to the funky **Sugar Bar**, housed in an old masonry Bank of Hawaii building. It's a narrow little pub decorated with surfing regalia and beer banners.

Put it in reverse and cross Goodwin to the old **Waialua Sugar Mill** with a huge and rusting cone-shaped boiler room. The mill is closed, although a few businesses occupy some of the outbuildings. Worth a stop here is **Hale'iwa Smokehouse,** a small market offering smoked fish and Hawaiian specialty foods; open daily 9 to 5.

Continue out Goodwin for half a mile, and at a T-intersection, go right onto the Farrington Highway. The terrain is level through there; the mountains—now the Wai'anae Range—are several miles inland. You'll travel through the open countryside of former sugarcane fields, passing a few banana and coconut stands and an occasional opulent plantation house, mixed with shabby homes. At the **Dillingham Field Glider Port**, two firms offer glider rides—Honolulu Soaring Club, (808) 677-3404, *www.honolulusoaring.com*; and Sailplane Ride Adventures, (808) 637-3147, *www.gliderrideshawaii.com*.

A few miles beyond, the paved road ends at a gravel parking area in **Ka'ena Point State Park**. There are no facilities here although low headlands above a rough lava beach provide good vantage points for watching incoming breakers. On a clear day, you can see east as far as Kane'ohe Bay and west toward Ka'ena Point. Although it has a few sandy coves among its lava ridges, this area is not a pretty place. These low headlands have been torn up by off-road vehicles. With no rangers present, the park is often littered, despite efforts by locals to keep it cleaned up. A rough jeep road used mostly as a hiking trail leads about four miles out to Ka'ena Point.

To get back to Honolulu, stay with Farrington Highway. It eventually blends with Highway 99 at Schofield Barracks, which then puts you on H-2 freeway.

THE LEEWARD COAST

This is the driest area of O'ahu—a low seacoast sloping gently down from the arid Wai'anae Range. And you may ask yourself, as you follow this mostly dreary drive, why have you sent us here? Except for a detour to the Ko'olina Lagoons area in the Ko 'Olina Resort development, there isn't much to see, except for a couple of scruffy, strung-out towns. However, it gets better toward the end of this allegedly scenic drive, so bear with us.

TRAVEL TIP: This area has some of O'ahu's roughest neighborhoods, and car break-ins are not uncommon. Don't leave anything of value in your vehicle.

To begin this drive, head west on H-1 from Waikiki past Barbers Point; the freeway eventually becomes Farrington Highway. Why two Farrington Highways? Originally, the road went all the way around Ka'ena Point, although it was never paved all the way. Both ends of the Farrington Highway become rough jeep trails as they approach the point; they're used mostly for hiking, see Chapter Nine, page 144.

If you'd like to see four interesting manmade lagoons, take the Ko 'Olina exit into **Ko 'Olina Resort** shortly after passing Barbers Point. Follow the main drive past the J.W. Marriott Ihiliani Resort to the **Ko 'Olina Beach Club**, a timeshare complex. At the far edge of this facility, turn right onto Waipahe Place and follow it to the **Ko'olina Lagoons**. These are four crescent-shaped enclaves sculpted in the shoreline by the developer. Although part of the resort complex, they're open to the public; see below, page 169.

Return to Farrington Highway and press westward and then northward on O'ahu's Leeward Coast. As we noted above, there's not much of interest along here. You'll pass through a series of scruffy run-together communities—**Nanakuli, Lualuaei, Ma'ili** and the largest, **Wai'anae** . Several public beaches are along here, although coast is flat and straight and not very appealing. What is appealing is the Wai'anae Range, whose terraced cliffs rise steeply to your right. Dry and brushy, they more suggest a scene from the American Southwest than O'ahu, except for the cobalt blue sea.

Past Wai'anae, the expressway narrows to two lanes. Just beyond the townlet of **Makaha**, it passes the U.S. Army's Ka'ena Point Satellite Tracking Station and terminates in the leeward portion of ❖ **Ka'ena Point State Park**. This is one of O'ahu's most remote and attractive public beaches; see below on page 170. Unlike the neglected windward section, this slice of the park has lawns, inviting sandy beaches, potties and beach showers.

Those impressive bluffs, still wildly rugged, are much greener here, since they receive some of the storm-driven rains that pummel O'ahu's North Coast. At the end of pavement is a parking area for a two-mile hike to Ka'ena Point, O'ahu's westernmost tip. Most of the route is a rough jeep road; more people hike it than drive it; see Chapter Nine, page 144.

Since you've reached the end of the road, your only option—other than hanging out at the beach or hiking to Ka'ena Point—is to turn around and retrace your path.

Oahu's Ten Best Beaches

Since we covered Waikiki and its beaches in earlier chapters, our Ten Best beach choices are outside the Honolulu/Waikiki area. Eight are on the windward side and two are leeward. We take them in order, heading east and then west from Honolulu.

Generally, you'll find calmer surf and sunnier weather on south and southeastern exposures while northern beaches are wetter and wilder. This is true particularly in winter when they catch the brunt of storms blowing in from the north. However, some of the northeastern public beaches are sheltered by bays and quite suitable for swimming.

For more detail on most of the beaches listed below as well as several others on the island, pick up a copy of *Hawaii's Best Beaches* by John R.K. Clark; see details in Chapter Ten, page 155.

Windward beaches

1 HANAUMA BAY

In Koko Head Regional Park off Highway 72; (808) 396-4229. Daily except Tuesday, 6 a.m. to 6 p.m. Modest fees for parking and beach access. GETTING THERE: It's about seven miles east of Waikiki on the Kalaniana'ole Highway.

O'ahu's most popular beach park outside Honolulu, Hanauma Bay offers some of the best snorkeling on the island. Since it's a nature preserve, both the coral and the fish among them are protected. Formed by an old crater whose seaward rim has eroded away, the bay is sheltered from the incoming surf, so it's a fine place for novice snorkelers. Further, it's an appealing park for swimming and sunning, with a beige sand beach shaded by palms. A beach hut provides rental equipment.

Park officials are so concerned about preserving the reef that visitors must view a seven-minute film with tips on safety and coral protection before they can go down to the beach. That beach can be reached by a long stroll from the visitor center, or by tram. For more on the Hanauma Bay, see Chapter Two, page 61.

TRAVEL TIP: Since it's one of O'ahu's most popular parks, Hanauma Bay is almost always crowded. Avoid it on weekends, since the parking lot fills up early. Further, you'll be snorkeling and swimming shoulder to shoulder with fellow visitors.

2 SANDY BEACH PARK

The park is about three miles beyond Hanauma Bay.

This large park at the base of Koko Crater has considerable appeal. The beach is nearly half a mile long, bordered by a grassy park the size of a pair of polo fields, with picnic tables and barbecues. The park's northeastern end is quite appealing, with palm trees sprouting from the sand, providing shade for sand-sitters and surfer-watchers. Even the park's two restroom facilities are interesting, for they're decorated with murals. One depicts Duke Kahanamoku and surfing scenes, and the other has an old Hawaiian scene with a hula dancer and fisherman.

The surf can get quite nasty here, so the beach is better for surfing and sunning than swimming. Incoming waves are particularly rough in winter.

3 KAILUA BEACH

In the town of Kailua. GETTING THERE: From Sandy Beach Park, follow Highway 72 about nine miles to the town of Kailua. At a T-intersection, turn right onto Kailua Road and then right again onto Kalaheo Road; the beach park is about two-thirds of a mile away. If you're coming directly from Honolulu/Waikiki, take Likilike Highway (Route 61) northeast across the island; it becomes Kailua Road.

This large park just beyond Kailua's business district is one of our favorite beaches, with rolling lawns and picnic areas shaded by palms and other tropical trees. It's missed by most visitors because it's not on a main highway. The long sandy beach is off-white and the water in shallow Kailua Bay is a pretty turquoise. The surf is fairly calm, since the beach is protected by the bay. However, it's rather breezy on this windward side of the island, so it's popular for windsurfing and the new sport of kiteboarding. Participants balance on chubby surfboards and are pulled along by large kites that resemble half-parachutes. They're colorful and fun to watch.

Kayak and small outrigger rentals are available, and paddlers can choose between an inland lagoon or the bay. The Ko'olau Range presents an imposing backdrop to this pretty place. Kailua Beach's sand is firm underfoot, so it's fine for strolling as well as sunning and windsurfing; see Chapter Nine, page 143.

4 KUALOA REGIONAL PARK

On the northwestern edge of Kane'ohe Bay. GETTING THERE: From Kailua Beach, follow Kalaheo Drive and Kane'ohe Bay Drive about six miles to Kamehameha Highway (Route 836). Turn right and drive about nine miles north along the Kane'ohe bayfront. From Honolulu, take Likelike Highway across the island, then go left on Kamehameha Highway.

Kualoa is the "the beach ignored" by many visitors because it isn't featured in most guidebooks. In fact, it's not even listed as a beach; it's called a regional park. We like this large park on the Kualoa Peninsula because of its wide expanses of shaded lawns and its narrow, gently sloping beach. The surf is calmed by Kane'ohe Bay, so it's a good family swimming area. And it occupies a dramatic setting, with the fluted cliffs of the Ko'olau Range rising just inland and a seastack called Chinaman's Hat offshore. The wide sweep of Kane'ohe Bay stretches to the right. The park has picnic tables, potties and a camping area. Although few visitors pause here, it's very popular with locals, particularly on weekends.

5 KAHANA BAY BEACH PARK

Opposite Kahana Valley State Park, about five miles north of Kualoa Regional Park.

Occupying the mouth of Kahana Valley, this park embraces a pretty crescent beach, with a surf somewhat gentled by its location in a narrow bay. It has grassy areas and picnic tables shaded by casuarinas and palms. Its sandy beach is suitable for swimming on calm days and strolling any day. There's a launch ramp at the far end, in case you happen to have something that floats strapped to the top of your car. The beach park has pit potties only, although there are full service restrooms across the highway at Kahana Valley State Park.

6 KAWELA BEACH

About fourteen miles northwest of Kahana Bay Beach Park and 1.5 miles west of Turtle Bay Resort; it's the first beach you see after passing the resort's entrance.

Most of Kawela beach and bay are on closed private land. However, this little crescent—unmarked by a sign—is open to the public. It's undeveloped, with no facilities, and the parking lot is potholed. However, the beach itself is exceptionally pretty. This cozy cove is shaded by casuarinas and palms, and the surf line is an inviting mix of sand and lava. You can choose between wading in the surf or checking out tidepools. The sea can get rough, however, so we don't recommend swimming. A cute little island, thatched with a few trees and shrubs, stands just offshore.

7 SUNSET BEACH

It begins about two miles beyond Kawela Beach and 3.5 miles past the turnoff to Turtle Bay Resort.

No sign marks Sunset Beach, although you'll know when you've arrived. This is surfer city, the home of wild Banzai Pipeline breakers and host to international surfing championships. The beach begins at the hamlet of **Kahikilani** and stretches for two miles along O'ahu's North Coast. You'll be hard-pressed to find a parking spot along its length on weekends and anytime during winter surfing competitions. Folks like us, who aren't about to try to hang ten or even five, are content to scuff along its grainy sand, watch the breakers slam in from the Pacific and admire those wild young surfers at play.

This is *not* a swimming beach when the surf is big, although it can be relatively flat on calm summer days. Most of the big surf rolls in between November and May when winter swells reach all the way down from the Gulf of Alaska. Much of Sunset Beach's length is behind shoreline homes, out of sight of the highway. However, a short stroll from any of several access points will put you on the sand. You can walk a mile or so in either direction. The famous "Banzai Pipeline"—in addition to describing the North Shore's wildest waves—is a specific area. Its monster winter waves break just southwest of **Ehukai Beach Park**, at the lower end of Sunset Beach.

8 PUPUKEA & WAIMEA BEACH PARKS

They're in and near the town of Waimea, just short of Waimea Falls Park, a couple of miles southwest of Sunset Beach.

We've combined these beach parks because they're linked by a short roadside path. Both have picnic tables, sandy and grassy areas and potties. A couple of surf shacks, a Foodland market and even a Starbucks are across the highway from Pupukea Beach, which is in the town of Waimea.

Pupukea is fascinating mostly for an offshore lava ridge, over which breakers break, particularly in winter. It is thus O'ahu's best storm-watching beach. Those big waves slam into the ridge and spew high into the air, eliciting exclamations from observers. A popular activity—but not on a stormy day—is to wade out from shore, safely behind that natural lava barrier, and get close to waves splashing over the top. Use caution, however, and stay on the inshore side. Waimea Bay Beach Park just to the west is one of the north shore's better winter surfing beaches. It occupies a pretty bay opposite the entrance to the popular tourist attraction of ❖ **Waimea Falls Park**.

Leeward beaches

Most of O'ahu's leeward beaches are rather flat and uninteresting. However, the beaches at Ka'ena Point State Park are worth the 45-mile drive from Honolulu. Four manmade lagoons just beyond Barbers Point are worthy of pause as well.

9 KO'OLINA LAGOONS

On O'ahu's southwest shore, just beyond Barbers Point Harbor. GETTING THERE: Head west from Honolulu on H-1 for about twenty miles until it blends into Farrington Highway at Barbers Point. After passing two traffic lights, exit right onto Ko 'Olina Drive and go left over the expressway to the Ko 'Olina resort. Follow the drive past the J.W. Marriott Ihiliani Resort to the Ko 'Olina Beach Club, a timeshare complex. On the far edge of the complex, turn right onto Waipahe Place and follow it to Ko 'Olina Beach Park.

Koʻolina Lagoons is a series of four crescent inlets along the shore-front of this large resort development. Although the resort is on private land, the lagoons are open to visitors, since all ocean beaches in Hawaiʻi are pubic. Ko ʻOlina Resort and the state share in maintaining the lagoons.

This is an exceptionally pretty area—too pretty to be natural, like a set for a South Pacific movie. The lagoons are oval enclaves sheltered from the rough surf by lava stone breakwaters. They're rimmed by sandy beaches that blend into putting green smooth lawns dotted with palms and palmettos. A concrete walking path ties the four lagoons to-gether, stretching about a mile between the Ko ʻOlina Beach Club timeshares and the Marriott resort. This is a good spot for families, since the protected lagoon waters are glassy calm.

10 KAʻENA POINT STATE PARK

From the Koʻolina Lagoons turnoff, follow Farrington Highway about twenty miles northwest to its end. The park is immediately beyond Kaʻena Point Satellite Tracking Station.

This end-of-the-road beach is appealing for several good reasons. It's remote and therefore uncrowded; it offers long stretches of soft beige sand, alternating with rugged lava shoals and tidepools; and it's backdropped by the dramatically terraced gray-green cliffs of the Waiʻanae Range. The sea here is quite pretty, ranging from turquoise to cobalt blue. It can be either gentle or violent, depending on the weather, so enter it with caution.

Park facilities include potties, beach showers and lawns. The paved road ends at a rough jeep trail, which continues about two miles to Kaʻena Point, Oʻahu's southernmost tip. It's a popular hiking trail; see Chapter Nine, page 144.

We visited the cultivated parts of the plain of Lahaina... The part bordering on the shore was pleasantly laid out in plantations of taro, sweet potatoes (and) sugar cane.

—Captain George Vancouver, 1793

Chapter Twelve

MAUI

IS IT REALLY WOWIE?

What is it with Maui? Why did the readers of *Condé Nast Traveler* and *Travel & Leisure* vote it the best island in the world? Why is it the most visited Hawaiian island outside of O'ahu? And why do we see Maui T-shirts on people who've never been there?

In seeking answers, we picked Maui as our first stop after completing our Honolulu/O'ahu research. We wanted to discover why it has been a cool place to be since the "Maui wowie" pot-smoking days of the 1960s. Although it isn't *our* favorite island—Hawai'i wins that prize—we soon understood why it's the favorite of so many others. It offers three opulent resort areas—Ka'anapali, Kapalua and Wailea; its popular town of Lahaina is rich in history and tourist lures; and Haleakala National Park, rising 10,000 feet above the sea, is one of the state's most fascinating landforms. Then there's a special charm to the not-so-hidden rainforest hamlet of Hana. It has been the chosen refuge of such luminaries as Charles A. Lindbergh, the Beatles' George Harrison, TV's Jim "Gomer Pyle" Nabors and comedian Richard Pryor.

That's some of the good news about Maui. The bad news—at least for those seeking to escape Waikiki crowds—is that it gets about two million visitors a year, which is twice as many as any other outer island. The main highway leading from the airport to Lahaina is often congested and unfortunately, it's mostly two lanes. Once you reach Lahaina, you'll find parking to be at a premium, unless you do as we do and drive a couple of blocks inland.

On the other hand, nearly seventy-five percent of Maui's terrain is relatively unpopulated. Since it's the second largest island after the Big Island, that provides a lot of roaming room. Its three planned resort areas aren't nearly as congested as Waikiki, and the resorts are more expansive, since there's more land available. So, the upside of Maui's downside is that it's less crowded than Waikiki, yet it has a enough of a population base—about 104,000—to provide all the essential services. It has several large shopping centers, plus a Wal-Mart, K-Mart and even Home Depot—not that you came here to buy sheetrock.

TO LEARN MORE: Contact the Maui Visitors Bureau, P.O. Box 580, Wailuku, HI 96793; (800) 525-6284 or (808) 244-3530; *www.visitmaui.com*. For Lahaina info: (888) 310-1117; *www.visitlahaina.com*.

Maui: GETTING TO KNOW YOU

As any guidebook will tell you, Maui is comprised of two volcanoes that emerged from the sea and eventually flowed together, forming a land bridge between them. This has earned it the practical and not very romantic nickname of the Valley Isle. That valley also is the least interesting part of Maui—a mix of pineapple and sugarcane fields and the site of its two largest towns, Kahului and Wailuku. Like the two volcanoes that formed the island, they have flowed together, creating a rather large population mass. Kahului is Maui's largest town, although Wailuku is the county seat and government center. These are essentially working class communities offering little of interest to visitors, except for their shopping facilities.

The second youngest of Hawai'i's main islands, Maui was born more than a million years ago when Haleakala rose from the sea, followed by a much smaller volcano to the northwest. Haleakala's wide alluvial skirts form about eighty percent of the island and this area is referred to as East Maui. Much smaller West Maui has been eroded into valleys and ridges. What remains of its original volcano forms the West Maui Mountains that rise above Lahaina.

Maui was named for a really cool demigod, who lassoed the sun to slow it down so the people would have longer days to work their taro patches. He was a little weird, however; legend says he made the lariat from his sister's pubic hair.

As with all of Hawai'i's islands, Maui has broad climatic extremes. Tradewinds bring frequent heavy rains to the northeastern flanks of Haleakala, creating the verdant rainforests around Hana. Those same storms pummel West Maui's northeastern exposure. The 'Iao Valley is one of the wettest spots in the islands, getting up to 400 inches of rainfall a year. The eroded, green-clad 'Iao Needle is a popular visitor attraction. The central flatlands are sheltered by Haleakala's mass and receive considerably less rain. West Maui's west coast is the driest of all; only a few inches of rain falls annually. It's also one of the warmest places in all of the islands. But you know what the say—it's a *dry* heat.

When Maui visitors arrive at Kahului International Airport, most of them set out in one of two directions—to West Maui with its lively tourist town of Lahaina and the Ka'anapali and Kapalua resorts; or east to the upscale planned resort community of Wailea.

TRAVEL TIP: Arrange in advance for a rental car at the airport, since it's far from Maui's tourist areas. A shuttle to Lahaina costs about $40 and a cab is around $50. Maui has several discount car rental companies but most don't provide airport pickup. Thus, renting from a national chain may be cheaper overall.

History-rich Lahaina

If you have time to visit only one town on Maui, make it Lahaina. The sleek resorts of next-door Ka'anapali seem to have had little effect on this old whaling capital, which rambles for about a mile along the beachfront. It's one of Hawai'i's most historic villages, dating from the sixteenth century, when the mild, dry climate and protected beaches made it a playground for the *ali'i*. It became a popular stop for whaling ships in the 1820s, and randy sailers turned it into the hell-hole of the Pacific—much to the shock of missionaries who arrived in 1823. The flavor of history remains in Lahaina. Its narrow streets are overhung with ancient banyan trees and many of its old buildings survive.

This is not to suggest that tourism hasn't impacted the old town. Indeed, it has inundated it, sweeping in from the Lahaina Roadstead—the narrows between Maui and Moloka'i—like a commercially-driven *tsunami*. Front Street is lined with scores of trinket shops, gift shops, galleries and tourist-targeting restaurants. The historic waterfront, which once hosted nearly 400 whaling ships a year, is now lined with pleasure boats and booths selling excursion tickets. Still, much of the past survives, such as the coral and brick Baldwin House, a missionary home turned museum; the venerable Pioneer Inn, the oldest continually operating hotel in the Islands; the 1859 customs and court house; and Banyan Tree Park, with its massive banyan tree planted in 1873.

Lahaina occupies a dramatic setting, between the ocean and tilted alluvial plains that rise up to green-clad ridges and valleys of the West Maui Mountains.

DRIVING MAUI

As we noted above, Maui was formed from two erupting volcanoes that oozed together to form a single island. A drive around their perimeters provides a good Maui sampler while taking you to some of its most remote areas. However, the complete loop drives aren't for everyone. The roads are very narrow and sections of the East Maui drive are rough and unpaved. For you timid drivers, you can book any of a number of tours that follow these routes, particularly West Maui's Hana Highway. Check with your hotel concierge or pick up a brochure.

NOTE: Listings in **bold face** marked with ❖ are described in more detail elsewhere; check the index for page numbers.

The Hana Highway — in reverse?

The Hana Highway is one of the most popular drives in all of Hawai'i. It's a sinuous route that winds through thick rainforests at the base of Haleakala along Maui's northeast coast to remote Hana. Then, for an adventurous few, it continue on, skirting the semi-arid wilderness of the south coast. About nine miles of the southern portion is graded dirt or gravel with occasional sections of asphalt. It gets rough out there, but it's navigable by a regular car during dry weather. We think it's more scenic than the popular Hana side. The rugged shoreline is almost always in view along the dry south coast, while the north road to Hana is mostly cloaked in rainforest.

TRAVEL TIPS: Avoid driving the dirt portion of this road during or immediately after a storm, and check on road conditions if it has been raining for several days. Washouts can occur and sharp rocks can emerge and puncture tires. To check on road conditions, call the Hana Public Works Department at (808) 248-8254. (The road is graded periodically to fill washboards and knock down rock projections.)

Many rental car companies prohibit taking their sedans on this road, urging you to rent a four-wheel-drive instead. And if you defy them? If you break down out there, you're on your own.

The complete East Maui loop is a long, tiring drive covering more than 100 miles with uncounted twists and turns, so you may want to consider overnighting in Hana. Accommodations range from small lodges and bed and breakfast inns to the famous—and expensive—Hotel Hana-Maui, see below on page 201.

Most travelers along the Hana Highway only drive to Hana and back, while a few do the complete loop. However, very few do what we suggest—run the route in reverse. And why do this thing backward? Because you're less likely to get stuck behind slow traffic, since most of it will be coming toward you. Also, you'll be on the coastal side of the road, affording better views. And finally, if you plan a single-day drive, you'll arrive in time to visit two very interesting diversions—Holy Ghost Church, whose gift shop closes at 1 p.m., and Tedeschi Vineyards tasting room, which closes at 5.

Begin by getting to Kahului. Go south briefly on Highway 350, then turn left onto Hanson Road to the ❖ **Alexander & Baldwin Sugar Museum**. It's beside Maui's only still-operating sugar mill. Continue past the mill to Pulehu Road and head south. This narrow country lane

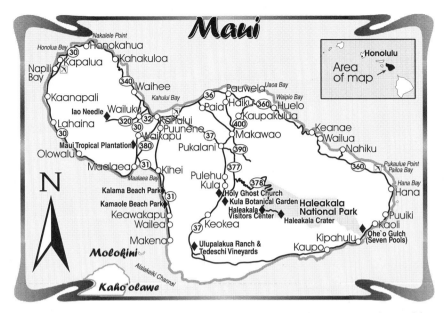

Nakalele Point
Honolua Bay
Honokahua
Napili Bay
Kapalua
Kahakuloa
Waihee
Kaanapali
Kahului Bay
Pauwela
Uaoa Bay
Iao Needle
Wailuku
Paia
Haiku
Waipio Bay
Huelo
Lahaina
Kahului
Kaupakulua
Keanae
Puunene
Maui Tropical Plantation
Waikapu
Makawao
Wailua
Olowalu
Pukalani
Nahiku
Maalaea
Kihei
Pulehu
Pukaulue Point
Pailoa Bay
Maalaea Bay
Kula
Hana Bay
Kalama Beach Park
Holy Ghost Church
Hana
Kamaole Beach Park
Kula Botanical Garden
Haleakala
National Park
Keawakapu
Haleakala
Visitors Center
Haleakala Crater
Puuiki
Wailea
Keokea
Kaoli
Makena
Ulupalakua Ranch &
Tedeschi Vineyards
Kipahulu
Oheʻo Gulch
(Seven Pools)
Kaupo
Molokini
Alalakeiki Channel
Kahoʻolawe

Honolulu
Area of map

N

rambles through cane fields, and then a mix of cactus and scrubby brush. The mass of often cloud-shrouded Haleakala looms to your left. (Note: After about four miles, fork right to stay with Pulehu.) Then the road widens and passes through an area of elegant country homes. Their occupants have—as you do—fine views up to the volcano and down to the valley of the Valley Isle, with both shorelines visible.

At road's end, go right on Kula Highway (Route 37) and then left onto lower Kula Road for the 1894 ❖ **Holy Ghost Church**. It's hard to miss, since it's the only church in Hawai'i with an octagonal shape. Exit the church yard, turn right and continue through the town of **Waiakoa/Kula**, built into the steep slopes of Haleakala's foothills. Merge back onto Highway 37 and continue southward. If you'd like to visit ❖ **Kula Botanical Garden,** a fine gathering of tropical plants terraced into a slope, turn right up the Haleakala Highway (Route 37). The garden comes up shortly, on your right.

Return to Highway 37 and press southward. The speed limit drops to 25 mph and the route becomes a curling narrow ribbon, winding through dryland forest, pastureland and cactus. From this slope 2,000 feet above the sea, called Upcountry Maui, you can look west toward **Kihei** and the resort complex of **Wailea**. Offshore are the islands of **Kaho'olawe** and tiny crescent-shaped ❖ **Molokini**. After five miles, you'll arrive at **'Ulupalakua Ranch**. Huge eucalyptus and cypress trees tower over this neatly tended complex, which has two items of visitor appeal—an old fashioned ranch store and the tasting room of ❖ **Tedeschi Vineyards**, Maui's only commercial winery.

Beyond the ranch, the narrow black ribbon—now labeled Highway 31—winds higher into the Haleakala foothills. It passes through a brushy, rumpled lava flow that reaches down to the faraway shore. About ten miles from the winery, the road's centerline disappears and the pavement becomes rough and bumpy, but easily navigable. It twists down to the seacoast and crosses several narrow lava-ribbed canyons on slender bridges. Then the route alternates between dirt, gravel and asphalt stretches for the next nine miles.

Shortly after hitting the first unpaved section, watch on your right for **St. John's Church**, with a Dutch barn look. It's generally closed, although you can poke about its rather barren grounds. As you approach the border of Haleakala National Park's coastal lowlands, you'll encounter the 1886 **Kaupo Store**, apparently held together by the peeling paint on its shabby boards. A sign reads: "Historical since 1925." It's part mini-mart and part museum; shelves are cluttered with old wall clocks, jugs, cameras, typewriters and just plain clutter.

Shortly beyond the store, opposite a pair of mailboxes, fork to the right down a rough gravel road. It delivers you to a wild and beautiful peninsula, where waves slam into a lava-ridged black sand beach. Standing forlorn on this windy promontory is the shabby little 1857 **Huialoha Church**. Only a few weathered pews are inside, although it's not really abandoned. Locals are trying to raise funds to restore it. Put a dollar or two in a donation box and make an entry in a journal on a small table. Some entries are quite touching, revealing that a few people make regular pilgrimages to this hauntingly remote place.

Just beyond milepost 37, the road hits pavement for good, and then it narrows and spills down to the base of steep rocky cliffs. The vegetation has begun to thicken, for you've rounded the bend to Maui's soggy northeast coast. Between mileposts 40 and 41, watch for a road to the right, leading to the 1864 **Palapala Ho'omau Congregational Church** and **Lindbergh's grave**. When you approach from this direction, no sign indicates the church or the grave, so you must be alert for that road. If you pass the small **St. Paul's Catholic Church** on the left, you just missed your turn. Go back two-tenths of a mile and you'll see a small sign indicating the church.

"The wings of morning"

It's about a quarter of a mile down this lane, and the final resting place of Charles A. Lindbergh is in the church cemetery. It's a large but simple plot covered with lava rocks. A granite marker bears this quote from Psalms 139: "...If I take the wings of the morning and dwell in the uttermost parts of the sea..."

A mile beyond the church turnout is the parking lot for the **Seven Sacred Pools**. They're more accurately and less romantically called the Pools of Ohe'o Gulch by the National Park Service. The pools— about twenty, not seven—are formed as a stream stairsteps through the natural basins of a lava flow, and they never were sacred. There is no record of *ali'i* or ancient spirits bathing here. This is the Kipahulu section of ❖ **Haleakala National Park**, with a small visitor center and friendly rangers who will relieve you of $10 per car. Ohe'o Gulch is a quarter of a mile beyond, reached by a roadside trail. From there, the Pipiwai Trail leads nearly two miles up through this series of pools to the imposing 400-foot Waimoku Falls.

Back in your vehicle, you'll cross Oheʻo Gulch, although there's no place to park here. Nine miles beyond, you'll enter what tourist promoters like to call "Heavenly Hana." Actually, **Hana** is more charming than heavenly—a quaint old town clad in thick green vegetation. Although remote, it is not uncrowded. Scores of people make the drive—coming from the other direction—to poke about its few stores and shops and buy T-shirts reading: "I survived the Hana Highway."

If your time is limited, plan at least two pauses in Hana. The **Hasagawa General Store** at the corner of Hana Highway and Mill Road has been run by the same family since 1902. It's open Monday-Saturday 7 to 7 and Sunday 8 to 6; (808) 248-8231. This is a tourist version of a true general store, selling everything from groceries to plumbing fixtures to postcards. From here, turn right off the main road and drop down to gorgeous little **Hana Beach Park** at the town's tiny harbor. Have a picnic in the park and stroll out to the end of the weathered pier. You'll enjoy fine views out over the rocky coastline and back to the lush green hills tilting toward the hidden heights of Haleakala.

From this point on, you'll be doing what many other Maui visitors do—driving the Hana Highway. Ahead of you is fifty-two miles of narrow, rainforest-cloaked road with about 600 curves and fifty-six one-lane bridges. If you've overnighted in Hana, most of the traffic will be in-bound. However, if you're completing this marathon drive in a single day, expect to be slowed by more timid drivers. Also expect rainfall; although Hana gets only about seventy inches a year (only?), more than a hundred annual inches saturate the thick forest beyond. We've made several Hana drives through the years and we've never had a completely dry run.

Many travelers and some travel writers call this one of the most beautiful drives in the world. It is indeed scenic, although what you will see here is mostly rainforest and some pretty waterfalls; the coast itself appears only occasionally.

Beyond Hana

Shortly after leaving Hana, follow a short road to **Waianapanapa State Park**; (808) 248-8016. You can stroll its beaches and follow a nature trail to a pair of lava tube sea caves. Another interesting stop is **Kahanu Garden**, reached by following Ulaino Road seaward for about 1.5 miles. It's one of four National Tropical Botanical Gardens in Hawaiʻi, open for tours weekdays from 10 to 2; (808) 248-8912; *www.ntbg.org/kahanu.html.*. The turnoff is between mileposts 31 and 32. Particularly impressive here is the forty-foot high **Piʻilanihale Heiau,** one of the largest ancient temples in the state.

About ten miles farther along the Hana Highway, a pretty waterfall tumbles into a jungle-clad ravine at **Puaʻa Kaʻa State Wayside.** At milepost 18, a road drops down to the quaint old fishing village of

Wailua. Grizzled clapboard houses hover around taro patches and banana groves. The 1870 **St. Gabriel's Church** is worth a look; it's made of local materials—coral with sand mortar. One of Hana Highway's finest vista points is just beyond, from the **Ke'anae Peninsula** and the village of Ke'anae. Turn coastward near milepost 17 for views of Haleakala above and the rugged coastline at your feet. Just beyond, left of the highway, is **Ke'anae Arboretum**, with six acres of tropical plants and trees along a pretty stream. It has no facilities or regular hours and it's free.

Kaumahina State Wayside between mileposts 12 and 13 has a picnic area and nice coastal views, and watch inland for **Puohokamoa Falls** near milepost 11. Just beyond **Kailua** near milepost 2, a short trail leads to **Twin Falls.** And no, the two-mile marker doesn't mean you're two miles from the end of Hana Highway. For reasons known only to highway planners, the route name changes from Highway 360 to Highway 36, starting a new set of markers. You have sixteen miles to go. Then, just when you thought the curves would never end, they do—beyond **Ho'okipa Beach Park**, a popular surfing area.

Once you've returned to the flatlands, explore the rustic old sugarcane town of **Pa'ia**, with a few shops, galleries and cafés tucked into stone and wood frame buildings. Then head inland on Baldwin Avenue (at the town's only stop light) to explore a pair of interesting churches. On the right, the **Holy Rosary Catholic Church** has an unusual display of old prints of biblical scenes mounted on marble plaques out front, plus classic *bas relief* Stations of the Cross inside. A bit beyond, on the left, the stone **Wawaoa Church** has dazzling leaded glass windows and an unusual interior of beamed, vaulted arch ceilings.

The wild west coast

For reasons not clear to us, virtually all tourist information sources urge people not to drive the narrow road looping the north coast of West Maui. Actually, it's all paved—unlike the Hana loop—and it has fewer curves. However, the second half of the road is one-lane and extremely narrow, so some folks may have second thoughts about driving it.

If you're hesitant, sign up with **Ekahi Tours** and leave the driving to a guide. The half-day Kahakuloa Valley tour includes lunch and a walk into that lush valley. Here, several native Hawaiians and a few social dropouts are farming the old Hawaiian way, raising taro and tropical fruits. Guides take visitors on a stroll through the steep terraced lands of Oliver Duklow, a former law enforcement officer and passive revolutionary who would like to see the old Hawaiian ways return. (He also does poi pounding demonstrations nightly at the Old Lahaina Luau; see below, page 190.) During the walk, guides fashion leis from ti leaves, pluck fresh bananas, papayas and passion fruit for their guests, and explain medicinal and other practical uses of native plants.

The firm also has Hana drive tours and sunrise trips to Haleakala. Contact **Ekahi Tours**; (808) 877-9775; *www.ekahi.com.*

TRAVEL TIP: Don't attempt this drive during or after a storm. Much of the road is notched into sheer cliffs, and rocks and boulders can come tumbling down from above. Landslides that temporarily block the road are not uncommon.

The drive—on your own or with Ekahi Tours—begins north of the Kapalua resort complex above Lahaina. The views of rugged seacliffs and surf crashing into lava seastacks are awesome. And like the south shore Hana drive, the ocean is almost always in view.

The route passes through a rainforest and then climbs to a high point above **Honolua Bay.** Views from here are impressive—back to Kapalua, across to Moloka'i and down to the restless sea, where breakers smash into a crescent cove. After several miles, just past milepost 39, watch for the rocky promontory of **Nakalele Point** and pull over to a wide spot for a look at a spouting horn.

A few miles beyond the blowhole, the two-lane road narrows to one and twists snakily down into the rustically cute village of **Kahakuloa.** It's an idyllic picture postcard hamlet, with a tiny church and a few homes tucked among the palms at the base of a lush valley. Despite its remote north coast location, tourists are beginning to discover it. Signs advertise coconut candy and "the planet's best banana nut bread." (It isn't.) A large tropical fruit stand offers locally-grown produce.

If you're on the Ekahi tour, you'll turn off the highway at mid-village and follow a bumpy road into the valley to Oliver's acreage.

Beyond Kahakuloa, the narrow road continues its torturous trip around West Maui, passing an amazing mix of flora—cactus, pasturelands, and rainforests in narrow canyons. To your left, the restless sea hammers the craggy coastline below.

You appear to be all alone, in one of Hawai'i's most remote wilderness areas. Then you round a bend and unexpectedly, civilization sprawls below. You're looking down onto Maui's thick waistline of sugarcane fields and the towns of **Wailuku** and **Kahului.** The road—still narrow—passes some stately hillside homes. The route is now called Kahaliki Highway, and if you turn right and uphill on Kahaliki Loop, you'll pass more of those expensive estates.

Kahaliki Highway soon blends into Highway 30 near Wailuku. If you've not done so yet, turn right to visit **'Iao Needle** in the soft green 'Iao Valley.

THE TEN BEST MAUI ATTRACTIONS

As we have done in most of the Waikiki/O'ahu chapters, we begin with our favorite attraction, and then list the rest in alphabetical order. Our number one choice is a no-brainer—one of Hawai'i's most interesting and most visited national parks.

PRICING: Dollar sign codes indicate the approximate cost of adult admission to various attractions and activities: *$* = under $10; *$$* = $10 to $19; *$$$* = $20 to $29; *$$$$* = $30 to $39; *$$$$$* = $40 or more. And you already know that prices are almost always less for seniors and kids.

☺ **KID STUFF:** This little grinning guy marks attractions and activities that are of particular interest to pre-teens.

1 HALEAKALA NATIONAL PARK

For information: P.O. Box 369, Makawao, HI 96768; (808) 572-4400; www.nps.gov/hale. Park Headquarters open 7:30 to 4; Haleakala Visitor Center open 6 to 3. Park admission: $$ per car or $ per person; free with Golden Eagle, Age or Access pass. No dining or lodging facilities or fuel in the park. GETTING THERE: Follow the Haleakala Highway southeast from Kahului. It's about forty miles to the visitor center near the summit. ☺

TRAVEL TIPS: The road to the summit of Haleakala is very steep and winding. Be cautious going up and even more so coming back down; drop your car into a lower gear to avoid brake fade. And dress warmly for the trip; it's about thirty degrees cooler up there than in Maui's lowlands. If you plan to do any hiking, take it easy. You're nearly two miles high and the air is as thin as a hooker's nightie.

Much of Maui's land mass was formed by Haleakala, a giant shield volcano. Over a period of half a million years, it grew from the ocean floor and ultimately reached 10,023 feet into the sky. In fact, the volcano *is* East Maui. Haleakala National Park occupies a 29,000-acre slice of this monster mountain, reaching from summit to sea. No road links the two elements. The misnamed **Seven Sacred Pools** are the chief attraction of the **Kipahulu** section, down on the coast just south of Hana; see page 176.

The bulk of the park is reached by a steep road that takes travelers from near sea level to more than 10,000 feet in about two ear-popping hours. The views are incredible as you drive toward the summit, and they just keep getting better. All of Maui lies at your feet and on a clear day, you can see Lana'i, Moloka'i, Kaho'olawe and even the distant island of Hawai'i. Once you reach the rest, the crater is an awesome thing, seven miles long, two miles wide and 3,000 feet deep. It's a fascinating moonscape of cinder cones, lava ridges and pockmark mini-craters.

Greeting the dawn from a viewpoint on the crater rim is a popular ritual, and many of these early-risers take a free-wheeling bike ride back down. It's a fun ride although it has become too popular. So many people book the trips that small squadrons of cyclists have to be time-released.

This is mostly a hikers' and a gawkers' park. Trails lead along high ridges and down into the crater. The best vistas are from the observation point and from the nearby Haleakala Visitor Center, which has a few exhibits on the flora, fauna and geology of the volcano.

Park Headquarters, several miles back down the mountain, has a surprisingly modest interpretive center. Here, you will learn about the area's two most famous indigenous items—the distinctive silversword plant, very common in the park; and the rare nene, Hawai'i's native goose. Only about 200 survive on Maui and most are in the park. Although the loose goose is rarely seen in the wild, you're guaranteed a sighting in the interpretive center; it's stuffed, of course.

2 THE ALEXANDER & BALDWIN SUGAR MUSEUM

3957 Hansen Rd., Pu'uenene; (808) 871-8058; www.sugarmuseum.com. Monday-Saturday 9:30 to 4:30; $. GETTING THERE: The museum is adjacent to the Pu'unene Sugar Mill just south of Kahului. Take Highway 360 south, then go east briefly on Hansen Road.

This interesting museum occupies a century-old former manager's house beside Maui's only still-operating sugar mill. Exhibits trace the development of Maui's sugar industry. That history began in 1878 when Samuel Alexander and Henry Baldwin engineered a fifty-mile ditch to bring water from the wet side of the island to irrigate the central flatlands. The museum has six rooms of artifacts, old photos, video presentations and a detailed scale model of a sugar mill. Displays focus on the thousands of contract workers brought from other South Seas islands, plus China, Japan, Puerto Rico, Portugal and Spain. They are of course forefathers and mothers of Hawai'i's ethnic diversity.

Visitors can taste a bit of the adjacent mill's partially-refined sugar and take a packet with them. The museum and mill are surrounded by 38,000 acres of sugarcane, one of the largest stands remaining in the islands.

3 ATLANTIS SUBMARINES

Lahaina waterfront; (808) 667-2224; www.go-atlantis.com. Operates daily from Lahaina Harbor, starting at 9. Major credit cards; $$$$$. ☺

One of several Atlantis craft operating in the Hawaiian Islands, this snug sub descends to more than a hundred feet, then cruises slowly past a pair of offshore reefs. All of its forty-eight passengers get window seats and good fish sightings are just about guaranteed. On our last cruise, we caught sight of a reef shark lurking in a shallow cave. Several schools of fish swirled about us and huge critter called an *olua* frequently flashed by, too fast to be photographed.

For the best fish sightings, pick a sunny day. The water is usually very clear off Lahaina, although it can get murky after heavy rains. Even under less than ideal conditions, lights mounted on the sub's sides brighten things. Some of the fish seem to glow in the light and they seem not to mind the presence of this big tin fish.

4 ʻIAO VALLEY STATE PARK

At the end of Iao Valley Road, just west of Wailuku; free. Hawaiʻi Nature Center open daily 10 to 4; (808) 244-6500; $. GETTING THERE: ʻIao Valley and the nature center are just west of downtown Wailuku. The entry road is an extension of Kaʻahumanu Avenue, Wailuku's main street. Coming from Lahaina, head toward Wailuku on Highway 30, then turn left onto Iao Valley Road. ☺

ʻIao Needle is one of Hawaiʻi's most photographed features—a conical spire rising 1,200 feet from the thick foliage of a rainforest valley. "Needle" is an overstatement, since it's a rather a chubby thing. It's almost always shrouded in mist because the ʻIao Valley is one of the wettest places on the island. This is the most imposing landform in the West Maui Mountains, a series of deeply eroded clefts with almost sheer walls. Its 5,788-foot Puʻu Kukui peak is soaked with more than 400 inches of rainfall a year. The "Needle" is a tough basaltic core that has withstood all that rain-driven erosion.

A short, steep trail leads from a parking area to an overlook just below the needle. Two streams cascade invitingly down this jungle-clad valley and many visitors—despite warning signs about slippery rocks—like to splash in the cool water.

Kepaniwai Heritage Gardens and the **Hawaiʻi Nature Center** are just outside the park entrance. Kepaniwai has several theme gardens and reconstructed houses or temples of the ethnic groups that have come to Hawaiʻi—Japanese, English, Korean, South Sea islanders and others. Unfortunately, most of the structures were rather shabby when we visited, and the prim English cottage was locked, being used for storage. The nature center has exhibits on the flora, fauna and geology of the ʻIao Valley.

5 HOLY GHOST CHURCH & KUKA GARDENS

Holy Ghost Church, Lower Kula Road, Waiakoa/Kula; (808) 878-1261; church open daily 9 to 4; gift shop open weekdays except Tuesday, 9 to 1 and after 9:30 Sunday mass; donations appreciated. Kula Botanical Gardens, Highway 377; (808) 878-1715; daily 9 to 4. Major credit cards; $. GETTING THERE: Both are in the Kula community en route to Haleakala National Park. Follow Highway 37 about eighteen miles south from Kahului, then shift onto Lower Kula Road in Waiakoa/Kula. Continue on Lower Kula until it rejoins the highway, then turn left onto Route 377 toward Haleakala; the botanical garden is about half mile up.

These two attractions would be worth a special drive even if you weren't going to Haleakala National Park, and you probably will. **Holy Ghost Church**—actually Holy Ghost Mission—is one of the most unusual churches in the islands, with a corrugated octagonal roof topped by a witch's hat bell tower. The interior is bright and airy and beautifully restored, with natural wood pews and multicolored *bas relief* Stations of the Cross. The hand-carved altar is gorgeous—white and polychrome with gold trim, with a *bas relief* Last Supper scene at its base. At the adjacent gift shop, ask for a loaf of *pao doce,*, a Portuguese bread so sweet it's like eating pound cake. Volunteers bake it every Monday and Thursday morning in the church's social hall, and there are usually a few loaves left over.

Kula is a predominately Portuguese community, settled in the early 1880s by sugar plantation workers who came from the Azores and Madeira Islands. The unusual church was designed by Father James Beissel, who arrived to minister to the community in 1882. Octagonal churches are not unusual in Portugal, although this is the only one in the Hawaiian Islands.

Kula Botanical Gardens just beyond the church is an attractive six-acre tropical preserve terraced up a steep slope. A path meanders past waterfalls and ponds, and through a covered bridge. The garden specializes in Polynesian flora such as protea, bromeliads, orchids and native koa and kukui trees. It also exhibits unusual flora from around the world, including a collection of poisonous plants. Among the garden's facilities are a picnic area, gazebo and a small aviary. A gift shop has a good selection of plant-related items, books and Hawai'i-theme giftwares, plus light snacks and beverages. Kula Botanical Gardens was established in 1968 as Maui's first educational preserve for tropical plants.

6 MAUI OCEAN CENTER

192 Ma'alaea Rd., Ma'alaea; (808) 270-7000; www.mauioceancenter.com. Daily 9 to 5; until 6 during July and August. Major credit cards; $$. GETTING THERE: It's at Ma'alaea Harbor, off Highway 30 midway between Lahaina and Wailuku. ☺

This fine aquarium is the largest in the state, dedicated to the display, study and preservation of Hawai'i's reefs and sea life. A trip through the center takes one from the coast to the deepest trenches of the Pacific—figuratively, at least. Visitors first encounter the shallow Surge Zone outdoors, then they enter the Living Reef exhibit, with forty aquarium tanks containing an impressive variety of sea life. The next "descent" is to Deep Hawaii, with videos of strange creatures thousands of feet down, and exhibits of deep dive vehicles, including the center's own Makali'i research sub.

Other exhibits focus on the early Hawaiians' almost mystical relationship with the sea; and on the humpback whale's long migration from Alaska to Hawai'i. (Clever bit: A stack of milk cartons symbolizes the nearly 100 gallons of milk that a baby humpback consumes daily.) New in 2003 is the Micro-World exhibit of plankton and other tiny things in the ocean. The center also has a touch pool for kids, a turtle lagoon and a sting ray cove. Naturalists are posted at various places to explain what folks are seeing. The facility has an attractive restaurant, an informal café and a very large gift shop.

7 MAUI TROPICAL PLANTATION

1670 Hono'api'ilani Hwy., Waikapu; (808) 244-7643. Country Store open daily 9 to 5; Plantation Café 11 to 2. Major credit cards. "Tropical Express" trams run 10 to 4; $. GETTING THERE: The plantation is on Highway 30, about midway between Ma'alaea Harbor and Wailuku.

This "plantation" is a tourist gimmick although it's a good one. The Country Store features Maui's best variety of specialty foods, and its tropical fruits—chubby apple bananas, pineapples, papayas and such—are even cheaper than in local supermarkets. If you want to ship pineapples home, the store probably has Maui's best prices. And naturally it sells the usual souvenirs and T-shirts.

The "Pineapple Express" is a tram that takes visitors through an area thickly planted with tropical fruits, flowers and flowering trees. It trundles past pineapple and taro patches, and beneath coconut palms and papaya trees. At mid-tour, the driver stops for a brief coconut shredding demonstration. In fact the entire tour is brief, only about forty minutes. You can save tram fare by walking the course, although you'll miss the narration.

8 TEDESCHI VINEYARDS

Highway 37 at 'Ulupalakua Ranch; (808) 878-6058; www.maui-wine.com. Daily 10 to 5; tours at 10:30 and 1:30; MV/VISA. GETTING THERE: The ranch complex and winery are about twenty-seven miles south of Kahului.

Maui's only commercial winery is worth a stop even if you don't know a Cabernet from a calabash and don't care. It's part of the handsome 'Ulupalakua Ranch complex, shaded by towering eucalyptus and Italian cypress trees. The tasting room is housed in a New England style clapboard cottage built for a royal visit by King Kalakaua in 1874. It has displays about the history of the ranch, the "Merrie Monarch," and present owner C. Pardee Erdman's work to restore much of the ranch's endemic dryland forest.

The wines? Well, this isn't exactly the Napa Valley, although the region's mild climate is suitable for the hybrid Carnelian grape from California. Tedeschi produces red, pink and sparkling wine from the Carnelian, as well as some fun pineapple wines. They're the best of the lot, suitable for picnics.

Also worth a stop is the old fashioned wooden-floored 'Ulupalakua Ranch Store. Note the comic life-sized carvings on its porch; they portray real folks who once worked here. The store has a few grocery items, souvenirs, cowboy hats and shirts. A small deli specializes in elk burgers; elk are raised on the ranch.

Alive and onstage

Of all outer island communities, only Lahaina has the tourist traffic to support live productions. Two shows perform regularly in the old whaling port and we herewith present our biased reviews.

9 'ULALENA

878 Front St.; (877) 688-4800 or (808) 661-9913; www.ulalena. com. Tuesday at 6 and 8, Wednesday-Saturday at 6 only; dark Sunday-Monday. Major credit cards; $$$$$. GETTING THERE: It's in the Maui Myth & Magic Theatre near the corner of Papalaua.

What's an *'ulalena*? It's a mystical rain that nurtured early people of Hawai'i and their legends, and this show attempts to capture its essence. It can best be described as kinetic art primitive, with primal dancing to a wild percussion beat that shakes this steeply tiered theater. The sets are both simple and dramatic; gauzy scrim curtains and inventive costuming give 'Ulalena its mystical edge. It's similar to a Cirque de Soleil production, but on a more ethereal level. In fact, two former members of that troupe helped create the show. 'Ulalena is not only the best live production on Maui, it's the best in the islands, surpassing anything on Waikiki. There is no dialogue and the singing and chanting are in Hawaiian, so read the program before the curtain rises.

The show begins with the emergence of a taro plant, who/which dances about like a baby Green Giant. Subsequent scenes trace the history and legends of Hawaiians, with dancers in art primitive costumes scampering about the stage, looking furtive and lost; I've felt the same way in Honolulu traffic. In a comic-tragic scene, Captain Cook arrives, played by a cocky little banty rooster of a performer. He introduces them to white man's ways, symbolized by a silly ring-toss toy and a musket. Later, masked and therefore faceless imported field workers surge onto the stage. The monarchy falls, then—in the show's nicest moment—the taro plant is reawakened by audience-induced rainfall.

It isn't what you think.

10 WARREN & ANNABELLE'S MAGIC SHOW

900 Front St., Lahaina; (808) 667-MAGIC; www.warrenandanna-belles.com. Nightly except Sunday at 6. Major credit cards; $$$$$. GETTING THERE: It's near the corner of Front and Papalua in the Lahaina Center. ☺

Most shows in Hawai'i—and most of them are in Waikiki—have Polynesian themes or music. However, this is a one-man comedy act that would play well in Las Vegas. In fact, Warren Gibson, who does sleight-of-hand tricks within inches of unbelieving eyes, is better than most Las Vegas magicians. He doesn't use mystery boxes or shrouds and he doesn't saw anyone in half. He simply uses his hands to make things disappear and reappear and, yes, his sleeves are rolled up. All the while, he keeps up a constant patter of one-liners and sight gags. He pulls a sponge rubber bunny from a hat and then an entire bowling ball. ("Bowler hat, get it?") His best feat is burning a $100 bill borrowed from a member of the audience; it reappears in a very strange place.

The show begins with the guests seated in a comfortable parlor. Here, patrons nibble appetizers and sip drinks while the invisible ghost of Annabelle entertains at a piano. A hostess invites request from the audience and Annabelle immediately plays them. But no one's sitting at the keyboard. Then guests adjourn to the intimate 78-seat theater, where Warren awaits.

THE TEN BEST MAUI ACTIVITIES

Haleakala National Park is our favorite Maui place to be, and greeting the sunrise there—for some masochistic reason—is our favorite thing to do. The other nine choices are in no particular order, except that we've grouped the walks together.

1 GREET THE DAWN AT HALEAKALA NATIONAL PARK

Park Headquarters open 7:30 to 4; Haleakala Visitor Center open 6 to 3. Park admission: $$ per car or $ per person; free with Golden Eagle, Age or Access pass. GETTING THERE: See above. ☺

Are we having fun yet? It is a popular ritual for Maui visitors to rise at an ungodly hour, drive for two or more hours up a twisting, winding road to the Haleakala summit viewpoint and sit shivering in the dark, waiting for sunup.

Sometimes, sunup is awesome; sometimes you'll wish you had stayed in bed. The sunrise is most striking when it's wreathed in golden-tinted clouds. On our last visit, the terrain below was blanketed in clouds, so sunrise was delayed for half an hour until it had cleared the cloud cover. It was as if Maui and returned and lassoed it again to slow it down. This prolonged our shivering, but when the sun finally arrived, it painted the clouds with a crimson lining. Then the cloud cover dissipated as if blown away by Maui's hot breath, and shafts of light spilled into Haleakala's crater. It was worth the wait.

TRAVEL AND BODILY WARMTH TIPS: Although it requires getting up even earlier, plan to arrive at the top of the crater an hour before sunrise. Whatever for? Because this spectacle is very popular and the summit parking lot will be filled if you wait until the last minute. Take a flashlight, since there are no lights at the vista point. Also, it's about thirty degrees cooler atop Haleakala than at Maui's beaches, so dress warmly for this sunrise experience. Since most of us don't fly to the tropics with a down jacket in our luggage, a borrowed blanket from your hotel room will work just fine.

2 PROWL THE LAHAINA WATERFRONT

Downtown Lahaina at Front, Hotel, Canal and Wharf streets.

The Lahaina waterfront and adjacent Banyan Tree Park are the town's historic and social centers, popular gathering places for locals and visitors. The park's dramatic centerpiece is the world's second largest banyan tree. (The largest is in the Indian Botanical Gardens in Calcutta.) Its air roots drop from thick upper branches and crawl back into the soil, forming a complex webwork of limbs and vines. The tree was planted in 1873 by Lahaina Sheriff William Owen Smith; it now stands sixty feet tall and shades two-thirds of an acre. It's carved with hundreds of initials of lovers and bratty children.

Arts and crafts fairs are held most weekends beneath the Banyan tree. Dozens of local artists and craftspeople display their wares, and many demonstrate on their skills. Food booths offer a variety of ethnic snacks.

The coral block **Old Lahaina Courthouse** on the square's harbor side was built as customs house and government center in 1859. The ground floor houses the Lahaina Visitor Center and gift shop, (808) 667-9193; and the Banyan Tree Gallery, where works of local artists are displayed and sold, (808) 661-0111; both are open daily 9 to 5. The Lahaina Historical Museum occupies second floor, with exhibits on the settlement of Maui. Operated by the Lahaina Restoration Foundation, it's open daily 10 to 4; (808) 661-3262.

The adjacent **waterfront**, where hundreds of whaling ships once anchored, hosts pleasure craft, charter boats and excursion boats. Stalls along the beachwalk offer everything from para-sailing to submarine rides to diving and snorkeling trips.

Moored on the north side of the waterfront is the *Carthaginian II,* a replica of a nineteenth century square-rigged brig. It's typical of the fast sailing ships that supplied the growing colonies in the Hawaiian Islands. It once served as a museum to early day shipping and whaling, although it's now closed to the public. In fact, the old ship may be scuttled, since it's a replica and not an original. The Lahaina Restoration Foundation is looking for an authentic ship that will reflect Lahaina's whaling days. So you may see the old *Carthaginian,* another ship or an empty spot beside the pier by the time you arrive.

3 SEE MAUI BY CHOPPER

Blue Hawaiian Helicopters, 105 Kahului Heliport, Kahului; (800) 745-BLUE or (808) 871-8844; www.bluehawaiian.com. Major credit cards; $$$$$. GETTING THERE: The heliport is at Kahului International Airport just east of town. ☺

Helicopter flight-seeing is not inexpensive in Hawai'i; prices range from about $100 to well over $200. However, a good flight can be quit spectacular. We chose Blue Hawaiian because the firm flies the new Eco-Star helicopter, which is quiet and roomy, with good visibility from its Plexiglas bubble cockpit.

Blue Hawaiian has a variety of flights and we chose its around the island trip, which rims east and west Maui. We passed over Kahului and Wailuku, then headed for the knife-edge West Maui Mountains. Above the 'Iao Valley, the pilot skimmed past the Wall of Tears, where six thin silvery streams cascade down steep slopes. The name was inspired by Kamehameha's defeat of a Maui chieftain in 1790. The route then took us over Lahaina and Ka'anapali, with the islands of Lana'i and Moloka'i hunkering offshore.

We later rimmed the coast off Haleakala National Park, looking down into its great shallow crater. The scene changed dramatically as we cruised over the verdant forests of Hana. We cruised above the ruggedly scenic coastline, thinking what a painless way this was to follow the Hana Highway. Our pilot pointed out a particularly craggy stretch of shoreline with slender seastacks that was used in the filming of *Jurassic Park*. He was bragging, of course; Blue Hawaiian did the all flying for the Maui scenes in the film.

4 SNORKEL OR DIVE AT MOLOKINI

Trilogy Cruises, Ma'alaea Harbor; (888) 225-MAUI; www.sailtrilogy.com. Half-day cruises depart daily at 6:15. Major credit cards; $$$$$. GETTING THERE: Ma'alaea Harbor is off Highway 30 about midway between Lahaina an Wailuku. Cruises leave from slip 99 on the east side of the harbor. ☺

Trilogy operates sleek catamarans, with a variety of trips off Maui and across the Lahaina Roadstead to Lana'i. The firm is noted for its onboard food as well as its cruises. Expect fresh cinnamon buns and fruit as a pre-launch snack and grilled teriyaki chicken, corn on the cob, salad and ice cream for lunch. Whenever there's a breeze, the crew likes to billow the catamaran's sails, and sailing is the ultimate form of cruising.

One of Trilogy's most popular trips is to the small tuff cone of Molokini, three miles offshore and just southeast of Wailea. Like a tilted teacup, it's a near-perfect crater with the north side dipped into the sea, providing an ideal shelter for sealife. Away from shore pollution and runoff, the water is remarkably clear; we could easily see more than a hundred feet down. Although the reefs aren't awesome, we saw a good number of fish. The trip accommodates both snorkelers and divers, and some of the SCUBA folks saw lobsters, a reef shark and an eagle ray. After snorkeling for about an hour, we sailed back to Maui and cruised into Ahihi-kinaʻu Cove, a green sea turtle preserve. We hit the water again and saw several turtles, along with a good assortment of reef fish. Incidentally, Molokini is one of Hawaiʻi's most popular snorkeling areas, so expect it to be crowded.

5 TOUR A PINEAPPLE PATCH

Kapalua Resort, 500 Office Rd., Kapalua; (808) 669-8088. Weekdays at 9:30 and 12:30. Major credit cards; $$$. GETTING THERE: The tour begins at the Kapalua Villas reception center. To reach it, follow Highway 30 nine miles north from Lahaina to Kapalua and turn left onto Office Road. The reception center comes up shortly on your right, just past the Honolua Store.

What's interesting about touring a pineapple field? How about all the pineapple you can eat, plucked right from the plant and "field peeled" by your guide's machete. Or watching workers follow behind the awkward-looking pineapple harvester, feeding fruit onto its fifty-foot-long boom. And being able to pick your own pineapple to take home.

The Maui Pineapple Company, now part of the Kapalua resort firm, has made this tour more interesting than it ought to be. Many of the guides are former pineapple workers, so they know what they're talking about. Vans take visitors to the fields high in the flanks of the West Maui Mountains; views down to Kaʻanapali, the Lahaina waterfront and islands of Lanaʻi and Molokaʻi are quite fine. Guests learn that the firm started planting pineapples in 1912 and it's the only grower left on Maui, farming about 3,500 acres. Its parent company now farms mostly tourists. Nearly all of the 1,500-acre Kapalua complex, including its three golf courses, covers former pineapple fields.

6 RIDE THE SUGARCANE TRAIN

975 Limahana Place, Lahaina; (800) 499-2307 or (808) 667-6851; www.sugarcanetrain.com. Lahaina departures daily from 11:05 to 4; $$; dinner train Thursdays at 5; $$$$$; major credit cards. GETTING THERE: The Lahaina depot is just north of town. Turn right from Highway 30 onto Hinau Street, go right again onto Limahana Place and follow it about two blocks to the end. ☺

Time was when this cute little red and black steam train ran through sugarcane fields, almost disappearing beneath the tall stalks. The sugar is gone although the train survives; it has hauled five million passengers since it started in 1969. Trains carried cane along this route to the now-defunct Pioneer Sugar Mill in Lahaina from 1890 until the 1950s.

This ride will mostly interest train buffs, since the coaches are pulled by a handsomely restored steam engine. Train fans like to gather and watch it do its slow-motion spin at the Lahaina Station turntable. It chugs off to Puʻukoliʻi Station near the Kapalua complex and returns to Lahaina, with a stop at Kaʻanapali. A conductor sitting in the middle car points out sights, plunks a banjo and sings as the train clatters and chugs along. However, the noise of the choo-choo and babble of passengers drowns out most of his narration and singing. The views are the same as you'd see driving between Lahaina and Kapalua, but it's more fun this way if you're a fan of old steam trains.

7 DO A LUAU

Maui's west coast is home to several luaus and these are our three favorites. Two are in Lahaina and the other is at Kaʻanapali's Royal Lahaina Resort. All three include open bars in the luau price. ☺

OLD LAHAINA LUAU, *Lahaina beachfront at 1251 Front St.; (808) 662-8688; www.oldlahainaluau.com. Nightly at 5:30. Major credit cards; $$$$$.* GETTING THERE: It's behind the Lahaina Cannery Mall. Go north on Highway 30 just past the Cannery, turn left onto Kapunakea Street and then left again onto Front Street.

The Old Lahania Luau occupies a grand site, on the beach overlooking the Lahaina Roadstead. Seating areas are separated by lava walls; purists can request mat seating down front and dine as the *aliʻi* dined a century ago. More than a luau, it's also a mini-craft fare. Locals create and sell their folk crafts and demonstrate tasks such as poi-pounding and tapa cloth making. The luau features the ceremonial unearthing of the *kalua* pig from the *imu.* And this is no staged event; the pig has been down there all day. Guests are invited to come by around 7 a.m. to watch it being buried.

Old Lahaina has a better food selection than most luaus, with a good mix of traditional and contemporary fare. Although the luau is buffet style, full trays of desserts and Kona coffee arrive at the tables at meal's end. During dinner, a Hawaiian combo provides soft music until the show starts. It's a wiggly history lesson, with a narrator telling the story of Hawaiʻi's Polynesian culture. This provides a fine excuse for sexy young women and muscular men to show off their traditionally costumed if scantily clad bodies.

THE FEAST AT LELE, *505 Front St., Lahaina; (808) 667-5353; www.feastatlele.com. Tuesday-Saturday starting at 6. Major credit cards; $$$$$. GETTING THERE: It's on the beach side of the 505 Front Street shops, at Front and Shaw just south of Lahaina Harbor.*

This "Feast" is more than a luau; it's a presentation of the cultures and some of the fare of Hawaiʻi, Tonga, Tahiti and Samoa. Some of the foods are typical of these areas while others seem more focused on showing off the skills of the kitchen staff. That's not a complaint; Chef James McDonald's cuisine is excellent. This is the best "luau" food you'll get in the islands. And unlike typical luaus, all service is at tableside; no standing in line for poi and *lau lau*.

Like the Old Lahaina Luau, the Feast at Lele is presented in a fine setting. It's just off the beach, with views of Lahaina Harbor, the dark profile of Lana'i and—on occasion—the lights of a visiting cruise ship. With tiki torches, candle-lit tables, Hawaiian sunsets, pleasant music and wriggling torsos—women's and men's—this is a romantic outing. The show is fun and sometimes sexy. The Tahitian dancing is particularly upbeat, and the program ends with the usual Samoan fire knife dancers.

ROYAL LAHAINA LUAU, Royal Lahaina Resort, Keka'a Drive, Ka'anapali; (808) 661-9119; www.Hawaiianhotels.com. Nightly starting at 5 to 5:30. Major credit cards; *$$$$$. GETTING THERE: Royal Lahaina Resort is at the northern end of Keka'a Drive. Go north from Lahaina on Highway 30, take the second left into Ka'anapali, then go right on Keka'a to the end.*

The Royal Lahaina Luau is a bit less expensive than the two above, and it also occupies a pleasing beachside setting. Like the Old Lahaina Luau, it features the traditional *imu* unearthing. In addition to the traditional *kalua* pork, Hawaiian sweet potatoes, salmon, poi and other fare, the luau features a kids' menu of hot dogs and macaroni. Tuesday, Wednesday, Friday and Sunday are "Family Nights" when a child under 12 eats free with each paying adult.

The show isn't as authentic as the two above, although it's fun. The emcee keeps the audience chuckling with a few jokes, and mass hula lessons. Tahitian hulas dominate the dancing, much to the pleasure of male guests, and naturally, the show ends with muscular young Somoans twirling fire.

Getting physical

After doing all those luaus, we now suggest three ways to shed some of the excess poundage.

8 TAKE THE LAHAINA WALKING TOUR

In downtown Lahaina, starting at the corner of Front and Dickenson. All level with long (1.5-hour) and short (45-minute) versions. FOR INFORMATION: Lahaina Restoration Foundation, 120 Dickson St.; office open weekdays 8 to 4; (808) 661-3262.

A walking tour of Lahaina's historic and cultural sites has been laid out by the Lahaina Restoration Foundation, which is responsible for much of the town's preservation. Map brochures showing thirty-one historic sites are available in the Lahaina Visitor Center. They're also in brochure racks around town and at the restoration foundation's office at Front and Dickenson, where the walk begins.

The map takes walkers to a pair of mission houses and to some old churches and shrines, plus several sites where bronze plaques mark former structures. Among its more interesting lures are the coral walled 1850s **Lahaina prison**, where randy sailors where thrown to sober up after a night the town; the Dr. Dwight **Baldwin missionary home**, with period furnishings and some of the doctor's fierce-looking medical implements; and the **Wo Hing Museum** in a Chinese Taoist temple, with history exhibits downstairs and the gaudy red and gold temple on the second floor. In the adjacent former cookhouse, visitors can watch jiggly old movie footage of Hawai'i shot by Thomas A. Edison at the turn of the last century.

9 WALK KA'ANAPALI

Along the Ka'anapali beachfront; about 1.5 mile round trip, all level. GETTING THERE: Start at Hanakao'o Beach Park, about 2.5 miles north of Lahaina, off Highway 30.

This paved path follows the landscaped shoreline between Ka'ana-pali's beach and its most opulent resorts. As you stroll, the offshore islands of Lana'i and Moloka'i will be your constant visual companions. You can leave your car at the **Hanakao'o Beach** parking lot. Or if you're really ambitious, park at the Lahaina Cannery Mall at the northern edge of Lahaina and add a couple of miles to your walk. You can follow a dirt path along the shoulder of the highway.

From Hanakao'o Beach Park, follow a paved path past an old cemetery and the **Kahana Canoe Club**. You'll soon reach the parking lot for the ❖ **Hyatt Regency's** Spa Moana. Walk through the parking lot to the beach to pick up the southern end of the shoreline path. Head north, passing in front of the gorgeously landscaped grounds of the Hyatt, with its complex water feature of streams and pools.

You'll next encounter the ❖ **Maui Marriott.** The **Ali'i Beachwalk Market & Pantry** at the Marriott's northern edge is a good place to pick up a snack and cup of designer coffee; it opens at 6:30 a.m. Next comes the **Ali'i Ka'anapali** condos, and then the ❖ **Westin Maui**, one of Ka'anapali's most opulent resorts, with an elaborate lagoon and pool complex. Immediately beyond, you'll pass in front of **Whalers Village**, with a couple of waterfront restaurants, **Leilani's** and **Hula Grill**, both open for lunch and dinner. The **Rusty Harpoon**, set back off the beach, is open for breakfast.

Check out the **Whalers Village Museum**, with exhibits indoors and out on the whaling industry. Displays include a huge whale skeleton, scale-model whaling ship and scrimshaw. The museum shop is open daily from 9 to 9:30; (808) 661-5992.

The ❖ **Whaler Resort** is at the shopping center's northern edge. Just beyond, the beach walk ends rather abruptly at the ❖ **Sheraton**

Maui, tucked against a steep lava cliff called Black Rock. That promontory marks the end of your walk. Before turning back, however, take the trail up to the Sheraton's Discovery Room atop the rock for a grand view of Ka'anapali Beach.

10 DO THE WAILEA COAST WALK

Three-mile round trip, all level; between the Fairmont Kea Lani and Ulua Beach. GETTING THERE: To reach Wailea from Kahului, go south on Highway 311, which blends into the Pi'ilani Highway (Route 31) at Kihei. Follow it into the resort, then turn left onto Wailea Alanui Drive. Go past the Fairmont Kea Lani and turn right onto Kauhaki Street. You'll find parking along here, near Polo Beach.

This is a pleasant stroll, along a concrete coastwalk above a mix of sandy and lava rock beaches. It takes you past four luxury resorts—the Fairmont, Four Seasons, Wailea Grand and Outrigger Wailea. You may want to detour inshore to see their attractive lobbies, landscaped pool complexes and other public areas. Most of these hotels provide courtesy ice water along the beach walk; they're intended for their guests although they probably won't mind if you help yourself.

Begin at Polo Beach and stroll north past the front of the ❖ **Fairmont Kea Lani**. As you walk, look offshore to the southwest for the tiny crescent of ❖ **Molokini** and the island of **Kaho'olawe,** once a naval gunnery range and now being cleaned up and returned to the Hawaiian people. Ahead, you can see the distant crests of the **West Maui Mountains**.

Just past the Fairmont, you'll encounter the lava stone base of an early Polynesian dwelling at **Wailea Point.** An upscale condo complex is just inshore. Here, the walk becomes a linear botanical reserve, the **Native Hawaiian Coastal Garden**, with scores of plants indigenous to the islands. You'll soon pass the ❖ **Four Seasons Resort** and then the ❖ **Grand Wailea Resort.** At the southern edge of the ❖ **Outrigger Wailea Resort** is a beach hut and espresso bar, in case you need a caffeine fix. Nearby, a coin-fed telescope invites peeks at the boats at play and at anchor in Molokini's bay. In winter, you might be able to scope out a humpback whale offshore.

Walk past the sloping green lawns of the Outrigger and continue a short distance to **Uhlua Beach**, a public park. If you want to turn strolling into window shopping, walk inland through the Outrigger complex to the **Shops at Wailea**, a very attractive mall.

THE TEN BEST MAUI RESTAURANTS

Maui offers Hawai'i's best dining variety outside of Honolulu, with some of the state's very best restaurants. In fact, the Zagat Survey's *Hawaii Top Restaurants* had more selections from Maui on its top twenty list than from O'ahu.

The closest thing this island has to a restaurant row is in the Hawai'i plantation style 505 Front Street shopping complex just south of the Lahaina waterfront. It has several restaurants, including **I'o, Pacific'O, Old Lahaina Café,** ❖ **Bamboo Bar & Grill** and **Hecock's,** plus the beachside ❖ **Feast at Lele.**

PRICING: Dollar sign codes indicate the price of a typical dinner with entrée, soup or salad, not including drinks, appetizers or dessert: **$** = less than $10 per entrée; **$$** = $10 to $19; **$$$** = $20 to $29; **$$$$** = $30 to $40; **$$$$$** = $41 and beyond.

1 DAVID PAUL'S LAHAINA GRILL

127 Lahainaluna Rd.; Lahaina; (808) 667-5117; www.lahainagrill.com. American nouveau; full bar service. Dinner nightly. Major credit cards; $$$$ to $$$$$. Reservations essential. GETTING THERE: It's at the corner of Lahainaluna and Front Street, a few blocks north of the banyan tree square.

Maui's best dining spot occupies the historic Lahaina Inn building, and the restaurant itself has made history since opening in 1990. It has won accolades from *Bon Appétit, Condé Nast Traveler* and *Food & Wine* magazines, and from local foodies, who annually select it as Maui's best restaurant.

Chef Paul's inventive menu changes constantly, so you may or may not find savories such as Maui onion-crusted *ahi* with vanilla bean jasmine rice, roasted breast of chicken with polenta, mahi mahi with spinach and garlic mashed potatoes, or Kona coffee roasted rack of lamb. The interior of the old building has been nicely restored, with polished wood floors, a marble topped bar and pressed tin ceiling. Splashy canvasses from Lahaina impressionistic artist Jan Kasprazycki add a contemporary touch.

2 THE BAY CLUB

Kapalua Bay Hotel, One Bay Dr., Kapalua; (808) 669-8008; www.starwood.com/kapalua. American-Mediterranean; mostly seafood; full bar service. Dinner nightly; jackets for gentlemen. Major credit cards; $$$$ to $$$$$.

Club indeed. The look is Hawaiian country club with dark woods, wicker furniture and louvered folding window walls that open to the sea. The clubby look is brightened by a Hawaiian mural along one wall. The Bay Club is part of the Kapalua Bay Hotel although it's in a free-standing bungalow about a quarter of a mile down the beach; shuttle service is available.

The menu is seafood-focused with Italian-Mediterranean accents. Some recent entrées were macadamia nut-crusted mahi mahi, seared *ahi* saltimbocca, a three-course lobster sampler, grilled veal chop, and Basque style rack of lamb. The restaurant also features a five-course tasting dinner, available with matching wines.

3 CHEZ PAUL

820 Highway 30 in Olowalu Village; (808) 661-3843. French; full bar service. Dinner nightly. Major credit cards; $$$ to $$$$. GETTING THERE: It's about six miles southeast of Lahaina.

Sitting alone across the highway from the surf, this might be mistaken—at a casual glance—for a beach restaurant. Step inside, however, and you're in a cozy French country inn, with brick walls, warm woods, café curtains, and tiny oil lamps on the tables. Cozy and dimly lit, it's one of Maui's most romantic restaurants. Chef/owner Patrick Callarec says his fare is "not classic French and not French nouveau, but just good food." Actually, it's French with tropical accents. Entrées include rack of lamb with mango chutney, lobster with saffron basil cream sauce, sautéed prime cut of beef, caramelized Pacific salmon, and *ahi* tuna with sweet peppers and onions.

4 KULA LODGE

Haleakala Highway, Kula; (808) 878-2518; www.kulalodge.com. American; full bar service. Breakfast, lunch and dinner daily. Major credit cards; $$ to $$$. GETTING THERE: It's on the road to Haleakala National Park, just north of the junction of Haleakala Highway and Crater Road.

High on the slopes of Haleakala, this rustic shingle-sided lodge and restaurant offers splendid views from its 3,500-foot perch, down to much of the rest of Maui. Foodies don't get too excited about the kitchen, which the Zagat Survey dismisses as "unpredictable." However, the food is generally well-prepared and served in one of the island's most pleasing settings. Menu offerings include catch of the day, shrimp scampi with scallions, lilikoi prawns, and sugarcane babyback ribs with Hawaiian herbs. The dining room has a homey look with maple furniture, although most diners are looking through the oversized windows to the view. It's a great place to watch the sunset. Outside, a brick path tilts down through a garden to little gazebos, where drinks and light fare are served in summer.

5 MAÑANA GARAGE

33 Lono Ave., Kahului; (808) 873-0220; www.themananaga-rage.com. Latin American; full bar service. Lunch weekdays and dinner nightly. Major credit cards; $$ to $$$. GETTING THERE: It's in downtown Kahului on the south side of Ka'ahumanu Avenue (Kahului's main street), on the ground floor of a green four-story office building.

The whimsical décor of this popular Kahului restaurant is more colorful than garage-like, with festive orange and dark blue trim and striking multicolored Murano glass ceiling fixtures. However, there is a metal garage door at one end, and check out the gas pump door handles and truck bumper foot rests at the bar. This fun place earned *Honolulu* magazine's best new restaurant award when it opened; *The New York Times* called it *industrial chic.* The menu is creative *Latino,* offering tasty curiosities such as guava tamarind-glazed salmon, fajitas with caramelized onions and peppers, macadamia nut-crusted fresh fish with mango chili sauce, and jerk chicken with black beans and red rice. Start with an order of warm cornbread made spicy with bits of chilies.

6 PLANTATION HOUSE RESTAURANT

In the Plantation Golf Course clubhouse at 2000 Plantation Club Dr., Kapalua; (808) 669-6299; www.theplantationhouse.com. Hawaiian with Mediterranean accents; full bar service. Breakfast, lunch and dinner daily. Major credit cards; $$$ to $$$$. GETTING THERE: Follow Highway 30 north from Lahaina to Kapalua. A mile past Office Road, turn right into the Plantation Golf Course. The restaurant is on the second floor of the clubhouse; drive beyond it, since parking is in the rear.

Plantation House is one Maui's most handsome restaurants, with teakwood tables and hand-carved chairs, warm tropical colors and a double-sided fireplace. Window walls open to a gorgeous view of the Plantation Golf Course, the Maui coastline and Moloka'i. And never mind its country club location; the restaurant is open to the hungry public. Chef Alex Stanislaw's kitchen creativity includes pork tenderloin with caramelized onions and Port wine reduction, oven-seared filet mignon with apple-smoked Maui onion confit, and prawn stir-fry with shiitake mushrooms. The wine list is extensive; it has earned the *Wine Spectator's* Award of Excellence.

7 ROY'S KAHANA BAR & GRILL

4405 Highway 30, Kahana; (808) 669-6999. Pacific Rim; full bar service. Dinner nightly. Major credit cards; $$ to $$$$. GETTING THERE: The restaurant is on the second floor in the Kahana Gateway shopping center. From Lahaina, follow Highway 30 about seven miles north to Kahana. The shopping center is on the northwest corner of the highway and Ho'ohui Road.

Roy Yamaguchi's "Asian fusion" cuisine has spread quickly since he opened his first restaurant in Honolulu in 1988. The Maui version is a large, spacious affair—actually two restaurants in one: the Kahana Bar & Grill and the smaller Nicolina. While the Kahana is stylishly cavernous and can get noisy, Nicolina is usually more quiet and it has an outdoor seating area. Yamaguchi's cuisine is a blend of Asian,

Mediterranean, French, Italian and whatever else he might like to include. Some recent examples from a daily-changing menu were hibachi grilled salmon with citrus ponzu sauce, blackened yellowfin tuna in mustard butter sauce, and Szechuan spiced babyback pork ribs.

8 SANSEI SEAFOOD RESTAURANT

115 Bay Dr., Kapalua; (808) 669-6286; www.sanseihawaii.com. Japanese/Pacific Rim; full bar service. Major credit cards; $$ to $$$. GETTING THERE: The restaurant is in the Kapalua Shops adjacent to the Kapalua Bay Hotel. From Lahaina, go north on Highway 30 about eight miles, turn left onto Napilihau Street, then right on Lower Honoapi'ilani Road. The shopping center is a few blocks up, on your left.

You'll like Sansei if you like inventive Asian fare—particularly seafood—and if you don't mind noisy dining. We like the former but are troubled with the latter. Obviously, most people aren't as fussy about noise as we are; Sansei is one of Maui's most popular and busy restaurants. The fare is Pacific Rim although the décor is essential Japanese, with rice paper paneled walls, folk art and historic prints of warriors and geisha.

Some of Sansei's inventive entrées are excellent while a few are simply too busy. Among the tastier ones are grilled fresh mahi mahi over greens with Japanese plum vinaigrette, Atlantic salmon topped with fresh tiger prawns, and shrimp and vegetable tempura with a spicy dipping sauce. Like sushi? Sansei has a separate sushi bar. Like bargains? The restaurant offers twenty-five percent discounts on dinner from 5 to 5:30.

9 SPAGO AT THE FOUR SEASONS

Four Seasons Resort, 3900 Wailea Alanui, Wailea; (808) 879-2999. Mediterranean/Pacific Rim; full bar service. Dinner nightly. Major credit cards; $$$ to $$$$. GETTING THERE: To reach Wailea from Kahului, go south on Highway 311, which blends into the Pi'ilani Highway (route 31) at Kihei. Follow it into the resort complex, go left on Wailea Alanui Drive briefly, then turn right into the Four Seasons.

Wolfgang Puck goes Hawaiian in this sleek Italian-modern restaurant with dark woods and warm tropical colors. The Four Seasons Spago is spacious and airy, with dining indoors and on a broad wraparound veranda. With stone accents, stylish lighting fixtures and art objects, it's one of Maui's more attractive restaurants. Coastal vistas are exceptional from the veranda and from the main dining room.

The menu is a Puckish version of Pacific Rim, with entrées such as roast Cantonese duck, grilled lamb chops with eggplant and chili-mint vinaigrette, roasted free range chicken, caramelized pork chops, pan seared *onaga*, grilled mahi mahi with pineapple ginger barbecue sauce, and 'opakapaka with macadamia nut crust.

10 WATERFRONT RESTAURANT

50 Haouli Street at Maʻalaea Harbor; (808) 244-9028. Hawaiian; mostly seafood; full bar service. Dinner nightly. Major credit cards; $$$ to $$$$. GETTING THERE: Maʻalaea Harbor is off Highway 30 midway between Lahaina and Wailuku. Drive through the harbor complex on Maʻalea Road, go right on Haouli Street briefly and turn into the Milowai Condominium complex. The restaurant is on the ground floor.

This family-owned seafood restaurant is more popular with locals than tourists, mostly because most visitors can't find it. One doesn't expect a fine restaurant to be in a condo complex. However, there it is, on the seaward side of the condos, providing nice views of the harbor. This is a serious seafood venue, featuring fresh fish prepared in a variety of ways, from simple sauté to *en papillote* (in parchment paper) to *en bastille*, jailed in an angel hair potato cage. And of course, there's the Hawaiian way, with Maui onions and fresh pineapple. Other menu items include jumbo scallops, scampi and lobster tail.

Affordable dining

Can't afford that three-course lobster sampler, with appetizer, designer wine and dessert? These Lahaina places offer decent fare—mostly—at very modest prices.

ALOHA MIXED PLATE: *1285 Front St.; (808) 661-3322; Hawaiian ethnic; wine and beer. Lunch through dinner daily. No credit cards; $. GETTING THERE: It's at the beachfront behind the Lahaina Cannery Mall. Go north on Highway 30 just past the Cannery, turn left onto Kapunakea Street and then left again onto Front Street.* □ "Paper plates and a million dollar view," said a *New York Times* writer about this simple open-air diner on a deck overlooking the beach. It's a fun place with modest prices and an unpredictable kitchen. It serves an interesting mix of Hawaiian, Japanese, Chinese, Spanish and Portuguese fare, including very inexpensive plate lunches. For a sampler, try the namesake Aloha Mixed Plate of *shoyu* chicken, teriyaki beef and mahi mahi. For dessert, an unbaked coconut-flavored flan called *haupia* is quite tasty.

BAMBOO BAR & GRILL: *505 Front St.; (808) 667-4051. Vietnamese and Thai; full bar service. Lunch and dinner daily. MC/VISA; $ to $$. GETTING THERE: It's in the 505 Front Street shopping center a few blocks south of the banyan tree square.* □ This simple café with a Polynesian-Asian look serves a tasty assortment of spicy Southeast Asian fare, and the prices are reasonable. Tummy-filling entrées such as lemongrass chicken and Thai curry go for less than $10. Bamboo does a thriving takeout business, so you can carry your booty to the beach or hotel room.

BJ'S CHICAGO STYLE PIZZA: 730 Front St.; (808) 661-0700. Pizza; full bar service. Lunch through late dinner daily. MC/VISA; *$ to $$*. *GETTING THERE: It's on the second floor of an old building just north of the banyan tree square.* ❑ You'll be hard-pressed to find a pizza parlor anywhere with a better view. BJ's second-story perch looks across Front Street to the harbor, boats at anchor and the island of Lana'i. Hold out for a table on the open balcony. This is a lively, up-beat place with nightly entertainment. And the pizza is quite fine, deep dish Chicago style with generous toppings.

LAHAINA FISH COMPANY: 831 Front St.; (808) 661-3472. American; mostly seafood; full bar service. Dinner nightly. Major credit cards; *$$ to $$$*. *GETTING THERE: It's downtown, about a block north of Lahainaluna Street.* ❑ To our knowledge, this place hasn't won any dining awards, although it serves relatively decent and fair-priced food. And we really like its location, built on a pier overlooking the Lahaina waterfront. The décor is tourist aquatic and the café is casual; come in your shorts and tank tops.

PIONEER INN: Wharf and Hotel streets; (808) 661-3636. American; full bar service. Breakfast through dinner daily. Major credit cards; *$$ to $$$*. ❑ Part of the oldest operating hotel in Hawai'i, it's more interesting for its waterfront location and rich Lahaina history than for its ordinary menu. The saloon style main dining room is decorated with a ship's figurehead, ceiling fans and a naughty painting of three fair-skinned nudes who seem in imminent danger of serious sunburns. Our preferred dining spot is on the patio overlooking the giant banyan tree and the Lahaina waterfront.

THE TEN BEST MAUI RESORTS

As it is with Maui dining, so it is with reclining. The Valley Isle has more resort choices than any other island except O'ahu. It has two of the three AAA Five Diamond resorts in the state; the other is on the Big Island.

Maui's high end vacation retreats are focused in three areas—Ka'anapali and Kapalua on the west coast of West Maui, and at Wailea on the western shore of East Maui. Unlike Waikiki, which gradually evolved, all three major Maui resort areas were started as master planned developments. They're a mix of hotels, condos, shopping complexes and of course—golf courses. Ka'anapali, immediately north of Lahaina, was the state's first major resort complex outside Waikiki, started in 1963.

Obviously, our Ten Best selections are pricey, with most nightly room rates starting around $300. If you seek more modest lodgings, check the bottom of this list. Also, Maui has two large and unplanned scatterings of small hotels, inns and condos—the Kahana area sandwiched between Ka'anapali and Kapalua; and the strung-out village of

Kihei north of Wailea. These west-facing beach towns enjoy the same climate as the planned resorts but with few of the amenities.

PRICING: Dollar sign codes indicate room price ranges for two people, based on high season (summer and winter) rates: **$** = a standard two-person room for $99 or less; **$$** = $100 to $149; **$$$** = $150 to $199; **$$$$** = $200 to $249; **$$$$$** $250 or more. **CREDIT CARDS:** All of the below listed cards accept most major credit cards.

In selecting our favorite Maui resorts, we've chosen those that are attractions unto themselves, even for non-guests. Not everyone can afford $350 a night, but anyone can explore a resort's facilities and enjoy its amenities. Our choices are based more on overall resort appeal than on the grandeur of individual rooms. Our top choice, in fact, doesn't have Maui's most opulent rooms, although it has its most striking public areas and great beach views.

1 WESTIN MAUI

2365 Ka'anapali Parkway, Lahaina, HI 96761; (800) WESTIN-1 or (808) 667-2525; www.westin.com. Very stylish beachfront resort with 759 rooms and suites; $$$$$. GETTING THERE: The Westin is in the heart of Ka'anapali, just north of Lahaina. Go north on Highway 30, turn left into the complex on Ka'anapali Parkway, continue briefly north and then turn left into the resort.

The focal point of our favorite Maui resort is its gorgeously landscaped 87,000-square foot lagoon area that extends down to the beachfront. It's busy with cascading waterfalls, streams and five swimming pools. A great people-watching place is the lagoon-side Colonnade Café, a takeout just north of the main lobby. You can get snacks and specialty coffees and settle at a table and converse with ducks, swans, flamingos and noisy macaws. Or stroll the hotel's wide corridors to admire its extensive art collection.

The hotel towers are coral pink with crescent balconies; think of the Westin as Maui's pink palace. The rooms, while not large, are comfortable with the usual resort amenities, and extras such as terry robes and slippers. All have nice views of something—the beach, the inner courtyard or the West Maui Mountains. Dining venues are OnO Surf Bar and Grill at poolside (Hawaiian); the *art moderne Tropica* Restaurant and Bar with shapes suggesting volcanic tipis (American *nouveau*); and the Colonnade Café.

2 FAIRMONT KEA LANI

4100 Wailea Alanui Dr., Wailea, HI 96753; (800) 257-7544 or (808) 875-4100; www.fairmont.com. A luxury 450-unit all-suite resort; $$$$$. GETTING THERE: To reach Wailea from Kahului, go south on Highway 311, which blends into the Pi'ilani Highway (route 31) at Ki-

hei. *Follow it into the resort complex, then turn left onto Wailea Alanui Drive and go about a mile to the Fairmont.*

The first thing to strike your eye is the Fairmont's dazzling white Moorish architecture. The North African look is a startling contrast to the hotel's extravagant green landscaping. The large breezeway lobby continues the look, with Moorish arches and a ceramic-tile trimmed fountain as a centerpiece. Marble floors with plush carpet add elegant touches. Broad flower-trimmed lawns tilt down toward a crescent-shaped sandy beach. Kea Lani is a family-friendly resort with a large children's pool and a Kids Place recreation facility.

Dining choices include the poolside Polo Beach Grill (American-Hawaiian), the Italian-modern Café Ciao with an adjacent deli and bakery, Nick's Fishmarket with a sleek Tuscan look (seafood); and the Mediterranean theme Kea Lani Restaurant (American-Hawaiian). The all-suite accommodations are spacious, stylish and expensive. All have distinctive crescent balconies to complement the Moorish look, plus kitchenettes with microwaves and living rooms with sofas and entertainment centers. For even more money, you can book one of Kea Lani's villas, each with private "plunge pools" and full kitchens.

3 THE FOUR SEASONS

3900 Wailea Alanui, Wailea, HI 96753; (800) 334-MAUI or (808) 874-8000; www.fourseasons.com. Opulent resort with 380 rooms and suites; $$$$$. GETTING THERE: The Four Seasons is just north of the Fairmont Kea Lani; see above.

The Four Seasons is one of two AAA Five Diamond resorts on Maui and it looks the part. An imposing palm-lined drive leads to this Italian-modern retreat, circling around a large spillover fountain. The huge lobby, supported by fluted columns, is open and inviting, with indoor-outdoor landscaping and tasteful art objects on display. A balcony off the lobby and above the pool complex is a fine people-watching spot, with comfy cushioned wicker armchairs. The extensive grounds, busy with pools, waterfalls and fountains, slope down toward a long sandy beach.

The Four Seasons rooms are upscale and spacious, with lanais, refrigerator-bars and amenities such as terry robes and down pillows. Most have ocean views. Bathrooms have eight-foot dual sink vanities, marble tubs and oversized showers for two. Restaurants are Spago (see above), the stylish and intimate Ferraro's (Italian), and Pacific Grill (American-Hawaiian). The resort also has a full service spa with ocean-view treatment rooms.

4 HOTEL HANA-MAUI

P.O. Box 9, Hana, HI 96713; (800) 321-HANA or (808) 248-8211; www.hotelhanamaui.com. A 66-unit luxury ranch style resort; $$$$$.

GETTING THERE: The resort is in the rainforest-clad village of Hana, reached by the famously twisting Hana Highway; see above, page 174.

This exclusive and extremely expensive hideaway set back off Hana's scenic seacoast is one of Maui's most historic properties. It was built by entrepreneurPaul Fagan in 1946 to lure visitors after the local sugarcane industry withered. For more than half a century, the hotel has been *the* hideaway for the rich and famous, including the politically famous. Caroline Kennedy honeymooned here and Hillary Clinton and her daughter Chelsea were recent guests. The low-rise cottage complex has been completely renovated and prices have increased a bit since Fagan charged $5 a night in 1946. Rack rates now start around $425.

The best lodgings are the Sea Ranch Cottages, upscale versions of Hawaiian plantation bungalows, decorated with hand-crafted artwork and traditional fabrics in soft Polynesian colors. Many have hot tubs and even private gardens. All lodgings have mini-bars and ceiling fans; air conditioning isn't necessary here. The main dining room off the lobby serves upscale American fare; other options are the nearby Hana Ranch Restaurant (American-Hawaiian), and the Hawaiian-Western style Paniolo Bar for light fare. The lodge has several tennis courts, a three-hole practice golf course, walking/running trails and riding stables.

5 HYATT REGENCY MAUI

200 Nohea Kai Dr., Lahaina, HI 96761; (800) 55-HYATT or (808) 661-1232; www.maui.hyatt.com. An 806-room luxury resort on Ka'anapali Beach; $$$$$. GETTING THERE: The Hyatt is at the south end of Nohea Kai. From Lahaina, enter the resort on Ka'anapali Parkway and turn right.

The forty-acre Hyatt complex rivals the Westin Maui as the most expansive resort on Ka'anapali. Its dramatic focal point is a huge open-to-the-sky lobby surrounded by the Atrium Tower, with rooms off suspended balconies. Two imposing leaf-glass chandeliers flank the entryway, multiplied by wall to ceiling mirrors. An excellent collection of Asian and Pacific art lines the resort hotel's wide flagstone-paved corridors.

The extensive grounds has a complex water course with a stream cascading over lava boulders, several swimming pools and water slides, including a new kids pool opened in 2003. Restaurants include the Swan Court with Pacific Rim fare; Cascades Grille and Sushi Bar (American/Japanese), Spats Trattoria (Italian), and the Pavilion Restaurant with poolside dining (American-Hawaiian). The fair-sized rooms are decorated with Polynesian prints and Hawaiian artwork. They have typical resort amenities and all have balconies with ocean, courtyard or mountain views.

6 KAPALUA BAY HOTEL

One Bay Dr., Kapalua, HI 96761; (800) 325-3589 or (808) 669-5656; www.starwood.com/kapalua. A mid-rise luxury hotel with 191 rooms and fourteen ocean-front villas; $$$$$. GETTING THERE: Take Highway 30 north about nine miles from Lahaina to Office Road and turn left into the Kapalua complex. Go downhill less than a mile, turn left at a T-intersection, then go south briefly and turn right into the hotel grounds.

This handsome hotel occupies a bluff overlooking Kapalua Bay, providing impressive views from many of the rooms and public areas. The look of the resort is light and airy, with whites and soft beiges throughout. Potted tropical plants bring a bit of the outdoors into the three-story atrium lobby. Rooms are similarly light and bright with Polynesian bamboo-style furniture. Luxury amenities include terry robes and slippers.

The landscaped grounds occupy a small peninsula leading out to lava-rimmed Kapalua Bay; there's a small sandy beach in a nearby cove. A sensuously cozy hot tub below the swimming complex has its own view of the ocean, tucked below a sheltering rock wall. Dining venues include the Gardenia Court with American-Hawaiian fare and live evening entertainment; the Terrace Dining Room, overlooking the beach and ocean; and the Bay Club (see above).

7 KAPALUA VILLAS

500 Office Rd., Kapalua, HI 96761; (800) 545-8088 or (808) 669-5234; www.kapaluavillas.com. Fully furnished one- to five-bedroom condos; $$$$$. GETTING THERE: To reach the reception center (guest check in), follow Highway 30 to Office Road and turn left; it's on your right, just past the Honolua Store.

If you'd like really settle into the Kapalua lifestyle, rent one of these spacious villas. They come completely equipped for living, with full kitchens, washers and dryers. Most are no more expensive than high end Kapalua or Ka'anapali resort rooms. The villas are terraced into gentle slopes, and many have views of at least a slice of the Pacific. All units have balconies and patios. Villa guests have access to Kapalua resort facilities, such as swimming pools, tennis courts and golf courses, including the Plantation Course, where the annual Mercedes Championships starts the PGA tour.

8 OUTRIGGER WAILEA RESORT

3700 Wailea Alanui Dr., Wailea, HI 96753; (800) OUTRIGGER or (808) 879-1922; www.outrigger.com. A luxury 524-unit beachside resort; $$$$$. GETTING THERE: See directions to the Fairmont Kea Lani

204 — CHAPTER TWELVE

above, then turn right onto Wailea Alanui, go past the Shops at Wailea, and left into the Outrigger.

The Outrigger is the least expensive major resort at the very pricey Wailea complex, with rates starting under $300 a night. It's appealing for families, with a youth program and a separate kids' pool. The resort occupies twenty-two landscaped acres above a lava-rugged tide-pool beach. When breakers slam into the rocks, it offers the most dramatic beach view in Wailea. Swimming and sunning beaches are a short walk in either direction.

The rooms are good-sized and nicely furnished and many have that imposing coastal view. The main restaurants are Hula Moons and Kumu Bar & Grill, both American-Hawaiian. The Outrigger could be called the "most Hawaiian" of Maui's resorts, with Polynesian crafts shows and demonstrations, Hawaiian entertainment nightly and luaus four nights a week. For shopping, the stylish Shops at Wailea are a short walk away.

9 RITZ-CARLTON

One Ritz-Carlton Dr., Kapalua, HI 96761; (800) 241-3333 or (808) 669-6200; www.ritzcarlton.com. A luxury mid-rise resort with 548 rooms and suites; $$$$$. GETTING THERE: Follow directions to the Kapalua Villas reception center (above), then go a short distance beyond and turn right.

Maui's other AAA Five Diamond resort, this gorgeous retreat exhibits the usual understated Ritz opulence, with stately and almost austere architecture, and a stylish interior of cut glass chandeliers, marble floors and thick carpets. Tasteful shops line wide corridors that are decorated with contemporary art. The oversized rooms have soft pastel colors, Polynesian artwork and light modern furniture; each has a balcony and most have ocean views.

The Ritz-Carlton occupies a 55-acre complex that blends into the Kapalua Bay Golf Course; there's a putting green immediately below the hotel. The large swimming pool is shaped like a *fleur de lys* to create individual bays, with depths for adults and kids. The resort isn't on the shore, although a path leads to a public beach park, where the Ritz maintains an activity hut for its guests; shuttles are available. The Ritz has many dining choices, including the Banyan tree (contemporary American), Kai Sushi Bar, the casual Terrace Restaurant (American), and the Beach House (light fare) down by the sea.

10 SHERATON MAUI

2605 Ka'anapali Parkway, Lahaina, HI 96761-1991; (800) 782-9488 or 661-0031l www.sheraton-hawaii.com. Luxury mid-rise resort with 510 rooms and suites; $$$$$. GETTING THERE: Follow directions *to the Ka'anapali complex and continue on Ka'anapali Parkway to the end of the street.*

After a major renovation that included replacing some of its hotel wings several years ago, the Sheraton is one of Ka'anapali's more appealing resorts. Particularly appealing is its "end-of-the-beach" location, in a shallow bay and tucked up against a lava ridge called Black Rock. It provides the resort with Ka'anapali's most sheltered beach; it's a good snorkeling and diving area. A path leads to the top of the promontory, providing a fine Ka'anapali view. The expansive 23-acre complex is dominated by a landscaped lagoon with lava-lined serpentine streams and a large swimming pool.

The hotel lobby is open and spacious, decorated with Polynesian art and crafts. Most of the rooms in the Sheraton's seven mid-rise towers have ocean views and all have balconies. They're are fairly spacious, with Polynesian décor and fabrics. For dining, Keka'a Terrace features Hawaiian regional fare; Teppanyaki Dan serves Asian-fusion; and Coral Reef issues steak and seafood.

Four affordable digs

If you seek lodging more affordable than our Ten Best resorts, check out these places in Lahaina and Ka'anapali.

OHANA MAUI ISLANDER: *600 Waine'e St., Lahaina, HI 9676; (800) 462-6262 or (808) 667-9766; www.ohanahotels.com. A low-rise 317-unit resort; $$ to $$$. GETTING THERE: It's in downtown Lahiana two blocks from the waterfront, near the corner of Prison Street.* □ This is our favorite Lahaina budget hotel, a Polynesian style retreat built round a landscaped pool. It's a brief walk to the harbor and Front Street, yet it's relatively quiet. However, request a room off the street because the old-fashioned louvered windows admit traffic sounds. Rooms start around $100 and kitchen units start at $130, with full kitchens around $160. Facilities include a pool, tennis courts and guest laundry.

PIONEER INN: *658 Wharf St., Lahaina, HI 96761; (800) 457-5457 or (808) 661-3636; www.pioneerinnmaui.com. Forty rooms in an historic hotel; $$ to $$$. GETTING THERE: It's just off the waterfront at Wharf and Hotel streets.* □ The rooms are spartan but they're inexpensive and the Pioneer Inn is in the heart of historic Lahaina, just steps from the waterfront. It's Hawai'i's oldest continuously operating hotel, built in 1901. Artifacts in the lobby and adjacent restaurant (listed above) make this a virtual museum of Lahaina's rowdy history.

ROYAL LAHAINA RESORT: *2780 Keka'a Dr., Lahiana, HI 96761; (800) 22-ALOHA or (808) 661-3611; www.hawaiianhotels.com. A Ka'anapali resort with 452 rooms; $$ to $$$$. GETTING THERE: It's at Ka'anapali's northern end. From Highway 30, take the second entrance into the complex and go right on Keka'a Drive.* □ This is Ka'anapali's most affordable large resort, with room specials starting round $150, Units at the adjacent Royal Hale are even less. Most rooms in both facilities have been renovated. While not posh, the Royal Lahaina has all the usual amenities, including three restaurants, a pool, shops and a luau (see above), and it's right on the beach.

THE WHALER ON KA'ANAPALI BEACH: *2481 Ka'anapali Parkway, Lahaina, HI 96761; (800) 922-7866 or (808) 661-4861; www.whalermaui.com. A 134-unit condo complex; $$$ to $$$$. GETTING THERE: It's beside Whalers Village.* ☐ The Whaler has the most affordable condo units on Ka'anapali, with studios starting around $200. It also has one- and two-bedroom units; all have complete kitchens. The Whaler right on the beach, with a swimming pool, spa and sauna, guest laundry and tennis courts. Several restaurants are a few minutes' walk away, in adjacent Whalers Village.

Through the glasses, the little fountains scattered about looked very beautiful. They boiled, coughed, and spluttered, and discharged sprays of stringy red fire. — **Mark Twain, visiting Kilauea in 1866**

Chapter Thirteen

THE BIG ISLAND
PLENTY OF ROOM FOR PARADISE

Hawi'i, the island, is in many ways the most impressive of the state's isles, and it's our personal favorite. Mark Twain, who spent several months exploring these islands, was certainly impressed. In 1866, in one of a series of travel letters published in California's Sacramento *Union*, he wrote:

Bound for Hawai'i, to visit the great volcano and behold other notable things which distinguish that island above the remainder of the group, we sailed from Honolulu on a certain Sunday afternoon, in the good schooner Boomerang.

He didn't enjoy the voyage, particularly after a shipboard rat scampered across his chest in his "coffin-sized" bunk. And then he noticed "a repulsive sentinel" perched on each end of his pillow, "cockroaches as large as peach leaves—fellows with long, quivering antennae and fiery, malignant eyes." Once ashore, however, he found the Big Island to be quite fascinating. He witnessed a Kilauea eruption, visited the beautiful bay of Kealakekua where Captain Cook was killed, and toured coffee and sugar plantations. During one trek, he chanced upon a pleasing sight:

At noon I observed a bevy of nude native young ladies bathing in the sea, and went and sat down on their clothes to keep them from being stolen. I begged them to come out, for the sea was rising and I was satisfied that they were running some risk.

You aren't likely to encounter such a sight when you explore the island of Hawai'i. However, you will find much of what Twain found: coffee plantations, Kilauea lava flows—possibly still warm—and the pretty bay of Kealakekua. There is much more here as well, such as two of the world's largest shield volcanoes, some of the state's most opulent resorts, even one of America's largest cattle ranches.

The reason the Big Island offers so much is because it has so much room. Although it's the youngest of the islands, Hawai'i is more than twice as large as all the others combined. Within this space, it produces more beef, coffee, papayas and macadamia nuts than the other islands, and it's the world's biggest producer of orchids. And it can absorb its 1.2 million annual visitors without seeming crowded.

Of course, size can have its drawbacks. After driving easily from shore to shore on O'ahu and Maui, you'll likely be frustrated by the distances involved in exploring the big island. If you're staying in the Kailua-Kona area, you'll have to cover nearly a hundred miles to reach the island's biggest attraction, Hawaii Volcanoes National Park. And it's a *slow* drive. You'll be on two-lane roads, often stuck behind locals who—unlike you—are in no hurry. Circling the island? It's about 220 road miles; don't try it in one day.

TO LEARN MORE: Contact the Big Island Visitors Bureau, 250 Keawe St., Hilo, HI 96720; (800) 648-2441 or (808) 961-5797; *www.bigisland.org.*

Hawai'i: Getting to Know You

What's intriguing about visiting here is that you're treading on some of the youngest land on the earth. And we aren't just referring to still-warm lava flows spilling from Kilauea. The Big Island broke the surface of the Pacific less than a million years ago. Considering that you can see Precambrian schist a *billion* years old in the bottom of the Grand Canyon, the landform that is Hawai'i is a geological infant.

This becomes evident when you explore the Kona and Kohala coasts and Hawaii Volcanoes National Park, areas where much of the land surface is still twisted black and brown lava, too young to have been broken down into soil.

How did the youngest Hawaiian island get so large? It was formed from a cluster of five volcanoes that rose from the ocean floor and flowed together. And two of these are really *big* mountains. Mauna

The Big Island

Area of map

Honolulu

Kamehameha I Birthplace
Hawi
Kapaau
Mahukona
250
Pololu Valley Lookout
270
Waipio Bay
Waipio Valley
Kukuihaele
240
Honokaa
Kawaihae
Kawaihae Bay
19
Paauilo
19
Umauma
Hapuna Beach State Park
Kamuela
190
Papaaloa
Maulua Bay
Parker Ranch
Ninole
Kohala Coast
Kakalau
Kiholo Bay
Waikii
Akaka Falls
Honomu
190
Mauna Kea
19
Papaikou
Puuanahulu
SADDLE ROAD
Hilo Bay
19
Rainbow Falls
Hilo
200
Kaumana
11
Kailua-Kona
180
Keauhou
Mountain View
130
137
Nanawale Bay
Captain Cook Monument
Mauna Loa
Pahoa
132
Kapoho
Kealakekua Bay
Captain Cook
Napoopoo
Mokuaweoweo Crater
Glenwood
130
Pohoiki
Honaunau
The Painted Church
Volcano House
137
Opihikao
Hookena
Pu'uhonua Honaunau National Historic Park
Kilauea Crater
Volcano
Kehena
Kaimu
Black Sand Beach
11
Hawaii Volcanoes National Park
Kalapana
11
Milolii
Papa
Pahala
N
Waiohinu
Punaluu
Southernmost Town in USA
Honuapo
Naalehu
Pohue Bay
South Point
Kaalualu Bay

Kea is the state's highest peak, at 13,796 feet; Mauna Loa is 13,677. And these are sea-level measurements. Taken from their base on the ocean floor, they're more like 31,000 feet tall. That's nearly *five miles!* Mauna Loa, the world's largest free-standing mountain, has a sea floor diameter of about ninety miles. If you sat it on Connecticut, it would cover the entire state.

The Big Island was a big player in Hawai'i's history and legend. Maui may have had its demigod who lassoed the sun, but Hawai'i is the home to Pele, the goddess of volcanoes. And without volcanoes, there would be no Hawaiian Islands. It may have been the first island settled by Polynesians, possibly as early as 200 A.D.

This is the birthplace of Hawai'i's first and greatest ruler, Kamehameha. Historians believe he witnessed the death of Captain Cook in 1778, and possibly was a participant. In 1791, he defeated his own cousin to become the ruler of the Big Island. He then began his island-hopping campaign to unify all of Hawai'i. He returned to spend his final years here, and he died in Kailua-Kona in 1819. Just a year later, when missionaries began arriving from Boston, the Big Island was their first landfall.

Like the other major islands in the Hawaiian archipelago, the Big Island has dry and wet sides. Soggy Hilo on the east coast gets nearly 130 inches a year while some areas of the Kohala coast on the western side receive as little as seven inches—about the same as Las Vegas. And like the Las Vegas desert, you'll find cactus, not orchids.

The Big Island is second to O'ahu in population, with about 120,000 residents. However, it has the fewest number of people per square mile. Hilo is the state's second largest city after Honolulu, with 38,000 people, then folks thin out quickly from there. Kailua-Kona's population is a distant second, with fewer than 10,000 souls. Everything else on else on the island is a hamlet.

From a visitor standpoint, Hawai'i has only two significant resort areas and they're both on the west coast. Which brings up a common geographical error made by some outsiders. You often hear references to the Kona Coast as the area where several large resorts are located amidst a massive fields of old lava. Nay, this is the *Kohala* Coast. The Kona Coast is just below there—the region south of Kailua-Kona. It's famous for its coffee plantations, the Captain Cook monument in Kealakekua Bay, and the former City of Refuge National Historical Park, now called by its Hawaiian name, which nobody can pronounce.

The Kohala Coast is the island's most popular and upscale resort area. Kailua-Kona has a few smaller resorts, condos and inns. Hilo is a distant third as a resort area, with a couple of midsize hotels and several inns and motels.

Since Kohala and Kailua-Kona get the majority of the island's visitors, it's home to the main airport—Kona International. Hilo has a smaller airfield. Flights from Honolulu serve both, and Kona also gets a few direct flights from the mainland and from Japan.

CIRCLING HAWAI'I

Hawai'i is the only island in the state completely encircled by paved roads. If you have the time—and the flexibility to make a couple or four overnight stops—this is the best way to orient yourselves to the Big Island. We'll describe a circle-island driving trip briefly, then list much of what you can see and do in greater detail below.

NOTE: Listings in **Bold face** marked with ❖ are described in more detail elsewhere; check the index for page numbers.

Our starting point is **Kailua-Kona**. Let's say that you've just picked up your rental car at Kona International and are heading south into town. At the outer edge of Kailua-Kona, go right on Palani Road, the town's main street, and drive two blocks to the beach. Palani swings southward and becomes **Ali'i Drive**, which passes through the heart of the Kona resort area. It's busy with hotels, cafés, shopping complexes and tourist trinket shops. You'll see frequent swatches of lava-ribbed and sandy beaches between the buildings; many have swimming and snorkeling areas.

At the Palani/Ali'i junction, find a place to park and check out the ❖ **King Kamehameha Hotel**, whose lobby walls are hung with portraits of Hawaiian royalty. Nearby is a small park with a sandy beach and the reconstructed **'Ahu'ena Heiau**. Here, Kamehameha I spent his final years, from 1812 until his death in 1819. The *heiau* is adjacent to the Kamehameha Hotel's luau grounds. Nearby is a sign marking the swim start of the **Iron Man Triathalon World Championship,** which brings contestants and crowds to Kailua-Kona every October.

From here, you can walk a few blocks and dip into the many shopping centers and cafés that line the upper end of Ali'i Drive. Within a short walk on your left is the lava block **Moku'aikauna Congregational Church**; it's the oldest in the state, completed in 1823 by that first group of missionaries. It's open daily 7:30 to 5:30; (808) 329-0655. Across the street is **Hulihee Palace**, built in 1838 by a brother-in-law of Kamehameha I. It's now a museum of Hawaiian history and royalty, open weekdays 9 to 4 and weekends 10 to 4; (808) 329-1877.

After exploring the area, retrieve your car and drive southward on Ali'i. Turn left into **Ali'i Gardens Market Place** where about twenty vendors have small open air stalls, selling everything from shave ice and produce to Hawaiian style clothing, crafts and souvenirs. Most shops are open Wednesday-Saturday 9 to 5; closed Sunday and Monday. About half a mile beyond, check out the 1855 **'Ohana Congregational Church**, with cut lava stone walls and a corrugated metal roof; it occupies a park-like setting just above the beach.

After a couple of miles, Ali'i Drive swings inland to become the Ali'i Highway, but only for a couple of blocks. At a traffic light, turn left onto Kamehameha III Highway, then go right onto Highway 11, the main coastal drive. It's time to wake up and taste the coffee.

Coffee break

For the next twenty miles, you'll be passing through the ❖ **Kona Coffee Belt,** America's largest coffee producing region. However, if you're picturing a caffeinated Napa Valley—a highway lined with coffee groves—think again. This region high on the flanks of Mauna Loa is a mix of small towns, scattered homes, banana groves, and mango and macadamia nut trees—plus many small coffee farms. Most of Kona's famous coffee is grown by more than 600 independent farms, averaging only about three acres. Some sell their beans to one of twenty or more roasters in the area, while a few roast and package their own coffee. The Kona Coffee Belt *is* similar to the Napa Valley in that several of these roasters offer tours and tasting. See below on page 221 for a detailed Kona Coffee tour.

The drive through coffee country is quite appealing, with its tropical farms and orchards sweeping down to the sea, and the green-mantled mass of Mauna Kea rising above, accented here and there with black swatches of lava.

It's also slow and congested—a two-lane road through a succession of small towns. Most have no identifying signs, so you may not know when you've left **Holualoa** and entered **Honalo** and then reached **Kainaliu, Kealakeua** and finally one you can pronounce—**Captain Cook.** Folks trying to reach Hawai'i Volcanoes National Park from Kailua-Kona will find this very slow going, and there's no alternative route. So, slow down and enjoy several interesting attractions along here. And watch for occasional scenic turnouts, where you can pause and enjoy the view down to the lava-edged coastline.

Just outside **Kealakeua,** between mileage markers 111 and 112, watch on the coastward side for ❖ **Greenwell Farms** coffee plantation, with a sales and tasting room open Monday-Saturday 8 to 5; closed Sunday; (808) 323-2275. Next door is the ❖ **Kona Historical Society Museum** in the old Greenwell Store; it's open weekdays 9 to 3; closed weekends; (808) 323-3222.

In the town of **Captain Cook,** take Napo'opo'o Road (Route 160) down to ❖ **Kealakekua Bay,** the pretty green-shrouded cove where the good captain met his demise. It's now a state underwater park and one of the best snorkeling spots in all the islands. Across the bay, you'll see the **Captain Cook Monument,** a white obelisk marking the spot of the great navigator's unfortunate end. It can be reached only by boat or by a two-hour hike. En route to the bay, a couple of lures are worth a pause. You can get your caffeine fix at the ❖ **Ueshima Espresso Bar and Roastery** that offers tours and tasting; daily 9 to 5, (808) 328-5662. Between the roastery and Kealakekua Bay is a reconstruction of the **Hikiau Heiau,** a terraced platform near **Napo'opo'o Beach Park**. Plaques here mark several events in the coming of outsiders to these islands.

Pu'uhonua who?

From here, follow Route 160 about four miles south to ❖ **Pu'uhonua o Honaunau National Historical Park,** open daily 8 to 5; (808) 328-2288. Some of you may remember it—before the National Park Service got historically picky—as the City of Refuge. It's a reconstruction of a major *ali'i* temple and a place of sanctuary for kapu breakers. Route 160 swerves away from the coast here to return you to Highway 11. En route, take a sharp left onto Painted Church Road for the charming little Gothic style St. Benedict's, built in 1899 and popularly known as the **Painted Church.** For more on the church, see below on page 224.

Back on Highway 11, you'll pass through the hamlet of **Kealia** and just below there, a rough but navigable two-mile road leads down to **Ho'okena Beach Park.** It's a fine swimming beach in a sheltered bay rimmed by coconut palms. A short walk north takes you to **Kealia Beach,** with some fairly good snorkeling spots.

Below Kealia, you'll finally shake the congestion of the Kona Coast's strung-out towns. Passing the scrubwood slopes of the **South Kona Forest Reserve,** you'll enter an area of ancient lava flows that spilled down from Mauna Kea. This is the Ka'u District of Hawai'i's southern tip. Thirteen miles below the Ho'okena Beach turnoff, near milepost 89, a steep paved one-lane road leads down to **Miloli'i.** It's a charming old fishing village where Hawaiians have merged past and present—hooking outboard motors to their outriggers to net mackerel. Just beyond is **Miloli'i Beach Park,** with offshore reefs that make it inviting for snorkeling and usually safe for swimming.

Beyond Miloli'i, the highway swings inland, cutting through old lava fields across the southern tip of Hawai'i. To reach that tip, called **South Point** or **Ka Lae,** turn right near milepost 70 and follow a narrow paved single-lane road through rolling grasslands. After twelve miles, you'll reach craggy cliffs above an often turbulent sea. You're now overlooking the southernmost point in the United States. According to legend, this is where Polynesians first stepped ashore on the Hawaiian Islands. If so, they picked a rough landing spot!

You'll see ruins of an ancient *heiau* near a U.S. Coast Guard lighthouse. A rough jeep trail—used more by hikers than jeeps—leads three miles down to **Green Sand Beach,** tinted by olivine sand.

Back on Highway 11, you'll pass through the hamlet of **Na'alehu,** whose primary significance is that it is America's southernmost town. For a cup of America's southernmost-brewed coffee and fresh fish caught off South Point, stop by **Na'alehu Coffee Shop.** It has been run by the same family since 1941; (808) 929-7238. The highway swings northeast from here, skimming the coast at **Whittington Beach Park** in the village of **Honu'apo.** Just beyond is the pretty palm-lined **Punalu'u Black Sand Beach Park.**

Volcano country

The route swings inland to begin a long, gentle climb through scrublands, grasslands and lava flows toward ❖ **Hawaii Volcanoes National Park.** Several small resorts and restaurants in and near the town of **Pahala** cater to park-bound travelers. For a brief side trip into lush **Wood Valley,** turn right onto Pikake Street in the middle of town. The valley is the site of the Tibetan Buddhist **Wood Valley Temple.** You must call ahead for permission to visit and to get directions; (808) 928-8539.

Beyond Pahala and just short of the national park entrance, turn onto a golf course road for **Volcano Winery.** You can taste fruit wines and drinkable whites made from the California hybrid Symphony grape. It's open daily 10 to 5:30; (808) 967-7479.

Continuing beyond the national park, Highway 11 passes through the town of **Volcano,** with more park-oriented lodgings and cafés. It then travels through one of the most volcanically active areas of the world. This is the **Puna Point** area, where entire villages have been buried by recent flows from Kilauea. Several small towns occupy this chubby eastern tip of the island. The Chain of Craters Road from the national park once reached Puna Point, linking with Highway 130, although it was cut off by a lava flow several years ago. The only way to reach these communities now is to continue northeast on Highway 11 toward Hilo, and then cut southeast on Highway 130.

In **Pahoa,** turn left onto Pahoa-Pohiki Road for **Lava Tree State Park** where a 1790 lava flow fried an *ohia* tree grove, creating an eerie fossil forest. A dirt road leads from here to the beach. Turn right onto Highway 137 for a pretty drive along a lava-encrusted coast. At **Kaimu**, you can see where a 1990 lava flow severed the highway. Backtrack up the beach on Highway 137, following it around **Cape Kumukahi**. Here, a devastating 1960 lava flow wiped out the village of Kapoho. It swept around **Cape Kumukahi Lighthouse**, surrounding the beacon, yet leaving it standing.

Hanging out in Hilo

Follow routes 132 and 130 back to Highway 11 and continue into the state of Hawai'i's second largest city, ❖ **Hilo.** You're now on the soggy side of the island and Hilo occupies a gorgeous setting at the base of narrow, green-cloaked canyons.

As you approach Hilo, Highway 11 becomes Kanoelehua Avenue. Shortly after passing **Hilo International Airport**, cross Kalanianaole Avenue (Highway 19) onto **Banyan Drive.** Shaded by ancient banyan trees, this pretty lane loops around the Waiakea Peninsula that thrusts into Hilo Bay. Continue around the peninsula and turn right onto Hilo Bayfront Highway (Route 19) and follow it west along Hilo Bay. The business district is just inland. The town has twice been hit by devastating *tsunami,* and the landscaped waterfront has a berm to protect it from future tidal waves. On a blustery day, you'll see waves crashing against this seawall and sometimes spilling onto the highway.

If you want to take a beach break, pause at one of the two beach parks along here—**Mo'oheau** and **Bayfront**, or go inland to **Wailoa River State Park** on a landscaped lagoon. The bayfront highway soon merges with Kamehameha Avenue. Backtrack briefly on Kamehameha to check out the ❖ **Pacific Tsunami Museum.** It's in an old bank building between Waianuehue Avenue and Kalakaua Street; open Monday-Saturday 10 to 4; (808) 935-0926. Nearby and definitely worth a stop is the ❖ **Lyman Museum** at 276 Haili St.; open Monday-Saturday 9 to 4:30; (808) 935-5021; *www.lymanmuseum.org*. From the *tsunami* museum, take Waianuehue three blocks inland, turn left onto Kapiʻolani Street and drive a block to Haili. From here, follow Waianuehue inland about 1.5 miles to ❖ **Wailuku River State Park** and **Rainbow Falls,** cascading down a 200-foot lava cliff.

TRAVEL TIP: For more detail on these attractions, see the Hilo listing below on page 229.

From Rainbow Falls, return to Highway 19 and press westward. You'll soon shed Hilo and swing north along the **Hamakua Coast,** called by local tourist promoters the **Heritage Coast.** This wet slope is a gorgeous mix of rainforests and plantation patches planted with macadamia, papaya and taro. Pretty beach parks line the shoreline. Watch for brown "Heritage Loop" and "Heritage Town" signs that take you on scenic or historic detours. The main highway and these detours pass through moss-draped jungle terrain where trees often form canopies over the roads. Views along here are splendid—down to rocky coves and up to lush canyons and waterfalls. Those green-clad ravines lead skyward toward the massive bulk of **Mauna Loa.** The route also passes a few rustic homes and rusting cars.

Shortly after leaving Hilo, fork right onto a route simply marked **Scenic Drive** and follow it through dense jungle and past a couple of weathered old towns. About 8.5 miles from Hilo, you'll encounter the **Hawaiʻi Tropical Botanical Gardens**, open daily 9 to 4; (808) 964-5233; *www.hawaiigarden.com.* About three miles beyond, the Scenic Drive rejoins Highway 19. Press onward, then turn inland for **Akaka Falls State Park**, a retreat with two cataracts spilling down from Mauna Kea—442-foot Akaka Falls and 400-foot Kahuna Falls.

The route continues along the base of wooded bluffs cut by more sheer-walled canyons. In **Umauma**, head inland for half a mile to **World Botanical Gardens**, open Monday-Saturday 9 to 5:30; closed Sunday; (808) 963-5427; *www.wbgi.com.* Beyond here, you'll pass two old plantation towns dozing in the sun—when it isn't raining: **Paʻauilo** and **Honokaʻa.**

At Honokaʻa, the route swings inland, travels through the upland country past Parker Ranch to Waimea, and thence to the Kohala Coast. Before completing your loop, however, follow Highway 240 about nine miles along the north coast to an overlook above the jungle-sheltered **Waipiʻo Valley**, a classic enclave of old Hawaiʻi. Sheltered by 3,000-foot cliffs, the valley can be reached only by a rough jeep road. Island tour operators offer trips down to this remote gathering of taro patches and sagging old homes. The two most active are **Waipio Valley Shuttle & Tours,** (808) 775-7121; and **Waipio Valley Wagon Tour,** (808) 775-9518. If you have the time, you can hike down; plan on several hours.

Cattle country

Back in Honokaʻa, Highway 19 travels thirteen miles through grassy *paniolo* country to **Waimea,** the neatly kept headquarters town of the 225,000-acre **Parker Ranch.** Stop by the ❖ **Parker Ranch**

Museum to learn about this large Hawaiian cattle spread, and perhaps arrange for a ranch or historic homes tour. The museum is open daily 9 to 5; (808) 885-7311; *www.parkerranch.com.*

To complete your around-the-island loop, head north from Waimea along the foothills of the **Kohala Mountains** to the North Kohala district and the charming old towns of ❖ **Kapaʻau** and ❖ **Hawi.** Kamehameha was born near here and his statue stands before the Kapʻau Civic Center. After area sugar mills closed in the 1970s, tourism came to North Kohalaʻs rescue, in the form of art galleries, cafés and the ❖ **Flum'in Da Ditch** adventure company; (808) 889-6922.

Go east from Kapaʻau through a string of rustic green-clad towns to road's end at the ❖ **Pololu Valley Lookout.** Pololu Valley is a smaller version of Waipiʻo Valley—lush, flat and green, alongside a flowing stream and sheltered by thousand-foot cliffs. From here, retrace your route through Kapaʻau and Hawi and pick up Highway 270. Just beyond Hawi, a dirt road leading from **Upolu Airport** will take you to the Big Island's most sacred temple, ❖ **Moʻokini Heiau,** and **Kamehameha's birthplace.** For specific directions, see below on page 226.

TRAVEL TIP: The road to the *heiau* and Kamehameha's birthplace may be impassable in wet weather, so check before you go.

From here, follow Highway 270 south to the busy port of **Kawaihae,** passing several small beach parks along the way. At Kawaihae, you'll merge onto Highway 19 that travels down the **Kohala Coast.** Pause for a look at **Lapakahi State Historic Park,** where rocky remnants of a 600-year-old fishing village have been preserved. Elements include fishing shrines, an old well, canoe shelters and foundations of houses. If no ranger is on duty, you can pick up a self-guiding pamphlet and wander about on your own. The historic park is open daily 8 to 4; (808) 882-6207.

Shortly after passing the busy port of **Kawaihae,** you'll encounter **Puʻukohola Heiau National Historic Site.** The visitor center is open daily 7:30 to 4; (808) 882-7218. Here, Kamehameha committed one of his most dastardly acts. He had been battling his chief rival and cousin, Keoua, for control of the Big Island. After completing a massive three-level temple in 1791, he invited Keoua here for peace talks. As soon as his rival stepped from his canoe, Kamehameha's stabbed him to death. His warriors then fell upon Keoua's retainers, killing all but two of them with swords and muskets. They hauled Keoua's body up to consecrate the new *heiau* in blood. Then, as prophesied by a *kahuna* from Kauaʻi, once Kamehameha's temple had been consecrated, he went on to unite all the islands.

The luxury coast

Below the national historic site begins the parade of luxury **Kohala Coast** resorts, interspersed with some of the Big Island's most attractive beach parks. Massive flows spilling down from Mauna Kea covered the Kohala Coast in a great petrified sea of lava, giving it a starkly dramatic look. The last flow was about 150 years ago. Developers have hacked roads through the rough lava and built some of the state's most elegant resorts. However, this is no busy Waikiki Beach. Only eight resorts stand along twenty miles of this otherwise dry and barren coastline. Each occupies its own personal cove, giving these grand hideaways a special intimacy.

This parade of luxury begins with the senior Kohala resort, the ❖ **Mauna Kea,** built in 1960 by Laurance Rockefeller. While the main structure is not imposing, its large collection of Asian art is definitely worth a look. Moving down the coast, you'll encounter the **Hapuna Beach Prince Hotel**, a modern retreat reached by an imposing palm-lined drive. Just below the Hapuna Prince is **Hapuna Beach State Park**, with a beige sand beach, tree-shaded grassy lawns, and swimming and snorkeling areas. It even has inexpensive A-frame cabins (bedding not included); (808) 974-6200.

A few miles beyond is the large **Mauna Lani Resort** development, a complex of condos, two golf courses and two luxury hotels, the ❖ **Mauna Lani Bay** and the ❖ **Fairmont Orchid Hawaii.**

Just below there is another large complex of condos, hotels and golf courses, the **Waikoloa Beach Resort.** Its major hotels are the ❖ **Outrigger Waikoloa** and the ❖ **Hilton Waikoloa**, built around an elaborate system of lagoons. Also of interest here is the **Waikoloa Petroglyph Field,** reached from **Kings' Shops** mall, just inside the entrance to the resort complex. Here again you'll see a vivid contrast— a short trail past rough boulders etched with ancient symbols, and surrounded by an emerald green golf course.

Pressing southward toward Kailua-Kona, pause at a viewpoint above **Kiholo Bay** to admire this dramatic terrain. This is a grand spot for viewing the Kohala Coast's jade sea, with its rough lava coastline etched here and there by crescent bays. Just below, palm-fringed Kiholo Bay is exceptionally pretty, with a black sand beach and a low offshore isle. This once was part of a fishpond, built by Kamehameha in 1810 and destroyed by a Mauna Kea lava flow in 1859. A gravel road leads down to the bay between mileposts 82 and 83. The last section is rough so you may want to park and walk to the beach.

Just south, you'll pass the turnout to the Kohala Coast's final resorts, which are studies in contrast. **Kona Village** is a series of simple—if quite comfortable—Polynesian style huts on a rough lava shoreline. The **Four Seasons Resort Hualalai** is the most opulent of the Kohala hideaways; the only resort on the Big Island with an AAA Five Diamond rating.

And then it's back to affordable reality. Highway 19 passes **Kona International Airport**, where our ambitious around-the-island safari began. If the luxury resorts you just saw are beyond the reach of wallet or purse, you'll find less costly digs in **Kailua-Kona.**

THE TEN BEST THINGS TO SEE & DO

As on Maui, the Big Island's most popular visitor attraction is its national park. And this one has been making headlines, with the ongoing eruption of Kilauea, the world's most active volcano. The next nine Big Island highlights represent a mixed list, from fun activities to historic and scenic attractions. They're presented in order of appearance, as you'd encounter them on two drives starting from Kailua-Kona—first to the south through Kona coffee country, and then north along the Kohala Coast and inland toward Parker Ranch.

PRICING: Dollar sign codes indicate the approximate cost of adult admission to various attractions and activities: **$** = under $10; **$$** = $10 to $19; **$$$** = $20 to $29; **$$$$** = $30 to $39; **$$$$$** = $40 or more.

☺ **KID STUFF:** This little grinning guy marks attractions and activities that are of particular interest to pre-teens.

1 GO CHASE A LAVA FLOW

For information: Hawaii Volcanoes National Park, P.O. Box 52, Hawaii Volcanoes, HI 96718-0052; (808) 985-6000; www.nps.gov/havo. Park admission $$ per car or $ per person; free with Golden Eagle, Age or Access pass. Kilauea Visitor Center open daily 7:30 to 5; Jagger Museum daily 8:30 to 5. GETTING THERE: The park entrance is south off Highway 11, about twenty-nine miles southwest of Hilo. ☺

In a world where geological changes are measured in centuries, this is one of the few places where you may see the earth shaped right before your eyes. Hawaii Volcanoes National Park is home to Pele and the world's most active volcano, headline-grabbing Kilauea. With luck, you may be able to see a lava flow changing the shape of the land. The park reaches through most the world's climate zones, from the sea to the subarctic heights of Mauna Loa. It covers 217,000 acres of Mauna Loa's southeastern flank. It can be cool up here, so bring a jacket.

The visitor center is located in a woodsy area, with little to indicate that steaming volcanism is but a few paces away. In fact the adjacent Volcano House hotel and restaurant sits on Kilauea's rim. The small visitor center has a few exhibits, mostly concerning lava, and it shows ongoing lava-erupting videos.

Although Kilauea has been erupting almost continuously for several years, don't expect to lean over the rim and see a burbling cauldron of lava. The most you'll see in that dark, steep-walled basin is a few steam vents. As of this writing, most of the action was happening in a vent on Kilauea's flanks called Pu'u. From there, magma has been flowing for several miles—mostly underground—and spilling into the sea, creating great hissing columns of steam. If this is still happening as you read this book, there are two ways to see living, glowing lava: Drive to the end of the Chain of Craters Road; or book a sightseeing flight that will take you over Pu'u Crater and down along the coast where the lava hits the sea.

Most of Hawaii Volcanoes National Park's highlights can be seen by driving its two roads—Crater Rim Drive just-mentioned Chain of Craters Road.

CRATER RIM DRIVE: This eleven-mile drive starts just outside the visitor center and loops around Kilauea, which technically is a caldera, not a crater. We suggest going clockwise so your car is on the inside lane, next to the rim. Frequent turnouts provide views down into that great black hole. If you have time, you can hike sections of the corresponding **Crater Rim Trail**. It alternately travels along the edge and then crosses the road to pass through *ohia* forests. Other trails drop down into the crater and criss-cross its dark, undulating floor.

The drive starts in a wooded area and then emerges onto the rim, keeping it in sight for most of the route. Signs along the way mark eruptions as recently as the 1980s—perhaps more recent by the time you arrive. Our favorite stop is **Halemaumau**, where a trail leads past dozens of steam vents to the lip of Halemaumau Crater. It's blacker, more steep-walled and even more sinister looking than Kilauea. Sulfur-stained and hissing steam, it's as outerworldly a place as one might find in this world.

At **Jaggar Museum** on the northwest side of Kilauea Caldera, displays focus on volcanology and particularly the geology of this area. Films of brilliant red splashes of lava are shown continuously. Kilauea views from an observation deck here are quite impressive.

CHAIN OF CRATERS ROAD: This road tilts 4,000 feet down to the sea, winding past a series of old craters that have begun to sprout vegetation. As you cruise downhill, you'll catch fine glances of "new" Hawai'i—a broad, undulating yet relatively level skirt of lava that has been building outward into the sea. Thus, the Big Island is getting even bigger. The **Mauna Ulu** vista point, a pagoda-shaped shelter near the 1,000 foot marker, is a particularly fine vantage point.

At the road's abrupt end, we were able to get within a few hundred yards of two sites where lava was hissing into the sea. Rangers in a portable visitor center—everything must be portable down there—advised people how close they could safely approach the action. They had used road markers to mark temporary trails over the rough lava flow.

When we visited, this part of the highway had been blocked just two months before. No, the lava wasn't still warm, although it was so new it resembled petrified dark, glossy chocolate pudding. The best time to see the drama of lava hissing into the sea—if it's still happening when you arrive—is after sundown. You aren't allowed close enough to lean over and see the spilling lava, although at night you can see its red-orange glow in the steam clouds.

TRAVEL TIP: If you plan a sundown trip, take good hiking shoes and a strong flashlight so you can negotiate the rough temporary trails over the lava in darkness. Get there well before sunset, since cars sometimes line the road for more than a mile.

2 FLY HIGH OVER HAWAI'I

Mokulele Flight Service, P.O. Box 830, Holualoa, HI 96725; (866) 260-7070 or (808) 326-7070; www.mokulele.com. Major credit cards; $$$$$. GETTING THERE: The company operates fixed-wing flights out of Kona and Hilo airports. ☺

The hottest attraction for flightseers on the Big Island is fresh, glowing lava. Itineraries vary, based on where it's flowing and glowing. Your choices are fixed wing aircraft and helicopters; both have advantages. Fixed wingers travel faster and can cover more territory, completely circling the Big Island and including overflights of what's hot at the volcano. Since they're less expensive to buy and operate, they're cheaper than chopper flights. On the other hand, helicopters can get closer to the action, flying lower and slower.

For our volcanic view, we chose the largest fixed wing operator on the Big Island. Our flight left Kona Airport, passed low over the Kailua-Kona waterfront, Captain Cook's monument the Kona Coffee Belt. Flying eastward, we began seeing black fingers of lava extending downward from the flanks of Mauna Loa. Cruising low off the coast, we passed the two areas where underground lava has been hissing into the ocean. Our pilot tilted inland, flying over a great black petrified river of hardened lava, then he slowly circled Pu'u vent, the source of Kilauea's latest hot temper tantrum. It was an awesome sight—hardening crusts of lava floating in a magma pool seamed with red streaks. An image came to mind: This was like an Arctic ice floe from hell.

The flight continued across the broad Pahoa peninsula, where angry black fingers had clawed into lush green countryside, sometimes burying villages in their wake. In one area, only a home's red tile roof was visible from its lava grave. Our small craft then scurried over Hilo, as green and inviting as the lava flow had been stark and sinister.

We rounded Hawai'i's northeast coast, winging alongside the island's steepest seacliffs, with majestic Mauna Kea rising above. Waipi'o Valley was particularly attractive from up here. Then we cut inland over the cliffs, crossed a mountain ridge and passed over a slice of the huge sprawl of Parker Ranch; we could almost smell the cattle from up here. On our homeward leg, we swung out over the Kohala Coast, passing its luxury resorts. They looked so green and inviting in their coastal enclaves at the base of the old Mauna Kea lava flow.

TRAVEL TIP: If you book a flight over an active volcanic area, particularly if it's often overcast, make sure you ask before boarding your airplane or chopper if clouds are covering what you want to see. Just because the firm says it's "safe to fly" on an overcast day doesn't mean you'll see anything; it means it's safe based on FAA regulations. Also, at the time of booking, ask about the firm's refund or rescheduling policy in case of poor visibility. On a recent "safe to fly" trip (not with Mokulele Flight Service), our helicopter pilot spent a good part of the flight going around in circles because the main attraction—an open vent spewing lava—was cloud-covered.

3 SNORKEL IN CAPTAIN COOK'S BAY

Fair Wind Snorkel & Dive, 78-7130 Kaleiopapa St., Kailua-Kona, HI 96740; (800) 677-9461 or (808) 322-2788; www.fair-wind.com. GET-TING THERE: Fair Wind cruises leave from Keauhou Small Boat Harbor at the end of Kaleiopapa Street, north of Kailua-Kona. Get specific directions when you book your trip. ☺

Idyllic Kealakekua Bay, rimmed by lush vegetation, has some of the state's best snorkeling. It's an underwater park, so the coral reefs and their resident fish are protected. The water is crystal clear and almost always calm in this sheltered cove. Visibility down to a hundred feet is common, although you'll see plenty of coral and fish much closer to the surface.

On arrival in the bay, the *Fair Wind* catamaran cruises right up to the Captain Cook Monument. You'll be so close that the inscription is legible. It then backs away and tethers to a submerged buoy to avoid disturbing the coral. Guests have nearly two and a half hours of snorkeling, with a lunch break of charcoal-grilled cheeseburgers. The *Fair Wind* is a fun boat, with a second-deck diving platform and a waterslide. Non-snorkelers can borrow innertubes and just play in the bay. Or they can receive quickie snorkel lessons from the crew. The *Fair Wind* also offers SCUBA diving, with advance reservations.

TRAVEL TIPS: The *Fair Wind* offers morning and afternoon cruises. If you really like to snorkel, take the morning trip, since both the sky and the water are more likely to be clear. If you're willing to skip lunch, you can stay in the water for the entire two and a half hours.

Just up from Keauhou Small Boat Harbor, walk through the narrow **Garden of Kamehameha Park** along the base of a low lava cliff. A plaque here marks the birthplace of Kamehameha III. Other signs identify native plants in this park strip.

4 WAKE UP & TOUR THE COFFEE COUNTRY

The Kona Coffee Belt, from Kailua-Kona south to Honaunau. For a detailed driving guide, check at visitor centers or contact the Kona Coffee Cultural Festival at (808) 326-7820; www.konacoffeefest.com. GETTING THERE: To begin the tour, drive to Kailua-Kona, follow Palani Road (Route 190) inland for 3.3 miles to Palani Junction and make a sharp right turn onto the Mamalahoa Highway (Route 180).

More than 600 small growers and a few big ones produce Kona's famous coffee on steep hillside slopes. You can visit many of these plantations and taste coffee as one would sample wine in California's Napa Valley. The best time to tour is during the August-February harvesting season, when you can watch the beans being processed and smell the heady aroma of roasting coffee.

Kona's Coffee Belt is about twenty miles long, starting at Palani Junction on Highway 180, then reaching southward along Highway 11 to Honaunau. A bonus in this tour is fabulous views down steep slopes to the ancient lava plateau of the Kona Coast.

Starting at the junction, you'll first encounter the **Ueshima Coffee Estate** at 75-5568 Mamalahoa Highway. Look for a large kiosk on your right, above a steeply tilted coffee grove. You can sample several coffee blends and stroll or drive down through the plantation. Ueshima is open daily 9:30 to 3; (808) 328-5662.

Continuing south on the road, you'll pass several more coffee farms, some offering tasting, sales and tours. Check out the charmingly funky town of **Holualoa** with old false front stores and corrugated roofed homes. Note the scruffy and hot pink **Holualoa Hotel** on your right and the weathered **Ferrari Coffee** tasting room and antique doll collection across the street.

A bit beyond Holualoa is our favorite small coffee producer, **Holualoa Kona Coffee Company** at 77-6261 Mamalahoa Highway. It's up to the left, near milepost 2. During harvest season, an employee will take a break and show you through the plantation, explaining the milling and roasting process. You'll see coffee beans in various stages of ripening; they're called "cherry" when they're ready to pick. Each tree must be plucked five to seven times since the beans ripen at different times.

More than coffee

Many plantations, including Holualoa, grow macadamia, papaya, banana and other tropical products. "Take a papaya with you," our guide said, handing us a three-pounder the size of a football. After watching the milling and sorting process, visitors are taken to the small "roastery" where beans achieve their darkened look and issue that heady aroma. Next door is Holualoa's combined packaging and sales room, where one can sample and buy various and coffees and remarkably tasty chocolate-covered coffee beans. Coffee samples are served in real mugs; most other plantations use styrofoam cups. Holualoa is open weekdays 7:30 to 4; (800) 334-0348 or (808) 322-9937; www.konalea.com.

Below Holualoa, the coffee route blends onto the main highway, Route 11. You'll encounter more coffee farms and tasting rooms, mixed with stores, homes and occasional cafés. Watch on your right between mile markers 111 and 112 for the **Greenwell Farms** sales and tasting room and the adjacent **Kona Historical Society Mu-**

BECOME A COFFEE "ROASTMASTER"

Ueshima Coffee Company allows visitors—by reservation—to roast their own special "private reserve" coffee. Guests are instructed in the art of coffee roasting, then they're given a bunch of beans and assigned to a roaster. Timing is critical. A few seconds too soon, and your coffee beans are pale and wimpy; a bit too long and they're almost black, suitable only for espresso. After the beans have been liberated from the roaster, they're packaged in sealed bags bearing the "roastmaster's" photograph (taken as the visitors arrive). The program, which lasts about an hour, includes a quick study in the cultivation and processing of coffee.

For a roastmaster reservation, call the Ueshima Coffee Company at (888) 822-5662 or (808) 328-5662. The roastery and coffee bar is at 82-5810 Napo'opo'o Road on the way to Kealakekua Bay. Visitors who haven't made a roastmaster reservation can still visit the roastery and coffee bar and sample Ueshima's various coffees; it's open daily 9 to 5.

seum. They're linked historically, since the plantation was established in the 1850s by Englishman Henry Nicholas Greenwell. His descendants donated the plantation store to the historical society. Greenwell Farms offers tasting and sales of its coffee, plus specialty foods and logo items. Tours of the plantation and mill are given "whenever a few people express an interest." This is a large operation compared Holualoa; Greenwell buys beans from 250 growers and produces thousands of pounds of coffee a year. The facility is open Monday-Saturday 8 to 5; closed Sunday; (808) 323-2275.

The next-door Kona Historical Society Museum, housed in the 1875 Greenwell Store, is open weekdays 9 to 3; (808) 323-3222. It has assorted exhibits and photos concerning the coffee industry. A nicely done fifteen-minute video documents the Kona Coast's history. The ruins of the original Greenwell home are adjacent to the museum.

The **Uchia Historic Farm** is a short distance beyond Greenwell, on the right just past the turnoff to Puiuhomua o Honaunau National Historical Park (Napo'opo'o Road). Here, you can take a one-hour tour of an old Japanese-Hawaiian coffee plantation and home, or a half hour tour of the home only. Tours start on the hour, from 9 to 1 and reservations aren't necessary.

Visitors are guided through a century-old plantation where the coffee bushes are shaded by towering macadamia trees. Guests receive a quick lesson in coffee bean picking. Later, they will use a hand-turned coffee mill to extract the pale white beans from the "cherries" they picked. The tour ends at the old wood-frame Uchia home and an adjacent processing mill. The home was occupied from 1913 until 1994, when it became part of the Kona Historical Society. It has been restored as a typical Japanese-Hawaiian home of the 1930s, with tatami mat floors, simple furniture and old family portraits.

5 SEE WHERE THEY SOUGHT REFUGE

Pu'uhonua o Honaunau National Historical Park, P.O. Box 129, Honaunau, HI 96726; (808) 328-2288; www.nps.gov/puho. Park admission $ per vehicle. Visitor center open daily 8 to 5; grounds open Friday-Sunday 6 a.m. to 11 p.m. and Monday-Thursday 6 to 8. GETTING THERE: From Kailua-Kona, follow Highway 11 about twenty-two miles south and turn seaward on Highway 160.

This was an early Hawaiian version of a safe house, where breakers of *kapus*, defeated warriors, and women and children could find refuge from enemies and possibly even irate husbands and fathers. It occupies a handsome little cove, with an elaborately reconstructed *heiau* where bones of *ali'i* were placed. Exhibits in the visitor center focus on the site's history and the customs of Hawai'i's early people.

A *heiau* has occupied this site since the 1500s, when the Kona district was ruled by Kamehameha's great grandfather Keawe. The last bones to be placed here were those of one of Kamehameha's sons in 1818. Then, after Kamehameha II abolished the *kapu* system the following year, this "place of refuge" fell to ruin. The historic park was established in 1961 and the *heiau*, temple platforms and several other buildings were restored or rebuilt.

A self-guiding trail leads through a sandy-floored palm grove to the sanctuary's various sites. This is a very calm and restful place, as a refuge should be. When you walk past a little cove where the *ali'i* once beached their canoes, watch for glossy dark rocks in the shallow surf. If one moves, it may be a green sea turtle. They like to hang out in this bay and they sometimes come ashore. They're protected by law so don't even think about approaching one. If the spirits of the *ali'i* don't berate you, a park ranger will.

En route to the historic park, stop by charming little St. Benedict's, the famous **Painted Church**. Turn right onto Painted Church Road about two miles down Highway 160, or follow directions above on page 212. The exterior is white clapboard although the interior is embellished with biblical scenes on the walls; palm-frond pillars supporting a starry ceiling. This was the work of Belgian priest Father John Velghe, who spent four years on the project. The church is open daily 8 to 5; (808) 328-2227.

6 STROLL THE KOHALA SHORELINE

Mauna Lani Resort, Kohala Coast. GETTING THERE: The resort is about thirty miles north of Kailua-Kona. Turn into the complex and follow signs to the Fairmont Orchid Hawaii.

The King's Trail extends more than twenty miles along the Kohala shoreline, from Hapuna Beach State Park south to Kona International Airport. It passes the ruins of several ancient *heiaus* and home sites, and it connects most of the coast's major resorts. There are missing links in the path; covering its entire length would require scuffing along a beach or scrambling over rough lava in some areas. You can't get lost, of course; there's only one shoreline.

For a brief hike that links a pair of resorts and passes several historic sites, start at the ❖ **Fairmont Orchid Hawaii** in the Mauna Lani resort complex. After parking, walk through the lobby and go down a level to the hotel's grassy lawn area. Then pick up a paved beachfront path and head south. It soon gives way to sand; follow along the surf line and, within less than a mile, you'll arrive at the ❖ **Mauna Lani Bay Hotel.** Pause to explore the handsomely landscaped grounds with a meandering water course stocked with tropical reef fish.

Then continue south across the hotel's grassy lawn areas and past the swimming pool. You'll soon encounter the first of two small sandy beaches. After crossing the first, head toward an elaborate complex of restored fish ponds, part of the **Kalahuipua'a Historic Park.** From here, you'll briefly follow a service road and then hit a second small beach near Mauna Lani's Beach House. Cross it and pick up a paved path that flanks a condo complex. The trail passes through a brief lava section, then it parallels a cart path on the Mauna Lani Golf Course. Shift up to the path and follow it about a quarter of a mile to a golf cart turnaround adjacent to the **Mauna Lani Point** condo complex. It marks the end of this section of the trail. You'll see several more historic plaques in this area, marking the sites of ancient Hawaiian houses and fishing camps.

7 VISIT KOHALA & FLUME DA DITCH

Flum'in Da Ditch, P.O. Box 190573, Hawi, HI 96719; (877) 449-6922 or (808) 889-6922; www.flumindaditch.com. Major credit cards; $$$$$. GETTING THERE: Hawi is near Hawai'i's northern tip. From Kailua-Kona, follow Highway 19 and then Highway 270 north along the Kohala Coast. If you're flumin' da ditch, when you reach Hawi, turn right onto Highway 250 (Hawi Road), then quickly left in front of a Japanese grocery; the office is behind. ☺

North Kohala is one of Hawai'i's most historic areas—the birthplace of Kamehameha. Two rustic old sugar towns, **Hawi** and **Kapa'au,** have become mini-tourist centers, with a few shops, boutiques and cafés in wood frame buildings. Two items of visitor interest are an adventure company that sends clients down a flume that once irrigated the sugarcane fields, and a famous bronze statue of Kamehameha, who was born near here in 1758. Hawi and Kapa'au bloomed in the 1880s when the Kohala Sugar Company planted hundreds of acres of cane and operated several mills in the area. The last one closed in the 1970s and they were on the verge of becoming shantytowns until tourists began arriving.

Flum'in da Ditch is a one-of-a-kind adventure—an inflatable kayak trip down an old irrigation channel. A combination of ditch, flume and tunnel, it was completed in 1906 after eighteen months of labor by Japanese workers. The trip covers about three and a half miles of the concrete-lined ditch. Participants ride in slender cigar-shaped kayaks, with a guide paddling up front and a volunteer passenger helping steer in the back. They pass through seven tunnels—the longest is 1,800 feet—and over a couple of flumes, although most of the route is in open ditch canopied by luxuriant rainforests.

Expect to get wet; the tunnels, blasted out of solid rock, drip and seep, and the self-bailing boats draw enough water to keep fannies soaked. There are no seats; participants sit bobsled style, leaning back and becoming quickly friendly with strangers during low-bridge portions of the trip. Speed is not the issue here; the boats move along at a leisurely pace. Guides describe the terrain along the way and offer bits of Hawaiian history and anecdotes.

TRAVEL TIP: If you're claustrophobic, you may not want to flume da ditch, since it passes through those dark tunnels.

After flumin' da ditch, drive two miles east to Kapaʻau to visit the Kamehameha statue. Cast in Paris in 1880, it was intended for the judiciary building in Honolulu, to mark the coronation of King Kalakaua. However, the ship bringing it to Hawaiʻi sunk and insurance money paid for a new statue. Meanwhile, the captain of the ill-fated ship found that the original had been salvaged off the Falkland islands. He bought it and North Kohala residents had it brought here to honor their famous son.

Continue east from Kapaʻau and you'll shortly reach the end of the road at the **Pololu Valley Lookout**. Sheltered by steep seacliffs, this pretty bowl-shaped valley was carved by a meandering stream that leads to a black sand beach. A half-mile trail leads down to the valley; it's often wet and slippery so hike with caution. If you chose not to go all the way, a partial hike down will improve the views.

Driving back from the lookout, you can visit the Big Island's most sacred shrine, **Moʻokini Heiau,** and **Kamehameha's birthplace**. However, you must bump along a dirt road. Just beyond Hawi, take the **Upolu Airport** turnoff, then follow a road about 1.5 miles to the *heiau*, which stands on a windy plateau high above the ocean. Now a national historic site, it's the largest temple on the island, used for centuries as a sacrificial ground by *aliʻi*. Less than half a mile farther along, after you pass through two gates, look for a plaque marking the site where the life of Hawaiʻi's greatest leader began in 1858.

TRAVEL TIP: The road to the *heiau* and Kamehameha's birthplace may be impassable in wet weather, so check before you go.

8 VISIT PANIOLO COUNTRY

Parker Ranch Museum, Highway 19, Waimea; (808) 885-7655; www.parkerranch.com. Daily 9 to 5; $. Historic Homes tours $; wagon tour of ranch $$; combination tickets available; (808) 885-5433. GETTING THERE: Waimea is in north central part of the island, forty miles from Kailua-Kona and fifty-seven miles from Hilo. Parker Ranch Museum is in Parker Ranch Center near the junction of routes 19 and 190.

Parker Ranch is one of those only-in-Hawai'i places that most people would never associate with Hawai'i. It's one of the world's largest cattle ranches, sprawling over 225,000 acres of the Big Island's northern uplands. It dates from 1847, although the story of Hawai'i cattle ranching began much earlier. Eighteen-year-old John Palmer Parker was a sailor aboard a Massachusetts schooner that called on the Big Island in 1809. He liked the look of the land so he jumped ship. Parker befriended Kamehameha I, who asked him to rid the island of cattle that had gone wild after they had been dropped off years earlier by Captain George Vancouver.

He began butchering them and salting the beef, and he eventually married Kamehameha's great granddaughter. In 1847, Kamehameha III allowed Parker to buy two acres of land for a small ranch. The king also helped him start the Hawaiian cowboy tradition by bringing three *vaqueros* from Mexico. They were considered Spanish by the Hawaiians, and the word came out *paniolo*. By the time of Parker's death in 1868, he had expanded his holdings to more than 200,000 acres. The ranch stayed in the family until Richard Smart, a sixth-generation Parker, died in 1992. His will left most of his holdings in trust to the Waimea community.

It's still a working cattle ranch, running about 35,000 head, tended by twenty-five *paniolo*. Under Smart's leadership, the ranch also became involved in land development and tourism. The company built the Parker Ranch Center in Waimea with a museum and Western store. The firm also has tours of two historic homes and wagon trips through the ranch.

Museum displays trace the history of the ranch and the history of Hawai'i, since they're closely linked. The most interesting exhibit is a reconstructed *paniolo* hut with saddles, bridles and simple bunkhouse furnishings. The home tour is perhaps more interesting than the small museum. Visitors are taken to Smart's 8,000-square-foot mansion and John Parker's smaller Cape Code style home. Smart's home is a virtual museum since he was a world traveler and a great collector of art and artifacts.

Waimea is a neat and prim town enjoying the Parker Ranch prosperity, with shops, a few galleries and some of the Big Island's better restaurants (see below). Since there's more than one Waimea in the Hawaiian Islands, the post office is called Kamuela, the Hawaiian pronunciation of "Samuel." It was named for Samuel Parker, the grandson of the ranch founder, who attended college with the future King Kalakaua. The flamboyant Samuel became a fixture in royal Hawaiian society and was given the honorary title of colonel. He was known around town as "Colonel Sam."

9 RIDE THE SADDLE TO THE STARS

Mauna Kea Observatory. Onizuka Center is open weekdays 9 to noon and 1 to 5, and weekends 9 to 6. Summit tours are at 1 on weekends and stargazing is offered nightly from 6 to 10; (808) 961-2180; www.onizukaspacecenter.com. Several tour companies do Mauna Kea tours; check brochure racks or ask your hotel concierge. GETTING THERE: Take Saddle Road (Route 200) east from Route 190 in North Kohala, or west from Hilo. At milepost 28, turn uphill toward the summit of Mauna Kea. ☺

Hawai'i's tallest mountain, Mauna Kea is home to the world's largest collection of astronomical observatories. Eleven countries operate a score of telescopes, including two of the world's largest. With its clear, thin air and lack of surrounding light pollution, the Mauna Kea summit is one of the best places on earth to probe deep space.

The Ellison S. Onizuka Center for International Astronomy is below the summit at the 9,200-foot level. It offers a free public program of exhibits, nightly stargazing and weekend summit tours. (However, you must have your own vehicle for the summit tour and four wheel drives are usually required.) You can reach the summit yourself if you're a skilled driver with the proper vehicle; see below. Most of the observatories are closed to the public, although Keck I—the world's largest telescope—and the University of Hawaii's observatory have visitors galleries, generally open Monday-Thursday 10 to 4. Summit tours include access to these galleries.

Part of the intrigue of this trip is driving Saddle Road, a narrow, paved lane that passes between Mauna Kea and Mauna Loa. It travels from the Kohala Coast up to wild scrub brush terrain at the 6,000-foot-high "saddle" between the two great mountains. If you continue east, it takes you down through verdant highlands of the Big Island's wet side to Hilo.

The drive up Mauna Kea begins at milepost 28, starting with a gradual 3,000-foot climb to the Onizuka Center. The summit is just over eight miles beyond. The grade steepens dramatically, twisting around some hairpin turns. Part of the summit road is paved; the rest is graded dirt.

This is one of the highest places on earth you can reach by car, and you may be tempted to reach for that old "top of the world" cliché. On a clear day, you can see most of the Big Island from up here, and other islands in the chain. On overcast days—not uncommon although the summit is almost always clear—you may get that feeling of being halfway to heaven, with a sea of clouds below you. (If you're careless driving back down, you may get all the way to heaven.)

TRAVEL TIPS: Dress warmly for the trip up Mauna Kea and take plenty of water, for hydration is essential at this altitude. (Bottled water and snacks are sold at the Onizuka Center.) If you've driven up from the coast, you will have gained nearly 14,000 feet in a couple of hours and your body will not be acclimated to this thin air. Take it easy as you explore the summit, and if you start feeling dizzy, headachy and short of breath—signs of altitude sickness—get down to a lower elevation.

The winding road to the summit is very steep, although it's navigable in passenger cars in good condition, driven by experienced drivers—*if* the road is dry. Otherwise, it's passable only by four-wheel drive. Winter snow is common up here, so don't try it in a regular car if there's snow or mud on the road. It is *critical* that you inquire at the visitor center for road conditions. As you drive, check for strange smells from your vehicle's engine and transmission, for this is likely the steepest climb it'll ever make. It might be wise to pull over and let it catch its breath a couple of times. And if it starts overheating, *stop!* On the return, make the descent in low gear; otherwise you'll fry your brakes and possibly boil away your brake fluid. This is not a good idea on the steepest grades that you'll probably ever drive.

10 EXPLORE HANDSOME OLD HILO

Big Island Visitors Bureau, 250 Keawe St., Hilo, HI 96720; (800) 648-2441 or (808) 961-5797; www.bigisland.org.

Many visitors overlook Hilo, perhaps discouraged by its 128 inches of annual rainfall. However, it has several tourist lures. And because of all that rain—Hilo is America's wettest city—this is one of the most scenic areas on the island.

Powerful *tsunami* savaged Hilo in 1946 and 1960, so waterfront businesses were moved inland. A seawall guards the pretty crescent bay and the area is landscaped with parks and gardens. Inland, many of Hilo's old brick homes and business have a New England or Victorian look, a legacy of missionary days.

This area is Hawai'i's tropical agricultural belt, where most of the island's macadamia nuts, anthuriums, orchids and papayas are grown. The town and the verdant slopes above are gorgeous on sunny days and the area does get a few. Hilo also is a bargain for visitors. Although not a major resort area, it has a couple of midsize hotels and many smaller motels and inns. Prices are much lower than on the Kohala Coast and Kailua-Kona. And it's much closer to Hawaii Volcanoes National Park.

Hilo's attractions include two museums, Banyan Drive and Rainbow Falls. The island-circling driving trip above provides directions to these sites. Here they are in more detail, in their order of appearance:

BANYAN DRIVE: *Starting at the junction of Kanoelehua Avenue (Highway 11) and Kalanianaole Avenue (Highway 19).* ☐ This pretty drive, shaded by ancient banyan trees, loops around parklike Waiakea Peninsula that thrusts into Hilo Bay. Among its green occupants are Naniloa Golf Course and the Oriental style Lili'uokalani Gardens. This also is Hilo's main resort district, rimmed by half a dozen small to mid-size hotels, including ❖ **Hilo Hawaiian Hotel.**

PACIFIC TSUNAMI MUSEUM: *130 Kalakaua Avenue, between Waianuehue Avenue and Kalakaua Street; (808) 935-0926. Monday-Saturday 10 to 4; modest admission fee.* ☐ Housed in the former First Hawaiian Bank building, this museum focuses on the two disastrous tidal waves that hit Hilo. Other exhibits concern *tsunami* in general. Films of *tsunami* are shown in the bank vault.

LYMAN MUSEUM: *276 Haili Street at the corner of Kapi'olani Street; (808) 935-5021; www.lymanmuseum.org. Open Monday-Saturday 9 to 4; modest admission fee.* ☐ This fine museum occupies the 1839 Lyman Mission House, the oldest frame building on the island. It presents a picture of early Hawai'i missionary life with furnished rooms, household items and other artifacts of the era. The adjacent Earth Heritage Gallery features exhibits on Hawaiian geology and natural history, including a mockup lava tube and magma chamber.

RAINBOW FALLS: *In Wailuku River State Park at Rainbow Drive and Waianuehue Avenue.* ☐ This imposing waterfall spills 200 feet down a lava cliff face—either trickling or thundering, depending on the state of the weather. A trail reaches an upper viewing platform. A one-mile drive farther along Wailuku River takes you to Boiling Pots, several kettle-shaped basins that churn merrily when runoff is heavy. Pe'epe'e Falls is just to the left. For yet another cataract, drive less than a mile up Waianuehue Avenue to Wai'lae Falls.

Dining: Ten Interesting Restaurants

Since the Big Island is so—well—big, we've spread our restaurant selections around to provide choices in various areas. Thus, this isn't a Ten Best list, but a Big Island sampler. Our choices are by region.

PRICING: Dollar sign codes indicate the price of a typical dinner with entrée, soup or salad, not including drinks, appetizers or dessert: $ = less than $10 per entrée; $$ = $10 to $19; $$$ = $20 to $29; $$$$ = $30 to $40; $$$$$ = $41 and beyond.

KOHALA COAST

1 BROWN'S BEACH HOUSE

Fairmont Orchid Hawaii Hotel in the Mauna Lani Resort; (808) 885-2000; www.fairmont.com. Hawaiian regional with Asian accents; full bar service. Dinner nightly. Major credit cards; $$$$ to $$$$$. Reser-

vations recommended. GETTING THERE: The Mauna Lani Resort is about twenty-three miles north of Kona International Airport.

Named for a legendary Hawaiian lady, Brown's Beach House provides one of the Big Island's finest dining experiences. This elegant restaurant isn't a beach house although it's certainly close to the beach. Most of the seating is outdoors and it's one of the island's most romantic restaurants. Candles light the tables and a Hawaiian combo plays rhythms to which a pretty hula girl sways. Floodlights highlight incoming breakers, just a few dozen yards away.

Service is attentive and the frequently changing menu offers tasty and innovative fare. Some recent examples were wok-seared lobster with lobster wonton ravioli sauce, crab-crusted 'opakapaka with wasabi mashed potatoes, and pan-seared new York steak with roast fingerling potatoes and soy mustard dipping sauce. For dessert, try the coconut crème brûlée, served in a chilled coconut, accompanied by macadamia nut biscotti.

2 THE CANOEHOUSE

Mauna Lani Bay Hotel in Mauna Lani Resort; (808) 885-6622; www.maunalani.com. Hawaiian regional; mostly seafood; full bar service. Dinner nightly. Major credit cards; $$$$ to $$$$$. Reservations recommended. GETTING THERE: See above.

The CanoeHouse has earned raves from Zagat, *Gourmet, Esquire* and *Bon Appetit.* Occupying a classic plantation style cottage near the beach, it's a pleasing study in dark woods, louvered doors and bamboo furniture. A large canoe hanging from the ceiling ratifies the name. Chef Alan Wong cut his culinary teeth here before moving on to Honolulu to open his own restaurant. The kitchen continues his creativity. Typical entrées include seafood risotto with Japanese pickled vegetables, onion-crusted tofu, chicken roulades with lobster and shiitake mushroom sauce, honey-glazed lamb chops, and seared peppered *ono* with Thai curried jasmine rice.

3 ROY'S WAIKOLOA BAR & GRILL

In the Kings' Shops at Waikoloa Resort, 250 Waikoloa Beach Dr., (808) 886-4321; www.roysrestaurant.com. Pacific Rim; full bar service. Lunch and dinner daily. Major credit cards; $$$ to $$$$. Reservations accepted. GETTING THERE: The Waikoloa complex is eighteen miles north of Kona Airport; the Kings' Shops are just inside the entrance.

This is trademark Roy Yamaguchi—a dramatically modern restaurant with dual open kitchens, splashy tropical prints on the walls, cane-back chairs and a large curving bar. It has indoor and outdoor dining areas. There's no ocean view here although the vista of an adjacent lake and golf course is pleasant. Some recent tastings from Roy's

"Euro-Asian" menu were braised pork roast with shiitake mushroom and soy saké juice, peanut-crusted 'opakapaka, caramel rum glazed rack of lamb with Maui onion mashed potatoes, and Chinese five spice mahimahi.

KAILUA-KONA AREA

4 KE'EI CAFÉ

*Highway 11 in Ke'ei; (808) 328-8451. Hawaiian regional; wine and beer. Breakfast, lunch and dinner daily. No credit cards; $$ to $$$. Reservations accepted. GETTING THERE: The café is about fifteen miles south of Kailua-Kona and three miles south of Captain Cook. Look for it on the right, immediately beyond milepost 106. (**NOTE:** The restaurant may move closer to Kailua-Kona, so call for directions.)*

If this locally popular restaurant is still in its original location when you arrive, don't let the shabby building dissuade you. Behind the façade of a former fish market is a charming little place with cheerful Hawaiian prints on the walls, café curtains and—for evening dining—seductively dim lighting. The menu is creative, without the creative prices of Kohala Coast restaurants. When we last dined, offerings included roast pork chops with peppercorn gravy and pineapple glaze, roast half chicken, *ono* with Thai red curry, seafood pasta, and *ahi* with mashed potatoes and passion fruit sauce.

5 KONA INN RESTAURANT

75-5744 Ali'i Dr., Kailua-Kona; (808) 329-4455. American with Hawaiian accents; full bar service. Lunch through dinner daily at the grill; dinner nightly at the restaurant. Major credit cards; $$ to $$$. Reservations accepted. GETTING THERE: It's in downtown Kailua-Kona at the corner of Ali'i Drive and Hualalai Road.

Remember the Hawai'i of yesterday? This is a classic old island-style restaurant with great aloha vibes and views of the Kailua-Kona waterfront. The main restaurant has lava stone walls and bamboo accents, with high back queens chairs. Most of the seating both in the restaurant and the casual grill is outside, the better to enjoy those fine coastal vistas. The kitchen isn't particularly creative although the fare is usually well-prepared and portions are generous. Among choices from the large menu are calamari or scampi or a combination thereof, spicy Hawaiian chicken topped with pineapple, top sirloin, and fresh fish done in assorted ways.

6 LA BOURGOGNE

77-6400 Highway 11, Kailua-Kona; (808) 329-6711. French; wine and beer. Dinner Tuesday-Saturday. Major credit cards; $$$ to $$$$. Reservations recommended. GETTING THERE: It's a couple miles from *downtown Kailua in Kuakini Plaza South. The restaurant us on the left, at the corner of Nilani Street, a couple hundred yards beyond mileage marker 119.*

Zagat calls Le Bourgogne Hawai'i's finest French restaurant and those who dine here heartily agree. Further, the entrées are reasonably priced and—a rarity—the wine list is both excellent and inexpensive. The place won't impress from the outside; it occupies a stucco building more suitable for a savings and loan office. Inside, it's very appealing, with a cozy dining room of wainscotting, green print wallpaper and brick accents.

The menu is classic, not cutesy French *nouveau*. Examples include *osso bucco* veal shank braised in red wine, sweetbreads of veal with Madeira sauce, fresh catch of the day with traditional French sauces, and sliced breast of roast duck with raspberries and pinenuts.

7 SIBU CAFÉ

75-5695 Ali'i Dr.; (808) 329-1112. Indonesian; wine and beer. Lunch and dinner daily. No credit cards; $$ to $$$. GETTING THERE: It's in Banyan Court in downtown Kailua-Kona, just south of Palani Road.

Sibu is a remarkably cute place with coral-peach walls decorated with Indonesian masks. And it's *tiny,* with just four tables inside and six more on Banyan Court. The menu is larger than the café, listing a variety of Indonesian and other Southeast Asian dishes. Its satays are particularly tasty and its curries are peppy. Some menu highlights include *gado gado*, which is a layered salad with brown rice, carrots, green beans, eggs and tofu with peanut sauce and lime juice; Balinese chicken filets with tarragon, garlic, onions and canola oil; and spicy pork with a cumin, coriander and garlic sauce simmered with chilis.

NORTH KOHALA & WAIMEA

8 BAMBOO RESTAURANT

Highway 270 in Hawi; (808) 889-5555. Hawaiian-Asian; wine and beer. Lunch and dinner Tuesday-Saturday and Sunday brunch. MC/VISA; $$ to $$$. GETTING THERE: It's in downtown Hawi near the corner of highways 250 and 270.

The Bamboo is typical of what's happening to this old sugar town. It's a charming combination restaurant, gift shop and art gallery in a 1911 woodframe building that once was a hotel. Settle into a comfortable chair, listen to soft Hawaiian background music and admire the tropical trim and works of local artists. The restaurant and gift shop are on the ground floor and the gallery portion is mostly on the second level. The menu is creative and eclectic, reflecting the town's ethnic roots. Some examples are marinated pork with tiger shrimp, pineapple barbecued chicken, Thai style fish with coconut milk and lemongrass, and kalua pork and cabbage.

9 MERRIMAN'S

Opelo Plaza on Highway 19, Kamuela-Waimea; (808) 885-6822; www.merrimanshawaii.com. Hawaiian regional; wine and beer. Lunch weekdays and dinner nightly. Major credit cards; $$$ to $$$$. Reservations recommended. GETTING THERE: Approaching Waimea from the south, the restaurant is on the left, at the corner of Opelo Road.

Legions of the faithful make the long drive to Kamuela to try the latest creations of Peter Merriman, the Big Island's best-known chef. Merriman's has been named its top restaurant for several years running. The look is appealing and simple, with bamboo and cane-back chairs, potted plants and Hawaiian prints on the walls. An open kitchen occupies the far end of the dining room.

Merriman uses organic locally-produced ingredients when possible. Some of his creations are sesame-crusted fresh island fish, grilled Kahuna beef with horseradish and goat cheese paté, fried *moi* in pineapple sesame sauce, and grilled chicken breast with coconut glaze and curry roast tomato.

HILO

10 SEASIDE RESTAURANT

1790 Kalanianaole Ave., Hilo; (808) 935-8825. American with Japanese accents; mostly seafood; wine and beer. Dinner nightly except Monday. Major credit cards; $$ to $$$. GETTING THERE: The restaurant is three miles east of downtown on Highway 19. Look for it on the right, opposite the eastern edge of Onekohakaha Beach Park.

This Japanese family-owned restaurant occupies an old corrugated roof house that could use some sprucing up. The dining room is equally basic, with long family-style tables and little adornment. The only views are of an adjacent aqua farm. So why do we recommend it? Because the fish is excellent, often fished out of the pond just before it's served. Seaside has been a local favorite for years. In addition to faultlessly fresh fish, it serves vegetarian pasta, steak and lobster, *paniolo* prime rib, teriyaki chicken and a vegetarian pasta.

RECLINING: TEN INTERESTING PILLOW PLACES

As with our restaurant selections above, this is not a Ten Best list, but a sampler of places to stay around the Big Island. They range from elegant and pricey to comfy and inexpensive. Most of our choices are on the Kohala Coast because that's where most visitors sleep.

PRICING: Dollar sign codes indicate room price ranges for two people, based on high season (summer and winter) rates: **$** = a standard two-person room for $99 or less; **$$** = $100 to $149; **$$$** = $150 to $199; **$$$$** = $200 to $249; **$$$$$** $250 or more. **CREDIT CARDS**: All of the below listed cards accept most major credit cards.

THE KOHALA COAST

Resorts on the Big Island's main resort area, the Kohala Coast, are carved out of a massive old lava flow that stretches more than twenty miles. If you've come to Hawai'i just to loaf in the sun, snorkel, swim and swing a golf club, you need go no further. Some of the resort complexes have fully-furnished condos as well as hotel rooms, making a self-contained vacation even more practical. We begin with our favorite Big Island resort, and our other choices follow in alphabetical order, by region.

1 HILTON WAIKOLOA VILLAGE

425 Waikoloa Beach Dr., Waikoloa, HI 96738; (800) HILTONS or (808) 886-1234; www.hiltonwaikoloavillage.com. Elaborate and extensive 1,240-unit resort; $$$$ to $$$$$. GETTING THERE: The Waikoloa Village Resort complex is about eighteen miles north of Kona International Airport on Highway 19.

This 640-acre resort, the largest in the outer islands, is our favorite place for families. With three hotel towers, an extensive complex of lagoons, swimming areas and waterfalls, a large art collection and even a monorail system, it rivals the most elaborate of Las Vegas resorts. And it's on da beach, man! Partly for convenience and partly for novelty, a monorail links the three hotel towers with the main lobby and convention center. Cute little boats follow a similar route along the hotel's lagoons. They're particularly romantic at night, and never mind that the boats are on tracks, a la Disneyland. (If only the operators would go through the motions of steering!)

The Museum Walk along hotel corridors take guests past a $5 million Asian-Polynesian art collection. Resort facilities include seven restaurants, a large spa, several swimming pools, tennis courts, a kids playground and youth program and DolphinQuest, where folks can get up close and personal with Flipper's kin. Two golf course are in the adjacent Waikoloa complex. One of the most appealing features of this resort is that it's relatively affordable. Rates start under $200 a night.

2 FAIRMONT ORCHID HAWAII

One N. Kaniku Dr., Kohala Coast, HI 96743; (800) 257-7544 or (808) 885-2000; www.fairmont.com. An opulent 539-room resort; $$$$$. GETTING THERE: It's in the Mauna Lani Resort complex about *twenty-three miles north of Kona Airport. Turn into the facility and follow signs to your right.*

The Fairmont Orchid is strikingly elegant, with a formal *porte-cochere* with a marble fountain, and a lobby embellished with Greek columns and crystal chandeliers. A large lawn area slopes down to the beach, which has a sandy cove for sunning and swimming, and a lava section for tidepooling. The resort's dining options are the Orchid Court, serving breakfast and dinner; the Grill, dinner only; and Brown's Beach House; see above). Rooms are nicely furnished with marble bathrooms and large tiled balconies. Resort facilities include the open-air Spa Without Walls, a fitness center and tennis pavilion. A 36-hole golf course is nearby.

The Fairmont Orchid is rather new—in name only. It was built as a Ritz-Carlton in 1990, then it became a Sheraton, and then the Orchid at Mauna Lani. It joined the Fairmont chain in late 2002.

MAUNA LANI CONDOS

In addition to two major hotels, the Mauna Lani resort complex has two condo communities, **Mauna Lani Point** and **Mauna Lani Terrace**. Units have full kitchens, separate bedrooms and even washer-dryers. Both are virtually surrounded by Mauna Lani's dual thirty-six hole golf course. At some units, it's so close that a short chip shot from the patio would get you onto a fairway. Guest check-in for the condos is behind the security office just inside the resort's main gate. **For information:** Mauna Lani Resort, 68-1310 Mauna Lani Dr., Suite 101, Kohala Coast, HI 96743; (808) 885-5022; *www.maunalani.com.*

3 KONA VILLAGE

P.O. Box 1299, Kailua-Kona, HI 96745; (800) 367-5290 or (808) 325-5555; www.konavillage.com. A Hawaiian style resort with 125 thatched bungalows; $$$$$. GETTING THERE: The village is about six miles north of Kona Airport.

We noted above that the large Kohala resorts are self-contained; places where vacationers never have to leave. Here, you can take that completely literally. Kona Village is a low-rise, palm-shaded complex on a beautiful lagoon. Lodgings are in 125 *hale* fashioned after various South Pacific dwellings. Everything is included—all meals, a weekly luau, activities, beach equipment and snorkel gear, a fitness center, tennis courts and even box lunches for hikers. All of this comes at a price, of course; rates start at more than $500 a night.

What Kona Village does not have are TVs, radios, clocks or phones in the units. However, these are not spartan Club Med-style digs. They're modern and comfortable rooms, recently upgraded as part of a $7 million renovation. Some of the *hale* are on stilts over the lagoon; these are some of the most romantic lodgings on the islands. Kona Village would be even more romantic—with its tiki torches, night beach walks and private cottages—except that it's popular for families. If you're seeking a really amorous escape, don't come to Kona Village during school vacation.

4 MAUNA KEA BEACH HOTEL

62-100 Kauna'oa Dr., Kohala Coast, HI 96743; (800) 882-6060 or (808) 882-7222; www.maunakeabeachhotel.com. Luxury low-rise resort with 310 rooms; $$$$$. GETTING THERE: The Mauna Kea is on the upper end of the Kohala Coast, about twenty-five miles from Kona Airport.

The first of the Kohala Coast resorts, the Mauna Kea has been outshined by newer and more glossy neighbors. However, it still has that understated elegance and faultless service that makes it a favorite retreat of the rich, famous and those who can afford the rates starting around $360 a night. (Since we were married on the beach here, we'll admit to having a special affection for the place.) The low-rise hotel sits on a gorgeous little crescent bay with a sandy beach on one end and tide-pool lava outcroppings at the other. Ocean-view rooms are tiered so guests have a view of the beach below and the sky above.

The hotel has an outstanding collection of Asian and South Pacific art, and the concierge can provide a self-guiding brochure. Regular tours are scheduled as well; call the hotel for times. Among the Mauna Kea's restaurants are the Pavilion, with mostly outdoor tables and a beach view, serving breakfast and dinner; the more elegant Batik Restaurant overlooking the pool and the beach, serving dinner only; and the Hau Tree and 19th hole for lunch. Resort amenities include a championship golf course, a tennis complex, spa and fitness center.

5 MAUNA LANI BAY HOTEL

68-1400 Mauna Lani Dr., Kohala Coast, HI 96743-9796; (800) 367-2323 or (808) 885-6622; www.maunalani.com. Luxury resort with 345 rooms and suites and five bungalows; $$$$$. GETTING THERE: It's part of the Mauna Lani Resort complex, about twenty-three miles north of Kona Airport. Turn seaward off Highway 19 and follow signs.

The Mauna Lani has a starkly dramatic swept-back exterior like the Mauna Kea, offering ocean and sky views from its balconies. The interior is quite posh, with an imposing three-story atrium lobby and distinctive "sheet fountains" cascading alongside a central stairway. The resort's most impressive feature is its elaborate water course, stocked not with the usual *koi* but with multicolored tropical fish. This stream meanders throughout the grounds and runs right through the lobby.

Nicely landscaped lawns tilt down to a small sandy beach. A trail leads south to a complex of restored fish ponds, part of the Kalahuipua'a Historic Park.

Among the resort's features are a large spa and fitness center, tennis courts, Hawaiian crafts classes and a kids' program. Dining choices include the Bay Terrace, serving breakfast and dinner daily; a poolside grill; and the Canoe House (see above). Rooms are spacious and handsomely furnished. And for *real* space, rent one of the 4,000-square-foot bungalows. Each has two bedrooms, a living room, lanai, private swimming pool, spa tub and personal butler service. It's all yours for $4,900 a night.

6 WAIKOLOA OUTRIGGER

69-275 Waikoloa Beach Dr., Waikoloa, HI 96738-5711; (800) 922-5533 or (808) 886-6789; www.outrigger.com. A resort complex with 545 rooms and suites; $$$$$. GETTING THERE: It's directly opposite the Kings' Shops.

This appealing retreat occupies one of the Kohala Coast's longest sandy beaches, a palm-studded crescent called Anaeho'omalu Bay. Typical of Outriggers, it carries a strong Hawaiian theme. A focal point in the lobby is a large, fanciful mural of Captain George Vancouver aboard his *HMS Discovery* being greeted by Hawaiians in a double-hulled canoe. The hotel chain's signature decorator piece, a varnished outrigger, is displayed nearby.

Hawaii Calls Restaurant, open to the beach, continues the Polynesian theme; it serves breakfast, lunch and dinner. Light fare is available poolside at Nalu's Bar from midmorning to sunset. Surrounding the pool is an extensively landscaped lawn area, with that long sandy beach and an ancient fishpond below. Guest rooms have all the usual resort amenities and most are angled toward the sea. Resort facilities include a spa, fitness center, tennis courts, kids' activities and Hawaiian cultural programs. Waikoloa's 36-hole golf course is nearby.

THE KONA COAST

Lodgings in and about the Kailua-Kona area are much smaller than those on the Kohala Coast and many are condos.

7 OHANA KEAUHAU BEACH RESORT

78-6740 Ali'i Dr., Kailua-Kona, HI 96740; (800) 462-6262 or (808) 322-3441; www.ohanahotels.com. A 311-unit beachside hotel; $$$ to $$$$$. GETTING THERE: Follow Ali'i drive about a mile south from downtown Kailua-Kona. The resort is on your right.

This midsize hotel sits just over the beach on the lower end of Ali'i Drive's "resort row." While not posh, it's neat and spotlessly clean, and it's affordable, with discount rates starting around $100. The hotel has a large comfortable lobby with inviting wicker chairs and a small gift shop. A particularly appealing spot is the Beach Bar, on pier over the water. Small coral reefs are just offshore and one often can see fish from the bar railing.

Kama'aina Terrace Restaurant, mostly with outdoor seating and coastal views, serves breakfast and Sunday brunch, and dinner nightly. Rooms are fair sized and rather modestly furnished; most of them have ocean views. Adjacent Keiuhau public beach has some good snorkeling areas.

8 KING KAMEHAMEHA HOTEL

75-5660 Palani Rd., Kailua-Kona, HI 96470; (800) 367-6060 or (808) 329-2911; www.konabeachhotel.com. A 450-unit hotel in downtown Kailua; $$ to $$$$. GETTING THERE: It's at the corner of Ali'i Drive and Palani Road.

The old "King Kam" could use a tuck here and there, but it's interesting, affordable and in a great location. It's at the Kailua waterfront, steps from a sandy beach and the historic Ahu'ena Heiau. This venerable lodging has been spruced up, and the old fashioned Polynesian style lobby displays portraits of Hawaiian royalty and assorted South Seas artifacts. It's worth a browse even if you aren't staying here. Rooms are modestly sized and very clean, with small refrigerators. Three restaurants and several shops and galleries are off the lobby. A luau is held near the waterfront Sunday through Thursday. Hotel facilities include a pool, spa and sauna and tennis courts.

HILO

9 HILO HAWAIIAN HOTEL

71 Banyan Dr., Hilo, HI 96720; (800) 367-5004 or (808) 935-9361; www.castleresorts.com. A 268-unit low-rise hotel; $$ to $$$. GETTING THERE: It's near the junction of highways 19 and 11 at Hilo's bayfront.

All rooms in this older, well-kept hotel have balconies with views of Hilo Bay. It's nicely located, within a short walk of the Banyan Drive parklands, Naniola Golf Course and public beaches. Queens Court Restaurant serves breakfast, lunch and dinner, with a Sunday brunch and weekend Hawaiian seafood buffet. Wai'Oli Lounge has entertainment most nights. A few Hawaiian artifacts are on display in the modest lobby. Facilities include a pool, gift shop and guest laundry.

...AND UP AMONG THE VOLCANOES

10 VOLCANO HOUSE

P.O. Box 53, Hawaii Volcanoes National Park, HI 96718; (808) 967-7321. An historic 42-unit hotel; $ to $$$. GETTING THERE: It's just inside the park gate, opposite the visitor center.

The Volcano House is old and tired, but the view! It's perched right on the edge of Kilauea Caldera. Ask for a crater view room and you can stare down into the black maw, watching steam rise ominously from its depths. When we last checked, crater-side rooms were only about $50 higher than non-view rooms, although they must be booked months in advance. For the budget-minded, a few rooms are available in the Ohia wing behind the hotel for under $100 a night.

Volcano House rooms are simple, clean and spartan, with no TV, phones or radios. The hotel has a couple of gift shops, a restaurant that serves breakfast, lunch and dinner and a cozy lounge with a crackling fireplace. It's quite inviting, since it can get chilly at this 4,000-foot altitude. Technically, the Volcano House is the oldest hostelry in the state. Overnight lodgings began here with a simple lean-to in 1865.

Kaua'i, from the sea, is green and rose, the bright volcanic earth showing through the rich vegetation which has caused its inhabitants to claim for it the name..."Garden Island."
— **Clifford Gessler, Hawaii, Isles of Enchantment, 1937**

Chapter Fourteen

KAUA'I
PARADISE IN A GARDEN

How nice it would be if we were like the island of Kaua'i—becoming more attractive with age. It's the oldest of Hawai'i's major islands and many say it's the most beautiful, with its lush vegetation and dramatic seacliffs. In a survey of *Travel & Leisure* readers a few years ago, it was voted the world's second best island, after Maui.

Formed from a single shield volcano called Wai'ale'ale, Kaua'i emerged from the sea five to six million years ago. With its long exposure to wind, sea and sun, it has eroded into deep canyons and the incredibly sheer seacliffs of Na Pali Coast. The elements have reduced Kaua'i's lava surface to rich soil that supports thick rainforests.

The oldest of Hawai'i's islands also may have been the first to be settled, although some anthropologists give that credit to the Big Island. If we are to believe Kaua'i's favorite legend, a society of *Menehunes*—think of them as Polynesian Leprechauns—were the island's first dwellers. These little people came from the mystic past—perhaps the lost continent of Mu—and were here when the first Polynesians arrived. Only two to three feet tall, they labored mightily to build fish-

ponds and the Menehune ditch above Wailea. Like true mystical dwellers of the forest, they came out only at night to do their labors. Where
they've gone, no one knows. Stay alert as you prowl the forests of this
mystical island; you may be able to report a *Menehune* sighting.

Kaua'i is small and rather remote, just thirty-three miles wide and
sitting by itself ninety miles northwest of O'ahu. Its isolation has been
an asset, except that it's the first island to be hit by storms blowing
down from the Gulf of Alaska. Its northwestern exposure is soaked by
condensing clouds, making it one of the wettest places on earth. Hurri-
canes Iwa in 1982 and Iniki in 1992 savaged the island with 100-mile-
an-hour winds, causing extensive damage.

However, its isolation and the stormy channel separating it from
the other islands kept Kamehameha's invasion forces from landing; it's
the only major island he didn't conquer. He finally convinced its ruler,
Kaumuali'i, to annex Kaua'i and neighboring Ni'ihau to his empire in
1810. When tourism started to develop in the Hawaiian Islands a century ago, ships didn't bother to cross that choppy channel, and it remains today one of the least "developed" of the major islands. And
therein lies most of its charm. Although it has enough of a population
base to offer essential services—about 58,000 people—it receives
fewer visitors than Maui or the Big Island. Enough tourists are drawn
here to support a few resorts but not enough to encourage a Waikiki or
Ka'anapali kind of development.

Kaua'i's residents like that just fine. Life moves at a slow pace along
the island's only two highways, although that's mostly because of traffic congestion. Kaua'i's economy is based more on agriculture than
tourism, although it does get about a million visitors a year. It produces coconuts, macadamia nuts, pineapples, papayas, guavas and a
little coffee. It has one of only two still-operating sugar mills in the
state and the only commercial taro patches. These endeavors keep
Kaua'i green; they help make it literally the Garden Island.

Much of its emerald beauty is natural, however. Thick tropical forest cloak its eastern foothills and the soggy heights of Wai'ale'ale. Half
of its total land is in forest preserves. Its tropical vegetation, crescent
beaches and sheer cliffs make it the darling of movie companies. More
films have been shot here than on any of the other islands, including
South Pacific, Raiders of the Lost Ark, Outbreak, Jurassic Park and—
good grief!—even Elvis Presley's *Blue Hawaii*. (See page 254.)

TO LEARN MORE: Contact the Kaua'i Visitors Bureau at (800) 262-
1400; *www.kauaivisitorsbureau.com*

Kaua'i: Getting to Know You

We find it amazing that Kaua'i's doesn't attract more visitors, since
it has some of the best attractions of all the islands. Its famous red-
walled Waimea Canyon and its awesome coastal cliffs are among the
most impressive natural wonders in the world. We have stood for long

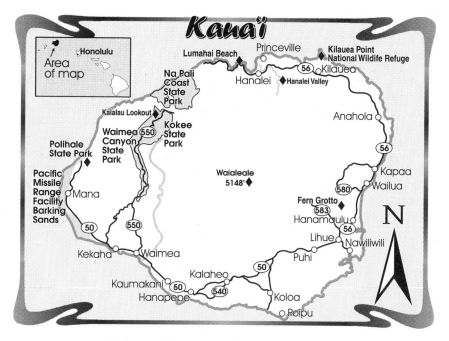

Kaua'i

Area of map — Honolulu

Lumahai Beach • Princeville • Kilauea Point National Wildlife Refuge
Na Pali Coast State Park • Hanalei • Hanalei Valley • 56 Kilauea
Kalalau Lookout • Kokee State Park • Anahola
Waimea 550 Canyon State Park • 56
Polihale State Park
Pacific Missile Range Facility Barking Sands • Mana
Waialeale 5148' • Kapaa / Wailua
580
Fern Grotto 583 • Hanamaulu • 56
Lihue • Nawiliwili
50 • 550
Kekaha • Waimea • Puhi
Kalaheo • 50
Kaumakani 50 • Hanapepe • 540 • Koloa
Poipu

N

moments at a Waimea Canyon overlook and had the place to ourselves. If this had been the *Pali* vista point above Honolulu, we would
have been shouldering through tour bus crowds. And Waimea's view is
much more impressive!

Virtually all of Kaua'i's population is limited to its coastal plains.
Two-thirds of the island is inaccessible only by hikers' boots. Only one
road penetrates the interior—a steep, winding lane leading up to
Waimea Canyon. No road—not even a dirt one—circles the island.

Because so much of Kaua'i remains in its natural state, it's popular
with outdoor types. Hiking trails wind among its forests and through
the wilderness of Waimea Canyon. The island's heavy rainfall has created the state's largest river system, so kayaking is popular. Surfing
and windsurfing are popular as well. The tamer waters of the south
coast attract novice and intermediate surfers and the wild waves of the
north coast draw the experts.

Like the other islands, Kaua'i has its wet and dry sides, although
the arid southwest coast is not as dry as the Big Island's Kohala Coast
or Maui's Lahaina-Ka'anapali region. Kaua'i's main tourist area is at
Po'ipu on the south coast. West from here, Highway 50 passes
through a relatively dry area with an appealing collection of old sugar
towns and some pretty beaches and bays. At **Waimea**, a road reaches
skyward to **Waimea Canyon.**

Kaua'i's eastern shore is the **Coconut Coast,** an area with enough
rain to keep it green but not enough to discourage some tourism.
Backdropped by emerald hills and canyons, it has several resorts and
condos and a scattering of small towns. The **North Coast** is the

greenest and prettiest part of Kaua'i. Despite a goodly amount of rain, it's home to several small resorts and one large and elegant one, **Princeville.** Beyond Princeville and the rustic tourist town of **Hanelei,** the road winds through some of the world's most gorgeous tropical scenery. And beyond that—beyond road's end—are the fabled cliffs of Na Pali Coast.

The least attractive part of Kaua'i is the first area that visitors see— the county seat of **Lihu'e** on the southeast coast. It's home to **Lihu'e Airport** and the island's only large shopping mall. Lihu'e is an old blue collar town that's slowly going modern. It has a certain amount of charm, with a fine historical museum, a few yesterday buildings, an old sugar mill and a plantation turned living history center. The island's worst congestion—and this is *real* congestion—is north from Lihu'e along the Coconut Coast through **Waipouli, Wailua** and **Kapa'a.**

DRIVING KAUA'I

As we noted above, Kaua'i has only two main highways—actually, just one that changes numbers. When you deplane at Lihu'e Airport and pick up your rental car, you can see all of accessible Kaua'i by following these highways and some short spur roads. We'll begin by going north and east from Lihu'e on Highway 56, and then south and west on Highway 50.

NOTE: Listings in **Bold face** marked with ❖ are described in more detail elsewhere; check the index for page numbers.

NORTH TO NA PALI

From the airport, head north on Kapule Highway (Route 51) toward Kapa'a and Princeville. It merges into Route 56 (Kuhio Highway) at the hamlet of **Hanamaulu.** Just beyond, turn right at the far end of **Wailua Golf Course** onto Leho Road and follow signs to **Lydgate State Park.** It's one of the island's more appealing public parks with grassy picnic areas and a beach that's a mix of sand and lava. This is a fine place for watching the waves roll in.

At the far end of the parking lot, Lydgate merges with **Wailua River State Park.** A short loop trail will lead you past **Hikina o Kala Heiau,** near the river's mouth. It's the first of seven abandoned shrines in the **Hauola Place of Refuge.** Most are little more than scatterings of lava boulders. A trail leads up the riverbank to the other temples.

As you return to the highway, you'll see **Smith's Tropical Paradise,** a tourist gimmick with a *faux* Polynesian village and real botanical gardens. It's open daily 8:30 to 4 and it presents luaus several nights a week; (808) 821-6895. At an adjacent dock, tour boats depart every half hour on one of Kaua'i's most popular—and corny—tourist activities, a trip up the Wailua River to the **Fern Grotto.** While the grotto is gorgeous—a lava cave dripping with thick ferns—the boats are crowded and noisy. Their loudspeaker narrations disrupt this otherwise peaceful and pretty stream. We prefer kayaking up the river; see below on page 254. However, if you must, two outfits conduct Fern Grotto tours—**Smith's,** (808) 821-6892, *www.smithskauai.com*; and **Waialeale Boat Tours,** (808) 822-9408.

Just beyond Smith's, cross the river and turn left onto Highway 380 for a look at another *heiau* and Opaeka'a Falls. The road travels up through gorgeous green countryside, headed toward the mountains. After a mile, stop at a scenic turnout for a view down to the emerald-shrouded Wailua River. You can explore a partially restored heiau here; it's one of the seven in Wailua River State Park. A bit farther up the road on the right, another turnout invites you to pause for a gander at **Opaeka'a Falls,** set back in a box canyon.

A gem of a village

Immediately beyond, turn left down a steep road for a real gem that's missed by most visitors and ignored by most other guidebooks—**Kamokila Hawaiian Village.** Sitting on the banks of the river, it's an authentically reconstructed early settlement, with grass shacks furnished with the simple items of a Polynesian yesteryear. A self-guided tour takes you past living quarters, a chief's house, small *heiau* and other structures. You also may see some traditional crafts demonstrations. The admission fee is very modest—$5 when we last visited, and easily worth it. Kayak rentals also are available. The village is open daily except Sunday 8 to 5; (808) 823-0559.

Continue inland through an emerald green agricultural region called **Waimea Homestead,** rich with macadamia groves and tropical fruit orchards. At the end of the road is **Keahua Forestry Arboretum** on the edge of the **Kaelia Forest Reserve.** The arboretum has two short trails winding through groves of mangos, monkeypods, eucalyptus and other tropical flora. And if you *really* want to hike, with a guarantee of getting wet, a trail leads from here up to soggy Wai'ale'ale. From the arboretum, head coastward and then turn left onto Highway 581, which travels through more of this lush agricultural region.

You'll soon enter the back door of **Kapa'a** on Route 56, the Kuhio Highway. It's basic blue collarsville and one of Kaua'i's fastest growing towns. In fact, it's the island's largest, with about 10,000 residents, nearly twice as many as Lihu'e. Kapa'a offers little of interest except a few good restaurants; see below. Unfortunately, it functions as a traffic plug between the western and eastern ends of the island. Worth a look on the far end of town is the **Kauai Products Fair,** with about fifty food and crafts booths. It's open Thursday-Sunday 9 to 5; (808) 246-0988; *www.kauaiproductsfair.com*.

As you continue along Kuhio Highway, look inland for the **Sleeping Giant,** a large green ridge that suggests a colossus in slumber.

Can't make him out? His head is just above Wailua and his feet extend northward.

Just past milepost 21 is the turnoff for the **Na'Aina Kai Botanical Garden,** reached by a brief drive down Wailapa Road. Tours through this elaborate garden are by reservation only, on Tuesday, Wednesday and Thursday; (808) 828-0525; *www.naainakai.com.* Ed and Joyce Doty have turned their 240 acres into twelve theme gardens, plus a hardwood forest and tropical fruit farm. Bronze statuary and water features add pleasing visual elements to this extensive layout, which visitors tour by tram and afoot.

The next attraction along this route, which requires no advance notice, is the **Guava Plantation** and visitor center, open daily 9 to 5; (808) 828-6121. Turn left onto Kuawa Road just short of Kilauea Lighthouse. It's a surprisingly appealing facility with a gift and specialty foods shop, and free samples of guava juice and several sauces and dips. You'll learn that Kaua'i produces sixty percent of the state's guavas and that they're good for you, with more vitamin C than oranges. A tropical garden and guava production plant are nearby. You may see huge wooden crates of just-harvested guavas, heading for certain death in the crusher. (The firm's guavas go into juice.) The facility also has a café serving guava specialties and light lunches.

Just beyond, at the turnoff to Kilauea Lighthouse, pause at the 1892 lava stone **Kong Lung Store.** This former general store is now a gift shop and gallery specializing in Asian art and artifacts. Out back are another gallery, a candle and soap works and Pan Hana pizza parlor and bakery. Baked goods are excellent although rather pricey; we have a problem with $2 pastries.

Nenes & boobies

Continue down the road to **Kilauea Lighthouse and Wildlife Refuge.** It's open daily 9 to 4, with a modest admission charge; (808) 828-1413. The refuge sits dramatically on a rocky point above the crashing surf. Among its attractions are a flock of nenes, Hawai'i's endangered state bird. Here, they're in danger of becoming roadkill; they waddle about like pet geese. Also practically underfoot—on a path leading to Kilauea Lighthouse—are nesting wing-tailed sheerwaters. They don't seem to mind all the tourists strolling past. Across a lava-ridged bay you can see hundreds of nesting red-footed boobies. They appear to be little more than white flecks; you can borrow binoculars for a better look.

This is one of the few good birdwatching areas on any of the main islands. Feral cats, egg-sucking mongeese and other predators have raised havoc with most other Hawaiian nesting sites. Inside the refuge's small visitor center, a large topographic map provides an excellent three-dimensional look at the Hawaiian Islands. The center also has a few exhibits on local bird life and a gift shop with a good selection of Hawaiiana books.

Five miles beyond the Kilauea turnoff, you'll encounter Kaua'i's only major planned resort community, **Princeville**, which appears to be one huge golf course. This immaculately manicured retreat has several stylish home complexes and two resorts—❖ **Hanalei Bay Hotel** and the ❖ **Princeville Resort**.

Return to the main highway, continue briefly north and you'll see the **Princeville Shopping Center** on the right. Just beyond on the left is the turnout for one of Hawai'i's best-known and most photographed vista points, **Hanalei Valley Overlook**. You've seen it before in photos and videos—a neat geometry of taro patches resembling Chinese or Balinese rice paddies, with brooding mountains—almost always misty and thus mysterious—rising above. This is a wildlife preserve where growers have been invited to plant taro patches, because they make excellent bird wetlands. With the coming of civilization and McDonald's, taro—from which poi is made—has gone out of style. Thus, most of these artificial wetlands had dried up. So the next time you force down a forkful of that bland, pale purple paste at a luau, remember that it's for the birds.

The highway drops down into the valley and brushes the edge of those taro patches, then it enters the old town of **Hanalei.** Many of its wood-frame false front and plantation style stores are occupied by shops, galleries and restaurants. Hanalei is in a gorgeous setting at the base of those impossibly steep mountains. If you need a designer coffee fix or shave ice, check out **Java Kai** and **Shave Ice Paradise**, sharing a bungalow near the old **Hanalei School**, which has been converted into a shopping center.

On the far side of town, watch on your left for the cute green shingle-sided 1834 **Wai Oli Hu'ia Church**. It's quite appealing, with a witch's hat bell tower, leaded glass windows and curved, polished wooden pews. Also worth a visit is the **Waioli Mission House**, built in 1836 and restored to its original look, complete with china and family portraits. Tours are conducted Tuesday, Thursday and Saturday from 9 to 3; (808) 245-3202.

Gentlemen, start your adjectives

And now, make ready your camera and your adjectives for a ten-mile drive along one of the world's most beautiful coastlines. It travels through the Kaua'i of reality and fable, where scenes from many movies have been shot. The narrow and winding road offers almost constant vistas of Hanalei Bay and Kaua'i's troubling sea and rough-hewn coast. This isn't a wilderness, however; tucked into the forest and along beaches are homes that range from opulent to funky.

Watch on your right for a sign indicating a turnout above **Lumahai Beach**. Here, Mitzi Gaynor tried to wash Rossano Brazzi out of her hair in the silly Hollywood version of *South Pacific*. Shortly beyond, the road drops down to the coast at the mouth of **Lumahai Stream.** You can park and walk back along this idyllic jungle-clad beach. Look but don't swim here; waves slam violently against the shore and career up into the river's mouth.

Pressing onward, you'll cross a couple of rickety-appearing one-lane wooden bridges. Just beyond milepost 8 is **Ha'ena Beach Park** with grassy picnic areas and a sandy beach. Immediately after passing through a cement creekbed crossing (sometimes wet), look to your left for a large dry lava cave. Next on the left is **Limahuli Garden**, open Tuesday through Friday and Sunday 9:30 to 4; (808) 826-1053; *www.ntbg.org/limahuli.html.* Tours are a bit expensive for a botanical garden, although they're worth it if you're a plant lover. One of four National Tropical Botanical Gardens in the state, Limahuli is terraced up a shallow ravine at the base of the great promontory of Mount Makana.

Immediately beyond, you'll enter ❖ **Ha'ena State Park**. This is the end of the road but not of your North Coast exploration. See the listing below on page 255.

TO LIHU'E & THE WEST COAST

Starting from the airport, follow Kapule Highway (Route 51) to Rice Street in **Lihu'e**. If you're returning on Highway 56 from the tour above, go left at the airport sign onto Route 51. At Rice Street, which is Lihu'e's main drag, turn left and follow it the to busy little port of **Nawiliwili Harbor** and **Kalapai Beach,** an inviting crescent of white sand. Now, reverse your route and follow Rice into the heart of town. Watch on your right for the old fashioned **County Government Center** with an appealing palm-shaded park in front. Next door, at Rice and Eiwa streets is the ❖ **Kaua'i Museum** open weekdays 9 to 4 and Saturday 10 to 4; (808) 245-6931.

A couple of blocks beyond, turn left onto Haleko Street and you'll shortly encounter the hulking old **Lihu'e Sugar Mill**; it's closed but worth a look. Return to Rice, turn left and go up to the Highway 50-56 junction. Go left onto Route 50, then within a block turn right onto Ho'omana Road for the 1881 **Lihu'e Lutheran Church**; (808) 245-2145. It's an exceptionally pretty church with glossy white pews, a white and gold trimmed altar and leaded glass windows. It was designed in the style of a ship, with a barrel-arch ceiling suggesting an inverted hull and a pulpit shaped like a forecastle.

If you seek a serious shopping break, return to Highway 50, continue west briefly and turn left on Nawiliwili Road for **Kukui Grove**. It has a Macy's, Sears, Longs and several smaller stores. A second complex with a Big K and Borders Books & Music is next door. A short distance down Nawiliwili Road on the left is ❖ **Grove Farm**, a former plantation that's now a museum and history center. If you'd to see the work of the *Menehunes*, continue on Nawiliwili for about a mile, go right onto Niumalu Road, then right again on Hulemalu Road for **Alakoko Fishpond**. It's part of the **Hule'ia National Wildlife Refuge,** where you might be able to scope out some shorebirds.

Return to Nawiliwili, follow it back to Highway 50, turn left and watch on your right for the entrance of **Kilohana**. Like Grove Homestead, it's a former plantation, although it has been fashioned into a rather grand estate. The gorgeously furnished main building contains ❖ **Gaylord's restaurant** and several shops and galleries. For a fee, you can book a carriage ride on the handsomely landscaped grounds or a wagon ride into nearby cane fields. Kilohana is open daily from 9:30, with various closing hours for the shops and restaurant; (808) 245-5608 or (808) 246-9529 for carriage rides and cane field tours.

To visit **Po'ipu**, Kaua'i's main resort area, turn south on Maluhai Road (Route 520) about six miles west of Kilohana. You'll pass through a **tree tunnel** of huge century-old cypress that form an overhead canopy. Just beyond is the old sugar plantation town of **Koloa**. It's evolving into a tourist lure, since it's rather quaint and it's on the highway to the Po'ipu resort area. At a T-intersection, check out a display about Hawai'i's sugar history in a small park. Nearby are an abandoned sugar mill and a demonstration garden of sugarcane varieties. Opposite the park on Koloa Street is the **Koloa History Center** in the Old Koloa Town Mall, with exhibits about plantation life and the various ethnic groups that came to work the cane fields.

The Po'ipu resorts

Go east briefly on Koloa Street for a look at two Japanese Buddhist temples, **Hongwanji Mission** and **Jodo Mission.** From here, follow Weliweli Road and the Ala Kin'oike Highway south to **Po'ipu**. It isn't a town but a collection of resorts along several scalloped coves of **Makahuna Point,** Kaua'i's southernmost tip. The most impressive of these is the ❖ **Hyatt Regency**, definitely worth a look. It shares this pretty coastline with several smaller resorts and condos. However, a few are still closed after being damaged by hurricane Iniki in 1992.

Follow the shoreline west to **Prince Kuhio Park,** marking the birthplace of Jonah Kuhio Kalanianaole. He would have inherited the throne if a white power group hadn't staged a coup that led to Hawai'i's annexation by the United States. The small park contains the remnants of the family home, a *heiau* and a fishpond. Just beyond is the **Spouting Horn,** one of Hawai'i's most impressive blowholes. This one not only blows, it hisses as incoming waves slam through a lava tube. Across from Spouting Horn is the visitor center for two of Kaua'i's three National Tropical Botanical Gardens, **McBryde** and **Allerton.** Advance reservations are required for tours; (808) 742-2623. The visitor center, occupying a renovated 1920s plantation home, is open Monday-Saturday 8:30 to 5; (808) 742-2433; *www.ntb.org.*

TRAVEL TIP: For more on this area, contact the Po'ipu Beach Resort Foundation, P.O. Box 730, Koloa, HI 96756; (808) 742-7444; *www.poipu-beach.org.*

Head back to Koloa and follow Highway 530 northeast to **Lawai,** where you'll again pick up Highway 50. Six miles west is charming little **Hanapepe,** a former sugar town whose two-block main street has become a mini art center. Several galleries, many owned by local artists, occupy wood-frame buildings. To reach them, fork to the right at the "Historic Hanapepe" sign. Every Friday night is "Art Walk" when the galleries are open from 6 to 9 p.m. Some offer refreshments, art demonstrations and even live entertainment. The ❖ **Hanapepe Café and Espresso Bar** is a Berkeley-goes-to-the tropics place that's both a gallery and a vegetarian restaurant; (808) 335-5011; *www.hanapepecafe.com.*

Pressing northwest on Highway 50, watch on your left for the turnoff to the ❖ **Gay & Robinson Sugar Plantation.** It offers tours of its mill and cane fields weekdays 8 to 4; (808) 335-2824. Even if you don't plan a tour, stop at the visitor center/gift shop to learn more about the island's sugar industry. As you approach Waimea, turn left into **Fort Elizabeth State Park,** the site of an 1815 Russian fortification. Not much remains except the tumbled ruins of old lava walls. Numbered posts are keyed to a walking tour pamphlet.

Waimea is yet another appealing old sugar town, with several plantation style homes and false front stores. It was here that Captain James Cook first set foot on the Hawaiian Islands. A small monument in Waimea Harbor marks the spot. Just past a tiny triangle of a park in the heart of town, turn right and follow Menehune Road a few blocks inland. Go left Puli Road for the **Waimea Shingon Mission,** set against a steep lava bluff. Its grounds are rimmed with ninety-eight altars that resemble shell casings or rockets awaiting launch. In fact they were erected in 1958 as a memorial to Japanese-Hawaiians lost during World War II, so their design is appropriate. The temple grounds, while interesting, are in desperate need of maintenance. Many of the altars—each with a figurine in its niche—are crumbling.

The work of little critters?

Continue up Menehune Road just over a mile until you see a swinging footbridge spanning the Waimea River. Look to your left for a bronze tablet marking the remains of the mysterious **Menehune Ditch.** Sections of its intricate masonry lining are still intact. Those who want to believe in *Menehunes* insist that it must have been built by the little people since Hawaiians at the time didn't have advanced stonemasonry skills. It's still used to carry water from the river to irrigate cane fields. While you're there, you may wish to fulfill a childish urge and take a wiggly walk across the swinging bridge.

Waimea is the gateway to Waimea Canyon. You can pick up information at the **West Kauai Technology and Visitor Center**, open weekdays 9 to 4 and Saturday 9 to 1; closed Sunday. It also has a few historical exhibits and displays concerning the area's efforts to attract high tech firms

Waimea Canyon ❖ is a short, steep drive from here and you have a choice of two routes. Follow Waimea Canyon Drive from town or continue west for three miles and take less-traveled Koke'e Road through cane fields. Or do a loop; the roads merge about seven miles up the mountain. We cover Waimea Canyon in detail below, so for the moment, continue west on Highway 50. You'll soon encounter **Barking Sands Pacific Missile Range**, on a long sand dune beach. It's named for a distinctive crunch the sand makes underfoot. Since the beach is on a military reservation, call (808) 335-4229 to see if it may be closed to the public because of security concerns. Also, tours of the facility may be available; call (808) 335-4740.

Following Highway 50 alongside Barking Sands, you'll run out of pavement seven miles from Waimea. However, should you be willing to bump your rental car over five miles of rough dirt road, you can explore **Polihale State Park**. Watch for a small sign indicating Polihale and follow it coastward through cane fields. The worst of the bumps—mostly potholes—are within the first 1.5 miles. Stay alert, since some of them are large enough to lose a cow. As you near the beach, you can turn left at a sign indicating a campground or continue straight ahead to road's end.

This is an awesome place. Row upon row of breakers roll onto this long, sandy beach, which is backed up by vine-covered dunes. A hike northward will take you to the beginning of ❖ **Na Pali Coast**, those towering seacliffs that seem to rise directly from the ocean. This is a grand place to watch the sunset. Ole Sol often settles behind offshore **Ni'ihau**, coloring its ever-present clouds and casting glittering ripples across the broad, scalloping surf line.

TRAVEL TIPS: Don't drive this road in wet weather—although rain is infrequent on this dry side of the island. During dry weather, be alert for loose sandy areas where you might get stuck. Your rental car contract may prohibit driving on this road. If you do get stuck, don't expect the company to rescue you.

If you'd like to spend the night, get a $5 camping permit from the Division of Parks office in Lihu'e. Camping is casual; there are no numbered sites and no park facilities. The office is at 3060 Eiwa St.; (808) 274-3444; *www.state.hi.us*, then click on "search" for state parks.

THE TEN BEST THINGS TO SEE & DO

Stately and mystical Waimea Canyon tops our list of Kaua'i's Ten Best attractions and activities. The next nine are an assortment, ranging from flying over our top attraction to kayaking the state's only major navigable stream. They're presented in order of appearance, as you'd encounter them on the two drive above.

PRICING: Dollar sign codes indicate the approximate cost of adult admission to various attractions and activities: *$* = under $10; *$$* = $10 to $19; *$$$* = $20 to $29; *$$$$* = $30 to $39; *$$$$$* = $40 or more.

☺ *KID STUFF:* This little grinning guy marks attractions and activities that are of particular interest to pre-teens.

1 EXPLORE WAIMEA CANYON

Waimea Canyon State Park, (808) 274-3444; and Koke'e State Park, (808) 274-3444. Koke'e Natural History Museum open daily 9 to 4; (808) 335-9975. GETTING THERE: Waimea Canyon is reached by following Highway 550 north from Waimea on the southeast coast. ☺

Oddly, one of America's most spectacular canyons isn't a federal reserve. The deepest of Mount Wai'ale'ale's many chasms, Waimea Canyon is contained in two contiguous state parks. It isn't as awesome and complex as Arizona's Grand Canyon, although it's pretty grand, with rusty-red terraced ridges and deep chasms marked by lush patches of green foliage.

To the east is Mount Wai'ale'ale, the wettest spot on earth, with an annual rainfall of 428 inches. Rainbows dance beneath its grim clouds, reaching deeply into the steep-walled chasm. To the west is the blue Pacific and the dark shape of Ni'ihau, as intriguing in look as it is in reality. It's privately owned and occupied by a few Hawaiians living in the old way. Only limited access is permitted, led by tour groups. Ni'ihau Helicopters offers overflights, (808) 335-3500; and HoloHolo Charters has a snorkel trip to its coast, (808) 848-6310.

To see the "Grand Canyon of the Pacific" by car, follow Waimea Canyon Drive north from Waimea. It climbs quickly through abandoned cane fields to woodlands and, within ten miles, to the western flank of the canyon itself. This lower portion is in **Waimea Canyon State Park**. Turnouts along the way—mostly unsigned—provide views of this 2,857-foot deep and mostly reddish chasm. It was carved by the Waimea River from the core of a collapsed volcano. At some of the turnouts, you can see the thin ribbon of river far below. The route also offers frequent glimpses back down to Kaua'i's west coast and Ni'ihau.

Waimea Canyon Overlook is the first signed turnout and the first with a good look into the heart of the canyon. Return to the main road and continue a couple of miles upward for **Pu'u Hinahina** lookout, offering the bonus of a view of Ni'ihau. Pressing onward, you'll enter **Koke'e State Park** and encounter **Koke'e Lodge**, on a broad forest-rimmed meadow, 3,600 feet above sea level. The only developed facility in either park, it has several rustic cabins, a souvenir shop and a restaurant open from morning through mid-afternoon. The cabins, very basically furnished, can accommodate up to six people. For lodging information, call (808) 335-6061. They're popular, so make reservations far in advance.

The adjacent **visitor center-museum** has several exhibits on Waimea Canyon and the Pali Cliffs. A detailed meteorology exhibit discusses Wai'ale'ale's unique soggy climate. Other displays focus on the flora, fauna and geology of the area. The museum has a rather good selection of Hawaiiana and nature books.

TRAVEL TIP: The lodge doesn't sell groceries, so if you're planning to stay in one of the cabins, you need to bring supper fare. Nights get cold at this altitude, so don't show up in beach wear.

A short distance beyond the lodge and museum is **Kalalau Lookout.** Here, you will see—not Waimea Canyon—but the bowl-shaped **Kalalau Valley** with silvery threads of waterfalls spilling down its sides, and **Na Pali Coast.** These sheer cliffs drop a dizzying 3,000 feet into the sea. At road's end, a final lookout provides another view of those razor-edged cliffs and mystical Wai'ale'ale—although it's almost always cloud-capped. When we were there last, a rainbow plunged into one of the thickly forested canyons, perhaps identifying the site of a Menehune pot of gold. Trails lead from here to **Alaka'i Swamp**, one of the world's highest bogs. It's actually a rainforest whose growth is stunted by poor soil.

TRAVEL TIP: It's best to make the Waimea Canyon drive early in the morning or late in the afternoon. Although Waimea is usually sunny, the upper reaches of the canyon are often cloud-covered at mid-day. Sunsets from up here can be spectacular.

2 FLY HIGH OVER KAUA'I

Air Kauai in Lihu'i; (800) 972-4666 or (808) 246-4666; www.airkauai.com. Major credit cards; $$$$$. GETTING THERE: Sightseeing flights leave from Lihu'e Airport; you'll get specific instructions when you make reservations. ☺

Having seen Waimea Canyon and Wai'ale'ale from the ground, you should next see it from the sky. Kaua'i has the best sightseeing flights in the islands because of the grandeur of its terrain. If you plan to go aloft, spend a little more for one of the one-hour around the island flights. The pilot will skim over the west coast with its surging surf and then head inland to the wilderness around Waimea Canyon. Because it isn't a national park, aircraft can fly below the canyon walls.

"We're going to go a little lower," our pilot said calmly as he dropped his chopper below the cliff tops. We flew into dead end canyons where waterfalls spilled hundreds of feet; our helicopter performed a slow pirouette so everyone had a good view.

The pilot then headed for Na Pali Coast. Those fluted cliffs are even more awesome from the air. Some plunge directly into the water; others have tiny crescent beaches at their feet. Again, we danced into canyons, seeking more waterfalls and dropoffs that would make a mountain goat dizzy. It was perfect day for flightseeing; a late sun cast strong shadows on the cliffs and broken clouds creating dappled patches of light.

The grandest part of the trip was yet to come. We flew into Wai'ale'ale crater, dipping under the perpetual cloud cap. The chopper hovered in dripping rain as we admired dozens of silvery waterfalls spilling down sheer walls. Those cliffs seem to be closing in on us. Yet as we left from one side of the crater, two other helicopters entered the other, looking no larger than dragonflies. We were indeed in an immense space!

3 KAYAK THE WAILUA RIVER

Secret Falls Tour by Kayak Kauai, Coconut Marketplace in Kapa'a; (800) 437-3507 or (808) 826-9844; www.kayakkauai.com. Major credit cards; $$$$$. GETTING THERE: Coconut Marketplace is on the east side of the highway in Kapa'a and Kayak Maui is in the rear, near Coconut Marketplace Cinema. ☺ ☺

There is nothing secret about Secret Falls—actually Uluhaki Falls. This pretty cataract on a tributary of the Waimea River is quite popular, reached by a short hike. However, it's considerably less crowded than the busy Fern Grotto. Kayak Kauai offers a combined river trip and hike to the falls. We like this firm because it uses real sea kayaks instead of the sit-upons used by most other companies.

The trip begins on the river's main channel, busy with those noisy Fern Grotto excursion barges and water skiers. Then the paddlers divert into a smaller stream, leaving the ruckus behind. It's easy to pretend that you're exploring a hidden jungle, gliding along silently, listening to bird calls and skirting the bank to pluck a hibiscus blossom. After a brief paddle, the group puts ashore and follows a one-mile trail through thick jungle alongside a cascading creek. Guides describe the flowers and trees along the way.

Uluhaki Falls is a broad bridal-veil cataract spilling from a mossy 100-foot cliff. Guests pick a comfortable rock and settled down for a lunch of sandwiches, Maui potato chips and fresh-cut pineapple. Some of the more brazen among them slip into the chilly pool at the base of the falls and swim beneath its silvery veil for a cold shower.

Kayak Kauai also offers trips along Na Pali Coast and up the Hanalei River, plus kayak, snorkel, surfboard and bicycle rentals.

4 GO TO THE MOVIES—KAUA'I STYLE

Hawaii Movie Tours, P.O. Box 659, Kapa'a, HI 96746; (800) 628-8432 or (808) 822-1192; www.hawaiimovietour.com. VISA/MC; $$$$$. Tours leave from Kapa'a; hotel pick-up can be arranged.

More than forty movies and TV shows have been filmed on Kaua'i, from the forgettable 1933 *White Heat* to the recent *Jurassic Park* and *Baywatch Hawaii* episodes. This company conducts van and four-wheel-drive tours to several of the locations. These aren't scholarly outings; they're fun and a little silly as guides urge patrons to join them in singing movie and TV themes. They salt their presentations with gossip about the stars and background on the film locations.

Onboard videos show scenes of the various films. The van trip takes guests to location sites for *South Pacific, King Kong, Jurassic Park, Raiders of the Lost Ark, The Wackiest Ship in the Army,* Elvis Presley's *Blue Hawaii* and the TV series *Gilligan's Island.* The four-wheel-drive trek goes high into the flanks of Wai'ale'ale for locations of *Flight of the Intruder, Dragonfly, Jurassic Park* and *Raiders of the Lost Ark.*

5 EXPLORE THE NORTH COAST

Ha'ena State Park and Ke'e Beach. For more information and hiking permits, contact the Division of Parks office at the State Office Building, 3060 Eiwa Street in Lihu'e; (808) 274-3444; www.state.hi.us. GETTING THERE: Ha'ena State Park is at the end of Highway 560, ten miles west of Hanalei. ☺

Ha'ena State Park is as far as you can go by highway on the gorgeously scenic North Coast. Beyond here, the sheer Na Pali block further progress—unless you're willing to hike. However, there is much to see here, including two 4,000-year-old lava caves and an ancient *heiau.* As you enter the state park, watch on your right for the first of two parking lots. Walk across the highway, go about half a block west and you'll see a trail leading uphill to the left; it ends at a huge, yawning crescent-shaped lava cave with a lake at the bottom. Scramble down to the lake's edge and sit quietly. When helicopters aren't buzzing along the coast, you can hear water dripping into this vast cavern.

Back to your car and you'll pass a second lava cave beside the road. Continue to the end for the main parking area, then stroll out onto **Ke'e Beach**. It's in an attractive reef-rimmed cove, with fine views west along the North Coast's seacliffs. Relatively sheltered, it's a good snorkeling and swimming area on calm days; lifeguards usually are on duty. Walk west toward the seacliffs, then follow a path up to the ruins of **Ka Ulu a Paoa Heiau,** a stone platform overlooking the beach.

If you come prepared to hike, the **Kalalau Trail** is one of the most spectacular in Hawai'i. It travels eleven miles along Na Pali Coast, cresting high ridges and dipping down to hidden beaches. However, this requires permits—which are limited in summer—and camping gear. You can sample the trail without a permit by hiking two miles to Hanakapiai Beach. The trail climbs to a Na Pali crest and dips down to the sea. Or just go part way; each step improves the views.

6 CHECK OUT KAUA'I MUSEUM

4428 Rice St., Lihu'e; (808) 245-6931; www.kauaimuseum.org. Weekdays 9 to 4 and Saturday 10 to 4; closed Sunday; $. GETTING THERE: The museum is in downtown Lihu'e at the corner of Rice and Eiwa streets.

Housed in the former library building, this museum is surprisingly appealing. It is in fact one of the better community museums in the islands. Displays begin at the beginning, with a geological look at the formation of Kaua'i. Other exhibits cover the arrival of the Polynesians and missionaries, life on a sugarcane plantation, and the flora, fauna and fishes of the island.

Particularly appealing is a diorama of Cook landing on Kaua'i. Another item of interest is a rain gauge from Wai'ale'ale's Wailea Ridge; it's so large that it looks like a milk can. In 1982 it measured 638 inches of rain, or nearly sixty feet! The museum has a rather extensive collection of Polynesian artifacts including a vintage outrigger canoe and royal dinnerware from Iolani Palace.

7 VISIT GROVE FARM

Grove Farm Homestead, 4050 Nawiliwili St., Lihu'e; (808) 245-3202. Tours Monday and Wednesday through Thursday at 10 and 1; $; reservations required. GETTING THERE: The farm entrance is half a mile below Kukui Grove shopping center, on the left, at the corner of Nawiliwili and Ahehe Street. A very small sign marks the lane, so be alert for it.

This tour provides one of Hawai'i's best opportunities to see a remarkably intact sugar plantation home. Established in 1864 by George N. Wilcox, a missionary's son, Grove Farm was owned by family members until the 1971. A trust now operates it as a living museum.

As you turn into the farm, you enter the Kaua'i of yesterday—a lushly landscaped eighty-acre estate. Its buildings border a polo field-sized lawn; this is one of those rare peaceful places within a stone's throw of a busy commercial area. The founder, a self-made millionaire and one of Hawai'i's first sugar barons, died a bachelor at the age of ninety-four. The tour takes you through Wilcox's spartan bachelor quarters, and then into the main house where his descendants lived in much higher style. It's a classic plantation mansion, furnished with varnished koa wood furniture and the objects of the wealthy.

As a mid-tour stop, guests are ushered into the kitchen, where one of the caretakers serves mint tea and tasty brown sugar cookies. Guests are then escorted around the extensive grounds. They're planted with banana, macadamia, avocado and citrus trees. Pens enclose chickens, ducks, geese and huge lazy pigs who lounge in the muddy shade of a sprawling avocado tree.

8 SNORKEL THE PALI COAST

Liko Kauai Cruises, Waimea; (888) SEA-LIKO or (808) 338-0333; www.liko-kauai.com. Major credit cards; $$$$. GETTING THERE: The cruises depart Kikialoa Harbor just north of Waimea, although check-in is at a office downtown. You'll receive specific directions when you book the trip. ☺

After seeing Na Pali Coast from air and land, you can view it from the sea by booking this firm's small, fast catamaran. It's an interesting craft, made of styrofoam and Fiberglas, the same material as surfboards. Although billed as a snorkel cruise, this is more interesting as an opportunity for an ocean view of those towering razor-edged cliffs.

As the craft heads for the North Shore, passengers may see spinner dolphins frolicking in the bow wash, or schools of flying fish. The catamaran cruises past Barking Sands Pacific Missile Range and shortly arrives beneath those towering 3,000-foot cliffs. Crewmen point out lush green valleys where Hawaiians lived in complete isolation well into the last centuries.

On calm days—mostly in summer—guests snorkel in bays at the base of the cliffs. At other times, the nimble catamaran cruises through offshore swells for a good look at Na Pali, then it returns to the more sheltered south coast for snorkeling. A choppy day can be spectacular, when rolling breakers slam into the shore, sending up salt spray that clings to the cliff faces like crystalline snow.

9 BIKE WAIMEA

Outfitters Kauai, Po'ipu; (888) 742-9887 or (808) 742-9667; www.outfitterskauai.com. Major credit cards; $$$$$. GETTING THERE: Outfitters Kauai is in Po'ipu Plaza; you'll receive specific directions when you book the tour.

Maui isn't the only island that has a downhill bicycling tour. On this outing, guests free-wheel down from Waimea Canyon, and it's much less crowded than Maui's popular Haleakala descent. Vans take guests up to **Waimea Canyon Overlook** for a gander down into that rust-red chasm. Then they're driven further up the road to launch their downhill descent. To avoid most of the traffic, the tour shifts from Waimea Canyon Drive onto less-traveled Koke'e Road. The scenery changes cyclists pass through climate zones, from thick woodlands to dryland forest to arid lowlands.

Riders stop to enjoy views back up the canyon, out to sea toward Ni'ihau and down to the rumpled alluvial fan of the southwest coast. Guides identify plants and point landmarks, and they may gather a few ripe pineapple guavas for their guests. They point out a silver-white puff that marks Kaua'i's only surviving sugar mill, operated by the Robinson family that owns Ni'ihau and nearly a quarter of Kaua'i.

In addition to this run, Outfitters Kaua'i has kayak trips offshore and on the Hule'ia and Wailua rivers, and it rents kayaks and bikes.

10 TOUR A SUGAR MILL

Gay & Robinson Sugar Plantation Tours, Kaumakani Avenue, Waimea; (808) 335-2824; www.grandtours-kauai.com. Weekdays 8 to 4; reservations required. Major credit cards; $$$$. GETTING THERE:

The plantation is just east of Waimea; turn coastward into the complex near milepost 19.

Just two sugar mills still operate in Hawai'i and this is the only one with a public tour. It begins in the visitor center in the former field office, where exhibits and artifacts tell the story of Hawaiian sugar production. Several specialty foods, company logo items and semi-refined brown sugar are for sale.

Vans or buses bounce visitors over cane-hauling roads to several different fields, where they see sugarcane at various growth stages. During the March to November harvest, visitors will see huge "push rakes" pushing down the mature stalks, which are stacked and hauled off to the mill in huge trucks. Our guide chopped sections of cane with a wicked-looking machete and passed this sweet and chewy "cane candy" among us. We learned that it takes three feet of cane to make a cube of sugar.

From the field, visitors adjourn to the big, noisy mill to watch giant rollers crush the cane to spill its juices into catch basins. They see giant kettles where the juice is cooked and centrifuges where it's separated into molasses and sugar crystals. Our guide scooped a pitcher into a centrifuge and offered another taste test—grainy unrefined sugar and cloyingly sweet molasses.

DINING: TEN INTERESTING RESTAURANTS

As in the previous chapter, this isn't a Ten Best list, but a Kaua'i dining sampler, with restaurant suggestions in several price ranges. Our choices are listed by region.

PRICING: Dollar sign codes indicate the price of a typical dinner with entrée, soup or salad, not including drinks, appetizers or dessert: $ = less than $10 per entrée; $$ = $10 to $19; $$$ = $20 to $29; $$$$ = $30 to $40; $$$$$ = $41 and beyond.

LIHU'E & THE COCONUT COAST

1 A PACIFIC CAFÉ

4-831 Kuhio Highway in Kauai Village Shopping Center, Kapa'a; (808) 822-0013. Hawaiian/Pacific Rim; wine and beer. Dinner nightly. Major credit cards; $$$. Reservations recommended. GETTING THERE: It's in central Kapa'a on the inland side of the street, near the Kauai Village Safeway.

Yes, it's "A Pacific Café" to put it first in the phone book. This storefront restaurant also is first in the taste buds of many foodies. Despite its shopping center location, it draws locals and visitors from afar. The large open dining area is casually sleek with a Polynesian-modern motif and paintings by local artists. There's no view and no outdoor dining area; merely excellent food. Recent examples from Chef

Jean-Marie Josselin's frequently changing menu were grilled moonfish with black olive polenta and shiitake mushrooms, lamb with red wine mint glaze and garlic mashed potatoes, and wok-charred mahimahi. For dessert, try the crème brûlée in a pastry shell or the macadamia nut torte topped with toasted coconut.

2 GAYLORD'S

Kilohana Plantation, Highway 50, Lihu'e; (808) 245-9593; www.gaylordskauai.com. Hawaiian regional; full bar service. Lunch Monday-Saturday, Sunday brunch and dinner nightly. Major credit cards; $$$ to $$$$. Reservations accepted. GETTING THERE: It's just west of Lihu'e, on the inland side of the highway.

Kilohana Plantation has been converted into a visitor attraction with shops, tours and a stylish restaurant. Gaylord's occupies a handsome space off a landscaped courtyard; all tables are open to the breezes. Some offerings from its American-Hawaiian menu include a "Food Rhapsody" of tiger prawns, sea scallops, lobster tail and local fish; herb-crusted rack of lamb; chicken Kaua'i sautéed with papaya and pineapple in a port wine macadamia nut cream sauce; and horseradish-crusted prime rib. For dessert, try the deep fried chocolate truffles or mango Lindsortorte. Gaylord's also has an elaborate Sunday brunch and twice-weekly luaus.

3 HAMURA SAIMEN

2956 Kress St., Lihu'e; (808) 245-2271. Japanese-Hawaiian; no alcohol. Midmorning through evening daily; open late on weekends. No credit cards; $. GETTING THERE: It's a block down from Rice Street, on the left.

Locals sitting at Hamura's U-shaped counters and slurping huge bowls of *saimen* (noodle soup) probably wonder what all the fuss is about. Tourists crowd into this scruffy café, looking for an empty stool. Actually, the *saimen* isn't *that* great unless you order special, with pork, wonton, Spam strips and a hard-boiled egg. Hamura's regular *saimen* is a bit bland. Accompany your soup with "barbecue"; that's what locals call *yakitori*, which is skewered chicken or beef. End your meal with a mild yet rich lilikoi pie. Then move along, please; someone's waiting for your stool. Hamura does takeouts and it has an adjacent shave ice parlor.

4 MEMA THAI CHINESE CUISINE

4-361 Kuhio Hwy. (Route 56), Kapa'a; (808) 823-0899. Southeast Asian; wine and beer. Lunch weekdays and dinner nightly. MC/VISA; $$ to $$$. GETTING THERE: It's on the western edge of Kapa'a, on the inland side of the highway, just beyond Halelio Road.

Kaua'i's best Asian restaurant, Mema is an attractive place with polished dark wood furnishings, Southeast Asian artifacts and potted plants. Servings are generous and the fare is uniformly excellent. The curry is *hot*, so you may want to ask that it be toned down. And request brown rice with your meal, not white. It's full flavored and subtly spiced, with a texture and taste that suggests huumus. Some worthy menu items are Thai chicken, pork, beef or seafood with red chili or coconut milk; Chinese sweet and sour chicken, beef, pork or seafood; and stir-fried cashew nut chicken or shrimp.

PO'IPU & THE SOUTHWEST COAST

5 THE BEACH HOUSE

5022 Lawai Rd., Lawai; (808) 742-1424. Hawaiian regional; full bar service. Dinner nightly. MC/VISA, AMEX; $$$ to $$$$. Reservations recommended. GETTING THERE: Follow Po'pu Road beachward from Koloa. The restaurant is just west of the Po'ipu resort area, toward Spouting Horn.

Kaua'i's celebrity chef Jean-Marie Josselin once owned this stylish oceanfront restaurant. Then, curiously, he moved on to a Kapa'a shopping center (above). Now owned by an island restaurateur partnership, it's still excellent, with Maui-born Chef Scott Lutey in the kitchen. Among his creations are seared crab-stuffed pork medallions, Chinese roast duck with Grand Marinier demi sauce, and ginger scallion-crusted 'opakapaka. He also specializes in kiawe grills such as marinated chicken and Cajun-spiced *ahi*. The restaurant has a sleek Polynesian look, although patrons' gazes are drawn mostly to the adjacent palm-lined beach.

6 DONDERO'S

Hyatt Regency, 1571 Po'ipu Rd., Po'ipu; (808) 742-6260; www.hyatt.com. Italian regional; full bar service. Dinner nightly. Major credit cards; $$$ to $$$$. Reservations accepted. GETTING THERE: Follow Po'ipu Road coastward from Koloa; the Hyatt is on the beach, near Po'ipu Bay Golf Course.

Classic Italian cuisine and a gorgeous Kaua'i beach setting make this one of the island's more elegant dining experiences. Dondero's is a handsome restaurant, with inlaid marble flooring, green tile accents and Mediterranean murals. It has tables indoors and out, with nice Po'ipu Beach views. A specialty is cioppino with Hawaiian accents, or try the fresh *ahi* or classic scaloppini. From the pasta side of the menu, order black ink linguine with scallops, shrimp, mussels, salmon and clams in cognac bisque sauce; or risotto rice with porcine mushrooms and asparagus tips. Finish with tirimisu or vanilla crème brûlée, with a flavored *grappa*.

7 HANAPEPE CAFÉ & ESPRESSO BAR

3830 Hanapepe Hwy., Hanapepe; (808) 335-5011; www.hanapepe-cafe.com. Vegetarian; no alcohol but wine can be brought in. Breakfast through mid-afternoon Tuesday-Saturday and dinner Friday only. MC/VISA; $ to $$. Reservations essential for Friday night. GETTING THERE: Hanapepe is about seventeen miles west of Lihu'e. Go inland at the "Historic Hanapepe" sign; the café is on the left.

This cute Berkeley-goes-Hawaiian café is an art gallery as well as the island's best vegetarian restaurant. Works of local artists, assorted prints, Hawaiian artifacts and potted plants decorate this busy place. It's housed in a former drugstore and the old soda bar is still intact, serving now as a coffee bar. Soft Hawaiian music rises above the pleasant chatter, and a slack-key guitarist plays during Friday night dinner. That dinner, timed to Hanapepe's weekly "Art Walk," is mostly Italian, featuring vegetarian lasagna, eggplant Parmesan and prima vera.

A breakfast specialty is frittata with eggs, smoked mozzarella and sautéed mushrooms. Lunch fare includes salads, excellent gardenburgers and a tri-plate special of Caesar, potato and pasta salad with focaccia bread.

PRINCEVILLE & HANALEI

8 CAFÉ HANALEI

Princeville Resort at 5520 Ka Haku Rd., Princeville; (808) 826-2760; www.princeville.com. Pacific Rim; full bar service. Breakfast, lunch and dinner daily, with a Sunday champagne brunch. Major credit cards; $$$ to $$$$. Reservations accepted. GETTING THERE: Turn into the Princeville complex and follow the main road to the end.

The Mediterranean style Princeville Resort occupies a glorious spot on Hanalei Bay, with misty peaks rising above, and silvery waterfalls spilling down their sides. Café Hanalei's window walls and terrace take full advantage of this splendid view. Live Hawaiian music is presented most evenings; it's one of the island's most romantic dining spots. Presented from the kitchen is fare such as steamed Hawaiian snapper with ginger and shiitake mushrooms, Macadamia-crusted chicken breast with guava butter sauce and grilled vegetables and—if you're feeling adventurous—broiled Japanese fresh water eel over steamed rice with shoyu sauce.

9 HANALEI DOLPHIN RESTAURANT

5-5016 Kuhio Hwy., Hanalei; (808) 826-6113; www.hanaleidolphin.com. American-Hawaiian; mostly seafood; full bar service. Lunch and dinner daily. MC/VISA; $$ to $$$. GETTING THERE: It's in downtown Hanalei on the north side of the highway.

The Dolphin is a pleasantly casual, prettily landscaped South Seas style restaurant. It has that proper old Hawaiian look, with a corrugated roof, ceiling fans and bamboo furnishings. Dining is indoors, on an outside deck and at picnic style tables alongside the Hanalei River. Soy sauce ginger Hawaiian chicken is a specialty, and the Dolphin's fresh fish is excellent. It also serves chicken teriyaki and honest steaks. Save room for a thick slice of banana-coconut-macadamia ice cream pie. The restaurant also has a serious fish market.

10 ZELO'S BEACH HOUSE & GRILL

In Ching Young Village at 5-8420 Kuhio Hwy., Hanalei; (808) 826-9700. Hawaiian regional; mostly seafood; full bar service. Lunch and dinner daily. MC/VISA; $$ to $$$. GETTING THERE: It's on the north side of the highway in downtown Hanalei, at the corner of Aku Road.

This lively café is a classic Hawaiian beach shack, with a tin roof, and a bamboo and palm leaf interior decorated with Polynesian art. An outdoor dining deck has a great a view of the mountains that rise green and misty above Hanalei. Zelo's is *the* place to party in town. The busy bar serves more than thirty tropical drinks and fifty specialty beers. From the kitchen emerges Haystack Prawns wrapped in shredded phyllo, wok-charred mahi mahi, and pan-blackened *ahi* with Cajun spices, plus an assortment of fresh fish, prime rib, steaks and chops.

FIVE FINE RESORTS

While Kaua'i ranks fourth behind O'ahu, Maui and the Big Island in tourist traffic, it has some of the state's finest resorts. We list below four of the best, plus an interesting cottage complex where vacationers an experience plantation-era Hawai'i.

PRICING: Dollar sign codes indicate room price ranges for two people, based on high season (summer and winter) rates: $ = a standard two-person room for $99 or less; $$ = $100 to $149; $$$ = $150 to $199; $$$$ = $200 to $249; $$$$$ $250 or more. **CREDIT CARDS:** All of the below listed cards accept most major credit cards.

1 HANALEI BAY RESORT

5380 Honoiki Rd. (P.O. Box 220), Princeville, HI 96714; (800) 827-4427 or (808) 826-6522; www.hanaleibayresort.com. A luxury low-rise resort with 234 units; $$$$ to $$$$$. GETTING THERE: Princeville is just east of Hanalei. Turn into the complex and watch for the sign; a road to the left leads to the resort.

It's a jungle in here. Established in the 1970s and since renovated, Hanalei Bay Resort is pleasantly smothered in lush landscaping. The 22-acre complex occupies a low bluff and views of Hanalei Bay and fluted green-clad mountains are striking. Units are furnished condos with kitchenettes or full kitchens; some have washer/dryers. All have decks and patios and many offer that incredible view. They're spacious and comfortable, with a Hawaiian plantation look. Soft floral prints, potted plants and silk flowers seem to bring some of that botanical jungle indoors. Paths lined with tropic plants lead to the various units. The resort is surprisingly affordable; rates start under $200.

In the main lodge, Bali Hai Restaurant (breakfast, lunch and dinner) has that splendid view of Hanalei Bay; it's a great place for watching the sunset. Resort amenities include swimming pools, tennis courts, spa treatments and a gift shop. Princeville's walking and cycling trails and two golf courses are nearby.

2 HYATT REGENCY KAUAI

1571 Po'ipu Rd., Koloa (Po'ipu), HI 96756; (800) 233-1234 or (808) 742-1234; www.kauai-hyatt.com. Luxurious beachfront resort with 602 rooms and suites; $$$$$. GETTING THERE: Take Highway 50 west from Lihu'e, go south on Route 520 to Koloa and follow Po'ipou Road south to the beach.

One of only two AAA Four Diamond resorts on Kaua'i, the Hyatt is the island's most expansive retreat. It recently was rated sixth on the list of *Condé Nast Traveler's* top ten Pacific Rim resorts. The look is luxurious old Hawai'i, with koa wood furnishings and art deco accents. The Hyatt spreads over fifty oceanfront acres. The garden-like complex has two swimming pools, meandering water courses and even a saltwater lagoon. A 500-yard beachfront has sandy sunning areas and lava-ridged sections that offer good snorkeling and tidepooling.

Amenities include a large spa, weight room, recreation paths and four tennis courts. The eighteen-hole Po'ipu Beach Resort Golf Course is adjacent. Rooms are fairly large, with Hawaiian décor. Dining options include Dondero's (see above); Tidepools on an island in the lagoon, dinner only; Ilima Terrace, breakfast, lunch and dinner; and Po'ipu Bay Grill and Bar, breakfast and lunch.

3 PRINCEVILLE RESORT

5520 Ka Haku Rd. (P.O. Box 223069), Princeville, HI 96722-3069; (800) 325-3589 or (808) 826-9644; www.princeville.com. A luxury low-rise resort with 252 rooms and suites; $$$$$. GETTING THERE: See Hanalei Bay Resort above. Turn into the Princeville complex and follow the main road to the end.

Kaua'i's second AAA Four Diamond Resort, Princeville occupies a stunning location above Hanalei Bay. It is at once sleekly modern and European classic, with cut glass chandeliers, Flemish tapestries and Italian art. Romanesque columns accent a vast marble floor lobby— one of the most impressive in the islands. Rooms are similarly opulent, with marble entries, light contemporary Italian furnishings and tropical floral prints.

Restaurants choices include Café Hanalei (above), and the stylish La Cascata, upscale Italian with upscale prices, serving dinner only. The restaurants, the lobby and a bar called the Living Room have fine views of Hanalei Bay and its surrounding mountains. Resort facilities include a swimming pool, spa, six tennis courts, horseback riding and a putting green. Thirty-six holes of golf are available on the adjacent Princeville complex.

4 RADISSON KAUAI BEACH RESORT

4331 Kauai Beach Dr., Lihu'e, HI 96766; (888) 333-3333 or (808) 245-1955; www.radissonkauai.com. An appealing low rise beachfront resort with 347 rooms and suites; $$$ to $$$$$. GETTING THERE: The Radisson is two miles north of Lihu'e Airport; turn right onto Kaua'i Beach Drive.

The Radisson is of Kaua'i's most affordable full-service resorts, with some special room rate starting around $100 night. There's a lot to like here. It sits just off the beach, with lots of sandy ocean frontage and two large swimming pools linked by a "lava ridge" grotto and waterfall. Free mai tais, a tiki lighting ceremony and Polynesian entertainment are presented nightly at poolside. It's a great place to watch swiveling hips in one direction and the sunset in the other.

The Naupaka Terrace serves breakfast, lunch and dinner; light fare is available at the poolside Driftwood Sand Bar and Grille. The Radisson has a few shops, a gallery of local artwork sharing space with an internet café, a health and fitness center, tennis courts, beachside trail and a water activity center. Rooms are comfortable and fair sized, with Hawaiian décor. Most have views of the courtyard pool complex and the beach beyond.

5 WAIMEA PLANTATION COTTAGES

9400 Kaumuali'i Hwy., Waimea, HI 96796; (800) 9-WAIMEA or (808) 338-1625; www.waimeaplantation.com. A cottage resort complex with fifty units; $$ to $$$$$. GETTING THERE: It's on the southwest coast, immediately beyond Waimea.

This appealing complex consists of renovated company houses brought from several sugar plantations. The cottages aren't luxurious but of course that would ruin the illusion. They're clean, comfortable and fully furnished, with complete kitchens. Although they're modern, they have period furnishings such as clawfoot tubs, pedestal sinks and wooden Venetian blinds. Most were built during the 1930s and 1940s. All have old fashioned porches; nice places to sit, listen to the surf and watch the sunset.

The complex is in a grassy 27-acre coconut palm grove a short walk from a salt-and-pepper sand beach. Amenities include a pool, volleyball court and guest laundry. The resort's plantation-style Waimea Brewing Company is open for lunch and dinner, serving American-Polynesian fare. It's Kaua'i's only brewpub; the best offering is Wai'ale Ale, full-flavored and medium bodied. The adjacent reception center has a small museum with some interesting exhibits on Waimea's sugar plantation days.

Imagination strives to revive, and cannot, the terrible scenes that took place on this land's end... It is all so quiet now, so exceedingly beautiful with its flowered meadows running down to the sea.
— **Author Kathryn Hulme,** on a 1958 visit to Kalaupapa

Chapter Fifteen

MOLOKA'I
HAWAI'I THE WAY IT WAS

It is perhaps unfortunate that Moloka'i is famous mostly for its Kalaupapa leper colony. It has given the island an undeserved reputation as a place of sorrow and suffering. Even its name sounds a bit foreboding, like "morbid," or "mournful."

We're not diminishing the accomplishments of the island's most famous citizen, Father Damien, who devoted his life to the colony. His work among the lepers stands as the single most valorous event in Hawai'i's history.

However, Moloka'i is much more than a place of lepers and their care giver. Were it not for Kalaupapa and the island's rather morose name, Moloka'i would be better known as one of Hawai'i's most appealing and places. It offers visitors a leisurely pace, yet with a variety of activities for those who want a little action. And it provides the true flavor of old Polynesia. Sixty percent of its 7,000 residents have mostly Hawaiian genes; that's higher than any island except privately-owned Ni'ihau.

We regard Moloka'i as a happy medium between Kaua'i and Lana'i. Kaua'i also has a slow pace and many attractions, although it suffers some traffic congestion. Lana'i has a *very* leisurely pace although there just isn't much to do there. Surprisingly, Lana'i receives more visitors than Moloka'i, about 85,000 a year, compared with 70,000.

It will strike you that Moloka'i is a special kind of place when you land at Ho'olehua Airport, which seems to be—and is—out in the middle of nowhere. As we left the airport, the driver of our hotel shuttle pointed a sign: *Aloha. This is Moloka'i. Slow down!*

"If someone passes us on the way to the hotel," the driver said, "he's probably from O'ahu."

No one did.

Getting around

Rental car rates are higher here than on most other islands. Budget (800-283-4387) and **Dollar** (800-567-6156) have airport outlets. A local firm called **Island Kine** (808-553-5242) has cheaper rates, but inquire if it has an airport pickup and dropoff charge. During busy periods, all three firms are likely to run out of vehicles, so book your wheels early. There is no regular airport shuttle service, although some hotels provide shuttles for guests. Two local firms, **Molokai Off-Road Tours & Taxi** (552-2218) and **Kukui Tours** (552-2282) have taxi service and backroad tours.

As an option to flying, you can reach Moloka'i aboard the *Maui Princess* ferry, with daily service from Lahaina for about $40. Cruise-drive packages are available that include a car rental. For information, call (808) 661-8397 or (808) 667-2585 for recorded schedule information; *www.mauiprincess.com*.

TO LEARN MORE: Contact the Molokai Visitors Assn., P.O. Box 960, Kaunakakai, HI 96748; (800) 800-6367 or (808) 553-3876; *www.visit-molokai.com* and *www.aloha-molokai.com*.

MOLOKA'I: GETTING TO KNOW YOU

If you fly in, your first impression of Moloka'i will be of a lumpy, low-lying island of pasturelands, abandoned pineapple and cane fields and brushy *kiawe* woodlands, marbled with rich red earth. This is typical of the western end. However, the eastern half is mountainous and lush, accented by 4,970-foot Mount Kamakou, Moloka'i's highest point.

For an island measuring only ten by thirty-eight miles, Moloka'i is rather diverse. The western half varies from cactus desert to dry grasslands and the island's western tip has one of the state's finest white sand beaches, **Papohaku.** The eastern half is a scenic wilderness of rainforest mountains, with the world's highest seacliffs; some rise more than 3,000 feet from the northeast shore. The stubby, low-lying Kalaupapa peninsula extends into the sea here, with this steep cliffs cutting it off from the rest of the island. It was this isolation that dictated its selection as a leper colony.

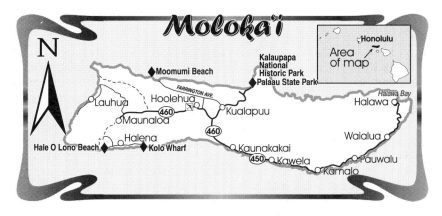

The lush, green southeast shore—traversed by Kamehameha V Highway—is marked with pocket beaches, lava ridges, ancient fish ponds, tiny Hawaiian villages and occasional small resorts. It's one of the prettiest drives in all the islands. Moloka'i's only town of size—and it's a pretty small size—is rustic **Kaunakakai** on the south central coast. With false front stores along its two-block-long main street, it seems transplanted from the American West.

This small island contains the state's highest waterfalls and most of its fishponds, the second largest cattle ranch and the world's tallest seacliffs. What it doesn't have is traffic lights, high rises or shopping centers, although it does have one fast food outlet, a KFC in the ranch town of Maunaloa. Residents call this gentle place "The Friendly Isle" and "The Most Hawaiian Island." We call it a nice place to enjoy the scenery and relax.

Legend and some historical evidence suggests that aquiculture may have started in this most Hawaiian place, since it has more fishponds than any other island. Moloka'i also is supposed to be the birthplace of the hula, although one has to question that. Some form of this dance has existed in Tahiti and other South Pacific islands for centuries and it was brought to the Hawaiian Islands by those early voyagers. And Moloka'i was one of the last to be settled; Polynesians from the Marquesas arrived here around the seventh century A.D.

However, Moloka'i honors this alleged event by sponsoring the annual **Ka Halo Piko** hula celebration the third Saturday in May at Papohaku Beach Park, featuring authentic hulas and ethnic music and food. Call (800) 800-6367 or (808) 553-3876 for details.

He didn't stop for hula lessons

The first outsider to visit Hulaland was Captain James Cook, in 1778. Unimpressed by its arid west end, he moved on. Kamehameha the Great, en route to his O'ahu invasion, conquered the island in 1795 almost as an afterthought, and moved on. The first missionaries came in 1832, although their descendants didn't develop extensive sugar and pineapple plantations as they had on the other islands.

A German immigrant named Rudolph Meyer arrived in the 1850s, married an *ali'i* and became manager of a large ranch owned by Kamehameha V. Moloka'i Ranch, still mostly intact, is Hawai'i's second largest, after Parker Ranch. Its 54,000 acres covers a third of the island and almost all of its western end. The ranch eventually wound up in the estate of Princess Pauahi Bishop, whose husband established Honolulu's famous Bishop Museum. A group of O'ahu businessmen bought the ranch in 1898, then Charles Cooke bought out his partners in 1908. It's now a privately held company and home to the Sheraton Molokai, the island's major resort.

In 1866, Kamehameha V banished the first lepers to the Kalaupapa peninsula, fearing the disease was extremely contagious. No facilities were built; they were merely dumped ashore to fend for themselves. Ten years later, Belgian priest Joseph de Veuster, who had taken the name of the martyred saint Damien, volunteered come and help the afflicted. He remained there for the rest of this life, which was tragically short. He cared for the lepers of Kalaupapa until he died of the disease in 1889, at the age of forty-nine. Father Damien is currently being considered for sainthood; he was elevated to the status of "Blessed Damien" in 1995 by Pope John Paul II.

Sugar and pineapple planters were late in coming to Moloka'i, and by the twentieth century, its population had shrunk to a thousand souls. In 1921, the Hawaiian Homes Act granted forty acres of land to anyone with more than fifty percent native blood. Moloka'i was one of the few places where land was still available, so several hundred Hawaiians came. About the same time, the sugar and pineapple planters finally arrived. Then with competition from cheaper foreign sources, most of the operations were shut down by the 1980s. Landowners turned to tourism for survival, although it hasn't developed here nearly as much as on other islands.

THE VERY BEST OF MOLOKA'I

☺ *KID STUFF:* This little grinning guy marks attractions and activities that are of particular interest to pre-teens.

There isn't ten of anything on the "Friendly Island." We offer instead a mix of places to see, things to do and drives to take. We begin with the island's most popular attraction—ironically, the place that gave it a bad name. We then string the remainder together in a simulated driving trip from the airport along the island's two main roads.

1 KALAUPAPA NATIONAL HISTORICAL PARK

For park information: P.O. Box 2222, Kalaupapa, HI 96742; (808) 567-6802; www.nps.gov/kala. For mule rides: **Molokai Mule Ride,** *P.O. Box 200, Molokai, HI 96757-0200; (800) 567-7550 or (808) 567-6088; www.muleride.com;* **$$$$$.** *For hiking permits and tours,*

Damien Tours; (808) 567-6171; $$$. GETTING THERE: Mule rides and hikes begin in Pala'au State Park, about ten miles north of Kualapu'u in central Moloka'i.

Kalaupapa is a flat tongue of lava extending 2.5 miles seaward from the base of almost sheer bluffs. Public access is only by air or a steep cliff-hanging trail. Independent exploration isn't permitted; one must go with a guided tour.

The most popular way to visit the park is by mule. It's a dizzying ride; the trail is more than three miles long, dropping 1,664 feet, with twenty-six switchbacks. It's so steep that most of it has been converted into stairsteps. Prepare your bottom for a long, bouncy trek as the mules clop and clunk down the path. The saddleback views from here are fantastic and foliage lining the narrow trail helps shield the sheer drop from nervous eyes.

TRAVEL TIP: The ride back up is considerably more smooth than the bouncy descent. You can opt to hike down, then take a mule up, although this requires special arrangement with the tour operators.

When we reached the bottom, we were struck by the beauty of this place, as are virtually all visitors. The peninsula is lushly vegetated and its scenic lava-ridged shoreline is washed by a restless surf. Those sheer cliffs rise dramatically to the heavens. Kalaupapa has two sections. The present facility is a charming New England style village on the peninsula's western half, while the original colony—now abandoned—is on the wind-battered eastern side.

Many victims of the ailment—now called Hansen's Disease and completely curable—still live in the village, by their own choice. Some work for Damien Tours, the firm that takes visitors around in battered old school buses. The most colorful of these is harmlessly cantankerous Richard Marks, who is probably somewhere in his seventies. He came here several decades ago to be with his leper father, decided to stay and eventually contracted the disease himself.

"When you get off the bus, stay the hell off the road because some of our drivers are half-blind," he snorted. During our tour, he stopped periodically to feed stray cats and dogs. Their masters had died and this crusty man says he hasn't the heart to have them put to sleep.

Tour stops include a monument to Mother Marianne Cope, who ministered to lepers here for many years; a waterfront pier where barges put in to supply the village; the 1909 Molokai Lighthouse; and the prim white St. Francis Church with an adjacent museum. The bus then bumps along an unpaved road to the site of the original colony. Again, the visitor is struck by the beauty of this place where thousands had suffered and died. Grassy lawns surround two old churches, the only structures left on this site. Thick rainforests reach inland to the base of the towering cliffs. A small sugarloaf island and a spired seastack are just offshore. This is as pretty a place as you'll find anywhere in Hawai'i.

The tour passes the small United Church of Christ, then it ends at the nearby "Damien Church," St. Philomena. It was built by Brother Victorian Bertrant in 1872, then rebuilt by Father Damien in 1888. Among its graves are Father Damien's original burial site. However, his body was removed to Belgium in 1936, despite strong local protest. Then in 1995, the bones of his right hand were returned to the Kalaupapa grave "after a triumphant tour of all the islands," according to a church flyer. Catholics sometimes do really weird things.

East from the airport

And now, the rest of the list. Assuming you've picked up a rental car from the airport, head east briefly and then turn north onto Route 481 for the hamlet of Ho'olehua. Go past the high school, turn right onto Lihi Pali drive and watch for a sign to a fun little attraction:

2 PURDY'S MACADAMIA NUT FARM

Lihi Pali Dr., Ho'olehua; (808) 567-6601. Weekdays 9:30 to 3:30 and Saturday 10 to 2; closed Sunday; free.

This is a good place to get cracking. Visitors to this tiny five-acre farm can practice their skills at cracking these thick-shelled nuts, either with a levered vice-like rig or a hammer. The trick is to crack the shell without squishing the nut, something I could achieve only with the vice. Visitors learn about the cultivation and production of macadamia nuts, and they're treated to a coconut tasting, dipping slivers of fresh coconut into macadamia nut honey and honey mustard.

In the small shack of a sales room shaded by 70-year-old macadamia trees, one can buy unroasted nuts and other nut-oriented foods and a few souvenirs. Raw macadamias are more richly flavored than processed ones, although they don't keep very long. The farm, owned by Tuddie and Kammy Purdy, sells its macadamias mostly to locals and tourists.

MOVING ON: From Purdy's, follow Lihi Pali Road south briefly until it intersects with Kala'e Highway (Route 470) at the hamlet of **Kualapu'u:**

3 MOLOKA'I COFFEE COMPANY

Route 470 and Lihi Pali Road, Kualapu'u; (800) 709-BEAN or (808) 567-9241; www.molokaicoffee.com. Weekdays 7 to 4, Saturday 8 to 4 and Sunday 10 to 4; free. Walking tours to nearby coffee groves weekdays only, whenever two or more show up. Major credit cards accepted in the gift ship.

Moloka'i Coffee Company's store has graphics and exhibits about this savory industry, plus tastings of a variety of coffees, such as Muleskinner, Moloka'i Gold and Hawaiian Espresso. This is a rustic, only slightly scruffy place with tables out front, where you can sit and enjoy Moloka'i breezes with your coffee. And of course, you can buy bagged coffee to go, plus Hawaiian specialty foods and souvenirs. The owners are working on an "instant wilderness" tour, taking visitors to a nearby rainforest; they're negotiating for access over some private land. It goes through a lush woodland of massive banyans and pines. Guests will learn about rainforest ecology and flora, and they can grab trailing creepers and swing about like George of the Jungle.

TRAVEL TIP: If you happen to be on the island the first weekend of November, catch the **Moloka'i Coffee Festival,** held at the Moloka'i Coffee Company. Festivities include a Miss Moloka'i Coffee Pageant, coffee baking contest, plantation tours, coffee picking contest and food booths. Call (808) 709-BEAN; *www.coffeehawaii.com.*

MOVING ON: Head uphill on Highway 470, which follows the coffee company's rainforest tour route. Watch on your left for the **Moloka'i Museum** and **Meyer Sugar Mill.** Most of the mill's equipment is intact, proving a quick study of the early days of sugar production. Hawaiian folk arts and crafts are the focus of an adjacent cultural center. Museum hours are Monday-Saturday 10 to 2; there's a modest admission charge; (808) 567-6436. And just up the hill, as you drive into thickening forest, is:

4 PALA'AU STATE PARK

At the end of Highway 470, ten miles northwest of Kaunakakai. For information: Hawaii State Parks, 90 Ainoa St., Kaunakakai; (808) 553-3204. ☺

This 234-acre park encompasses a densely wooded area of the cliff tops above Kalaupapa Peninsula. The park, thick with silvery-needled ironwood trees, is worth a visit even if you don't plan to descend to the leper colony. A short trail leads to the Kalaupapa Lookout, for a view of the colony 1,600 feet below. From here, it appears as a neat and prim village, sitting on its peninsula, rimmed by scalloped breakers. A sign at the lookout quotes a Robert Louis Stevenson comment after he visited the colony: "They were strangers to each other, collected by common calamity, disfigured, mortally sick, banished without sin from home and friends."

Another trail, longer and steeper, leads to Phallic Rock which, if you have a clean mind, also resembles the head of a turtle. It's one of several designated phallic rocks on these islands, suggesting that the early Hawaiians were a rather randy lot. This phallus symbol comes with a legend, about a man admiring a beautiful young woman, who is admiring her own reflection in a pool. The man's wife comes by and objects to his voyeurism. Angered by her jealousy ("Geez, I was just looking!"), he hurls her off a cliff. But he tumbles after her and both are turned to stone. This rock is all that remains of the husband. A sign indicates that it isn't entirely original: "The rock's present form is a natural configuration which has been carved to some extent."

Women wanting to become pregnant can increase their odds—say legends—by spending the night here. The legend doesn't specify with whom.

MOVING ON: From Pal'au State Park, follow the highway back down from the mountains, and turn right onto Route 460 for Kaunakakai. As you near town, note the large grove of towering coconut trees; they were planted by Kamehameha V, who once owned much of Moloka'i. You've heard of an auto row, but how about a church row? Beyond the grove, the highway is lined with a row of seven small churches, representing assorted denominations.

5 KAUNAKAKAI TOWN

Moloka'i's metropolis is a village of just a few hundred souls. Several pleasantly scruffy stores and shops line a short section of Ala Malama Avenue, which is a block off the highway. These are worth a peak:

Molokai Fish & Dive, (808) 533-5926 □ This attractively cluttered store sells surfboards, souvenirs and interesting locally-fashioned T-shirts, and it rents kayaks, surfboards, boogie boards and snorkel equipment. Its owners conduct kayak cruises along Moloka'i's coast; see the listing below.

Kanemitsu Bakery & Coffee Shop, (808) 533-5855 □ It's more bakery than coffee shop, featuring savory specialties such as apple-cinnamon bread, pineapple bread, strawberry cinnamon muffins and macadamia nut *lavosh*. And don't leave the premises without a sackful of macadamia nut cookies.

Big Daddy's Store & Restaurant, (808) 533-5841 □ Daddy's is a minimart selling groceries, a few deli items and shave ice. An adjacent dining room serves Japanese and American entrées.

Ovieto's Lunch Counter, (808) 533-5014 □ This is a scruffy, locally popular Filipino café noted for its roast pork. To reach it, drive up the two-block main street, then fork left.

Kamakana Gallery, (808) 533-8520 □ This shop is upstairs in Molokai Center, between Ala Malama Avenue and the highway. It sells made-in-Molokai arts and crafts such as quilts, paintings, framed scenic photos, calabash bowls and carvings.

After leaving town, go east briefly on Highway 450, then turn seaward onto Wharf Road for **Kaunakakai Wharf.** This is Moloka'i's lifeline, where barges from O'ahu bring essential goods. Go to the end of the pier and enjoy a view of some of the rest of Hawai'i—Maui, Lana'i, Kaho'olawe and O'ahu.

MOVING ON: Back on Highway 450, you're now positioned to begin one of the prettiest coastal drives in all of the islands:

6 THE SCENIC SOUTHEAST COAST

Kamehameha V Highway. Twenty-seven miles, from Kaunakakai to the Halawa Valley. ☺

This is the most scenic drive on Moloka'i; its vistas surpass the more famous Maui drive to Hana. The road twists and winds, and shrinks down to one-lane in spots, although it's all paved and easily navigable by an ordinary car.

Kamehameha V Highway initially travels along a pretty seacoast busy with modest houses. Maui's Ka'anapali beach resorts and the town of Lahaina are visible across Maui Roadstead. About two miles out of Kaunakakai, note the classic Polynesian style **Hotel Molokai,** an appealing beachside resort; see below. A couple of miles further, at coconut palm-lined **Oneali'i Beach**, you'll see the first of several coral and lava-walled **fish ponds**, where the ancients trapped fish and practiced aquiculture. Look skyward as you drive; the steep slope of **Mount Kamakou** towers above.

Continuing along, watch on your right for the **Church of St. Joseph's**, built by Father Damien in 1876 and restored in 1995. The interior is simple and white, with a plain altar and crucifix. It's no longer an active church, although it's lovingly kept by local residents. A statue of Father Damien is out front, usually wreathed by flower, shell or kukui nut leis.

Beyond the church, the highway sheds most of the houses and begins climbing steeply through pasturelands and forest, with the rocky coastline almost always in view. Near milepost 25 is the hidden resort of **Pu'u o Hoku Ranch**, with a few lodging units tucked into a thick forest; see below. Beyond the ranch, the highway drops from its high point and snakes twistily down into the **Halawa Valley**. As you enter this broad, steep-walled valley, you'll pass the cute little white and green **Ierusalema Hau** (Jerusalem Church). The interior is quite charming, with polished burlwood pews and an altar adorned with lace curtains and flowers. The front is busy with flower gardens, bougainvillea, papayas, banana and coconut palms and other tropical plants.

Pavement ends just beyond the church, and a short sandy road bumps out to a parking area for **Halawa Bay**. The setting is stunning; Halawa Valley is cradled by steep seacliffs streaked by 500-foot **Hipuapua Falls** and 250-foot **Mouala Falls**. The beach is a mix of sand, lava stones and beach grass and a river feeds into the small crescent bay. A popular hiking trail leads two miles to **Mouala Falls**. It starts near a picnic pavilion, passes Ierusalema Hau and several taro patches and fruit trees in the valley floor, then it begins climbing toward the falls. There has been an ongoing dispute over access, since private property and several jungle-clad homes lie between the trailhead and the falls. When we last visited, you could get hiking permits at the Pu'u o Oku Ranch. The lower portion of the trail is a bit hard to follow, since there are several other paths and roads in the area, so ask for specific directions.

West from the airport

7 MAUNALOA & MOLOKAI RANCH

Sheraton Molokai Ranch, 100 Maunaloa Hwy., Maunaloa; (808) 552-2791; www.molokai-ranch.com.

If you head west from the airport, you'll travel through the mostly rolling terrain of Molokai Ranch. The ranch center, Maunaloa, is a prim little town of green woodframe buildings with red roofs. Some are old and restored; others are new, with the same "plantation-*paniolo*" look. The town has a general store, two gasoline pumps, a movie theater, and a couple of shops and cafés.

The only fast food parlor on Moloka'i is here, a **KFC** which—as if wanting to belong—exhibits old photos of the town when it was an active ranching center. Across the highway, the **Big Wind Kite Factory** builds, displays and sells an imposing variety of kites. Adjacent is the **Plantation Gallery**, a curio, art and souvenir shop that's amazingly cluttered. Both are open Monday-Saturday 8:30 to 5 and Sunday 10 to 2. Nearby is the **Village Grill**; see below. Modest former ranch hands' homes, now mostly occupied by resort employees, are terraced above the small business district.

Surrounding Molokai Ranch still runs a few head of cattle. The cowboy look is preserved in the **Sheraton Molokai** resort complex, with its rough-walled General Store, Great Hall and several rustic lodgings. Have a meal or a drink in the handsome Great Hall, which houses the Maunaloa Dining Room and Paniolo Lounge. Like the general store, it has that rustic look of leather, stone and natural wood. A great stone fireplace seems right out of a Western ranch lodge, except for the idealistic painting of a pretty Hawaiian girl above.

8 THE WEST COAST

Kaluakoi Road from Maunaloa to Kepuhi Bay.

Go east briefly from Maunaloa, then turn northwest on Kaluakoi Road and follow it four miles to **Kepuhi Bay**. The road travels through dry scrublands to a resort area that started and then stalled as Moloka'i's economy sagged. It has a few lodgings, and they're generally modestly priced. Most of this land, sold to developers several years ago, was bought back by the Molokai Ranch company in 2001.

If you're looking for lodging, check out **Kaluakoi Villas** (see below), **Ke Nani Kai** condos (800-888-2791), or the small **Paniolo Hale** (800-367-2984); all are on or near Kepuhi Bay. The largest resort, **Kaluakoi Hotel**, was closed at press time.

Just south of Kepuhi Bay is **Papohaku Beach Park**, Moloka'i's largest beach. This white sand strand is three miles long and it averages a football field deep. To reach it, drive past Kaluakoi Hotel and follow Kaluakoi Road down to the shoreline.

This is an appealing beach with low sand dunes, clusters of *kiawe* trees and views across Kaiwi Channel to O'ahu. This is a particularly romantic spot at night, when you can see the glowing lights of Honolulu. Swimming is good here on calm days, but the surf can be rough. Stay on the beach and enjoy the view if the waves are high. Facilities include picnic areas, potties and rinse-off showers. The road leads about three miles south to several other beaches.

Outdoor lures

9 NATURE CONSERVANCY RESERVES

Nature Conservancy of Hawaii, P.O. Box 220, Kualapu'u, HI 96757; (808) 553-5236; www.nature.org.

Much of what's appealing about relatively undeveloped Moloka'i is its wilderness. The Nature Conservancy has established three preserves here to ensure that they remain undeveloped. Two of them, Kamakou Preserve in central Moloka'i and Mo'omomi Preserve on the arid northwest coast, are open to the public. Both require four-wheel-drives, which can be rented from Budget and Island Kine; see above on page 267. However, you should first contact the Nature Preserve office on Moloka'i for directions and entry permits.

Kamakou Preserve is a 2,774-acre site high on the flanks of Mount Kamakou. It contains 250 plant species, most found nowhere else in the world. A boardwalk leads through a swampy area, lush with native plants, birds and insects.

Mo'omomi Preserve is an arid sand dune area on Moloka'i's rarely visited northwest coast. It's the most untouched sand dune beach in the Hawaiian Islands. Visitors may spot sea turtles and Hawaiian shorebirds such as plovers and sanderlings, and perhaps even large frigatebirds offshore.

10 KAYAKING THE COAST

Molokai Fish & Dive, P.O. Box 576, Kaunakakai, HI 96748; (808) 533-5926; www.molokaifishanddive.com. Daily departures starting at 8 a.m.; $$ to $$$$. GETTING THERE: The shop is in Kaunakakai; see above.

Molokai Fish & Dive offers kayaking trips, either self-guiding rentals or guided—along the base of the world's highest and most spectacular seacliffs. The firm can drop you a selected point and leave you with a cell phone, so you can call for a pickup. The water offshore is relatively shallow, and the wind is usually at your back during morning trips, so even the most intimidated should feel secure. And with a one-day notice, the firm can arrange guided trips.

The fluted cliffs, cut by lush green valleys and rising as much as 3,250 feet, are awesome, particularly from a kayak's-eye-view. However, there's much more to see on this trip. Depending on where you put in, you can paddle leisurely past reefs, ancient fish ponds and crescent beaches. You can rent snorkeling gear so you can put ashore, then slip into the water to explore the reefs.

Another firm offering kayaking is **Molokai Rentals & Tours**. It also does snorkel trips, guided forest hikes and bike tours. It rents kayaks, surfboards, camping gear, snorkeling and water play equipment, and it can arrange for rental cars, jeeps and lodgings. For information: HC01 Box 28, Kaunakakai, HI 96748; (800) 553-9071 or (808) 553-5663; *www.molokai-rentals.com.*

WHERE TO DINE & RECLINE

There aren't ten significant restaurants or resorts on Moloka'i, although we did find five each. The combined lists begin with our favorites, followed by the rest in alphabetical order.

Dining

Another guidebook author stated unkindly that "a gourmet would starve to death on Moloka'i," which isn't quite true. The Maunaloa Dining Room issues very creative fare. And we found four other restaurants that—while not of gourmet quality—serve tasty food.

1 MAUNALOA DINING ROOM

Sheraton Molokai Lodge, 100 Maunaloa Hwy., Maunaloa; (808) 660-2824. Pacific Rim; full bar service. Breakfast, lunch and dinner daily. Major credit cards; $$$ to $$$$. GETTING THERE: The lodge is adjacent to Maunaloa on Moloka'i's west end.

The dining room in the Sheraton's Great Hall serves the island's most creative fare. Among dinner entrées are *paniolo* steak with Hawaiian seasonings, lemongrass-mango breast of chicken, saffron Pacific snapper, and shrimp and scallop skewers with black bean sauce over angel hair pasta. The dining room has a handsome Hawaiian—*paniolo* look. Indoor and outdoor tables provide nice views down across the ranch's grasslands to the distant sea. Lighter fare is available in the Western style Paniolo Lounge.

2 HOTEL MOLOKAI DINING ROOM

Hotel Molokai, Kamehameha V Hwy., Kaunakakai; (808) 553-5347; www.hotelmolokai.com. Hawaiian regional; full bar service.

Breakfast, lunch and dinner daily. Major credit cards; $$ to $$$. GET-TING THERE: Hotel Molokai is two miles east of Kaunakakai.

Hotel Molokai's Puʻu Hoʻomaha dining room-bar has a pleasing South Seas look with bamboo and rattan décor and flickering tiki torches. The open-air restaurant overlooks the hotel's swimming terrace and a sandy beach. Come for the Friday night "Music and Grinds" session, when a several residents—mostly seniors—play traditional and contemporary Hawaiian music. Occasionally, one of them may push away from the table and do a bit of hula. The restaurant also has Hawaiian entertainment several other nights. The menu features an assortment of fresh fish, coconut shrimp, steaks and a few pastas. Or come just for the Hawaiian music, *pupu* platters and tasty tropical drinks.

3 MOLOKAI PIZZA CAFÉ

Kahua Center on old Wharf Road, Kaunakakai; (808) 533-3288. Eclectic menu; wine and beer. Lunch through dinner daily. No credit cards; $ to $$. GETTING THERE: Wharf Road is just south of town.

This is a very popular island gathering spot. Most visitors miss it because they miss the Wharf Road turnoff as the head for east end beaches and scenery. Those who find it find a cozy café serving much more than pizza. The busy menu includes fresh fish, babyback ribs, a few pastas and gyro sandwiches. For even more variety, go for one of the theme days: Sunday for prime rib, Wednesday for Mexican fare and Thursday for Hawaiian plates. The café is cutely decorated with children's art.

4 THE VILLAGE GRILL

Maunaloa Highway in Maunaloa; (808) 552-0012. American-Hawaiian; full bar service. Lunch weekdays and dinner nightly. Major credit cards; $$ to $$$. GETTING THERE: Maunaloa is in west Molokaʻi.

This *paniolo* style grill in one of Maunaloa's old buildings offers pleasing views across the strait to Oʻahu. Tables are indoors around a handsome old brass bar and on a wraparound screen porch. Light fare such as plate lunches, Oriental chicken and soup are served at noon. At night, the grill specializes in Hawaiian style tableside heated-stone cooking, with beef, chicken and fish. It also has more conventional entrées, including catch of the day and prime rib.

5 ZIGGY'S

Kamehameha V Highway, Kaunakakai; (808) 553-8166. American-Hawaiian; full bar service. Lunch through late dinner daily. MC/VISA; $ to $$. GETTING THERE: It's just east of town at the corner of the highway and Maunaloa.

This popular local spot serves light fare, plus generous *pupu* plates. It's very inexpensive, with most dishes well under $10; *pupu* platters that will feed a small crowd are in the low teens. Kitchen offerings include teri burgers, teriyaki chicken, jalapeno poppers, deep fried shrimp and thick pork chops. You can choose between a lively and sometimes noisy bar with a TV and couple of pool tables, or a quieter, simply decorated Naugahyde dining room.

Reclining

6 SHERATON MOLOKAI LODGE

100 Maunaloa Hwy. (P.O. Box 259), Maunaloa, HI 96770-0259; (877) 726-4656 or (808) 552-2791; www.molokai-ranch.com. A 22-unit ranch resort; **$$$$$**.

Units in this *paniolo* style resort are charmingly rustic, with leather trim, quilted bedspreads, and Hawaiian accents. Bathrooms are modern, but with old fashioned clawfoot tubs and oval rugs. All have front porches or patios; many provide views down a green slope toward the ocean. The Great Hall lounge and dining room (see above) and the General Store—which serves as the reception center—have the same rustic Western-Hawaiian look. Resort amenities include a pool, riding stables, Hawaiian ethnic programs and cultural hikes.

7 HOTEL MOLOKAI

Kamehameha V Hwy. (P.O. Box 1020), Kaunakakai, HI 96748; (808) 367-5004 or (808) 545-3510; www.hotelmolokai.com. Traditional South Seas style hotel with rooms and kitchenettes; $ to $$. GETTING THERE: The hotel is just east of Kaunakakai.

This is a classic Hawaiian resort, rustic and charming yet well kept, and remarkably inexpensive. Lodgings are in pitched-roof South Seas style huts and rooms start around $80; they're even less with internet specials. They have cheerful Polynesian décor; all have refrigerators and balconies. The hotel's most appealing feature is its open-air restaurant and bar overlooking a swimming pool and the beach. Hawaiian style entertainment is presented most nights, and locals gather for a "Music and Grinds" session Fridays; see above. Facilities include a pool and sundeck, guest laundry and a gift shop.

8 KALUAKOI VILLAS

1131 Kaluakoi Rd. (P.O. Box 350), Maunaloa, HI 96770; (800) 367-5004 or (808) 552-2721; www.castleresorts.com. A low-rise condo complex; $$ to $$$$. GETTING THERE: It's part of the Kaluakoi Resort facility on Moloka'i's west end, four miles beyond Maunaloa.

Kaluakoi Villas has very affordable studios, one- and two-bedroom suites and cottages. While not fancy, units are fully furnished, with kitchens or kitchenettes. All have private lanais or balconies and many have ocean views. Resort facilities include a swimming pool and barbecue area, guest laundry and a gift shop. Adjacent beach areas offer swimming (on calm days), sunning, hiking and snorkeling.

9 KAUPOA BEACH VILLAGE

100 Maunaloa Hwy. (P.O. Box 259), Maunaloa, HI 96770-0259; (877) 726-4656 or (808) 552-2791; www.molokai-ranch.com. Forty beachside "tentalows"; $$$$$. GETTING THERE: Part of the Sheraton Molokai Resort complex, the village is reached by shuttle from the hotel, or rental cars can be driven down.

This may be the most expensive tent you'll ever sleep in, although the environment may be worth the $250-plus per night. Kaupoa Beach Village is a Polynesian style retreat on a remote sand and lava shoreline. It's a grand place for tidepool exploring, hiking, or just lying in a hammock on a grassy knoll above the beach. An amateur astronomer conducts stargazing sessions, and a native Hawaiian cultural expert leads walks to a nearby *heiau* and ancient dwelling platforms. Water sports gear is available at a beach hut.

Lodgings are spartan—woodframed tents with showers, beds and very rudimentary furnishings. Hawaiian-style dining is outdoors, with tables just off the beach; a meal plan is optional. Although this is a remote place, you're not quite cut off from the outside world. There's a phone and internet access in the reception center.

10 PU'U O HOKU RANCH

Kamehameha V Hwy. (P.O. Box 1889), Kaunakakai, HI 96748; (808) 558-8109; www.puuhoku.com. Cottage style ranch resort; $$ to $$$. GETTING THERE: It's on Moloka'i's east coast at milepost 25.

This 1930s style resort is in a gorgeous wooded setting, part of a 14,000-acre organic ranch. Although it's not on the beach, Halawa Valley and Bay are a short drive away. The resort has two rustically furnished cottages with kitchens, living rooms, TV, phones and lanais. The Grove Cottage has four bedrooms and a fireplace; the Sunrise Cottage has two bedrooms. The ranch also has an eleven-room lodge, although it was being rented only as a complete unit when we last checked. It's a great buy at $1,000 a night if you have twenty friends. Cottages have weekly rates that average out to just over $100 a night. The ranch's facilities include a swimming pool and store; horseback riding is available.

Chapter Sixteen

LANA'I

POSH RESORTS, NOT PINEAPPLES

When the languid little island of Lana'i presents its July Pineapple Festival, it supposedly has to borrow pineapples from Maui. This is an interesting commentary on an island that once was the world's largest producer of that fruit. Its pineapple fields in recent years has shrunk from 16,000 to thirty acres.

Of all the main islands of Hawai'i, Lana'i is where less is more. It's the smallest inhabited island except for off-limits Ni'ihau; it has the smallest population—about 3,200; it has the least amount of asphalt— thirty miles of paved road; and it has the smallest number of towns— one. Less is more here because those who live on Lana'i and those who choose to visit like it that way.

We can't say that Lana'i is particularly impressive physically. It's mostly arid and low-lying, without the climatic or terrain extremes of other islands. Rainfall varies from ten to forty inches; most of the incoming storms are blocked by neighbor Maui. Lana'i has no rainforest, although its higher ridges are wooded, mostly with introduced species such as eucalyptus and Norfolk pines. Much of the lowland landscape appears barren because of abandoned pineapple fields, although some areas are being replanted in pastureland, oats and alfalfa.

The island is noted mostly for outdoor pursuits, such as hiking, mountain biking, jeeping, kayaking, snorkeling and scuba diving. In fact, Lana'i is rated as one of the top ten snorkel and scuba sites in the world by *Skin Diver Magazine.* Four-wheel-driving is popular over Lana'i's network of unpaved roads. The island even offers deer hunting. The axis deer was introduced by early ranchers and hunting is permitted to keep them from eating what's left of the vegetation.

All of the above is not to suggest that a visitor has to rough it to enjoy a Lana'i vacation. This is home to two of America's the most highly rated resorts, the Manele Bay and the Lodge at Ko'ele. And should you want a permanent hideaway—and have the funds to afford one—several luxury villas have been built above the lodge. All of this is the work of Castle and Cooke, the company that owns ninety-eight percent of the island. When the company's pineapple industry was ruined by outside competition, it followed the example of several other large Hawaiian landholders and went into the tourist business.

Lana'i's venture into tourism received international publicity when Microsoft zillionaire Bill Gates married Melinda French on the Manele Bay golf course on New Year's Day, 1994. Ironically, no other tourist could stay on Lana'i on that day. To ensure privacy and keep the pesky press away, Gates booked every hotel room and tied up every rental car. A Seattle television reporter was arrested for trespass as he tried to approach the hotel. He sued for violation of his civil rights and Gates and the island's corporate owners paid him an undisclosed settlement. Gates later apologized to the reporter, so he isn't really such a bad guy. He and his wife have returned for vacations without renting the whole damned island. However, we're straying from our story.

TO LEARN MORE: Contact Destination Lana'i, P.O. Box 630700, Lana'i City, HI 96763; (800) 947-4774 or (808) 565-7600; *www.visitlanai.net.*

Lana'i: GETTING TO KNOW YOU

Early Hawaiians called Lana'i the "Forbidden Island" because it was inhabited by evil spirits. Maui's high chief Kaka'alaneo banished his delinquent son Kaulua'au to this haunted place for chopping down his breadfruit trees. The kid redeemed himself by driving the spirits away—as Bill Gates did centuries later—making the island safe for habitation, and maybe even tourism.

A few Hawaiian settled here, although the population was never much larger than it is today. James Cook sailed by its barren shores in 1779, and kept going. Kamehameha the Great conquered the island a few years later and spent some time at Kaunolu Bay on the south

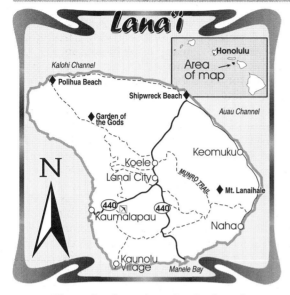

coast. Mormon missionaries arrived in 1835, and they later assigned one of their members, Walter Murray Gibson, to buy land for a church agricultural operation. What they didn't know was that he was secretly buying it for himself. Naturally, he was excommunicated. But he had himself an island!

Gibson brought in settlers, who introduced cattle and goats that began ravaging Lana'i's fragile environment. They also introduced axis deer for sport and like the goats, they soon got out of hand. Gibson went on to become active in Hawaii politics and Lana'i was passed on to other owners. In 1911, some ranchers hired New Zealander George C. Munro to manage their holdings. A botanist by trade, Munro worked to rid the highlands of feral goats and replanted the area, mostly with Norfolk pines, which remain the island's trademark tree.

In 1922, James Drummond Dole bought Lana'i for $1.1 million and turned it into one large pineapple patch. Not the son of a missionary as many assume, he was a cousin of Stanford Dole, who *was* a missionary descendant and Hawai'i's first territorial governor. James Dole came to O'ahu from Massachusetts in 1899. He pioneered Hawai'i's pineapple growing and canning industry and eventually controlled eighty percent of the world's market.

Dole imported mostly Filipinos to harvest his pineapples and their descendants are the island's largest ethnic group. Through mergers and buyouts, Lana'i eventually became the property of Castle & Cooke, the corporation that owns it today.

Getting there

Despite an assumed remoteness, Lana'i isn't really way out there. It's just nine miles from Maui and ten miles from Moloka'i. Lana'i Airport is served by several daily flights from O'ahu and from other islands by **Hawaiian Airlines**, (800) 367-5220; and the prop-jets of **Island Air**, (800) 652-6541. A more appealing approach is aboard the Lahaina to Lana'i passenger ferry, operated by a firm called **Expeditions**; (808) 661-3756. The ferry runs five times a day and the fare is $50. It puts in at Manele Harbor, near Lana'i's largest resort. Car and jeep rentals are available from **Dollar Rental Car**, (800) 800-3665; and **Avis Rent-a-Car** (800) 230-4898.

Lana'i is shaped like a pork chop and measures only nine by thirteen miles. Its highest point is 3,370-foot **Mount Lana'ihale**, which caps a ridge on the southeastern side. On the southwest, around **Palaoa Point**, seacliffs rise from a thousand to two thousand feet. Most of the interior, the **Palawi Basin**, is a plateau a thousand or more feet high. This is where the vast majority of its residents live, not along the coast, as on most of the other islands.

Sitting almost in the middle of the plateau is **Lana'i City**, the island's only town. It's a cool place—literally and figuratively—a classic company town of woodframe and false-front buildings. At 1,645 feet above sea level and fanned by breezes, it rarely suffers the heat of other Hawaiian communities.

From Lana'i City, paved roads gallop off in four directions. Route 440 goes south to **Manele Bay**, the island's fishing and pleasure boat harbor; and west past **Lana'i Airport** to Kaumalapa'u Harbor, where barges bring supplies from O'ahu. Route 430 travels northeast through the island's ridgeline to **Shipwreck Beach**, a popular recreation area. En route, it passes the **Munro Trail** that leads to a lookout at the island's highest point. Polihua Road reaches north from Lana'i City to the **Garden of the Gods**, where weather has sculpted spires, ridges and boulders. From there, trails lead to **Polihua Beach** and **Ka'ena Point** on the island's northwest tip.

THE VERY BEST OF LANA'I

We noted in the previous chapter that there isn't ten of anything on Moloka'i. This is even more true with Lana'i, so we'll group its attractions, activities and places to dine and recline in a single Ten Best list.

The best things to see & do

1 EXPLORE THE SEA WITH TRILOGY

Trilogy Lana'i, (888) MAUI-800; www.visitlanai.com. Most trips leave from Manele Harbor. ☺

Trilogy Cruises, which operates out of Maui, has several watersports activities on Lana'i. One of the more popular is its **Morning Snorkel Sail** on Monday, Wednesday, Friday and Saturday. It's more than a snorkeling trip; Trilogy's trimaran cruises beneath the high cliffs of the southeast coast, often accompanied by dolphins and flying fish. Best seats in the house are on a canvas tarpaulin stretched between the hulls forward, although you're likely to get a faceful of water. The crew picks one the island's better snorkeling spots, usually Shark Fin Cove at the base of those coastal cliffs. The trip includes a light lunch and snorkeling gear.

The firm runs its **Lanai Adventure Scuba** trip on Monday, Wednesday and Friday. Divers explore coral reefs and lava caves along the south and west coast. Outings include gear, snacks and a dive master. Its **Ocean Kayak** trips depart daily except Saturday, exploring the south shore Kahekili Ho'e area, with several sea caves and lava tubes; and Shipwreck Beach on the east coast. The outing includes single or double kayaks, snorkel gear and lunch.

2 EXPLORE THE LAND BY JEEP

Lana'i City Services, P.O. Box 630610, Lana'i City, HI 96763; (800) JEEP-808 or (808) 565-7227.

Working with Dollar Rental Car, Lana'i City Services offers jeep tours over the island's rough terrain. Or visitors can rent their own vehicles and follow the firm's *Jeep Safari Drive Guide*. Tours follow five routes or combinations thereof: Shipwreck Beach, the Munro Trail, Garden of the Gods, Polihua Beach and Luahiewa petroglyphs.

The most popular is a combination tour that begins with a drive over coastal Mountains to **Shipwreck Beach,** where the hulk of an old liberty ship protrudes just offshore. No, it wasn't a casualty of World War II; it got stuck on a reef as the Navy was towing it through the channel between Lana'i and Moloka'i. Nearby is the foundation of a lighthouse built in 1929; a trail leads from here to some ancient petroglyphs. From here, the tour returns to the ridge and follows the thickly wooded **Munro Trail** to Lana'ihale, the highest point on the island. It then swings back through Lana'i City and heads out to the **Garden of the Gods,** site of strangely eroded boulders and ridges.

3 HIKE OR DRIVE THE MUNRO TRAIL

Extending ten miles southeast and then west from Keomoku Road above Lana'i City. It can be a long and difficult hike, or a relatively easy if sometimes sloppy jeep drive.

Named in honor of the New Zealand botanist who worked to restore Lana'i's ravaged plant life, the Munro Trail travels through the island's most interesting terrain. Despite the name, it's a road and not a trail and it's more popular with jeepsters than hikers. However, if you can arranged to be dropped off at the trailhead above Lana'i City, you might prefer hiking it, so you can stop and smell the flowers. If you prefer to jeep it, see the "Jeep Safari" listing above for details on a rental.

The road/trail twists and winds through thick growth along Lana'i's southeast ridgeline. It's the island's only tropic woodland, although most of the flora has been introduced. About 200 yards from the trailhead, bear to the left at a fork to keep on course. After two miles, the trail descends into **Maunalei Gulch,** and you'll get occasional views offshore. Here, islanders battled unsuccessfully against invaders from the Big Island in 1778. Watch for a short trail to an overlook for **Hau-ola Gulch,** the island's deepest canyon.

From here, the trail begins a steep climb and—nearly eight miles from its starting point—it reaches the island's high point, **Mount Lana'ihale.** This is one of the best vantage points in the state; you can see portions of every other major island except Kaua'i. About half a mile beyond, you'll get a nice gander down to **Lana'i City.** Then the trail drops off the ridge and intersects with Manele Road.

4 EXPLORE THE GARDEN OF THE GODS

Eight miles north of Lana'i City on Polihua Road.

The Garden of the Gods is something unique to the Hawaiian Islands. It's an area of huge boulders and eroded spires, ridges and buttes that seem transplanted from the American Southwest. To be frank, if you have explored the Southwest, this place is small by comparison. Its features would be dwarfed by most of America's red rock formations. However, it is intriguing, particularly in the early morning or late afternoon, when shadows accent its outerworldly shapes. The mineral-rich formations create a palette of red, brown, ocher, soft yellow and even lavender. Come during early morning or late afternoon light for the most dramatic effects.

Although this looks to be the work of the ages, the Garden of the Gods was created within recorded time, not by some wild force of nature but by overgrazing. When vegetation was gnawed down to the dirt, winds carried off the soft red volcanic soil, lowering the terrain by as much as nine feet to expose these harder shapes.

TRAVEL TIP: The road to Garden of the Gods is dirt and gravel and often ribbed by erosion. Inquire about conditions before taking a conventional vehicle, and don't try it during or after a rain.

5 PROWL ABOUT LANA'I CITY

Lana'i's only town is a collection of modest former plantation workers' homes—mostly well-tended—with walls and corrugated tin rooftops painted in soft beiges. The business district, Lana'i City Commercial Square, consists of a several wood frame buildings around a two-block plaza. The plaza, called Dole Park, is lush and green, planted with Norfolk pines.

Stores and shops rimming the plaza provide most of the essentials for residents and browsing for visitors. The 1946 **Richard's Shopping Center** on the south side is not really a shopping center but a midsize general store; (808) 565-6488. **Gifts with Aloha** at Eighth and Houston sells art and crafts by locals, plus resort wear and specialty foods; (808) 565-6589. Another art shop, not on the plaza but behind the nearby Lanai Hotel, is **Heart of Lana'i Art Gallery**, with a selection of paintings and sculptures, including many by locals;

(808) 565-6678. The **Lana'i Playhouse** on the plaza's northeast corner shows current films, and it hosts assorted public events.

If strolling about this charming old town works up an appetite, you have several choices. **Blue Ginger Café** is a locals' favorite, occupying an old corrugated roof structure at Seventh Street and Ilima Avenue; it serves breakfast and lunch; (808) 565-6363. **Pele's Other Garden** on Eighth Street near Kiele Avenue, is decorated with state license plates and assorted other odds and ends; it's open for Lunch and dinner, with tables inside and on a small front porch; (808) 565-9628. The **Coffee Works**, just off the square at Ilima and Sixth, is open from early morning through lunchtime, featuring light fare and specialty coffees; (808) 565-6962.

The best places to dine

PRICING: Dollar sign codes indicate the price of a typical dinner with entrée, soup or salad, not including drinks, appetizers or dessert: *$* = less than $10 per entrée; *$$* = $10 to $19; *$$$* = $20 to $29; *$$$$* = $30 to $40; *$$$$$* = $41 and beyond.

6 THE FORMAL DINING ROOM

The Lodge at Ko'ele, Lana'i City; (808) 565-4580; www.lodgeatkoele.com. Contemporary American; full bar service. Dinner only. Major credit cards; $$$$ to $$$$$. Reservations recommended; jackets required for gentlemen.

The name says it; this is the most formal dining space on an island known for its informality. In decor and cuisine, it rivals any restaurant in Hawai'i. Zagat's *Hawaii Top Restaurants* gives the Dining Room its highest rating for food, service and decor, and it topped a recent *Condé Nast Traveler* readers' poll as Hawai'i's best restaurant.

It has the stately look of an elegant tropical living room, with a distinctive carved wood chandelier, orchid-laden vases, crackling fireplace, beam ceilings and windows on the lodge's handsomely landscaped grounds. The seasonal menu is American with Mediterranean and Pacific Rim accents. It features beautifully presented entrées of venison, rack of lamb, ragout, fresh island fish and poultry, served with island vegetables, herbs and fruits.

7 HENRY CLAY'S ROTISSERIE

Hotel Lanai, 828 Lana'i Ave., Lana'i City; (808) 565-7211; www.hotellanai.com. American-Cajun; full bar service. Dinner only. MC/VISA; $$ to $$$. Reservations recommended.

If you can't afford the prices at the Formal Dining Room, retreat to the nearby Hotel Lanai for the island's next best restaurant. Although the hotel is charmingly funky, the restaurant's fare is contemporary with spicy Cajun accents. And why not? Chef Henry Clay Richardson, who happens to own the hotel, is a New Orleans native. Featured on his menu are seafood gumbo, fresh local fish prepared with spicy authority, rotisserie-roasted chicken and—a local specialty—venison prepared in a variety of ways. Ragin' Cajun shrimp, available as an appetizer or main entrée, is one of the best dishes.

The restaurant's look fits the rest of the hotel, with knotty pine walls, wood plank floors, light natural wood furniture and two cheery fireplaces. Prices are modest and portions are generous.

The best places to recline

PRICING: Dollar sign codes indicate room price ranges for two people, based on high season (summer and winter) rates: *$* = a standard two-person room for $99 or less; *$$* = $100 to $149; *$$$* = $150 to $199; *$$$$* = $200 to $249; *$$$$$* $250 or more.

TRAVEL TIP: The company that owns the island operates a free shuttle that runs to all of the below-listed hotels.

8 MANELE BAY HOTEL

P.O. Box 630310, Lana'i City, HI 96763; (800) 321-4666 or (808) 565-7700; www.manelebayhotel.com. Luxurious low-rise resort with 250 rooms and suites; $$$$$.

Picture yourself in a lush tropical garden that cascades down toward the sea. Or maybe even picture Bill Gates and his bride having this gorgeous place all to themselves. In our "Superlist" in Chapter One, we picked Manele Bay as the best resort in all of the islands. *Condé Nast Traveler* and the Zagat Survey almost agree, both rating it number two in the state. This splendid retreat is a pleasing ramble of low-rise buildings surrounded by lush landscaping above a small crescent bay. The grounds are busy with floral gardens, waterfalls, streams and koi ponds. Particularly appealing are five theme gardens—Chinese, Bromiliad, Japanese, Hawaiian and Kamai'ina. A trail leads from the hotel past an ancient *heiau* and home sites to a sheltered swimming and snorkeling beach.

The hotel's public areas have an interesting Asian-Hawaiian theme, with murals, artifacts and richly carved woods. Check out the six-panel mural in the lower lobby, depicting preparations for a fanciful Chinese wedding. It was painted in honor of another fanciful wedding—Bill and Melinda Gates' marital merger on New Year's Day, 1994. Guest rooms are spacious, with European style furnishings and cheerful Hawaiian decor. Dining choices are the elegant Polynesian style Ihilani, dinner only; the oceanview Hulopoe Court, breakfast and dinner; and the Pool Grille, lunch through late afternoon.

Resort facilities include a golf course, swimming pool complex, a large spa and tennis courts.

9 THE LODGE AT KO'ELE

P.O. Box 630310, Lana'i City, HI 96793; (800) 321-4666 or (808) 565-7300; www.lodgeatkoele.com. Elegant country style resort with 102 units; $$$$$.

In contrast to the extravagantly opulent Manele Bay Hotel, the Lodge is elegantly simple. Yet it is no less refined, with a classic plantation theme. And it, too, has won numerous awards. With a pine tree-lined drive and an old fashioned split-rail fence enclosing a horse paddock out front, it suggests an elegant New England resort instead of a Hawaiian retreat. The lobby is a grand hall with lofty ceilings and twin stone-faced fireplaces. Among the lodge's appealing places of quiet repose are the Music Room, decorated with musical instruments, and the Library, with a goodly selection of books and current magazines.

The lodge's hotel wings border the formal Ko'ele Garden, with ornamental hedges, palms and pines, croquet courses and an 18-hole putting green complete with water hazards. A cascading stream leads to small ponds busy with multicolored koi. At the rear of the garden, a greenhouse is filled with orchids and other fragrant tropical blooms. The lodge's rooms have four-poster beds with floral print spreads that match cushions on the wicker furniture. Ko'ele's dining choices are the Formal Dining Room (above), and the adjacent Terrace Restaurant, serving breakfast, lunch and dinner. Amenities include a golf course, pool, spa and fitness room, riding stables, lawn bowling and croquet.

10 HOTEL LANAI

P.O. Box 630520, Lana'i City, HI 96763; (800) 795-7211 or (808) 565-7211; www.hotellanai.com. An historic renovated eleven-unit hotel; $$ to $$$.

From two sublimes, we end this book by going to the affordable— which we need after many months of research! This charming clapboard hotel, now owned by Henry Clay Robinson, was built in 1923 as a guest house for visiting dignitaries. The rooms are small, but think of them as cozy and cute, with wooden floors, ceiling fans and Hawaiian quilt bedspreads. Most share double lanais, except for number two, which has its own personal front porch. For more privacy, you can rent a small one-bedroom cottage on the grounds.

Hotel Lana'i's small front room and pub are popular gathering spots for island locals, who like to kick back with a beer and "talk story" (the local term for campfire talk). Occasionally, someone brings a ukelele. It's easy to be drawn into this affable group, to share lies and maybe even a song or two, and experience a bit of rural Hawai'i.

We can't think of a more agreeable way to end our visit to paradise.

INDEX: Primary listings indicated by *bold face italics*

Remarkably useful DiscoverGuides
By Don & Betty Martin

Critics praise the "jaunty prose" and "beautiful editing" of travel, wine and relocation guides by authors Don and Betty Martin. They are recent winners of a gold medal for best guidebook of the year in the annual Lowell Thomas Travel Writing Competition. Their DISCOVERGUIDES are available at bookstores throughout the United States and Canada, or you can order them on line at **www.amazon.com, bn.com** or **borders.com.**

ARIZONA IN YOUR FUTURE

It's a complete relocation guide for job-seekers, retirees and "Snowbirds" planning a move to Arizona. It provides essential data on dozens of cities, from recreation to medical facilities.　　*— 272 pages; $15.95*

THE BEST OF DENVER & THE ROCKIES

Discover the very finest of the Mile High City, from its Ten Best attractions, museums and parks to its leading restaurants and lodgings, and then explore attractions of the nearby Rockies.　　*— 256 pages; $16.95*

THE BEST OF PHOENIX & TUCSON

Head for the Sunbelt to explore Arizona's two largest cities. Discover their Ten Best attractions, desert parks, walking and biking trails, restaurants, resorts, dude ranches and much more!　　*— 272 pages; $16.95*

THE BEST OF SAN FRANCISCO

Our perennial best seller takes you through the streets of everybody's favorite city, pointing out its best attractions, museums, hidden lures, restaurants, cheap eats & sleeps and more! The book also covers the best of Oakland and the Ten Best regional side trips.　　*— 280 pages; $16.95*

THE BEST OF THE WINE COUNTRY

Where to taste wine in California? More than 350 wineries are featured, along with nearby restaurants, lodging and attractions. Special sections offer tips on storing and serving wine.　　*— 352 pages; $16.95*

CALIFORNIA-NEVADA ROADS LESS TRAVELED

This is a "Discovery guide to places less crowded." It directs travelers to interesting yet uncrowded attractions, hideaway resorts, scenic campgrounds, interesting cafes and other discoveries.　　*— 336 pages; $15.95*

HAWAI'I: THE BEST OF PARADISE

Discover the very best of Hawai'i in this guide to America's tropical paradise. The book covers Honolulu's and Waikiki's top attractions, restaurants, resorts, shopping areas and more. It then takes readers to the Outer Islands to discover their very best lures.　　*— 296 pages; $16.95*

LAS VEGAS: THE BEST OF GLITTER CITY

This impertinent insiders' guide explores the world's greatest party town, with expanded Ten Best lists of casino resorts, restaurants, attractions, buffets, shows, pubs, clubs and more! — *296 pages; $16.95*

NEVADA IN YOUR FUTURE

It's a complete relocation guide to the Silver State, with useful information for job-seekers, businesses, retirees and winter "Snowbirds." A special section discusses incorporating in Nevada. — *292 pages; $16.95*

SAN DIEGO: THE BEST OF SUNSHINE CITY

Winner of a Lowell Thomas gold medal for best travel guide, this lively and whimsical book features the finest of sunny San Diego, featuring its Ten Best attractions, restaurants and much more. It also features the Ten Best attractions in San Diego County and the best lures of nearby Tijuana and the Baja Peninsula. *—236 pages; $16.95*

SEATTLE: THE BEST OF EMERALD CITY

This upbeat and opinionated book directs visitors to the very best of Emerald City's attractions, activities, restaurants and lodgings. It then takes readers on interesting side trips to the Ten Best attractions elsewhere in Western Washington. *—236 pages; $15.95*

THE ULTIMATE WINE BOOK

This handy little pocket-sized book takes the mystique out of wine. It covers the subject in three major areas—Wine and Heath, Wine Appreciation and Wine with Food. And it does so with good humor, poking harmless fun at wine critics. *—194 pages; $10.95*

WASHINGTON DISCOVERY GUIDE

This handy statewide guidebook steers motorists and RVers from the Olympic Peninsula to Seattle to the Cascades and beyond, with details on attractions, restaurants, lodging, camping and more. And it features driving directions from one attraction to the next. *—464 pages; $17.95*